Medieval English Lyrics

MEDIEVAL ENGLISH LYRICS

A Critical Anthology

edited
with an introduction and notes
by
R. T. DAVIES

NORTHWESTERN UNIVERSITY PRESS
1964

R0137634644

CEN CHUM

*First published in the U.S.A. 1964 by Northwestern University
Press under arrangement with Faber and Faber Limited, London.*

Library of Congress Catalog Card Number 64-10994

Second Printing: United States of America 1964
Third Printing: United States of America 1967
Fourth Printing: United States of America 1969
Fifth Printing: United States of America 1972
Sixth Printing: United States of America 1988

ISBN 0-8101-0075-4

Contents

Contents

Contents

Contents

Contents

Contents

Preface

Many more than can be named here have contributed in one way and another to the making of a book which, the longer I think of it, seems the less my own. To all who have been of so much help to me—some of them without knowing it—and, in particular, to those of my colleagues who work regularly in the Staff Reading Room of the Harold Cohen Library in the University of Liverpool, I am most grateful. There is one, however, who has been outstandingly generous and whose help I acknowledge with special pleasure. It is Mr. Brian Nellist, William Noble Fellow in our University. The benefit of his learning, good judgement and understanding of things medieval is to be found on almost every page of this book, particularly in the Appendix, and it would be a work vastly inferior were it not for him. Miss Joyce Bazire, Professor Kenneth Muir, Dr. Miriam Allott and Mr. Kenneth Allott have criticized my drafts with kind thoroughness and improved the book in countless ways. Dr. J. Linskill gave me expert advice on the difficulties of no. 70. The publisher's readers were constructively critical of many details, and our Medieval Society, with Professor C. N. L. Brooke in the chair, discussed, to my great gain, what I had to say about several of these poems. I am indebted to the staffs of many libraries, but, in particular, to those of the manuscript rooms in the British Museum, the Bodleian and the Cambridge University Libraries. Mr. M. A. F. Borrie, Mr. A. B. Scott and Mr. H. S. Pink of these departments, Mr. W. O'Sullivan of the Library of Trinity College, Dublin, Miss D. Coates, Librarian of the Marquess of Bath, and Mr. D. P. Whiteley of the Pepys Library, Magdalene College, Cambridge, have been specially helpful, and so, too, have the staff of the Harold Cohen Library, and particularly among them Mr. A. N. Ricketts and Mr. D. F. Cook. To Lady Talbot de Malahide, the Marquess of Bath, Lord Harlech, and the authorities of the following bodies I am grateful for permission to print poems from documents in their keeping: The British Museum, the Bodleian Library, the Cambridge University Library, the National Library of Scotland, the Huntington Library, California, the Glasgow University Library, the

Preface

Edinburgh University Library, the Library of Lincoln Cathedral, the Kongelige Bibliotek, Copenhagen, the National Library of Wales, Trinity College, Cambridge, Corpus Christi College, Oxford, Lincoln's Inn, London, Merton College, Oxford, St. John's College, Oxford, Magdalene College, Cambridge, Gonville and Caius College, Cambridge, Balliol College, Oxford, Magdalen College, Oxford, St. John's College, Cambridge, Trinity College, Dublin. My own University of Liverpool gave me a grant towards my expenses for which I am most grateful, and Miss M. Burton, Miss M. Cleator, Miss A. Garfield and Mrs. P. Elliott, Secretaries in our Faculty of Arts, have patiently spent themselves, skilfully unravelling my manuscript and typing what they eventually found.

Introduction

This general introduction has four parts. The first shows what some of the poems are like and what issues their proper reading may raise; the second is a short, selective history of the medieval English lyric; the third considers some of the kinds of lyrics and some of the influences on them; and the fourth is a guide to this book and an explanation of what I have tried to do in it.

I

With many of these poems the reader who does not know medieval as intimately as later literature will feel himself immediately at home. He will find in them kinds of character and situation with which, in other guises, he is already familiar: Besse Bunting, the miller's maid, of no. 113, red-lipped in her white skirt with her thoughts all on pleasure; Jack, the cleric of no. 108, who seduces a girl after evensong; and the nimble-witted magician of no. 175, the only man able, by his skill and guile, to win the rich baron's daughter who,

> wold have no man
> That for her love had sought her—
> So nice she was.

Sentiments and associations abound that might be those of the poetry of yesterday if not of today:

> When the nightegale singes,
> The wodes waxen grene;
> Lef and gras and blosme springes,
> In Averil, I wene.
> And love is to mine herte gon
> With one spere so kene (no. 10).

Familiar in a different way, it is the mature art of poets in a sophisticated society, unfalteringly confident of their powers, which produces both the delicacy of the wit in no. 90, where a penitent lover promises his confessor to return the kiss he has stolen, and the

13

noble and large resonance of Dunbar's Resurrection hymn, no. 147. On the other hand, nos. 75, 84 and 171 have, in what are probably folk-poetry elements, a compelling freshness and, like no. 15, that concrete and earthy particularity which characterizes Shakespeare's maidens bleaching their summer smocks in *Love's Labour's Lost* and, in the *Tempest*, his sun-burn'd sicklemen in their rye-straw hats. In its central stanzas no. 66 has immediately recognizable and mysterious powers of evocation which are essentially poetic, apparently requiring no aid from learned exegesis. And such are the adjustments that have been made in this edition to the spelling, punctuation and lay-out of the verses, that, even were their content alien, with the glosses that have been provided at the foot of the page it should be little more difficult to read many of these poems than to read Shakespeare.

These lyrics are conspicuously varied; their range frequently surprises. But they were written by a diversity of people in the course of four centuries, by learned men in serious and in trivial mood, and by women running comfortable households in the country, by court entertainers and by civil servants, by noblemen and by saints. The earliest poem in this anthology existed as long before the last as the last before us. If the poems written in contempt of the world oppress the reader he can refresh himself with a carol, or, according to his inclination, he can be devout, or entertain himself like a gentleman.

For these reasons, if for no other, it is not surprising that many medieval lyrics are less immediately effective than others, and that some require in the modern reader an educated historical imagination. This is not necessarily any more true of them than of the poetry of any past age, nor is the fact that a number of these lyrics, which are expressly traditional and conventional, demand that the reader shall adjust himself to their mode as well as inform himself about their meaning. In any age, many of these poems would be regarded by contemporary readers as of a different sort from some of those already mentioned, the impact of which is immediate. Even such a poem as no. 66, 'I sing of a maiden that is makeles', is the richer for historical and critical exposition, and how it was read by contemporaries and with what expectations is a question for discussion.

The first and last stanzas of this poem are adapted from a longer and inferior thirteenth-century work in which there is no hint of how the miraculous and momentous entry of God, the King of kings, into the womb of a virgin is represented as an event as natural and imperceptible as the falling of dew. So long as one knows that it is to the Incarnation of Christ that the poem refers, the fresh and tender wonder of the central stanzas and the exultation of the first and last speak to the modern reader, without any exposition, through the sensuous and familiar imagery of dew and stillness, maidens and ladies, and a king who comes quietly to his mother's room. So long as this is appreciated, what is known of the literary, ecclesiastical and other associations which this poem may have had for contemporary readers or hearers may be considered without much risk of stifling its beauty beneath a load of pedantry. Nor need there be in an appreciation of the potentialities of the imagery in this poem any suggestion that all these associations were present in the mind of any one contemporary reader.

April and the springtime was a season constantly occurring in medieval poetry. It is mentioned in the thirteenth-century source of no. 66 but with a different and only introductory function:

> Nu this fules singeth and maketh hure blisse,
> *Now these birds sing and rejoice,*
> And that gres up-thringeth and leveth the ris,
> *And the grass thrusts up and branches grow leafy.*
> Of on I wille singen that is makeles,
> *I shall sing of someone who has no equal (mate),*
> The King of alle kinges to moder he hire ches.
> *The King of all kings chose her for his mother.*

But, in another thirteenth-century lyric, spring is intimately associated with tender love for Jesus:

> Nu I see blostme springe,
> I herde a fuheles song,
> A swete longinge
> Mine herte thureth-ut (*through*) sprong. . . .
> Of Jesu Christ I singe. (C.B. *13c.*, pp. 120–2, no. 63.)

Such an association of spring with the up-welling of love is also, as so commonly in the middle ages, a feature of secular love poetry, whether it be, for example, the more formal and more obviously conventional as in no. 13,

> Betwene Mersh and Averil,
> When spray beginneth to springe,

The lutel fowl hath hire will
On hire lud to singe.
Ich libbe in love-longinge (etc),

or the more popular and unpretentious, as in no. 113,

In Aprell and in May
When hartes be all mery,
Besse Bunting, the millaris may (*maid*) . . .
She cast in hir remembrance
To passe hir time in daliance.

When a gentleman was stirred by the spring it was evidence of his *gentil*, or appropriately fine and noble, heart, as Chaucer says in his *Knight's Tale*:

The sesoun priketh every gentil herte
And maketh him out of his slep to sterte
And seith, 'Aris! and do thine observaunce.'

Chaucer also associates the upsurging of life in the world without with that in the world within in the opening lines of his *Prologue to the Canterbury Tales* where the romantic desire of ordinary folk 'to goon on pilgrimages' or of *palmeres* 'for to seken straunge strondes' is related to the season,

Whan that Aprill with hise showres soote
The droghte of March hath perced to the roote,
And bathed every veine in swich licour,
Of which vertu engendred is the flour.

This is the season of fertility and renewed life when, with the warmth and rain, the earth brings forth new vegetation: just so, it is appropriate to pray in the words of an antiphon in an Advent service, 'Let the clouds rain down righteousness and the earth be opened and bring forth a Saviour'.

Another outstanding feature of 'I sing of a maiden' is the formal movement of the middle stanzas:

He cam also stille
Ther his moder was,
As dew in Aprille
That falleth on the grass.

Introduction

He cam also stille
To his moderes bowr,
As dew in Aprille
That falleth on the flowr.

This repetition with partial variation is a stylistic device common
in the ballads, as in this instance from a version of 'Sir Patrick Spens':

They had not sailed upon the sea
A league but merely three,
When ugly, ugly were the jaws (*waves*)
That rowd (*rolled*) unto their knee.

They had not sailed upon the sea
A league but merely nine,
When wind and weit and snaw and sleit
Came blawing them behind.

Since it is in part from this ballad-like feature that the power of the
poem springs, it is likely that the dew, the stillness and the coming
to his mother, three times re-iterated like an incantation, have con-
nections with folk tradition.

The services and the learned tradition of the Church also contri-
bute to the meaning of the poem.[1] Biblical and liturgical imagery,
in general, are like that of this poem in that they have an imme-
diate impact: such characteristic Christian figures as darkness and
light, fathers and sons, washing, feeding and making free are the
coin of everyday life. This simple and familiar imagery becomes for
one who devoutly reads the Scriptures or takes regular part in the
daily round of the Church's worship the natural vehicle of profound
and complex religious experience. Some of the Advent services,
which, of course, all look forward to the Incarnation and the descent
of God into the womb of a virgin, have references to dew and rain
descending from the heavens, and, in particular, the Lord is said to
come down into the womb of the Virgin expressly as dew on the
grass. A common figure for Mary was a flower, which was often
associated with chastity, and another was a branch bearing the flower
of the Incarnate Lord.

Such images as these have also a special significance. Those who

[1] For all the images referred to in this and the next paragraph see Appendix under
Dew, Fleece of Gideon, Lily, Rose, Rod, and see also note to no. 66.

explained the Scriptures in the middle ages interpreted them alle-
gorically: it was assumed that whatever was done or said in the Old
Testament must in some way pre-figure the New, and it was the
task of men of learning to expound the meaning, for example, of
the burning bush seen by Moses or of the love poem, the *Song of
Songs*, in allegorical terms. Thus, in their tradition, the dew which
fell on the fleece of Gideon in chapter six of *Judges* and was mentioned
in some of the Advent services was an allegory of the word of God
descending upon Mary, and, thus, Mary was represented by a
flower not only because of its general poetic propriety but, in parti-
cular, because the reference to the 'lily among thorns' in the *Song
of Songs* was, in biblical exegesis, applied to her, as was the reference
to the 'rose plant in Jericho' of *Ecclesiasticus*. When she was said
to be a branch that bears a flower it was because the 'rods' of Aaron
and of Jesse had borne flowers in the Old Testament, prefiguring
her bearing of Jesus in the New. In this same tradition the stillness
in this poem may be interpreted as that of the silent Christmas night
or of a conception and birth immensely significant to the clerical
mind because it was entirely free from all concupiscence; April was
the first month of the medieval year and the first month of Mary's
pregnancy,[1] and the month in which spring renews the earth may be
interpreted as that in which begins the new age of man's redemption.

These are the terms in which the poem may be read in the eccle-
siastical tradition. But neither these terms nor those of any other
tradition exhaust, on their own, the meaning of a poem which,
paradoxically, is perfectly clear and obviously beautiful. Were it
possible to discover who the poet was or for what audience he wrote
one might be clearer about how it was intended the poem should
be read. The manuscript in which it is written may contain the
repertoire of a travelling entertainer (pp. 19, 29): it includes both
secular and religious poems, ballads, carols and other songs; three
are in Latin and a number contain Latin lines. Such is their diversity
that, if anything, the company which 'I sing of a maiden' keeps
confirms the impression of the modern scholar that it is a poem
which reflects not one but several traditions. Better perhaps, it might
be said, this is a poem which, simply because it is such sheer and
universal poetry, can be seen to have meaning in the terms of various

[1] The Feast of the Annunciation is 25 March which was counted in the middle
ages as New Year's Day and commonly referred to by the old Roman designation
of the eighth of the calends of April.

poetic traditions, each of which may, in practice, have been quite sharply differentiated.

It is not certain, however, that the book in which no. 66 is found —or any such book—was that of a travelling entertainer or that its user was clerical or lay. There exist no accounts of 'minstrel' performances, nor of their repertoires. Indeed, such evidence as exists has led R. L. Greene to conclude that they were not singers at all but only instrumentalists![1] The names of some of them are known but, with the possible exception of Laurence Minot of the fourteenth century, who was probably a travelling entertainer, none can be identified as the composer of particular poems. It is impossible to generalize at length and boldly about performers or audiences as it is, also, for lack of evidence, about a number of other aspects of the medieval verse in this anthology. And yet, in accounting for the conspicuous differences between so many of these poems and in trying to read them right, it is inevitable that some attempt should be made to discriminate between the diverse traditions in which they were written.

In trying to do so it is usual to call some of these poems 'popular'. By 'popular' is meant something that met the taste of people in general and not of one group only—say, the court or the learned, who must often have found what was popular uninteresting, distasteful or wicked—and something that was generally current and had 'caught on'. Carols, in general, were popular and have no particularly courtly or elaborately sophisticated or learned features (pp. 35–6). Transmission was sometimes oral, sometimes written, but most popular songs, as is true today, were probably learnt by hearing. Music was catchy and tuneful, and the subject might be topical. Ballads as much as ballades were probably not popular in this sense, but it is not always possible to discriminate definitively between popular poetry and what is probably the separate category of folk-song. Whether or not it should be called folk poetry, there is certainly a kind of poetry distinguished by its style—for example, advance by repetition with partial variation; or by its content, which is like that of folk-lore; or by its atmosphere, which is peculiar to itself, and for which other traditions can barely account. Poetry of this sort may well be regarded as distinct from that of most of the carols, though they sometimes show its influence as in nos. 84, 171, 164. Indeed, with regard to the last of these, the Corpus Christi

---

[1] Greene, *Selection*, pp. 18–20.

Carol, if not so much with regard to the first two, which have as their subject the Holly and the Ivy, in the light of present knowledge it is most uncertain what is the nature of the commixture or where to draw the line.

But whatever the traditions in which a poem is written an attempt has been made throughout this anthology to show that it was often conventions of one sort or another that these poets were using with more or less vitality and originality. The emphasis put since the romantic movement on originality or spontaneity in poetry and on the personality of the poet makes for injustice towards most of these lyrics. Most of them are anonymous: it was not thought important to preserve the author's name. They were written about avowedly conventional topics in avowedly conventional ways: their content was traditional and their expression through an accepted rhetoric. The ridiculous or tedious consequences of this at the hand of a mechanical and uncreative poet can be compared with those where, at the hand of the true artist, the same conventions have come to life, in two love poems, nos. 23 and 25. The organization and quality of the detail in no. 23 is quite different from that in no. 25.

Few matters in medieval literature were more obviously conventional than those of love between the sexes, but just as conventional, too, were matters of religious love. Not only is the temperature of no. 34, addressed to the Mother of God and probably by William of Shoreham, very low, but it is a matter for discussion to what extent its conventional images are much more than a recognized currency for a common and simple rhetorical game in which their value is precisely and only in their allegorical equivalence to Mary. So conventional are these figures that some may doubt, in view of the manner in which they are used and the time at which these English poems were written, how clear poets or audiences were about what underlies them or how much they were interested in it. Certainly little attempt is made in these English poems to analyse theologically. In this they are quite unlike the Latin poems of Adam of St. Victor[1] which were intended, presumably, for a professional audience. In the English poems, also, little attempt is made to explore the peculiar propriety of some of the figures, and when implications, whether emotional, intellectual or suggestive, seem to have been regarded as insignificant, and when few if any occasions are taken

[1] The abbey of St. Victor, near Paris, was famous for its learning, piety and poetry. Adam lived in what was probably its greatest age, the twelfth century.

even to realize an image concretely, the modern reader may feel that some of these poems are deprived by the poets' inadequacy of sensuous body and complex meaning. He may think that what he regards as poetic qualities are not much sought after.

On the other hand, St. Augustine, for example, writing in the fourth and fifth centuries, had affirmed how much more pleasurable it was, though he did not know why, to hear a truth conveyed allegorically rather than in plain words;[1] and, presumably, though allegorical figures may not, from the poetical point of view, be fully realized in these poems, the pleasure St. Augustine took in them may also have been taken by learned contemporary readers. They—and the less learned, too—may well have felt the mysterious splendour of the figures, particularly when used as glorious titles in the attempted high style of no. 104, 'The infinite power essenciall', and, despite the inertness of their expression in William of Shoreham's no. 34, have supposed that the very abundance of these marvellous aspects of her mystery honoured Mary in what is primarily a hymn offered to her in prayer: it celebrates her as a lover might his mistress, reciting her excellences point by point and entreating her merciful aid.

There is, in fact, some difference in the use of these titles and figures. In no. 107, for example, not only do they expand the appeal to Mary's mercy but they are also a slow sequence, on each member of which the devotee may dwell in momentary meditation. These collocations of titles are very like litanies in which a principle of organization is often hard to find. Indeed, many of the references made to Mary grow out of devotion to the Mother of God and are to be found, as we have already seen (p. 17), in the services of the Church and in formulas of prayer (e.g., nos. 11 and 12 and Appendix under *Queen, Mother and daughter*). The use of imagery which is, among other things, biblical and liturgical, contrasts completely, as we have seen in no. 66, 'I sing of a maiden' (pp. 15–19), with its use in the poems just discussed, and no. 71, 'Adam lay ibounden', is completely free from Marian rhetoric in its expression of joy at the offence against God that made Mary necessary: it is immediately fresh and compelling. Its mode of advancing by partial repetition

---

[1] 'De doctrina christiana', ii, 6, *P.L.* xxxiv, cols. 38–9: quotes *Song of Songs*, iv, 2: Num aliud homo discit, quam cum illud planissimis verbis, sine similitudinis hujus adminiculo audiret? Et tamen nescio quomodo suavius intueor sanctos, cum eos quasi dentes Ecclesiae video praecidere ab erroribus homines, etc.

with an addition (e.g. ll. 1–2) suggests popular origins, but at its heart is a sentiment thoroughly in the tradition of the Church and formulated in the 'Exultet', which is sung in the Easter Eve ceremonies and refers to the 'felix culpa' or 'happy fault' of man's first parents.

Even though their method and content is conventional, warmth of feeling is also a characteristic of many religious lyrics. For example, though Friar William Herebert's no. 28 has a thoroughly traditional theme, exploring the paradoxical 'gret wonder' of the Incarnation whereby 'one woman was mother to her father and her brother', so that it would not be surprising if the modern reader took this evident delight in the preposterous for a mere venture of metaphysical wit, in fact the point in the second stanza to which this exploration is leading fetches out its nature and purpose. It is a meditation to evoke in the devotee a deep and warm movement of intimate dependence on God: 'thou my sister and my mother, and thy son is my brother—who should then be afraid?' Indeed, an understanding of their character as devout meditation is the key to many of the religious poems in this anthology. It is entirely characteristic that their imagery and aspirations, as well as their method, should also be found in the Latin writings of St. Augustine and of the devotional tradition stemming from the eleventh century (in which were written works felt to be so much like St. Augustine's that they were wrongly attributed to him). It was a tradition of affective piety in which stood the *Song of Songs*, interpreted as the love-song of Christ for the soul, the hymn, 'Jesu dulcis memoria' (Mone, i, p. 329), the writings of Franciscans and Cistercians, and works rightly or wrongly attributed to SS. Anselm, Bernard and Bonaventura, and Richard and Hugh of St. Victor (note 1, p. 20). Poems in this tradition do not appeal to the intellect through theological elaborations and subtleties but inflame the heart through a contemplation of the physical Passion and poignant consideration of its implications for a sinner.[1]

On the other hand, no. 5, 'Of on that is so fair and bright', no.

---

[1] The prose meditations of 11c. (?) ascribed to SS. Augustine and Anselm are representative of this tradition and are frequently cited in the notes. They can be read in a translation of 1701 by G. Stanhope. For accounts of the tradition see: A. Wilmart, *Auteurs spirituels et textes dévots du moyen âge latin* (Paris, 1932); chapter 5 of R. W. Southern's *The making of the middle ages* (London, 1953); introduction to *Poems of John of Hoveden*, ed. F. J. E. Raby (Surtees Society, 1939).

66, 'I sing of a maiden', no. 71, 'Adam lay ibounden', and no. 147, Dunbar's Resurrection hymn, do not need allowances made for them. They are poetry and not piety in verse. And, though they are less poetically successful, William Herebert's no. 27, 'What is he, this lordling, that cometh from the fight?' and the anonymous meditation on the Passion, no. 45, show artistic activity which has the potential of poetry though their intention may have been to further religious practice. The concentration and reorganization done by Friar Herebert and the use, by the anonymous poet, of such rhetorical features as reiteration of names and key words, and his adoption of conventional images, such as prayer as a chain and love as an archer, are in the service of public and private piety, but they are the same stuff as poetry is made of. Generally speaking, many anonymous English poems that can be compared with Latin analogues make no unfair showing: it is the greatest of the Church's hymns to which English lyrics cannot aspire, as well as the poetry of particular Latin poets of special genius such as Adam of St. Victor or John of Hoveden. On the other hand, there is nothing in Latin like 'I sing of a maiden' or 'Adam lay ibounden': these are peculiarly English and peculiarly good.

Many Latin poems were translated into English, particularly by Franciscans, for use in preaching and public worship or private devotion. On the other hand, some religious poems are attempts by Franciscans to use secular lyrics for the same purposes. St. Francis had conceived of his disciples as *joculatores Dei*, 'God's minstrels', and this vision inspired their writing of poetry both in Latin (note 24) and in the vernacular. William Herebert and James Ryman were Franciscans, and a number of lyrics in this anthology are, significantly, from a collection of sermon materials in Latin and English arranged under one hundred and forty-three topics by John of Grimestone, who was almost certainly a Franciscan.[1] But it should not be forgotten that only three or four friars are known by name as authors of lyrics and that there is no evidence, for example, that the many

[1] According to Bale (16c.) Herebert died in 1333. Seventeen of his pieces survive in the one MS. Most are paraphrases of Latin hymns, etc. There are one hundred and sixty-six pieces in the MS. that contains Ryman's name and the date 1492 and one hundred and nineteen are carols. Greene says he was thus responsible for a quarter of all the known carols up to 1550. There are several tunes in this MS. For the fundamental relationship between religious lyric and the homiletic tradition, and for exploration of countless topics and images in this anthology, see G. R. Owst's *Literature and pulpit in medieval England*, 2nd edn. (Oxford, 1961).

verses of Friar Ryman were in the slightest acceptable to those for whom, presumably, this popularizer intended them. Friar Thomas of Hales's 'love-song' to Jesus (C.B. *13c.* p. 68, no. 43), written in the thirteenth century and among the first in the devotional tradition described above, was still influential in the later fourteenth century: but it is, nevertheless, most unattractive as a poem and is not included in this anthology. It is, however, an important example of the intimate relationship between medieval secular and religious love lyrics in that it begins by saying that a certain holy woman has asked the poet to make her a love-song addressed to the truest of all true sweethearts, and in that, during the course of it, the poet, acclaiming virginity as the most precious of gems, says that it is 'full of fin amur': 'refined love' between the sexes was the ideal of countless writers of secular lyrics and romances (p. 44).

It was the Franciscan Bishop of Ossory, Richard de Ledrede, who, in the fourteenth century, so disapproved of his clergy's delight in popular, vernacular songs that he wrote pious Latin words for them to sing to the same tunes (p. 31). Another instance of a churchman's attempt to minimize the evil of secular lyrics and to use them for devout ends is in a sermon of the early thirteenth century (p. 31) which takes as its text the popular lines,

> Atte wrastlinge my lemman I ches (*chose*),
> And atte ston-casting I him forles (*lost*).

It discovers in them a spiritual meaning: for example, in order to come to true bliss we are called to wrestle with the world, the flesh and the devil, and, for example, by *stone* is signified the hard hearts of men and women. It may well be that this allegorical interpretation fell, in its own day, on very stony hearts, but such indisputable evidence that the allegorical method was explicit is to the modern reader a most useful measuring stick when assessing claims that such a popular song as no. 33 must be taken allegorically. It so happens that this very poem, 'Maiden in the mor lay', is one of those which the Bishop of Ossory classed as shamefully secular, and for which he wrote new and acceptable words. The bishop may have been too obtuse to perceive that there was at least a layer of devout meaning in the vernacular lyric, or too astute to allow the possibility of interpreting the poem piously to excuse the enjoyment of it vulgarly. But it is more likely that the simplest explanation is right and that, since he condemns it, there is no religion in the poem at all.

Introduction

The highly conventional character of medieval religious poetry is that, also, of the secular poetry of, for example, Geoffrey Chaucer and Charles of Orleans, and of a unique cluster of secular poems, known as the Harley lyrics (p. 28, note 1, and pp. 32–3), written down at the beginning of the fourteenth century. In particular, this early, probably thirteenth-century verse, and the fourteenth- and fifteenth-century verse of the court poets is characterized by a cultivated use of appropriate formulas and figures of speech. In Chaucer's no. 53 it was a convention that comparisons with such precious stones as crystal and ruby should convey how precious were the features of a lady, and that love should wound a heart and that the lady's medicine should heal it. With rhetoric like this and, in particular, with a contrived lofty manner and a sustained high tone, many modern readers are ill at ease.

> O! ghost formatt, yelde up thy breth att ones!
> O! carcas faint, take from this liif thy flight!
> O! bolled hert, forbrest thou with thy grones!
> O! mested eyes, why faile ye not youre sight? (no. 88)

But this should not surprise readers of Elizabethan poetry, and, in one degree or another, rhetoric is in daily use, unnoticed, when something is put forcibly by saying, 'he had a face like thunder' or 'she went on and on', or when abstractions are thought about as in 'his thoughts were twisted'. The point is that many medieval poets used rhetoric with a deliberate and elaborate skill that was appreciated as much for its technical brilliance as for its appropriateness to a noble subject, a noble kind of poem, and a noble audience.

In Chaucer's no. 54 there is both this noble eloquence in a high style and a decasyllabic line, and also the accomplished dignity of elaborate stanzas in the ballade form.

> Hide, Absolon, thy gilte tresses clere;
> Ester, ley thou thy mekenesse all adown;
> Hide, Jonathas, all thy frendly manere;
> Penalopee, and Marcia Catoun,
> Make of youre wifhode no comparisoun;
> Hide ye youre beautes, Isoude and Heleine;
> My lady cometh that all this may disteine.

Chaucer probably introduced ballades and roundels into English (pp. 43–4) and the rime-royal stanza, of which this just quoted is an example. But another of his complex stanza forms, that of the *Monk's Tale*, is found already among the Harley lyrics (pp. 25, 28; no. 26). Aiming at Chaucer's effect, some of his successors often used means that he never employed and, praising, for example, 'fresch anamalit termes celicall' (*heavenly words like bright enamel*: Dunbar's 'Goldin Targe'), or the 'aureat ditees' of Homer and the 'sugred tonge' of Cicero (Lydgate's no. 97), crammed their lines with polysyllabic Romance words, intending thereby to elevate their tone and make them glorious with a borrowed glitter and a Latin sonority. Dunbar's no. 144 is an example of the aureate, as it is generally known and as he called it, at its most artificially accomplished, misguided though it is. The hymn addresses the Blessed Virgin,

> Hodiern, modern, sempitern
> Angelicall regine.

No. 104 is an example of the style which is less consistently ambitious but more typically ridiculous in its self-conscious affectation:

> Phebus persplendent made his abdominacioun,
> *Bright-gleaming Phoebus abdicated,*
> Devoiding all in tenebrosite.
> *Getting rid of all in darkness.*

These later poets were, in one degree or another, aware that their monosyllabic and heavily consonantal native language was an inadequate vehicle for their growing poetic aspiration and the achievement, among other things, of those effects which they enjoyed in both Ancient Latin and the Latin hymns of the Church.

But, as in Dunbar's no. 145, many a medieval poem is just as characteristically colloquial and homespun. In his *Canterbury Tales* Chaucer chose to offer the reader several kinds of tale: there was not only a noble poem about the interests of noble people, such as the 'Knight's Tale', but also a vulgar poem about the interests of vulgar people, such as the 'Miller's Tale', and both were written in appropriately different styles. In the same way, Dunbar, a deliberate artist of singular versatility and with an exceptional relish for words, offers, in no. 145, another kind of poem than his no. 144: it is one that exploits another sort of theme in another and appropriate sort of language and is, in this sense, just as artificial as no. 144 and, incidentally, just as open to the possible charge of misguided or even ridiculous excess.

Introduction

Many a medieval poem has the strength and freshness of common life and something of that liveliness of dialogue for which Geoffrey Chaucer is frequently admired:

> 'What helpeth thee, my swete lemman,
> *What do you gain, my sweetheart,*
> My life thus for to gaste?'
> *From making my life desolate like this?*
> 'Do wey! thou clerk, thou art a fol,
> *Get away, you cleric, you're a fool,*
> With thee bidde I noght chide (etc.).'
> *I've no wish to quarrel with you (etc.). (no. 9)*

In no. 89 the poet trusts to have 'More joy than ther be stiches in my shert', and in no. 140 garments are said to hang on an uncomely lover 'As it were an olde gose had a broke winge'. No. 122 begins with the brusque, colloquial impetuosity that convinces most modern readers of sincerity:

> Yet wulde I nat the causer fared amisse,
> For all the good that ever I had or shall.

These are the best lines in the poem and the most assured, whereas, in the last stanza, having lost the initial impetus of speech rhythm, the poet finds himself stumbling and fumbles for any regularity at all. On the other hand, in the last lines of no. 173 there is a simple dignity which is that of the natural utterance of any man imagined in this position:

> And when I awoke, by Heven Kinge,
> I wente after hur, and she was gone;
> I had nothing but my pilowe in my armes lying,
> For, when I awoke, ther was but I alone.

The full extent to which medieval lyrics were 'literary' poems, rather than songs to be sung, cannot, in most cases, be readily determined. For one thing, in very round figures, only some two hundred survive with musical settings, and, of these, a good half are polyphonic carols. This paucity of music is the rule throughout the period and it is typical that, whether or not Chaucer's lyrics were ever sung—for which there is little evidence—no music for them survives today. It is not clear whether we are to conclude from this that the public for verse was incomparably greater than that for written music, or that music was less frequently written down than words. Generally speaking, 'literary' and 'musical' lyrics are not very dissimilar, as may be seen by comparing, for example, those carols that have music and those that have not. Such music as there is, including the earliest (e.g. nos. 2, 3, 4, 12) and that which accompanies the simplest poems, is frequently elaborate and may be for two or three voices. It seems rarely to be the outcome of much feeling for words in themselves, and what evidence we have does not often add up to the joint composition of words and music by one man.

If anything, musical rhythm was probably determined by the rhythm of the words and it is not, therefore, possible to use such music as there is to discover how these poems were meant to sound. The question of prosody in medieval poetry is a very difficult one in any case, but not least in many of these lyrics. It should be remembered, first, that in poems up to, say, the mid-fifteenth century, final 'e', was often still pronounced, and that, wherever this was so, it must still be pronounced to do justice to the rhythm of a line. Secondly, it should be remembered that whatever may or may not have been a particular poet's concern with the number of syllables in a line, he was probably more at home with the stress rhythms of English speech and of the native alliterative poetry than with any others. These two points remembered, most poems will provide few difficulties and the reader who tackles these poems, confident that he will be able to feel out their rhythm, will frequently discover that it will readily find itself.

These poems have been preserved in a variety of ways, chiefly in manuscripts though the earliest versions of some few are in print (e.g. nos. 160 and 161). Some were recorded by what seems happy accident in odd corners of books with which they have nothing to do (nos. 4, 113, 121, 72, 172) or have survived, for example, among odd fragments on a narrow strip of parchment used as part of a binding (no. 2). Some have been collected into anthologies: thus, what are now known generally as the Harley lyrics (pp. 25, 32–3) are found in the B.M. MS. Harley 2253 with a variety of other works in Latin, Anglo-Norman and English, in both verse and prose.[1]

[1] For example, saints' lives and fabliaux, *King Horn* and *The Sayings of Saint Bernard*. The MS. was probably written in the West Midlands, perhaps in Leominster or Hereford, between about 1315 and 1325. Another such anthology is in the Vernon MS. in the Bodleian, a vast collection the provenance of which is quite unknown (e.g. nos. 42, 43 and 48).

Some collections belonged to religious houses such as Reading Abbey (no. 3) and some to individual clerics such as John of Grimestone (p. 23; e.g. nos. 46 and 50). Some lyrics are in commonplace books belonging to laymen, rag-bags serving many uses and containing in various assortments secular and, in some cases, religious lyrics mixed with such things as narrative poems and prose chronicles, genealogies and deeds, medical prescriptions, prophecies and mere lists of events and places: that containing, for example, nos. 175, 177, 178, was written, perhaps, between 1500 and 1535, and belonged to Richard Hill who married the daughter of a haberdasher and was at one time 'servant with Mr. Wyngar, alderman of London', a grocer; while that containing, for example, nos. 148 and 151 was compiled about 1500 by one of the Newtons who were of Cheshire, comfortable in fortune, and related to many of the county's leading families.[1] Some poems have been recorded in song-books or choir repertoires: in what is known as Ritson's MS, from the west country, which contains no. 155, there are songs for many kinds of civil and religious occasions such as might connect the book with, say, Exeter Cathedral; a printed book of twenty songs with only the bass parts contains no. 182.[2] Again, some lyrics come from what may have been the repertoires of some sort of travelling entertainer. They are found in books measuring $4\frac{1}{2}'' \times 6''$ which could have been readily carried about.[3] Some belong to collections of the work of one or two distinguished authors (p. 33). Some are in manuals of devotion and prayer-books (e.g. nos. 45 and 61). By whatever means, however,

---

[1] Robbins has argued that the MS. containing, for example, nos. 134 and 137 belonged to the Finderns, 'one of the leading county families' of southern Derbyshire. It was written by various people, some women, 1450–1550. No. 108 is from a commonplace book apparently belonging to a Wymundus London, and no. 153 from a book owned by John Colyn, a mercer.

[2] Stevens suggests that the MS. containing no. 181 and only the tenor and counter-tenor parts for some two dozen songs was used by a professional court-musician. Further choir repertoires: see note 2 p. 36. Further song-books, see notes 156, 157 and 180.

[3] B.M. MS. Sloane 2593 contains seventy-four lyrics (e.g. nos. 66, 71, 75) of which some fifty-six are carols, and, of the rest, three are in Latin. There is no music. It is attributed by Greene (*Selection*, p. 173) to the monastery of Bury St. Edmunds. Bodl. MS. Eng. poet. e.1 contains seventy-five English and Latin songs (e.g. nos. 133 and 138) of which sixty-three are English carols. There is one tune. Greene (*Selection*, p. 179) attributes the MS. to Beverley Minster. It has also been suggested that St. John's College, Cambridge, MS. S. 54 may have been of the same sort as these two (e.g. Stevens, *Early Tudor Court*, p. 118).

these lyrics have been recorded there is a certain element of good fortune in their preservation, for unlike poems printed in books, of which some hundreds of copies may have been printed, these lyrics were, probably, in many cases, written down once and once only, in versions that are unique props against the ruining of time.

II

A saint has pride of place as the first English lyrist (no. 1), which is appropriate enough since so many medieval lyrics that have survived are religious. But Saint Godric cannot have been the only poet composing verses within a hundred years of the Norman Conquest, and a comment made by a chronicler who records a fragment of poetry at least as early as St. Godric's implies the existence in his day of another sort of verse with another function. Thomas of Ely quotes[1] these four lines and says that they, and others, were sung publicly in dances and remembered in wise sayings:

> Merye sungen the muneches (*monks*) binnen Ely
> Tha (*When*) Cnut King rew ther by;
> 'Roweth, knites, noer the land,
> And here we thes muneches saeng.'

Thomas calls King Canute their author. We do not know to what sort of poem they originally belonged, but it may well be that, at least in Thomas's day, they were the burden of a dance-song. But whereas ecclesiastical decrees against dances with song are memorials to their existence on the Continent long before the Norman Conquest, no such evidence exists in England. There is no sign of dance-song in Old English literature.

From the twelfth to the fourteenth centuries, however, from St. Godric's day until Chaucer's, several scraps of evidence suggest that there existed a range of popular poetry now almost entirely lost. To begin with, in the twelfth century, Gerald of Wales describes a delightful episode that was ecclesiastically horrifying, when a parish priest, having heard dancers singing all night about his church a song including the refrain, 'Swete lemman, thin are' (*Sweetheart, have mercy*) mistakenly incorporated the line in his mass next morning. In the early thirteenth century two lines, which, according to

---

[1] *Liber Eliensis*, ed. D. J. Stewart (London, 1848), p. 202.

Robbins,[1] occur also in a fourteenth-century manuscript, formed the subject of a sermon which was mentioned earlier on p. 24:

> Atte wrastlinge my lemman I ches (*chose*),
> And atte ston-casting I him forles (*lost*).

The preacher says that these words are said in his country, among other songs worth little, when people go 'into the ring', that is into a ring-dance. Some one hundred years later, nos. 31 and 33, 'Maiden in the mor lay' and 'Ich am of Irlaunde', were scribbled down among several other pieces of similar verse, some of which are in French, fascinating and chance relics left stranded on the shore by a tide that has long-since receded:[2]

> All night by [the] rose, rose,
> All night by the rose I lay,

and

> [Trip]pe a lutel with thy fot,
> And let thy body go.

Finally, between 1317 and 1360, as was mentioned on p. 24, Richard de Ledrede, Bishop of Ossory, in Ireland, disapproving of the shameful songs they were singing, composed for the minor clergy of his cathedral some sixty pious lyrics in Latin to be sung, instead of the secular English and French words, to the same popular tunes.[3] Several of these Latin poems are preceded by a line or two of the vernacular lyrics to indicate what tune is meant. One of them is the first line of no. 33, 'Maiden in the mor lay', which, as we have seen, was recorded elsewhere in what is probably its entirety; but, for the rest, there exist only these fragments of what were almost certainly popular love poems. They are the few chinks in a wall of silence cutting us off from what was doubtless a whole world of song.

> Alas! how shold I singe?
> Yloren (*lost*) is my playinge.
> How shold I with that olde man
> To leven, and let (*leave*) my lemman,
> Swettist of all thinge?

[1] R.H.R. *Sec. Lyrs.*, p. xxxix: in Camb. Univ. Lib. MS. Ii.3.8. Sermon ed. M. Förster in *Anglia*, xlii, pp. 152–4.

[2] ed. W. Heuser in *Anglia*, xxx, pp. 173–9.

[3] R.H.R. *Sec. Lyrs.*, pp. xxxv–xxxvi; Greene, p. cxviii, and Greene, ' "The maid of the moor" in the *Red Book of Ossory*', *Speculum*, xxvii (1952), pp. 504–6.

It is probably from this world that nos. 66 and 164, for example, derive so much of their peculiarly English strength.

Various reasons, holding more or less water, can be suggested why such popular, secular poetry was not written down: if it was part of a minstrel's repertoire he would not wish it to be readily available to other entertainers; on the other hand, the more popular a song the less likely it is that anyone would need to write it down to remember it; it is in the nature of folk-song to be transmitted orally; parchment was expensive and unlikely to be used for popular songs, while cheaper forms of record, such as wax tablets, even if used must have been impermanent; and in their devoted lives, clerical scribes would be unlikely to spend monastic time and materials on the ephemeral entertainments of the contemptible world.

In this period between the Norman Conquest and Chaucer's day, with the exception of political poems (e.g. nos. 7 and 26) there were recorded not only very few popular, but also very few sophisticated secular lyrics. Nos. 2, 3, 4, 18(?), 19 and the lyrics in the Harley manuscript, of which nos. 7, 9, 10 and 13 are examples, are almost all that are to be found. The Harley collection (p. 25 and p. 28, note 1), made in the early fourteenth century, is, therefore, from this point of view, quite exceptional. As well as longer works, it includes about equal numbers of religious and secular lyrics, but of the two dozen or so that are religious or moral, some twenty are found also in other manuscripts, whereas of those that are secular, every one is unique. This indicates that the secular lyrics had a much narrower circulation. On the other hand, lyrics of this manuscript were originally in several different dialects, which suggests, rather, that there may have existed many more than the compiler selected for his collection (since they must thus have come from far and wide), and, also, that they were the product of no one group or community such as the King's court, or a gentleman's household, or a monastery. The authors of these early secular lyrics—which may all have been by different men—are quite unknown, but they would seem, in general, to have been deliberate artists making poetry in much the same way as, though less successfully than, Chaucer a century or so later. Presumably they modelled their verse on that of the troubadours for here are elaborate stanza forms like those of the continental poets, conventional images and sentiments, rhetorical formulas and subjects like theirs. But here also are native English characteristics, for example, frequent alliteration, such alliterative formulas as 'stark ne stour' (no. 14, l. 4), in no. 15 the homely language, the local scene and perhaps the rhythm of the line, and in no. 25, the popular burden. It is unlikely that any of these early poems were by court poets—such as, in a later age, were Geoffrey Chaucer, Charles of Orleans or William Dunbar—who wrote for an aristocratic audience highly conscious of decorum and the entertainment proper for a gentleman. Some, at least, were probably written by clever clerics, as is suggested by the religious company which they keep in this collection and by having among their number one that has for subject a clerical love-affair (no. 9).

The sporadic incidence of sophisticated secular lyrics before Chaucer's day may be due to a possible lack of English interest in the manifestations of that refined love which was the subject of so many French lyrics that afforded a model, or to the fact that English did not become the language of court or of the government of the country until Chaucer's day, so that, in either case, little such lyric poetry was written. Until the 1370's and 80's the predominant languages were Latin and French, and it was not until this time, also, that questions of love really came into their own in any form of English literature. Such poetry of this sort as was written may have been recorded in collections destroyed, as were so many manuscripts, in the sixteenth century; but it seems more likely that it was not until Chaucer's day and after that lay scribes and new tastes in those who could afford to employ them, or could now write themselves, made the recording of secular lyrics increasingly likely. For one thing, perhaps, the new high style and the noble forms of ballade and roundel made their preservation in a fine manuscript seem more appropriate.

The nature and significance of this high style and of these forms new in Chaucer's[1] poetry have already been considered on pp. 25–6.

[1] Geoffrey Chaucer (1340's (?)–1400) came of an Ipswich family of wholesale wine merchants and customs officials. He is first heard of in the service of Elizabeth, wife of Prince Lionel, and did not, himself, become a merchant though he was later closely connected with commerce as controller of customs 1374–86. A J.P. and M.P. As a courtier, in his earlier days he served the King in his household, travelled as a diplomat and fought against France; in his later years he supervised some of the King's palaces and estates. His wife, Philippa, waited on the Queen, and his treatise on the Astrolabe (an astronomical instrument) is addressed to 'little Lewis, my son'. He is generally supposed to have been writing the *Canterbury Tales* soon after he left the Customs House but he never completed this dramatic sequence of diverse stories. *Troilus and Criseyde*, in five books of rime-royal stanzas, is complete and is one of the most profound and moving philosophical poems in the language and one of the most perceptive psychological studies of people in love (pp. 40–1, 44–5).

Introduction

Though the greatest poet of the English middle ages said he had written 'many a song', there remain only some twenty of his lyrics. On pp. 25–6 I have also considered the developments—in particular 'aureation'—of the one hundred and fifty years before the publication of Tottel's Miscellany and the advent of the great sonneteers. In the work of Chaucer and some one or two of his successors, such as William Dunbar and Robert Henryson,[1] are to be found so many of the characteristics of the poetry, variously, of Spenser, Shakespeare, Milton and Pope that it is clear why Dryden called Chaucer the father of English poetry. In the earliest, consistently accomplished instances of the characteristic English verse line, Chaucer achieved the confident and expansive copiousness of the sonnets and dignified stanzas of the Elizabethans. And though, as has been said, the poetry of Chaucer is in the same tradition as that in which many of the early secular lyrics were written, there is no reason to think Chaucer was aware of continuing in it: he made a fresh start, in many respects, learning direct from France and also from Italy.

His age, however, experienced a renaissance wider than this. It was a time when native traditions also came back into their own: in particular, in such poems as the *Morte Arthure*, *Sir Gawain and the Green Knight* and *Piers Plowman* there was revived and developed for new ends the English alliterative style based on the stress rhythms of speech which derived, ultimately, from long before the Norman Conquest and the songs of the French love-poets. The fifteenth-century poem, no. 115, is a good instance of its characteristic robust vigour and solidity:

> Swarte-smeked smethes, smatered with smoke,
> Drive me to deth with den of here dintes.

But it is, when thus full-blooded, a style generally unsuitable for lyric poetry, even if by that is meant no more than a short poem, and no. 115 is unique. On the other hand the poetry of a John Lydgate[2] or of nos. 135, 148, 173, or 176, which makes poor sense

---

[1] William Dunbar: dates of birth and death unknown; a priest, who received a pension from James IV of Scotland (1488–1513) and in his court was a poet of a rich and gay aristocratic society, closely linked to France. Though several Robert Henrysons are known of, none can be certainly identified with the man whose name is attached to a number of poems and who is mentioned as a poet now dead in Dunbar's no. 146. Since that poem was printed in 1508 he may be presumed to have lived during the last half of 15c.

[2] Lydgate died about 1450, a monk of the Benedictine abbey at Bury St.

rhythmically in terms of classical prosody or syllabic counting (how, for example, should line 3 of no. 97 be read?), sometimes makes more if not perfect sense in terms of broken-down alliterative metre without alliteration, but with rhyme, and with two halves in each line and two stresses in each half:

> Put in a som all marcial policye,
> Compleet in Afric and boundes of Cartage
> The Theban legioun, examples of chevalrye,
> At Rodamus River was expert ther corage (no. 97).

It is also true that Chaucer's own poetry probably derived fundamentally far more from the native tradition than appears on the surface.

One development of the fifteenth century that is generally considered of special importance is that of the carol. Poems that are called 'carols' in the fifteenth and sixteenth centuries could be sung and were made of uniform stanzas and a burden. The burden began the poem and was repeated after each stanza. The dominant form was that in nos. 67, 68, a stanza riming a, a, a, b, linked by the shorter last line to the burden riming b, b. Carols were not essentially Christmas songs. On the other hand, carols became specially associated with Christmas, perhaps because it was such an elaborate and long festival (note 78) or perhaps partly in an endeavour by the pious (e.g. the Franciscans) to redeem them from paganism. They may sometimes have been transmitted orally but, typically, they were written down (p. 19 and note 129).

Until the fifteenth century no English poem can be found which anyone in its day explicitly called a 'carol'. When the word 'carol' is used in the fourteenth century it is more often than not associated with dancing as well as with song. Illustrations in manuscripts and descriptions in literature show that, in France, for a couple of centuries before this, the *carole* was a ring-dance with song in which the dancers circled, hand in hand, while the burden was sung, and then danced on the spot for the stanza. Until about Chaucer's death in 1400 this dance was very fashionable in England: 'ring-dances' and 'carols' seem to have been danced by ordinary folk and by ladies and gentlemen, but we know scarcely at all to what words

Edmunds. Nearly 150,000 lines of his verse exist, characteristically dull. For questions of rhythm mentioned here see C. S. Lewis, 'The fifteenth-century heroic line', *Essays and Studies of the English Association*, xxiv (1938), pp. 28–41.

or tunes they danced.[1] It is most unlikely that it was to any of the carols in this anthology—at least, as they are written down. Only some quarter or so of the more than five hundred carols in English that remain have music and it is generally polyphonic both for burden and stanza: it is not simple dance-song but learned harmony.

Many religious carols may have been used as processional hymns but there is no certain evidence that they were. They are recorded in manuscripts which contain choir repertoires in Latin and English (p. 29),[2] and their basic form, of a burden with uniform stanzas, is also that of the processional hymn (no. 29). It is, however, uncertain how far, if at all, English carols, at any rate of the fifteenth and sixteenth centuries, grew out of Latin hymns or, on the other hand, out of vernacular dance-songs (from which, it has been suggested, the Latin hymns themselves also originally derived). Of English poems in carol form before the early fifteenth century there remains only a handful of such varied poems that no simple conclusions about their origins are possible: the earliest are nos. 13(?), 19, 25, 29(?) and 31(?), while nos. 37 and 38 from Friar Grimestone's notebook represent the very few there are of the mid- and later fourteenth century. On the other hand, there are poems in Latin and Italian from at least the thirteenth century, and in French from much earlier, which have the same general form as the fifteenth-century English carol and, very often, precisely that stanza form and rhyme scheme which is predominant in it.[3]

What has been said about developments in the form and style of Chaucerian and post-Chaucerian secular lyrics applies also to religious, but it remains for the last few paragraphs of this brief and selective historical survey to consider the religious lyrics separately. Many things have already been said about them on pp. 17–18, 20–2,

[1] Such odd scraps of dancing songs as remain are described on pp. 30–2: but it is not certain whether they have what has come to be regarded as the literary form of a carol. Not all dances were 'carols'.

[2] Manuscripts containing Choir repertoires suggesting processional use of carols: Bodl. MS. Arch. Selden B.26; B.M. MS. Egerton 3307; B.M. Additional (Ritson) MS. 5665. See Stevens, *Carols*, p. xiv and C. K. Miller, 'The early English carol', *Renaissance News*, iii (1950), pp. 61–4. In general see Greene's introduction and his *Selection*, pp. 44–5; R.H.R. 'Middle English carols as processional hymns', *S.P.*, lvi (1959), pp. 559–82 and introduction to his *Christmas Carols*. Estimates of number of carols with music in R.H.R. 'Two new carols, Hunterian MS. 83', *M.L.N.*, lviii (1943) and his *Christmas Carols*, pp. 3–4, and Greene, *Selection*, p. 1. The music for a number of carols is printed in Stevens, *Carols*, and R.H.R., *Christmas Carols*.

[3] Greene, *Selection*, pp. 8–9 and 40–1.

24 which would also be in place here. Only three new points will now be made. First, from any period in the middle ages far more religious lyrics have been preserved than secular. With respect to the later centuries, for example, Robbins has said[1] that, excluding the poems of Chaucer, Lydgate and Hoccleve, it would be difficult to add to the two hundred and ten items of the fourteenth and fifteenth centuries in his anthology of secular lyrics more than about another hundred; whereas Brown has said[2] that it would have been possible to make a collection of religious lyrics ten times the size of that in his fifteenth-century anthology alone, which contains one hundred and ninety-two items.

Secondly, some of the earlier religious lyrics enjoy a restraint and spareness that has a quality a little like that of Simone Martini or Giotto, the late thirteenth- and early fourteenth-century Italian painters, roughly contemporary with them. Instances are the ballad-like poem, no. 18, about the betrayal of Jesus by Judas, the Nativity poem, no. 32,

> Gabriel, fram Hevene King
> Sent to the maide swete,
> Broughte hire blisful tiding,
> And faire he gan hire grete,

the dialogue between Mary and Jesus on the Cross, no. 24, 'Stond well, moder, under Rode', and even the more expansive and lamentatory, no. 8, which has the 'Ubi sunt' theme, 'Where beth they beforen us weren?' (note 83; p. 40). All but the first of these, which is more likely to have popular connections, are certainly poems in the learned tradition. They are neither exercises in theological analysis nor mere accumulations of ecclesiastical conventionalities, but poetry of an unassuming dignity, intelligently organized and simply moving. There is the same significant simplicity in the song to Mary, no. 5,

> Of on that is so fair and bright,
> Velud maris stella,
> Brighter than the dayes light,
> Parens et puella,

which is another poem clearly belonging to the tradition of Latin learning and worship and using some of the Marian titles and allusions that can elsewhere be so mechanical. But it has a superbly gay

---

[1] R.H.R. *Sec. Lyrs.*, p. xxii.   [2] C.B. *15c.*, p. xviii.

movement, freely alternating between English and Latin in a complex stanza and with unfaltering step. How integral the form of this stanza is to its success is shown by comparing the poem with the inferior fifteenth-century 'carol' version not included in this anthology (C.B. *15c.* no. 17).

The third point is that in the last half of the fourteenth century and in the fifteenth century there developed a religious poetry of pathos and passion. It was not new, for it grew in the devotional tradition stemming from the eleventh century considered on p. 22. Moreover, in such thirteenth- and early fourteenth-century poems as the love-song of Friar Thomas of Hales, mentioned earlier on p. 24, and the love-song to Jesus in the spring, of which the opening lines are quoted on p. 15, and the Harley lyric, 'Swete Jesu, King of blisse' (*Harley*, pp. 51–2, no. 15), tender longing for 'Jesu, lefman swete' is stirred by the recital of some features of his suffering on the Cross, feet and hands pierced with nails, and head bloody. But the degree of pathos and the quantity of poems of which it is a characteristic are certainly features of this later period. Among the poems of Mary and the Passion of Jesus, no. 24, of the thirteenth century, cited above as an example of restrained feeling, sparely expressed, may be compared with no. 112, a more elaborate poem which fully and poignantly explores the heart-breaking potentialities of a situation chosen for its sentimental power. There is a tendency for such poems to lack obvious shape, and to be flabby, as is particularly seen in the work of Richard Rolle,[1] which furnishes probably the most famous but not the earliest examples of this mode. The warmth and passionate eagerness of no. 36, and its tender iteration of the name of Jesus, are typical. But in 'Quia amore langueo', no. 62, probably written about the end of Chaucer's life-time and a prime example of this type of poetry at its best, sentiment is not only evoked but controlled, and the warm and tender love involved in the imagery of family relationships has an intellectual toughness, an element of wit, because of the theology of the Incarnation which is presupposed. It is all the more fitting that this fine poem should be the last mentioned in this section of the introduction since, from the point of view of time, it comes from the heart of the English middle ages

[1] Left Oxford University at eighteen to become a hermit and live as a contemplative in his home country of Yorkshire. Moved about considerably, however, in days of great political and military disorder, and died at Hampole in 1349, probably at about the age of fifty.

and is in that learned tradition, both with respect to style and subject, which, sometimes with justification, the modern reader might think unlikely, in the terms of one of its own conventional images, to bear the flower of true poetry.

III

Robbins[1] has estimated that translations from Latin form some tenth of the extant medieval English lyrics but, as we have seen (pp. 26, 32–4), it was not until the late middle ages that English and Scottish poets tried to convey in the vernacular the stylistic qualities of the great medieval Latin poems. In earlier times, however, the accentual Latin verse, stemming from the popular poetry of the latter days of the Roman Empire, must have directly influenced the rhythm of the English lyric and music appropriate to Latin rhythms and stanza forms must have moulded the rhythms and stanza forms of the English translation to be sung to it (nos. 29, 32, 40, 117). A number of English stanza forms are the same as those in Latin: that they are borrowed from Latin is very likely where the English is a translation, and it has been argued that the English carol itself derives from Latin hymns (see p. 36), though it may be that both Latin and English forms developed separately and similarly from the same roots in popular song.

Of the four hundred and seventy-four carols in his great collection, Greene has counted two hundred and two which include Latin lines or phrases. Such inset Latin, whether in carols or elsewhere, is sometimes a commonplace, sometimes a special composition to meet a particular need, but sometimes taken from hymns used in church services, proses (a part of some masses between epistle and gospel) and antiphons (which were sung before and after the psalms). More important than all such forms and formulas was the influence exercised on the content of English lyrics by the general learned tradition of the Church, which was conveyed in Latin, whether, for example, through the Scriptures or the Fathers, the twelfth- and thirteenth-century devotional writers or through the services themselves.

Many English religious lyrics are in Latin genres. Of these, with the exception of James Ryman's, there are very few poems of the

[1] 'Middle English versions of "Christe qui lux es et dies",' *Harvard Theological Review*, xlvii (1954), pp. 55–63.

Introduction

Resurrection or Trinity, and Dunbar's magnificent Resurrection hymn, no. 147, might suggest that the former theme, at any rate, had to await the development in the vernacular of the appropriate 'high' style. To the best of my knowledge, lullabies of the Child Jesus (e.g. nos. 35, 38, 77), a form in which the Passion is foretold, are found first in the fourteenth century in English. Poems of Mary—hymns in her praise, for example, or songs of her joys—abound in English and have already been considered on pp. 17–18, 20–2.

One of the most important of the Latin kinds is the complaint of Christ or his mother. From the later eleventh century onwards there was reflected in a new form, the *planctus*, or complaint, a fresh emphasis on the human suffering of the Passion (see pp. 22, 38). Sometimes *planctus* are found attached to the authorized liturgy, but they probably originated as independent poems. Sometimes Christ utters the lament; but more usually, and in the earliest, it is the Blessed Virgin as she stands at the foot of the Cross. For such complaints by Mary, the Sorrowing Mother, the Gospel accounts themselves afford no material. But it was in the twelfth century, also, that there grew a special devotion to the Blessed Virgin, and meditation on her part in the drama of redemption, aimed at stirring the believer's heart, would naturally supply appropriate sentiments. Nos. 44, 112, for example, are complaints of Mary. To the best of my knowledge, complaints of Christ in verse form do not occur in English until the fourteenth century. In Latin there seem to be none earlier and only one or two later.[1] (For example, nos. 41, 46, 47.)

Another of the most important Latin kinds is the poem in contempt of the world. Such a poem reflects medieval man's profound awareness of change and insecurity in the world and his life in it. He regarded this as one of the consequences of the Fall, brought about by the disobedience of Adam and Eve in eating the forbidden fruit, and as a law of that part of the universe which, in the Ptolemaic system, lay beneath the sphere of the moon, itself the planet of change. Over this area of chronic instability ruled the Goddess Fortune, herself a late Roman and pagan goddess, but incorporated into the Christian vision of countless medieval thinkers and artists. She was often represented turning a wheel, symbol of earthly and

---

[1] Such complaints resemble Christ's reciting to sinners, on the Day of Judgment, the sufferings he had endured for them in a 6c. sermon of Caesarius of Arles (*P.L.*, xxxix, col. 2207) or God's complaint in 8c. Old English poem on Last Judgment in the 'Exeter Book'.

human mutability, herself, perhaps, blindfold, so that at one time a king might be coming to power, at another reigning, and, at another, as surely, suffering a fall. Chaucer's *Monk's Tale* is a collection of illustrations of this activity of Fortune in the lives of the great. Sometimes Fortune was represented with two faces, like Janus, one ugly and one beautiful, sometimes seated insecurely on a sphere. To achieve stability and peace the Christian was bidden to put no trust in things of the world or of man, glorious and strong and clever as they might be, but only in things of Heaven; and, to this end, to use his reason, his will and God's grace.

The Scriptures and the Fathers amply contributed to this tradition of Contempt of the World, while tragic awareness of the transience of things is characteristic of Old English literature, and few works of any sort have had a greater effect on later writers than the *Consolation of Philosophy* of Boethius (late fifth and early sixth centuries). This is a consideration, among other things, of the apparently unjust and unreasonable action of Fortune.[1] But it was not until it received a new and selective emphasis in the later eleventh and in the twelfth centuries—a time when more men began to write about more things—that contempt of the world appears to have become a common literary form. At the other end of the middle ages, a particular emphasis on death and the personification of it increased both in Latin and vernacular literature and in the visual arts[2] of the fourteenth century. In the fifteenth century, for example, there grew from earlier origins the iconographic convention of the Dance of Death, in which skeletons were represented 'arresting' the living, perhaps a ploughman, a lady or a bishop, as Death does in no. 109. Men of the later middle ages evinced a disproportionate and morbid concern with death. Nos. 8, 35, 43, 48, 60, 83, 127 and 131 are examples of poems in contempt of the world.

[1] The goddess Fortune: see H. R. Patch, *The goddess Fortune in mediaeval literature* (Cambridge: Harvard Univ. Press, 1927). Tradition of contempt: *Book of Job*; 4c.: St. Ambrose, 'Liber de bono mortis', *P.L.*, xiv, col. 573: Quid enim est aliud haec vita nisi plena laqueorum? . . . lacrymae, dolores (etc.); 7c.: St. Gregory, 'Moralia' (commentary on *Job*), *P.L.*, lxxv, col. 509 ff.; 11c., 12c.: Bernard of Cluny, 'De contemptu mundi', *Anglo-Latin satirical poets of the twelfth century*, ed. T. Wright (London, 1872), vol. ii, pp. 7 ff.; attributed to St. Bernard, 'Meditationes de cognitione humanae conditionis', *P.L.*, clxxxiv, col. 490: Nihil aliud est homo quam sperma fetidum, saccus stercorum, cibus vermium. Post hominem vermis, post vermem fetor et horror. Sic in non hominem vertitur omnis homo; etc., etc.
[2] E. Mâle, *L'art réligieux de la fin du moyen âge en France* (Paris, 1931), pp. 347 ff.

Introduction

Another aspect of the Latin tradition which will probably cause surprise is that represented by drinking songs. To the best of my knowledge there are no drinking songs among English folk-songs nor are there any in the French or 'courtly' tradition, but there are some among the student poetry of the *Carmina Burana*, those Latin songs in a manuscript collection, formerly in the Benedictine monastery of Benediktbeuern, which were written down in the later thirteenth century. In that collection there are many poems in the various genres represented in this anthology, such as poems in contempt of the world. There are also satires and love poems, and, when it is remembered that Latin was as much their authors' everyday language as the vernaculars, it is not surprising that the Latin songs have much in common with vernacular popular poetry. But, with regard to drinking songs, this would not seem to be so. There was, among the 'clerks', a tendency to riot and parody, irreverence and vulgarity, which showed itself, especially in fourteenth- and fifteenth-century France—and in England, to a lesser extent and rather earlier—even in burlesque of the words and ceremonies of church services.[1]

The 'clerks' were not alone responsible, however, for another kind of medieval poetry, that of satire on women, which was common from the twelfth century onwards. Anti-feminist literature was often written by celibate churchmen, it is true, who may have known the satire of the Ancient World against women and who regarded them as the deceiving descendants of Eve, through whom man had lost Paradise; but it was written, on the other hand, within the tradition of secular love, by Deschamps and Chaucer, for example, in the fourteenth century, and by the continuator of the *Roman de la Rose*, Jean de Meun, in the century before.[2] Underlying the formal satire there might be ascetic contempt of the world, but there might be, on the other hand, that antagonism between the sexes which is still as much a part of life today as simple attraction. The sophisticated, in particular, as was characteristic in the middle ages, made out of the entertaining diversity of sex relationships a courtly game. Satires on women, then (e.g. nos. 123, 135) are in both Latin and French traditions.

From the time of the Norman Conquest, 'France' and England

[1] E. K. Chambers, *The mediaeval stage* (Oxford, 1903), vol. i, pp. 274–335.
[2] F. L. Utley, *The crooked rib, an analytical index to the argument about women in English and Scots literature to the end of the year 1568* (Columbus: Ohio State University, 1944).

had many things in common, but forms of lyric poetry that are peculiarly French seem to have had only a limited effect in England. Many medieval poems contain a 'refrain'—a recurrent element repeated as part of each stanza—or a 'burden'— a recurrent element at the beginning of a poem which is repeated after each stanza and independently of it: in the opinion of most historians, this suggests that the form of these poems originated in a dance, however stylized or literary they may have eventually become. Their evolution can probably be best seen in the case of the carol for the development of which there is far more evidence in France than in England.

A French form often found, however, in English is the *chanson d'aventure*.[1] It has a narrative setting: the poet begins by describing his going out into the country, often in the spring; he may meet a woman and take part in a dialogue with her, as in no. 19 (in which case the form is sometimes called a *pastourelle*), or make love to her, with or without success; he may simply report the overheard complaint of the woman, for example, at her having no lover or against her unhappy marriage. Nos. 20 and 38 are further examples.

The French poets Machaut, Froissart, Deschamps, and Christine de Pisan, roughly contemporaries of Chaucer, wrote a variety of *ballades*. They are in some respects a fixed form, consisting of three stanzas with or without a shorter fourth stanza called the *envoi*. Stanzas may, however, have as few as seven lines or as many as ten, and lines may be of eight or ten syllables. The last line of each stanza is repeated, and the rhymes, which are no more than three or four, are carried throughout the poem. It was probably Chaucer who introduced the *ballade* form into English. English does not provide as many possibilities as French of rhyming one sound throughout an entire poem and English (and Scottish) poets modified the ballade accordingly. A further adaptation was the adding of many more stanzas. Nos. 53, 55 are ballades.

Chaucer also probably introduced into England the *rondeau* or roundel. Written by Deschamps and Machaut, it was a form in which one or more lines occurred among the other lines three times. There may be as many as fourteen or as few as seven lines, altogether (depending partly on how many lines are repeated), with two rhymes throughout. The manuscripts of nos. 52 and 57 do not make clear how many lines are to be repeated. It would seem that in the *rondeaux* of Villon in the later fifteenth century the refrain was

[1] H. E. Sandison, *The 'chanson d'aventure' in Middle English* (Bryn Mawr, 1913).

reduced to a repetition of the opening words only and it is this form that is used by Wyatt in no. 184. In this he drew freshly on French models and did not derive, simply, from his English forebears.

Ballades and roundels form a very small proportion of extant medieval English lyrics and are the work, almost entirely, of Hoccleve and the major writers mentioned above.

Since French was the language of Court and ruling class and Latin that of Church and learning, and to many medieval Englishmen two or three languages were as natural as one, 'macaronic' poems—made of lines or half lines in several languages, regularly arranged—are not uncommon. Their pleasure is in the piquancy of the strange mixture and the cleverness of the dove-tailing. No. 70 is a macaronic poem.

But it was, perhaps, in the literature of love that secular France and England had most in common. In the late eleventh and earlier twelfth centuries love between the sexes received such a new and particular emphasis in the literature, first of southern and then of northern France, that it was tantamount to the beginning, in what was a formative period for many aspects of European culture, of another of the basic medieval traditions. Our modern American and European civilization is still very much dominated by some aspects of it.

One aspect of particular importance in the middle ages was a cult of refined, sometimes called nowadays courtly, love, characterized by the concept of the lover as a humble servant, the woman he loved as a sovereign and often unattainable lady, and the love between them as ennobling (see, e.g., nos. 141, l. 2; 86, ll. 2, 7; 9, l. 2; 13, l. 23; 53, l. 1; 54, l. 7; 89, ll. 1–2; 91, l. 8; 148, l. 1; 154, ll. 18–19). In French literature, more often than in English, this love was for another man's wife. But the inaccessibility of the woman might be simply the result of her *danger*, that stimulating self-containment and aloof power, which could be caprice, and which prevented or deferred physical fulfilment (so that she was often called merciless), while, at the same time, it intensified the lover's desire and increased his sensibility. It could embolden him in battle and provoke effort to please her, for example, by improving his manners; but it could also result in abandonment to sentimental self-pity and despair (see, e.g., nos. 21, ll. 13–24; 25, ll. 37–68; 142, ll. 3–7; 93; 13, l. 8; 186, l. 2; 165, ll. 1–4; 57, l. 16; 143; 70, l. 29). Such attitudes were conventions in literature, whatever was the case in life. Poems in this tradition often have characteristics in common with poems of religious love, and the two are often difficult to distinguish (pp. 20, 24). On the other hand secular love, it was often said, unlike the love of God, was bound to involve unhappiness if only because of its association with the Goddess Fortune (pp. 40–1).

Most of the love poems in this anthology evince the conventions of the general tradition if not always those of the more refined and courtly: the association of love and spring, nos. 23; 10, ll. 1–5; 13, ll. 1–6; the wounding by love, nos. 21, l. 25; 9, l. 60; 10, ll. 5–6; 57, l. 3; 141, l. 2; that love is *derne*, no. 21, l. 43; madness, no. 9, l. 11; 186, l. 27; 4, l. 3; and paradoxical, no. 88, ll. 1–6; no. 99; that the mistress alone is *bote of bale* or a physician, nos. 10, ll. 23–4; 53, l. 7; that the lover cannot sleep, nos. 13, l. 21; 186, l. 11; 19, ll. 2–3; 165, l. 9; and burns, nos. 53, l. 22; 186, l. 10; 70, l. 35. (And see note 25.)

Several poems, in particular no. 25, are rather descriptions of a conventional beauty than poems of love.[1] Their details are in the rhetoric books and in previous writers of love literature and scarcely derive at all from observation: the lady is white, nos. 21, l. 1; 13, l. 27; gold, no. 21, l. 2; has grey eyes, no. 21, l. 24; arched eyebrows, no. 21, l. 26; long sides, no. 91, l. 19; slender waist, nos. 13, l. 16; 91, l. 19. There are some variations which may be new; for example, the black eye of Alisoun in no. 13, l. 14 is exceptional.

There is one kind of poetry which is neither French nor Latin in origin and with which this section must conclude. It is the ballad. Ballads are narrative poems. Classically, their style is elliptical and characterized by that repetition with partial variation which advances action or creates atmosphere and drama. Dialogue is typical, terse and telling. A ballad is objective and impersonal and conveys nothing of the teller's feeling nor reflects his relations with his audience. It is generally transmitted orally and is meant for saying or singing. Since ballads are a kind of poetry of their own and essentially different, despite resemblances, from the rest of the poems in this anthology, only one of them is included and that for special reasons (p. 32; note 18).

IV

The lyrics in this book range from the mid-twelfth to the mid-sixteenth centuries, from the earliest known after the Norman

[1] D. S. Brewer, 'The ideal of feminine beauty in mediaeval literature', *M.L.R.*, (1955), pp. 257–69.

Introduction

Conquest until the poetry of Wyatt.[1] His verse was first published, in selection, fifteen years after his death and then became associated exclusively with the work of the Elizabethans. But in their Italianizing of English, Sidney and Spenser drew freshly for both form and content on foreign models rather than on Wyatt and did not do so until a quarter of a century after his poems were published. Scottish poems are included because their affinities to those in the strictly English dialects—and not least their affinities of language—far outweigh what differentiates them.

By a 'lyric' is meant simply a shorter poem, and the word is used only because it is shorthand which is understood by most people in this general sense. For the most part, I have chosen lyrics for their quality and interest as individual poems in the same way that more modern poems might be chosen for an anthology. I have taken into account that it is often harder to construe medieval lyrics and that there is more obvious need in reading them to use a trained historical imagination, but I have not necessarily made allowance for what different expectations of poetry may underlie the writing of some, if not all, of these poems. In a few cases I have included a poem rather because of its interest in literary or cultural history. While this anthology should be primarily a collection of enjoyable medieval lyrics—it would not have been made were this not so—I intend that the commentary required for their full and proper appreciation should make an illustrated introduction to medieval English literary studies. For all these reasons I have included the poetry of well-known authors, but, although some of their best is much superior to many anonymous poems that have been given a place, it has sometimes been excluded for the sake of due proportion and the representation of a variety of topics, kinds and styles.

The arrangement of the poems is roughly chronological. Few, however, can be dated precisely, and the date at the head of each poem is generally derived from that of the source of the base text (p. 47) which is, in most cases, the earliest known. Many poems were probably composed much earlier than they were recorded. Though I have thought it best not to speculate (except rarely, as,

---

[1] A member of the turbulent court of Henry VIII, Wyatt was several times imprisoned. He was a trusted ambassador and a soldier. A man of letters and said by Leland to have been at Cambridge, he translated a work of Plutarch and wrote satires and a version of the penitential psalms. He was unhappily married and died in 1542 at the age of thirty-nine.

for example, in the case of the Harley lyrics among which are at least two poems (nos. 7 and 26) which must clearly have been written earlier than they were recorded in the MS. while no. 24, for example, is found also in MS. Digby 86 of the later thirteenth century), I have, on the other hand, seen little point in dating poems within a few years and have, instead, at best placed most in either the 'earlier', 'mid' or 'later' parts of a century. After taking into account these rough chronological groups I have arranged the poems largely for the reader's varied pleasure and he should be careful not to let himself be misled into thinking that because, for example, no. 62, 'Quia amore langueo' or no. 83, 'Why is the world beloved, that fals is and vein' are found in this anthology after Chaucer and on pages headed 'fifteenth century', they could not have been current in his day. There are dangers in a roughly chronological arrangement, but the difficulties of any other proved much greater.

Glosses at the foot of the page are intended to be complete for each poem, and there is no general glossary. To save space only the first occurrence of a word in each poem is glossed, but if there are two occurrences, two line references are given, and if there are more, then the first, followed by 'etc.'. If a line or a poem is particularly difficult it is translated in full.

The texts have all been taken direct from the original manuscripts or first printed texts, or from photographs of them, unless otherwise stated. The source of the base text of each poem is listed in the notes on individual poems at the back of the book. I have departed from this text only in infrequent circumstances, making each emendation on its own merits. In general, these departures, unless trivial or obviously appropriate, are noted among the glosses at the foot of the page, together with whatever support there may be in other manuscripts. Reference in any note to *the MS.*, without qualification, is to that manuscript in which the base text is found. I have supplied each poem with a title which is, generally, of my own invention, but I have used a line from the poem where I have thought the poem more likely to be known by it.

Modern punctuation and use of capital letters have been introduced throughout. With regard to spelling I have had these major considerations in mind: that the appearance of a page can do much to help a reader to be at home with its contents, and that medieval spellings (not to speak of the arrangement of poetry on the page of a manuscript and the absence of punctuation) are, for the modern reader, either unnecessarily repulsive, or misleadingly quaint; that medieval scribes were commonly inconsistent spellers, even within any one poem, as well as free assimilators to their own dialect of a poem in another, even at the cost of rhyme; that expert philologists do not know for certain what sounds all these various spellings represent nor, in all cases, on what syllables the stresses fell; that there are involved in this anthology the spellings of a variety of dialects over a period of four hundred years in which major sound changes occurred; that comparatively few readers of the lyrics in this anthology are ever likely to know properly what the experts think particular spellings represent, and it would be altogether beyond the scope of this book to attempt to teach them; but that, on the other hand, 'modernizing' spelling often gives a false impression of a modern meaning, so that what would have been automatically 'looked-up' for its old sense when oddly spelt, when made to seem contemporary is not suspected by the disarmed reader; that greater knowledge than I have would be necessary to justify amending spelling with great boldness, and that a hundred and one difficulties crop up as soon as anyone attempts it, not least questions of consistency, particularly in view of the variety of dialect and period; and that, all other things being equal, such evidence as medieval scribes have left us of the rhythm of a poem and of how a poem sounded to them is best left intact even for the non-specialist reader.

What I have done in the light of these major considerations will probably offend everybody in some way but not all in the same way. It will be asked why, if I have allowed myself to take this liberty, I have not also allowed that. In dealing with spelling, as in establishing a text, I have treated each case on its own merits. In general, however, *th* is printed instead of *ð* or *þ*, *y* or *gh* instead of *ʒ*, and, with regard to *u*, *v*; *y*, *i*; *w*, *u*; *i*, *j*; *c*, *k*, the text conforms as far as possible to today's practice, always bearing in mind the considerations above—so that, for example, if a modern spelling would disguise an old meaning I have been as inconsistent as a medieval scribe and kept the spelling of the manuscript. In general, spelling within a poem or between poems written in the same hand is, as far as possible, made uniform. In a few early texts I have been more conservative, but in most poems obviously unstressed syllables have been made to conform to modern usage; *sch* is generally represented by *sh*; *sal*, for example, becomes *shall*; *hool* becomes *whool*; *wel*, *well*; *fresshist, freshest*; *taucht, taught*; *quhen, when*; *ouris, houris*; *hit, it*; *com, comb*; *forte, for to*; *wit, with*; *wrecched, wretched*; *wikked, wicked*; *siknes, sickness*; *byleue, belefe*; *crist, Christ*; *iugged, judged*; *stiuart, stiward*; *byfel, befell*; *nicht* (except in 'Scottish' poems) or *nitht* or *niht* or *nist, night*; and so on. I have made no alterations that, to my knowledge, seriously modify the predominant sounds in any line, and—except that such common words as *mine* and *thine* are so spelt though they sometimes have no *e* in the manuscript—no alteration that could affect rhythm. I have left untouched even those final 'e's' that are sometimes called merely scribal. For the linguistic specialist who is skilled in interpreting spelling as sound and to whom any variation may be significant there are editions of all these poems that give him all he needs. The texts in this anthology are not intended peculiarly for him. But, on the other hand, it has been my intention to modify the spelling of the originals no more than is possible to achieve a measure of consistency or a more modern appearance without losing anything which from the literary point of view is linguistically vital.

The notes on individual poems at the back may each have three parts. The first is a general preface to the poem setting it in its proper context, explaining it and making some critical observations. The second, if relevant, gives detailed references which substantiate and expand the first part. In the third part are cited the number of the poem in Brown and Robbins' *Index of Middle English Verse*, if it is included in it, and the source of the base text. When referring to the folios of a manuscript on which a poem is to be found, only that folio is cited on which it begins. In Brown and Robbins' *Index* there are generally listed all the known records of each poem (and, in most cases, all have been examined in determining the text in this anthology): these are not, therefore, generally repeated here but are given only if the poem is not included in the *Index* or if reference has to be made to them in the textual notes. Although the *Index* lists principal editions at the time of its publication there have been others since then and therefore all are listed here.

There are many cross references throughout, indicated simply by enclosing in brackets the appropriate page numbers to be turned to—for example (p. 561)—or the appropriate number of the poem (no. 251), or the appropriate note (note 210).

Twelfth Century

I

ST. GODRIC

A cry to Mary

Sainte Marye Virgine,   mid 12c.
Moder Jesu Christes Nazarene,
Onfo, schild, help thin Godric,
Onfang, bring heyilich with thee in Godes Riche.

Sainte Marye, Christes bur,   5
Maidenes clenhad, moderes flur,
Dilie min sinne, rix in min mod,
Bring me to winne with the self God.

St. Mary, the Virgin, Mother of Jesus Christ of Nazareth, receive, defend and
help your Godric, (and,) having received (him), bring (him) on high with you in
the Kingdom of God. St. Mary, chamber of Christ, virgin among maidens, flower
of motherhood (? see note 1), blot out my sin, reign in my heart, and bring me
to bliss with that selfsame God.

8. the, *one MS.* thy, *but others omit altogether;* self, *so several MSS. but this MS.*
selfd.

2

How long this night is

Mirie it is, while sumer ilast,   earlier 13c.
With fugheles song.
Oc nu necheth windes blast,
And weder strong.
Ey! ey! what this night is long!   5
And ich, with well michel wrong,
Soregh and murne and fast.

It is pleasant, while summer lasts, with the birds' song. But now the storming
wind comes on and severe weather. Alas! how long this night is, and I, because of
very great wrong, grieve, mourn and fast.

7. fast, *not in MS., which is torn.*

3

Sumer is icumen in

Sing! cuccu, nu. Sing! cuccu.   earlier 13c.
Sing! cuccu. Sing! cuccu, nu.

Sumer is icumen in—
Lhude sing! cuccu.
Groweth sed and bloweth med   5
And springth the wude nu—
Sing! cuccu.

Awe bleteth after lomb,
Lhouth after calve cu,
Bulluc sterteth, bucke verteth,   10
Murie sing! cuccu.
Cuccu, cuccu,
Well singes thu, cuccu—
Ne swik thu naver nu!

Sing! now, cuckoo. Spring has come in—sing loud! cuckoo. The seed grows and the meadow flowers, and now the wood is in leaf. Sing! cuckoo. The ewe bleats for her lamb, the cow lows for her calf, the bullock leaps and the buck breaks wind. Sing, tunefully! cuckoo, cuckoo, you sing well—now don't ever stop!

4

I live in great sorrow

Foweles in the frith,   later 13c.
The fisses in the flod,
And I mon waxe wod:
Mulch sorw I walke with
For beste of bon and blod.   5

Birds in the wood, the fish in the river, and I must go mad: I live in great sorrow because of the best creature living.

4. Mulch, *MS.* multh (?).

5

A hymn to Mary

Of on that is so fair and bright,   13c.
Velud maris stella,
Brighter than the dayes light,
Parens et puella:
Ic crye to thee—thou se to me—   5
Levedy, preye thy sone for me,
Tam pia,
That ic mote come to thee,
Maria.

Levedy, flowr of alle thing,   10
Rosa sine spina,
Thu bere Jesu, Hevene King,
Gratia divina.
Of alle thu berst the pris,
Levedy, Quene of Parais   15
Electa;
Maide milde, moder es
Effecta.

All this world was forlore
Eva peccatrice,   20
Till our Lord was ibore
De te genitrice.
With 'Ave' it went away,
Thuster night, and cometh the day
Salutis.   25
The welle springeth ut of thee
Virtutis.

In the MS. the stanzas are ordered: 1, 3, 2, 5, 4, but the letters 'a' and 'b' written in the left margin opposite stanzas 5 and 3 above suggest an alteration of order was intended.

1. on, one. 2. *Like the star of the sea.* 4. *Mother and maiden.* 5, 8. Ic, *I.* 6 etc., Levedy, *Lady.* 7. *So devoted.* 8. mote, *may.* 11. *Rose without thorns.* 12. Hevene, *of Heaven.* 13. *By divine grace.* 14. *You are best of all.* 15. Parais, *Paradise.* 16. *Chosen.* 17–18. *Gentle maid, you are proved a mother.* 19. forlore, *utterly lost.* 20. *Through Eve, the sinner.* 22. *Of you, the mother.* 24. Thuster, *Dark;* cometh, *MS.* com3 (?). 25. *Of salvation.* 27. *(The well) of virtue.*

Well he wot he is thy sone,
Ventre quem portasti;
He will nought werne thee thy bone,   30
Parvum quem lactasti.
So hende and so god he is
He haveth brought ous to blis
Superni,
That haveth idut the foule put   35
Inferni.

Of care, conseil thou ert best,
Felix fecundata;
Of alle wery thou ert rest.
Mater honorata.   40
Besek him with milde mod,
That for ous alle sad his blod
In cruce,
That we moten comen till him,
In luce.   45

28. wot, *knows.* 29. *Whom you carried in your womb.* 30. *He will not deny you your request.* 31. *Whom, when little, you fed at your breast.* 32. *So gracious and so good he is.* 34. *Of Heaven.* 35–6. *Who has shut the foul pit of hell.* 37. *In trouble you are the best counsellor.* 38. *Fortunate and fruitful one (Mary).* 40. *Honoured mother.* 41. *Implore him with gracious heart.* 42. sad, *shed.* 43. *On the Cross.* 44–5. *That we may come to him in the light.*

6

Pity for Mary

earlier 13c.

Now goth sonne under wod:
Me reweth, Marye, thy faire rode.
Now goth sonne under Tre:
Me reweth, Marye, thy sone and thee.

1. wod, *wood (of the Cross).* 2. *I feel pity, Mary, for your fair face.*

7

Against the Barons' enemies

Richard, thah thou be ever trichard,   about 1265
Tricchen shalt thou nevermore.

Sitteth alle stille and herkneth to me!
The King of Alemaigne, by my leaute,
Thritty thousand pound askede he   5
For to make the pees in the countre—
And so he dude more.

Richard of Alemaigne, whil that he wes king,
He spende all his tresour upon swiving.
Haveth he nout of Walingford o ferling!   10
Let him habbe ase he brew—bale to dring—
Maugre Windesore.

The King of Alemaigne wende do full well:
He saisede the mulne for a castel;
With hare sharpe swerdes he grounde the stel—   15
He wende that the sailes were mangonel
To helpe Windesore.

The king of Alemaigne gederede his host,
Makede him a castel of a mulne post,
Wende with his prude and his muchele bost,   20
Broghte from Alemaigne mony sory ghost
To store Windesore.

---

1. thah, *though;* trichard, *deceiver.* 2. Tricchen, *Cheat.* 4. *Trust me, the King of Germany.* 7. *And he asked for more as well.* 9. swiving, *'women'.* 10–11. *He shall have not a farthing from Wallingford (where he had a castle) (?): let him have what he brewed— misery for his drink.* 12. Maugre, *In spite of.* 13, etc. wende, *thought.* 14, 19. mulne, *mill.* 15. *With their sharp swords he made the position secure.* 16. mangonel, *catapult (for use in a siege).* 20. prude, *pride;* muchele, *great.* 21. ghost, *person.* 22. store, *garrison.*

By God that is aboven ous, he dude muche sin
That lette passen over see the Erl of Warin:
He hath robbed Engelond, the mores and the fen,   25
The gold and the selver, and iboren henne,
For love of Windesore.

Sire Simon de Montfort hath swore by his chin,
Hevede he now here the Erl of Warin,
Shulde he never more come to his inn,   30
Ne with sheld, ne with spere, ne with other gin,
To help of Windesore.

Sire Simon de Montfort hath swore by his top,
Hevede he now here Sire Hue de Bigot,
All he shulde quite here twelfmoneth scot—   35
Shulde he never more with his fot pot
To helpe Windesore.

Be thee luef, be thee loth, Sire Edward,
Thou shalt ride sporeles o thy liard
All the righte way to Dovereward—   40
Shalt thou nevermore breke foreward,
And that reweth sore.

    Edward, thou dudest ase a shreward,
    Forsoke thine eme's lore.

26. iboren henne, *carried (it) hence.* 29, 34. Hevede, *Had.* 30. inn, *dwelling.* 31. gin, *device.* 35. *He would pay off a year's reckoning (i.e. give them board and lodging for a year in prison?).* 36. pot, *push, kick.* 38. *Whether you like it or not.* 39. *without spurs on your grey horse.* 40. *to Dover.* 41. foreward, *agreement.* 42. *And that is a great pity.* 43. *you acted like a scoundrel.* 44. eme's lore, *uncle's teaching (i.e. Simon de Montfort's).*

8

Contempt of the world

Where beth they, beforen us weren,   later 13c.
Houndes ladden and havekes beren,
And hadden feld and wode?

Where are they who lived before us, who led hounds and carried hawks, and owned field and wood?

The riche levedies in hoere bour,
That wereden gold in hoere tressour,   5
With hoere brighte rode?

Eten and drounken and maden hem glad;
Hoere lif was all with gamen ilad:
Men keneleden hem beforen.
They beren hem well swithe heye,   10
And, in a twinkling of an eye,
Hoere soules weren forloren.

Where is that lawing and that song,
That trailing and that proude yong,
Tho havekes and tho houndes?   15
All that joye is went away,
That wele is comen to weylaway,
To manye harde stoundes.

Hoere paradis hy nomen here,
And now they lien in helle ifere: 20
The fuir it brennes evere;
Long is 'ay!' and long is 'ho!'
Long is 'wy!' and long is 'wo!'
Thennes ne cometh they nevere.

Dreye here, man, thenne, if thou wilt,   25
A luitel pine that me thee bit,
Withdraw thine eyses ofte.

The great ladies in their chambers, who wore gold in their head-bands and whose faces shone?
They ate and drank and entertained themselves; their life was spent wholly in pleasure: men kneeled before them. They carried themselves most proudly, and, in the twinkling of an eye, their souls were utterly lost.
Where is that laughter and that singing, that trailing of garments, and that proud gait, those hawks and those hounds? All that joy has vanished, that happiness has turned to misery and (many) hard times.
They took their paradise here, and now they lie in hell together: the fire burns without end; long lasts their 'ah!' and long their 'oh!' long their 'alas!' and long their 'woe!'—they shall never come out of that place.
Then, man, suffer here, if it is in you, the little pain enjoined you, deny yourself comforts often.

25. Dreye, *MS.* dreჳy.

They thy pine be ounrede,
And thou thenke on thy mede,
It shall thee thinken softe.   30

If that Fend, that foule thing,
Thorou wicke roun, thorou fals egging,
Nethere thee haveth icast,
Oup and be god chaunpioun!
Stond! ne fall namore adoun   35
For a luitel blast.

Thou tak the Rode to thy staf,
And thenk on him that thereonne yaf
His lif that wes so lef.
He it yaf for thee: thou yelde it him,   40
Ayein his fo that staf thou nim,
And wrek him of that thef.

Of righte bileve thou nim that sheld,
The wiles that thou best in that feld
Thine hond to strengthen fonde.   45
And kep thy fo with staves ord,
And do that traitre seyen that word,
Biget that murie londe.

Thereinne is day withouten night,
Withouten ende strengthe and might,   50
And wreche of everich fo,

Though your torment is severe, if you think about your reward (the pain) is bound to seem to you little.
If the foul Fiend has cast you down through his wicked words, through his deceitful temptation, up, and be a good champion! Stand! and fall down no more at a mere puff of wind.
Take the Cross for your staff, and remember him who gave his precious life on it. He gave it for you: yield it to him, take that staff against his foe and avenge him on that thief.
Take that shield of right belief and, while you are in that field, try to strengthen your hand. And keep your foe at the end of the staff(?) resist your foe with the point of the staff (?) and make that deceiver say that word (of surrender?) and gain that happy land.
There is day and never night, unending strength and might, and vengeance on all enemies,

Mid God himselven eche lif,
And pes and rest withoute strif,
Wele withouten wo.

Maiden, moder, Hevene Quene,   55
Thou might and const and owest to bene
Oure sheld ayein the Fende.
Help ous sunne for to flen,
That we moten thy sone iseen
In joye withouten ende.   60

Amen.

eternal life with God himself, and peace and rest without conflict, well-being without any pain.
Maiden, mother, Queen of Heaven, you might and are able and ought to be our shield against the Fiend. Help us to avoid sin so that we may see your son in endless joy. Amen.

9

A cleric courts his lady

'My deth I love, my lif ich hate,   later 13c.,
For a levedy shene;   earlier 14c.
He is bright so dayes light,
That is on me well sene:
All I falewe so doth the lef   5
In somer when it is grene.
Yef my thoght helpeth me noght,
To wham shall I me mene?

'Sorewe and sike and drery mod
Bindeth me so faste,   10
That I wene to walke wod,
Yef it me lengore laste.

'*I long to die and hate living, because of a beautiful lady; she is radiant as the day-light which my present state makes clear: I fade as a leaf does in summer when it is green. If thinking is no help to me, to whom shall I make my complaint?*
'*Sorrow and sighing and a melancholy mood bind me so fast that I expect to go mad if it goes on any longer.*

My sorewe, my care, all with a word,
He mighte awey caste.
Whet helpeth thee, my swete lemman,   15
My lif thus for to gaste?'

'Do wey! thou clerk, thou art a fol,
With thee bidde I noght chide.
Shalt thou never live that day
My love that thou shalt bide!   20
Yef thou in my bowre art take,
Shame thee may betide.
Thee is bettere on fote gon
Then wicked hors to ride.'

'Weylawey! Why seist thou so?   25
Thou rewe on me, thy man:
Thou art ever in my thoght
In londe wher ich am.
Yef I deye for thy love
It is thee mikel sham!   30
Thou lete me live and be thy lef,
And thou my swete lemman.'

'Be stille, thou fol—I calle thee right—
Cost thou never blinne?
Thou art waited day and night   35
With fader and all my kinne.
Be thou in my bowr itake,

She could, with one word, cast away my sorrow and care. What do you gain, my sweetheart, from making my life desolate like this?'
'Get away! you cleric, you're a fool, I've no wish to quarrel with you. You'll never see the day when you'll have my love. If you are caught in my room you'll be disgraced (?) may you be disgraced (?). Better be safe than sorry. (It's better for you to walk than to ride a bad horse.)'
'Alas! why do you say so? Have pity on me, your man: you are always in my thoughts wherever I am. If I die for your love how shameful for you! Let me live and be your love, and you my own sweetheart.'
'Be quiet, you fool—the right name for you—can't you ever stop? You are spied on, night and day, by my father and all my relations.

33. right, *MS.* ript.

Lete they, for no sinne,
Me to holde and thee to slon,
The deth so thou maht winne.'   40

'Swete ledy, thou wend thy mod,
Sorewe thou wolt me kithe.
Ich am all so sory mon
So ich was whilen blithe:
In a window ther we stod,   45
We kuste us fifty sithe;
Fair beheste maketh mony mon
All his sorewes mithe.'

'Weylawey! Why seist thou so?
My sorewe thou makest newe.   50
I lovede a clerk all par amours,
Of love he wes full trewe.
He nes nout blithe never a day,
Bote he me sone seye.
Ich lovede him betere then my lif—   55
Whet bote is it to leye?'

'Whil I wes a clerk in scole,
Well muchel I couthe of lore.
Ich have tholed for thy love
Woundes fele sore,   60
Fer from hom and eke from men,
Under the wode-gore.
Swete ledy, thou rewe of me—
Now may I no more.'

*If you are caught in my room they won't hesitate out of fear of any sin to hold
me and kill you, so that you shall die.'*
'*Sweet lady, please change your mind or you will make me so unhappy. I am as
sorry a man as I was happy before: standing in a window we kissed fifty times; a
fair promise makes many a man hide all his sorrows.'*
'*Alas! why do you say so? You renew my sorrow. I loved a cleric as a true lover,
and in love he was most faithful. There was never a day that he was happy unless
he could see me. I loved him better than my life—what's the use of lying?'*
'*While I was a student I knew a great deal of lore (pun? "learning" and "lore of
love"). I have suffered for your love countless wounds, far from home and civiliza-
tion, under the forest. Sweet lady, please have pity on me—I can go on no longer.'*

61. hom, *not in MS.*

'Thou semest well to ben a clerk,   65
For thou spekest so stille:
Shalt thou never for my love
Woundes thole grille.
Fader, moder and all my kun,
Ne shall me holde so stille,   70
That I nam thine and thou art mine,
To don all thy wille.'

*' You seem well-suited to be a cleric, for you speak so quietly: for you there'll be no
suffering dreadful wounds for my love. Father, mother and all my relations shall
not keep such firm hold on me but I shall be yours and you mine, to do all your
will.'*

IO

Fairest between Lincoln and Lindsey

When the nightegale singes,   later 13c.,
The wodes waxen grene: earlier 14c.
Lef and gras and blosme springes,
In Averil, I wene.
And love is to mine herte gon   5
With one spere so kene:
Night and day my blod it drinkes;
Mine herte deth me tene.

Ich have loved all this yer
That I may love na more;   10
Ich have siked mony sik,
Lemmon, for thine ore.
Me nis love never the ner,
And that me reweth sore.

*When the nightingale sings, the woods grow green; believe me, leaf and grass and
blossom springs in April. And love has gone to my heart with so sharp a spear: it
drinks my blood night and day; my heart is hurting me.*
*I have loved all this year so that (? what?) I can love no more; I have sighed many
a sigh, sweetheart, for your favour. Love is not any the nearer me, which grieves
me greatly.*

Swete lemmon, thench on me:　　　　　　15
Ich have loved thee yore.

Swete lemmon, I preye thee
Of love one speche.
Whil I live, in world so wide
Other nulle I seche.　　　　　　　　　20
With thy love, my swete lef,
My blis thou mightes eche:
A swete kos of thy mouth
Mighte be my leche.

Swete lemmon, I preye thee　　　　　　25
Of a love-bene.
Yef thou me lovest, ase men says,
Lemmon, as I wene,
And, yef it thy wille be,
Thou loke that it be sene.　　　　　　30
So muchel I thenke upon thee
That all I waxe grene.

Betwene Lincolne and Lindeseye,
Northamptoun and Lounde,
Ne wot I non so fair a may　　　　　　35
As I go fore ibounde.
Swete lemmon, I preye thee
Thou lovie me a stounde.
I wole mone my song
On wham that it is on ilong.　　　　　　40

Dear sweetheart, think about me: I have loved you for so long.
Dear sweetheart, I pray you for one word of love. As long as I live I will not seek
another throughout the whole world. You could increase my happiness with your
love, my dear: a sweet kiss from your mouth might be my physician.
Dear sweetheart, I pray of you a lover's request. If you love me, as men say,
sweetheart, as I think, and if it is your wish, please see that it is shown. I am
falling ill with thinking so much about you.
Between Lincoln and Lindsey, Northampton and Lound, I know no maid so fair
as I go in love-fetters for. Dear sweetheart, I pray you to love me a little while. I
will sadly sing my song about the cause of my complaint.

Thirteenth Century

11

Thanks and a plea to Mary

Levedy, ic thonke thee,   13c.
Wid herte swithe milde,
That god that thu havest idon me
Wid thine swete childe.

Thu art god and swete and bright,   5
Of alle otheir icoren.
Of thee was that swete wight,
That was Jesus, iboren.

Maide milde, bidd I thee
Wid thine swete childe,   10
That thu herdie me
To habben Godis milce.

Moder, loke one me,
Wid thine swete eyen,
Reste and blisse gef thu me,   15
My levedy, then ic deyen.

1, 16. Levedy, *Lady;* ic, *I.* 2. swithe, *very;* and 9. milde, *gracious, gentle.* 3. *For that good you have done me.* 6. *Chosen from among all others.* 7. wight, *creature.* 9. bidd, *pray.* 11. herdie, *shelter.* 12. *To have God's Mercy.* 14. eyen, *eyes.* 15. gef, *give.* 16. then, *when;* deyen, *die.*

12

In praise of Mary

Edi be thu, Hevene Quene,   13c.
Folkes froure and engles blis,
Moder unwemmed and maiden clene,
Swich in world non other nis.

Blessings upon you, Queen of Heaven, the comfort of men and bliss of the angels, Mother without spot and pure virgin, such as no other in the world is.

On thee it is well eth sene 5
Of alle wimmen thu havest that pris.
My swete Levedy, her my bene,
And rew of me yif thy wille is.

Thu asteye so the dais-rewe
The deleth from the derke night; 10
Of thee sprong a leme newe
That all this world haveth ilight.
Nis non maide of thine hewe
So fair, so shene, so rudy, so bright.
Swete Levedy, of me thu rewe, 15
And have mercy of thine knight.

Spronge blostme of one rote,
The Holy Ghost thee reste upon;
That wes for monkunnes bote,
And here soule to alesen for on. 20
Levedy milde, softe and swote,
Ic crye thee mercy: ic am thy mon,
Bothe to honde and to fote,
On alle wise that ic con.

Thu ert erthe to gode sede; 25
On thee lighte the Hevene dews;
Of thee sprong the edi blede—
The Holy Ghost hire on thee sews.
Thu bring us ut of care, of drede,
That Eve bitterliche us brews. 30

You are most obviously the best of all women. My sweet Lady, hear my prayer, and have pity on me if it is your will.
You ascended as the first streak of day that separates from the dark night (Appendix, 'Dawn'); from you sprang a new light that has lit the whole world. There is no maid like you, so fair, so beautiful, so fresh, so radiant. Sweet Lady, pity me and have mercy on your knight.
Blossom sprung from a root (that of Jesse), the Holy Ghost rested on you: that was for the healing of mankind and to deliver their souls once and for all (?). Gracious Lady, mild and gentle, I cry to you for mercy: I am your man with every part of me, in every way that I am able.
You are earth for good seed; on you the dew of Heaven came down; from you sprang that blessed fruit—the Holy Ghost has sown it in you. Bring us out of the fear and dread that Eve has brewed for us in bitterness.

Thu shalt us into Hevene lede—
Welle swete is the ilke dews.

Moder, full of thewes hende,
Maide, dreigh and well itaught,
Ic em in thine lovebende,   35
And to thee is all my draught.
Thu me shilde from the Fende,
Ase thu ert fre, and wilt and maught:
Help me to my lives ende,
And make me with thine sone isaught.   40

Thu ert icumen of heghe cunne,
Of David the riche king.
Nis non maiden under sunne
The mey be thine evening,
Ne that so derne loviye cunne,   45
Ne non so trewe of alle thing.
Thy love us broughte eche wunne:
Ihered ibe thu, swete thing!

Selcudliche ure Louerd it dighte
That thu, maide, withute were,   50
That all this world bicluppe ne mighte,
Thu sholdest of thine boseme bere.
Thee ne stighte, ne thee ne prighte,
In side, in lende ne elleswhere:
That wes with full muchel righte,   55
For thu bere thine Helere.

You will lead us to Heaven—most sweet is that same dew (? see l. 26).
Mother, full of gracious virtues, maiden, patient and well-taught, I am in the bonds
of your love, and leaning wholly to you. Shield me from the Fiend, you who are
noble, and will, and can: help me until I die, and reconcile me with your son.
You are come of exalted race, descended from David, the great king. There is no
maiden under the sun who can equal you, nor love so profoundly (? secretly), and
who is so true in everything. Your love brought us eternal bliss: praise to you,
sweet thing!
Our Lord arranged it marvellously so that you, maid, without knowing a man,
should bear in your womb the one whom all this world could not encompass. You
felt no stabbing or pricking in your side or loins or anywhere else: that was entirely
right, for you bore your Saviour.

Tho Godes sune alighte wolde
On erthe, all for ure sake,
Herre teyen he him nolde
Thene that maide to ben his make: 60
Betere ne mighte he, thaigh he wolde,
Ne swetture thing on erthe take.
Levedy, bring us to thine bolde
And shild us from helle wrake.

                               Amen.

When God's son wished to come down on earth, all for our sake, he would not take to him a servant superior to that maid to be his lover: he could not find a better though he wanted to, nor take a sweeter thing on earth. Lady, bring us to your abode and shield us from vengeance in hell. Amen.

13

Alison

Betwene Mersh and Averil,   latcr 13c.,
When spray beginneth to springe,   earlier 14c.
The lutel fowl hath hire will
On hire lud to singe.
Ich libbe in love-longinge   5
For semlokest of alle thinge—
He may me blisse bringe;
Ich am in hire baundoun.

    An hendy hap ich habbe ihent!
    Ichot from Hevene it is me sent.   10
    From alle wimmen my love is lent,
    And light on Alisoun.

Between March and April, when the twigs come into leaf, the little bird has her wish and sings with her voice. I live longing with love for the fairest of all—she may bring me happiness; I am in her power.
Fair fortune has come my way! I know it is sent me from Heaven. My love is taken away from all women and has settled on Alison.

On hew hire her is fair inogh,
Hire browe browne, hire eye blake;
With lossum chere he on me logh,   15
With middle small and well imake.
Bote he me wolle to hire take,
For to ben hire owen make,
Longe to liven ichulle forsake,
And feye fallen adoun.   20

Nightes when I wende and wake—
Forthy mine wonges waxeth won—
Levedy, all for thine sake,
Longinge is ilent me on.
In world nis non so witer mon   25
That all hire bounte telle con:
Hire swire is whittore then the swon,
And fairest may in toun.

Ich am for wowing all forwake,
Wery so water in wore,   30
Lest eny reve me my make,
Ich habbe iyirned yore.
Betere is tholien while sore
Then mournen evermore.
Geynest under gore,   35
Herkne to my roun!

In colour her hair is abundantly beautiful, her brow brown, her eye black; with lovely face she laughed upon me, with her waist slender and well-turned. Unless she will take me to her, to be her own mate, I will not live long but fall down, doomed.

At night when I turn and lie awake—therefore my cheeks grow pale—lady, desire has come upon me all for your sake. There is no man so wise anywhere who can tell her goodness (? beauty): her neck is whiter than the swan and she is the fairest maid alive.

I am worn out with lying awake in love, weary as water in a troubled pool, lest any one should rob me of my mate whom I have longed for for so long. It is better to suffer badly for a while than feel sorrow for ever. Kindest of women, listen to my song.

14

The penitent hopes in Mary

Now skrinketh rose and lilye-flour,   later 13c.,
That whilen ber that swete savour,   earlier 14c.
In somer, that swete tide.
Ne is no quene so stark ne stour,
Ne no levedy so bright in bour,   5
That Ded ne shall by glide.
Whose wol flesh lust forgon
And Hevene blis abide,
On Jesu be his thoght anon,
That therled was his side.   10

From Petresbourgh in o morewening,
As I me wende o my pleying,
On my folye I thoghte.
Menen I gon my mourning
To hire that ber the Hevene King,   15
Of mercy hire besoghte:
'Ledy, preye thy sone for ous,
That us dere boghte,
And shild us from the lothe hous
That to the Fend is wroghte.'   20

Mine herte of dedes wes fordred,
Of sinne that I have my flesh fed
And folewed all my time:

Now the rose and the lily wither that once bore that sweet smell in summer, that sweet time. There is no queen so mighty and strong, nor lady so bright in her chamber, whom Death shall not creep up on. Whoever will forgo bodily delight and wait for the bliss of Heaven, let his thoughts be straightway on Jesus whose side was pierced.

As I went out from Peterborough one morning to enjoy myself, I thought about my folly (illicit love?). I go to express my grief to her who bore the King of Heaven and begged her for mercy: 'Lady, pray for us to your son who bought us dear, and defend us from the hateful house made for the Fiend.'

My heart was very afraid for what I had done, for the sin that I have fed my body and that I have followed all my time:

That I not whider I shall be led,
When I ligge on dethes bed,   25
In joye ore into pine.
On o Ledy mine hope is,
Moder and virgine:
We shulen into Hevene blis
Thurh hire medicine.   30

Betere is hire medicine
Then eny mede or eny wine,
Hire erbes smulleth swete.
From Catenas into Divelin
Nis ther no leche so fine   35
Oure sorewes to bete.
Mon that feleth eny sor,
And his folye wol lete,
Withoute gold other eny tresor
He may be sound and sete.   40

Of penaunce is his plastre all,
And ever serven hire I shall,
Now and all my live.
Now is free that er wes thrall,
All thourh that Levedy, gent and small—   45
Heried be hir joyes five.
Wherso eny sek is
Thider hye blive;
Thurh hire beth ibroght to blis
Bo maiden and wive.   50

so that I have no idea whither I shall be led when I lie on my death-bed, into joy
or into torment. My hope is on a Lady, mother and virgin: through her medicine
we shall enter into the bliss of Heaven.

Her medicine is better than any mead or wine, her herbs smell sweet. From Caith-
ness to Dublin there is no physician so fine to cure our sorrows. That man that
feels any grief and will leave his folly, can be sound and content without any gold
or treasure.

Such a man's plaster is penitence, and I shall ever serve her now and all my life.
Now he is free who was before a slave, all through that Lady, noble and slender—
praise to her five joys (no. 20). Wherever any one is sick, let him hasten to her
quickly; through her both maiden and wife are brought to happiness.

For he that dude his body on Tre
Of oure sunnes have piete,
That weldes Hevene boures.
Wimmon, with thy jolifte,
Thou thench on Godes shoures: 55
Thah thou be whit and bright on ble
Falewen shule thy floures.
Jesu have mercy of me,
That all this world honoures.
              Amen.

You who rule the chambers of Heaven (being their Queen) have pity on our sins for the sake of him who gave his body on the Tree. Women, in your gaiety, think on God's pains: though you are fair and your face is radiant your flowers shall wither. Jesu, whom all the world honours, have mercy on me. Amen.

58. me, MS. vs.

15

The Man in the Moon

Mon in the mone stond and strit;   later 13c.,
On his bot-forke his burthen he bereth.   earlier 14c.
It is muche wonder that he na down slit—
For doute leste he falle he shoddreth and shereth.
When the forst freseth muche chele he bid.   5
The thornes beth kene, his hattren to-tereth.
Nis no wiht in the world that wot when he sit,
Ne, bote it be the hedge, whet wedes he wereth.

The man in the moon stands and strides; he bears his burden (? bundle?) on his forked stick. It is a great wonder that he doesn't slip down—for fear of falling he trembles and veers. When the frost freezes he endures much cold. The thorns are keen, his clothes tear to pieces. There is no person in the world who knows when he sits down, nor, except for the hedge (on which he has been working or from which he has been stealing, and which 'knows' his clothes because it tears them (?)), what clothes he wears.

Whider trowe this mon ha the wey take?
He hath set his o fot his other toforen.   10
For non hihte that he hath ne siht me him ner shake:
He is the sloweste mon that ever wes iboren.
Wher he were o the feld pitchinde stake,
For hope of his thornes to dutten his doren,
He mot mid his twibil other trous make,   15
Other all his dayes werk ther were iloren.

This ilke mon upon heh whener he were,
Wher he were i'the mone boren and ifed,
He leneth on his forke ase a grey frere:
This crokede cainard sore he is adred.   20
It is mony day go that he was here.
Ichot of his ernde he nath nout isped.
He hath hewe sumwher a burthen of brere,
Tharefore sum hayward hath taken his wed.

Yef thy wed is itake, bring hom the trous,   25
Sete forth thine other fot, strid over sty.
We shule preye the hayward hom to our hous,
And maken him at eise for the maistry,
Drinke to him derly of full god bous,
And oure dame douse shall sitten him by.   30
When that he is dronke ase a dreint mous,
Thenne we schule borewe the wed ate baily.

Where do you think this man has made his way(?)? He has put his one foot before the other. He is never moved by any exertion or anything he sees. He is the slowest man that ever was born. Whether (or not?) he was making stakes fast in the field in the hope of stopping up his gaps (?) with his thorns, he must make other bundles (of brushwood, say, or briars, to protect the newly planted hedge from animals (?)) with his two-edged axe, or all his day's work would be lost.
Whenever it was this same man arrived above (?), whether (or not?) he was born and brought-up in the moon (?), he leans on his fork like a grey, Franciscan friar; this crooked idler is very much afraid. It's a long time ago that he was here. I know he has not been successful in his errand. He has somewhere cut a bundle of briars and therefore some keeper of hedges has taken his pledge for payment of a fine.
If your pledge is taken, bring home the bundles, set your other foot forward and stride over the path. We shall ask the hedge-keeper home to our house and make him extremely comfortable, drink to him affectionately in first-class drink, and our sweet missis shall sit beside him. When he is drunk as a kitten, then we will redeem the pledge from the bailiff.

This mon hereth me nout, thah ich to him crye·
Ichot the cherl is def—the Del him to-drawe!
Thah ich yeye upon heh, nulle nout hye: 35
The lostlase ladde con nout o lawe.
Hupe forth! Hubert, hosede pie.
Ichot th'art amarscled into the mawe.
Thah me tene with him that mine teth mye,
The cherl nul nout adown er the day dawe.   40

This man hears me not, though I cry to him: I know the fellow is deaf—to hell
with him! Though I cry out loud, he will not hurry. The lazy lad knows nothing
of law (?). Go on! Hubert, magpie in trousers (?). I know your belly is stuffed
full (?). Though my teeth grate with anger at him, the man will not come down
before day dawns.

16

When Death comes

Now is mon hol and soint,   13c.
And uvel him comit in mund.
Thenne me seint aftir the prest,
That wel con reden him to Crist.
Afteir the prest boit icomin,   5
The feirliche Deit him havit inomin.
Me prikit him in on ful clohit,
And legget him by the wout.
Amorwen, both in sout and norit,
Me nimit that body and berrit it forit.   10
Me gravit him put other ston;
Therin me leit the fukul bon.

Now man is whole and sound, and evil comes into his soul. Then the priest is sent
for who is well able to guide him to Christ. After the priest has come, dreadful
Death has seized him. He is dressed in a foul cloth and laid by the vault. Next day,
in whatever part of the world it may be, that body is taken and carried forth. There
is made for him a grave or a tomb; in it is laid the deceiving bone.

6. inomin, *here and in nine other places I have accepted the readings and reconstruction*
of Carleton Brown.

Thenne sait the soule to the licam,
'Wey! that ic ever in thee com.
Thu noldes, Friday, festen to non,   15
Ne, the Setterday, almesse don,
Ne, then Sonneday, gon to churche,
Ne Cristene werkes wurche.
Neir thu never so prud,
Of hude and of hewe ikud,   20
Thu shalt in orthe wonien and wormes thee tochewen,
And of alle ben lot that her thee were ilewe.'

Then says the soul to the body, 'Alas! that I ever entered you. You would not on Fridays fast until noon, nor on Saturdays give alms, nor on Sundays go to church, nor do Christian works. Never mind how proud you were, famous for your skin and complexion, you shall dwell in earth and worms shall chew you thoroughly, and you shall be loathsome to all who were dear to you here.'

17

How Death comes

Wanne mine eyhnen misten,   13c.
And mine heren sissen,
And my nose coldet,
And my tunge foldet,
And my rude slaket,   5
And mine lippes blaken,
And my muth grennet,
And my spotel rennet,
And mine her riset,
And mine herte griset,   10
And mine honden bivien,

When my eyes get misty, and my ears are full of hissing, and my nose gets cold, and my tongue folds, and my face goes slack, and my lips blacken, and my mouth grins, and my spittle runs, and my hair rises (? falls, note 17) and my heart trembles, and my hands shake,

And mine fet stivien—
Al to late! al to late!
Wanne the bere is ate gate.

Thanne I schel flutte   15
From bedde to flore,
From flore to here,
From here to bere,
From bere to putte,
And te putt fordut.   20
Thanne lyd mine hus uppe mine nose.
Of al this world ne give I it a pese!

and my feet stiffen—all too late! when the bier is at the gate. Then I shall pass from bed to floor, from floor to shroud, from shroud to bier, from bier to grave, and the grave will be closed up. Then my house rests on my nose. I don't care one jot for the whole world.

14. the, *MS.* 3e.

18

Judas sells his Lord

It wes upon a Scere Thorsday that oure Lord aros;   about
Full milde were the wordes he spec to Judas: 1300

'Judas, thou most to Jurselem oure mete for to bugge;
Thritty platen of selver thou bere upo thy rugge.

'Thou comest fer i' the brode stret, fer i' the brode strete, 5
Summe of thine cunesmen ther thou meist imete.'

Imette wid his soster, the swikele wimon.
'Judas, thou were wurthe me stende thee wid ston.

1. *Maundy Thursday.* 3. *you must go to Jerusalem to buy our food.* 4. *Carry thirty pieces of silver on your back.* 6. *There you may meet some of your relations.* 7. *He has met his sister, the crafty woman.* 8. *you deserve to be stoned with stones.*

'Judas, thou were wurthe me stende thee wid ston,
For the false prophete that tou belevest upon.'   10

'Be stille, leve soster: thine herte thee tobreke.
Wiste mine Lord Christ, full well he wolde be wreke.'

'Judas, go thou on the roc, heye upon the ston;
Ley thin heved i' my barm: slep thou thee anon.'

Sone so Judas of slepe was awake,   15
Thritty platen of selver from him weren itake.

He drow himselve by the top that all it lavede ablode:
The Jewes out of Jurselem awenden he were wode.

Foret him com the riche Jew that heiste Pilatus:
'Wolte sulle thy Lord that hette Jesus?'   20

'I nul sulle my Lord for nones cunnes eiste,
Bote it be for the thritty platen that he me bitaiste.'

'Wolte sulle thy Lord Christ for enes cunnes golde?
Nay ! bote it be for the platen that he habben wolde.'

In him com oure Lord gon as his postles seten at mete.   25
'Wou sitte ye postles, and wy nule ye ete?

'Wou sitte ye postles, and wy nule ye ete?
Ic am abought and isold today for oure mete.'

Up stod him Judas: 'Lord am I that frec?
I nas never o' the stude ther me thee evel spec.'   30

---

10. tou (*thou*) *you*. 11. *Be quiet, dear sister: I wish your heart would break*. 12. *If my Lord Christ knew he would be sure to have vengeance*. 13. heye, *high*. 14. *Lay your head in my bosom*. 15. Sone so, *As soon as*. 17. *He tore his hair so that it all ran with blood*. 18–22. *The Jews from Jerusalem thought he was mad. The great Jew who was called Pilate came forward: 'Will you sell your Lord who is called Jesus?' 'I will not sell my Lord for any kind of property, unless it be for the thirty pieces of silver that he entrusted to me.'* 24. habben wolde, *would have*. 25–6. *In came our Lord as his apostles sat at table. 'How is it you sit, apostles, and why won't you eat?'* 28. *I am bought and sold today for our food*. 29. frec, *not in MS.*, man. 30. *I was never where ill was spoken of you*.

Up him stod Peter and spec wid all his mighte:
'Thau Pilatus him come wid ten hundred cnightes,

'Thau Pilatus him come wid ten hundred cnightes,
Yet ic wolde, Lord, for thy love fighte.'

'Stille thou be, Peter! Well I thee iknowe: 35
Thou wolt fursake me thrien ar the cok him crowe.'

32. Thau, *Though.* 36. ar, *before.*

19

The singing maid

Now springes the spray,   about 1300
All for love I am so seek
That slepen I ne may.

Als I me rode this endre day
O' my pleyinge,   5
Seih I whar a litel may
Began to singe,
'The clot him clinge!
Way es him i' love-longinge
Shall libben ay!'   10

Son I herde that mirye note,
Thider I drogh:
I fonde hire in an herber swot
Under a bogh,
With joye inogh.   15
Son I asked, 'Thou mirye may,
Why singes tou ay?'

1. Now (*that) the twigs come into leaf.* 2. *sick.* 4. *As I rode out the other day; MS.*
this endre dai als i me rode. 5. pleyinge, *not in MS.* 6. Saw; *and* 16. may, *maid.*
8. *May the earth (of the grave) stick to him (?) waste him (?);* clinge, *MS.* clingges.
9–10. *Unhappy is the man who must live always longing with love.* 11, 16. Son, *As soon*
as, at once; mirye, *joyful.* 12. *Thither I went.* 13. in, *not in MS.;* herber, *arbour; and*
18. swot(e), *pleasant, sweet.* 15. inogh, *in plenty.* 17. tou, (*thou) you.*

Than answerde that maiden swote
Midde wordes fewe,
'My lemman me haves bihot   20
Of love trewe:
He chaunges anewe.
Yiif I may, it shall him rewe
By this day!'

19. Midde, *With.* 20–1. *My loved one has promised me true love.* 23–4. *If I can, he shall regret it for this day.*

20

The five joys of Mary

Ase I me rod this ender day,   later 13c.,
By grene wode to seche play,   earlier 14c.
Mid herte I thoghte all on a may,
Swetest of alle thinge.
Lithe, and ich ou telle may   5
All of that swete thinge.

This maiden is swete and fre of blod,
Bright and fair, of milde mod;
Alle he may don us god,
Thurh hire besechinge.   10
Of hire he tok flesh and blod,
Jesus, Hevene Kinge.

With all my lif I love that may:
He is my solas night and day,
My joye and eke my beste play,   15
And eke my love-longinge.
All the betere me is that day
That ich of hire singe.

1. *As I rode out the other day.* 2. *To seek pleasure by the green wood.* 3. Mid, *With;* etc., may, *maiden.* 5. *Listen, and I can tell you.* 7. fre, *noble.* 8. *Radiant and fair and gracious of heart.* 9. he, *etc.,* she. 10. *Through her intercession.* 12, 60. Hevene, *of Heaven.* 15. *My joy and also my greatest pleasure.*

Of alle thinge I love hire mest,
My dayes blis, my nightes rest;   20
He counseileth and helpeth best
Bothe elde and yinge.
Now I may, yef I wole,
The fif joyes minge.

The furst joye of that wimman,   25
When Gabriel from Hevene cam,
And seide God shulde become man,
And of hire be bore,
And bringe up of helle pin
Monkin that wes forlore.   30

That other joye of that may
Wes o Christesmasse day,
When God wes bore on thoro lay,
And broghte us lightnesse.
The ster wes seie before day,   35
This hirdes bereth witnesse.

The thridde joye of that levedy,
That men clepeth the Epiphany,
When the kinges come wery
To presente hire sone   40
With myrre, gold and incens.
That wes mon become.

The furthe joye we telle mawen,
On Estermorewe, when it gon dawen,
Hire sone, that wes slawen,   45
Aros in flesh and bon.
More joy ne may me haven,
Wif ne maiden non.

---

19. mest, *most.* 22. *Both young and old.* 23. *Now, if I will, I can.* 24. minge, *mention.* 29. of . . . pin, *from hell torment.* 30. *Mankind that was utterly lost.* 32. o, on. 33. *When God was born in perfect light* (?). 34. lightnesse, *light.* 35. The ster, MS. (?) ʋestri; seie, *visible.* 36. This hirdes, *These shepherds.* 37, 55. levedy, *lady.* 38. clepeth, *call.* 43. mawen, *may.* 44. *On Easter morning, when dawn broke.* 47. me, *one.*

The fifte joye of that wimman,
When hire body to Hevene cam,   50
The soule to the body nam
Ase it wes woned to bene.
Christ leve us alle with that wimman
That joye all for to sene.

Preye we alle to oure Levedy,   55
And to the sontes that woneth hire by,
That he of us haven mercy,
And that we ne misse
In this world to ben holy,
And winne Hevene blisse.   60

                    Amen.

51. nam, went. 52. As it was accustomed to be. 53. May Christ allow us all with that woman. 56. And to the saints that dwell with her. 57. he, (Christ).

21

The white beauty

A waile whit ase whalles bon,   later 13c.,
A grein in golde that godly shon,   earlier 14c.
A tortle that mine herte is on
In townes, trewe.
Hire gladshipe nes never gon   5
Whil I may glewe.

When he is glad
Of all this world namore I bad
Then be with hire mine one bistad
Withoute strif.   10
The care that ich am in ibrad
I wite a wif.

A beautiful woman, white as whale's bone (ivory?), a bead of gold that fair one shone, a turtle-dove that, among all others, my heart is set on, true. Her joy shall never pass away while I can make songs.
When she is glad, I ask no more in the whole world than to be alone with her without strife. The trouble that I live with I blame on a woman.

A wif nis non so worly wroght
When he is blithe to bedde ibroght.
Well were him that wiste hire thoght,   15
That thriven and thro.
Well I wot he nul me noght:
Mine herte is wo.

How shall that lefly sing
That thus is marred in mourning?   20
He me wol to dethe bring
Longe er my day.
Gret hire well, that swete thing
With eyen gray.

Hire eye haveth wounded me, iwisse,   25
Hire bente browen that bringeth blisse;
Hire comely mouth, that mighte kisse,
In muche murthe he were.
I wolde chaunge mine for his
That is here fere.   30

Wolde hire fere be so free,
And wurthes were that so mighte be,
All for on I wolde yeve three
Withoute chep.
From helle to Hevene and sonne to see   35
Nis non so yeep,
Ne half so free:
Whose wole of love be trewe do listne me.

There is no woman so beautifully made when she is brought happily to bed. It would be good for him who knew her mind, that woman so fine. I know well she will not have me at all. My heart grieves.
How can the man who is thus afflicted with sorrow sing well? She will be my death long before my day. Greet her well, that sweet thing with grey eyes.
Her eyes have wounded me, indeed, her arched eye-brows that bring happiness. The man who might kiss her comely mouth would be most happy. I would change mine (mistress (?) lot (?)) for his who is her lover (?) husband (?).
If her lover (?) husband (?) would be so generous and there were what would be worth exchanging with, I would give three of them all for the one and not bargain. From hell to Heaven and between sun and sea there is none so wise nor half so noble: listen to me whoever will be true in love.

24. eyen, MS. eʒenen.

Herkneth me, I ou telle.
In such wondring for wo I welle;⁣ 40
Nis no fur so hot in helle
All to mon
That loveth derne and dar nout telle
Whet him is on.

Ich unne hire well and he me wo, 45
Ich am hire frend and he my fo:
Me thuncheth mine herte wol breke atwo
For sorewe and sike.
In Godes greting mote he go,
That waile white. 50

Ich wolde ich were a threstelcok,
A bounting other a lavercok,
Swete brid.
Betwene hire kurtle and hire smok
I wolde ben hid. 55

Hear me, I tell you. I suffer for sorrow in such distress of mind. There is no fire in hell so hot as the man who loves secretly and dare not tell what is the matter with him.
I wish her well and she me woe, I am her friend and she my enemy: it seems to me my heart will break in two for sorrow and sighing. With God's welcome may she go, that white beauty.
I wish I were a song-thrush, a bunting or a lark, sweet bird (fair lady?). Between her kirtle and her smock I would be hid.

22

The Crucifixion

I sike when I singe⁣ later 13c., earlier 14c.
For sorewe that I se,
When I with wipinge
Beholde upon the Tre,

1, etc. sike, *sigh.* 3. wipinge, *weeping.*

And se Jesu, the swete,   5
His herte blod forlete
For the love of me;
His woundes waxen wete,
They wepen stille and mete—
Marye, reweth thee.   10

Heye upon a downe,
Ther all folk it se may,
A mile from uch towne,
Aboute the midday,
The Rode is up arered: 15
His frendes aren afered
And clingeth so the clay;
The Rode stond in stone,
Marye stond hire one,
And seith, 'Weylaway!'   20

When I thee beholde,
With eyen brighte bo,
And thy body colde,
Thy ble waxeth blo;
Thou hengest all of blode,   25
So heye upon the Rode,
Betwene theves two.
Who may sike more?
Marye wepeth sore,
And siht all this wo.   30

The nailles beth too stronge,
The smithes are too sleye;
Thou bledest all too longe,
The Tre is all too heye;
The stones beth all wete.   35
Alas! Jesu, the swete,

---

6. forlete, *lose*. 8, 35. wete, *wet*. 9. mete, *fitly*. 10. reweth, *it grieves*. 11. Heye, *High*. 13. uch towne, *all human habitation*. 17. *And become dull-spirited as clay.* 19. hire one, *on her own*. 22. eyen, *eyes*; bo, *both*. 24. ble, *face*; blo, *ashen, leaden*. 25. of blode, *bloody*. 30. siht, *sees*. 31, etc. beth, *are*. 32. sleye, *skilful*.

For now frend hast thou non,
Bote Seint Johan, mourninde,
And Marye, wepinde,
For pine that thee is on.   40

Ofte when I sike,
And makie my mon,
Well ille thah me like,
Wonder is it non
When I se honge heye   45
And bittre pines dreye
Jesu, my lemmon,
His wondes sore smerte,
The spere all to his herte
And thourh his sides gon.   50

Ofte when I sike
With care I am thourhsoght;
When I wake, I wike,
Of sorewe is all my thoght.
Alas! Men beth wode   55
That swereth by the Rode,
And selleth him for noght
That boghte us out of sinne.
He bring us to winne,
That hath us dere boght!   60

40, 46. pine(s), *suffering(s), torment(s); on, in.* 43. *Though I am very much distressed (by it).* 45. honge, *hang.* 46. dreye, *suffer.* 48. smerte, *(I see) smart.* 50. gon, *(I see) go.* 52. thourhsoght, *pierced.* 53. wike, *grow weak.* 55. *Men are mad.* 59. *May he bring us into joy.*

23

Lenten is come with love to toune

Lenten is come with love to toune,   later 13c.,
With blosmen and with briddes roune,   earlier
That all this blisse bringeth.   14c.

1–2. *Spring has come with love among us, with flowers and with the song of birds.*

Dayeseyes in this dales,
Notes swete of nightegales,   5
Uch fowl song singeth.
The threstelcok him threteth oo.
Away is huere winter wo
When woderofe springeth.
This fowles singeth ferly fele,   10
And wliteth on huere wynne wele,
That all the wode ringeth.

The rose raileth hire rode,
The leves on the lighte wode
Waxen all with wille.   15
The mone mandeth hire ble,
The lilye is lossom to se,
The fennel and the fille.
Wowes this wilde drakes,
Miles murgeth huere makes,   20
Ase strem that striketh stille.
Mody meneth, so doth mo;
Ichot ich am on of tho
For love that likes ille.

The mone mandeth hire light,   25
So doth the semly sonne bright,
When briddes singeth breme.
Deawes donketh the dounes,
Deores with huere derne rounes
Domes for to deme.   30
Wormes woweth under cloude,
Wimmen waxeth wounder proude,

4, etc. this, *these.* 6, 10. Uch fowl, *Each bird.* 7. *The song thrush wrangles all the time.*
8. huere, *their.* 9. *woodruff.* 10–11. *Vast numbers of birds are singing and warbling in their*
abounding joy; wynne, MS. wynter. 13. *The rose puts on her rosy face.* 14. *The leaves*
in the bright wood. 16, 25. *The moon sends out her radiance.* 17. lossom, *lovely.* 18. fille,
wild thyme. 19–22. *These wild drakes make love, animals (?) cheer their mates, like a*
stream that flows softly. The passionate man complains, as do more; doth, MS. doh.
23–4. *I know that I am one of those who is unhappy for love.* 27. breme, *strongly.*
28–32. *Dews wet the downs, animals with their cries that we do not understand, for telling*
their tales. Worms make love under ground, women grow exceedingly proud.

So well it wol hem seme.
Yef me shall wonte wille of on,
This wunne wele I wole forgon,   35
And wiht in wode be fleme.

33–36. *so well it will suit them. If I don't have what I want of one, I will abandon all this happiness and quickly be a fugitive in the woods.*

24

The Mother and her Son on the Cross

'Stond well, moder, under Rode.   later 13c.,
Behold thy sone with glade mode—   earlier 14c.
Blithe moder might thou be.'
'Sone, how shulde I blithe stonde?
I se thine fet, I se thine honde,   5
Nailed to the harde Tre.'

'Moder, do wey thy wepinge.
I thole deth for monkinde—
For my gult thole I non.'
'Sone, I fele the dedestounde: 10
The swerd is at mine herte grounde,
That me bihet Simeon.'

'Moder, thou rewe all of thy bern:
Thou woshe away the blody tern—
It doth me worse then my ded.'   15
'Sone, how may I teres werne?
I se the blody stremes erne
From thine herte to my fet.'

2. mode, *heart.* 7. do wey, *stop.* 8, etc. thole, *suffer.* 9. gult, *sin.* 10. dedestounde, *hour of death (?) death-pang (?).* 11–12. *Luke ii, 25–35; The sword that Simeon promised me has gone to the bottom of my heart.* 13. *have pity on your child.* 14. tern, *tears.* 15. *It does me more harm than death would (to see your tears).* 16. werne, *restrain.* 17. erne, *run.*

'Moder, now I may thee seye,
Betere is that ich one deye   20
Then all monkunde to helle go.'
'Sone, I se thy body beswungen,
Fet and honden thourhout stongen—
No wonder thah me be wo.'

'Moder, now I shall thee telle,   25
Yef I ne deye thou gost to helle:
I thole ded for thine sake.'
'Sone, thou art so meke and minde,
Ne wit me naht, it is my kinde
That I for thee this sorewe make.'   30

'Moder, mercy, let me deye!
For Adam out of helle beye,
And his kun that is forlore.'
'Sone, what shall me to rede?
My peine pineth me to dede.   35
Lat me deye thee before.'

'Moder, now thou might well leren
Whet sorewe haveth that children beren,
Whet sorewe it is with childe gon.'
'Sorewe, iwis, I con thee telle!   40
Bote it be the pine of helle,
More sorewe wot I non.'

'Moder, rew of moder care,
For now thou wost of moder fare,
Thou thou be clene maiden-mon.'   45

20. ich one, *I alone;* etc., deye, *die.* 21. Then, *Than.* 22. beswungen, *scourged.*
23. stongen, *pierced.* 24. *No wonder though I am distressed.* 26. Yef. *If.* 28. minde,
thoughtful. 29. *Do not blame me, it is natural for me.* 31-6. *Order of stanzas: see note*
24. 32. beye, *to redeem.* 33. kun, *family;* forlore, *utterly lost.* 34. *what shall I do?*
35. pineth, *tortures.* 38. *What sorrow (they) have who bear children.* 39. gon, *to go.*
40, 53. iwis, *indeed.* 41. Bote, *Unless;* pine, *torment.* 42. wot, *know.* 43. *have pity on a*
mother's grief. 44. *For you know now the way of a mother.* 45. *Though you are a pure*
virgin.

'Sone, help at alle nede
Alle tho that to me grede,
Maiden, wif and fol wimmon.'

'Moder, may I no lengore dwelle.
The time is come I shall to helle.   50
The thridde day I rise upon.'
'Sone, I will with thee founden.
I dcye, iwis, for thine wounden,
So soreweful ded nes never non.'

When he ros tho fell hire sorewe,   55
Hire blisse sprong the thridde morewe:
Blithe moder were thou tho.
Levedy, for that ilke blisse,
Besech thy sone of sunnes lisse—
Thou be oure sheld ayein oure fo.   60

Blessed be thou, full of blisse,
Let us never Hevene misse,
Thourh thy swete sones might.
Louerd, for that ilke blod
That thou sheddest on the Rod,   65
Thou bring us into Hevene light.
                    Amen.

46. at alle nede, *in all necessities.* 47. tho, *those;* grede, *cry out.* 48. fol wimmon, *prostitute.* 50. shall, *must* (*go*). 52. founden, *go.* 54. *There was never so sorry a death.* 55, 57. tho, *then.* 58. Levedy, *Lady;* and 64. ilke, *same.* 59. of sunnes lisse, *for remission of sins.* 60. ayein, *against.* 64. Louerd, *Lord.*

25

Love for a beautiful lady

Blow, northerne wind,   later 13c.,
Send thou me my sweting,   earlier 14c.
Blow, northerne wind,
Blow, blow, blow!
88

Ichot a burde in bowre bright   5
That sully semly is on sight,
Menskful maiden of might,
Fair and fre to fonde.
In all this wurhliche won
A burde of blod and of bon   10
Never yet I nuste non
Lussomore in londe.

With lockes lefliche and longe,
With frount and face fair to fonde,
With murthes monye mote he monge,   15
That brid so breme in boure.
With lossom eye grete and gode,
With browen blisful under hode—
He that reste him on the Rode
That leflich lif honoure!   20

Hire lure lumes light
Ase a launterne anight,
Hire ble blikieth so bright,
So fair he is and fine.
A swetly swire he hath to holde,   25
With armes, shuldre ase mon wolde,
And fingres faire for to folde—
God wolde he were mine.
. . .
He is coral of godnesse,
He is rubye of rightfulnesse,   30

5–28. *I know a beautiful lady, radiant in her chamber, who is most comely to look
on, a gracious maiden with power over me, fair and noble to enjoy. I never yet
knew a more lovely lady alive through all this splendid world.*
*With beautiful long hair, a forehead and a face fair to enjoy, with many pleasant
things must she be compared, that damsel so excellent in her chamber. With lovely
eye, large and good, with brows most happy under her hood—may he that
remained on the Cross honour that beautiful one (?).*
*Her cheek shines alight like a lantern by night, her face gleams bright, so fair she is
and fine. She has a lovely neck to embrace, with arms, shoulder as you would
wish, and fingers fair to clasp—would God she were mine.*

6. sully, *MS.* fully (?). 28, 29. *Two stanzas omitted.* 30. *virtue.*

He is crystal of clannesse,
And baner of bealte.
He is lilye of largesse,
He is parvenke of prowesse,
He is solsecle of swetnesse,   35
And ledy of lealte.

To Love, that leflich is in londe,
I tolde him, as ich understonde,
How this hende hath hent in honde
On herte that mine wes: 40
And hire knightes me han so soght,
Siking, Sorewing and Thoght,
Tho thre me han in bale broght
Ayein the poer of Pees.

To Love I putte pleintes mo,   45
How Siking me hath siwed so;
And eke Thoght me thrat to slo
With maistry yef he mighte;
And Sorewe sore in balful bende
That he wolde for this hende   50
Me lede to my lives ende
Unlahfulliche in lighte.

Hire Love me lustnede uch word
And beh him to me over bord,
And bed me hente that hord   55
Of mine herte hele:

37–56. I told Love, who is pleasant, how, as I understand, this fair creature has captured a heart that was mine: and her knights have so attacked me, Sighing, Sorrowing and Thinking, the three have brought me into torment against the power of Peace.

To Love I put more complaints, how Sighing has so followed me; and, also, Thinking has threatened to slay me with force if he could; and Sorrow has threatened that he would, for this fair creature, lead me in dire bondage to the end of my life, unlawfully and openly.

Love of her listened to my every word and bent towards me over the table, and bade me seize that treasure of my heart's health:

31. purity. 32. banner of beauty. 33. generosity. 34. periwinkle of excellence. 35. marigold. 36. lady of loyalty.

'And besecheth that swete and swote,
Er then thou falle ase fen of fote,
That he with thee wolle of bote
Dereworthliche dele.'   60

For hire love I carke and care,
For hire love I droupne and dare,
For hire love my blisse is bare,
And all ich waxe won.
For hire love in slep I slake,   65
For hire love all night ich wake,
For hire love mourning I make,
More then eny mon.

57–60. '*And implore that sweet and lovely one, before you fall as mud from a
foot, that she will lovingly grant you a remedy.*'

   61. *grieve and sorrow.* 62. *pine and cower.* 64. *And I grow all sickly, pale.* 65. *I be-
come weak.*

26

The death of King Edward I

Alle that beth of herte trewe   about 1307
A stounde herkneth to my song:
Of del that Deth hath dight us newe,
That maketh me sike and sorewe among;
Of a knight that wes so strong,   5
Of wham God hath don his wille.
Me thuncheth that Deth hath don us wrong
That he so sone shall ligge stille.

All Englond aghte for to knowe
Of wham that song is that I singe: 10

   1, 54. beth, *are.* 2. stounde, *while.* 3, etc. del, *grief;* and 63. dight, *appointed, sent.*
4. sike, *sigh;* among, *at times.* 7. Me thuncheth, *It seems to me.* 8. ligge, *lie.* 9, 15.
aghte, *ought.*

Of Edward King that lith so lowe,
Yent all this world his nome con springe;
Trewest mon of alle thinge,
And in werre war and wis.
For him we aghte oure honden wringe—   15
Of Christendome he ber the pris.

Before that oure King wes ded
He spek ase mon that wes in care:
'Clerkes, knightes, barouns', he saide,
'I charge ou by oure sware   20
That ye to Engelonde be trewe.
I deye—I ne may liven na more.
Helpeth my sone and crowneth him newe,
For he is nest to ben icore.'

. . .

The messager to the Pope com   25
And seyde that oure King was ded.
His owne hond the lettre he nom—
Iwis, his herte wes full gret.
The Pope himself the lettre redde,
And spek a word of gret honour: 30
'Alas!' he seide, 'is Edward ded?
Of Christendome he ber the flour.'

The Pope to his chaumbre wende:
For del ne mighte he speke na more;
And after cardinals he sende,   35
That muche couthen of Christes lore,
Bothe the lasse and eke the more,
Bed hem bothe rede and singe.
Gret del me mighte se thore,
Mony mon his honde wringe.   40

---

11. lith, *lies.* 12. *Through the whole world his fame has run.* 13–14. *A man most true in everything, prudent and wise in war.* 15. *For him we ought to wring our hands.* 16, 32, 70. ber the, hadest, pris, flour, *was pre-eminent.* 19. Clerkes, *Clergy.* 20. *I charge you by your oath.* 24. *For he is next to be chosen.* 24, 25. *Two stanzas omitted.* 27. *With his own hand he took the letter.* 28. *Indeed his heart was very full.* 33. wende, *went away.* 36. *Who were most learned in theology.* 37. eke, *also.* 38. *Told them to perform services.* 39. *Great sorrow was to be seen there.*

The Pope of Peyters stod at his Masse,
With ful gret solempnete,
Ther me con the soule blesse.
King Edward, honoured thou be;
God lene thy sone, come after thee, 45
Bringe to ende that thou hast begonne—
The Holy Crois, imad of tree,
So fain thou woldest it han iwonne.

Jerusalem, thou hast ilore
The flour of all chivalerye, 50
Now King Edward liveth na more.
Alas! that he yet shulde deye.
He wolde ha rered up full heye
Oure baners that beth broght to grounde.
Well longe we mowe clepe and crye, 55
Er we a such king han ifounde.

Now is Edward of Carnarvan
King of Engelond all aplight.
God lete him ner be worse man
Then his fader, ne lasse of might 60
To holden his pore men to right,
And understonde good consail,
All Engelond for to wisse and dight.
Of gode knightes darh him nout fail.

Thah my tonge were mad of stel, 65
And mine herte iyote of bras,
The godnesse might I never telle
That with King Edward was.
King, as thou art cleped, 'Conquerour',
In uch bataille thou hadest pris. 70

41. Peyters, *Poitiers*. 43. *Where (Edward's) soul was commended to God.* 45–6. *May God grant (that) your son (who) comes after you may bring to fulfilment what you have begun.* 47. imad, *made*. 48. *You wanted so very much to have won it.* 49. ilore, *lost*. 50. *The choicest of all knights.* 55. *We may call and cry a very long time.* 56. Er, *Before.* 58. aplight, *in truth.* 59–64. *May God grant him never to be a worse man than his father, nor less mighty in preserving justice among his people, and that he may receive good counsel to guide and manage all England. He must not lack good knights.* 65. Thah, *Though.* 66. iyote, *made*. 69. cleped, *called*. 70. uch, *each*.

God bringe thy soule to the honour
That ever wes and ever is,
That lesteth ay withouten ende,
Bidde we God and oure Ledy
To thilke blisse Jesus us sende.   75

                              Amen.

74. Bidde, *Pray*. 75. thilke, *that same*.

27

WILLIAM HEREBERT

The knight stained from battle

What is he, this lordling, that cometh from   earlier
    the fight?   14C.
With blod-rede wede so grisliche idight,
So faire icoyntised, so semlich in sight,
So stifliche yongeth, so doughty a knight.

'Ich it am, ich it am, that ne speke bote right,   5
Chaunpioun to helen monkunde in fight.'

Why, thenne, is thy shroud red with blod all imeind,
Ase troddares in wringe with most all bespreind?

'The wringe ich habbe itrodded all mysulf on,
And of all monkunde ne was non other won.   10

*Who is he, this young lord, who comes from battle, with blood-red raiment so
terribly arrayed, apparelled so fair, so goodly to look at, (who) goes so sturdily(?),
so valiant a knight?*
'*It is I, it is I, who speak only the truth, the champion to heal mankind in battle.*'
*Why, then, are your clothes all mixed with blood, like those who tread in the
wine-press all spattered with grape-pulp?*
'*The wine-press I have trodden all on my own, and there was no other hope for
all mankind.*

Ich hem habbe itrodded in wrethe and in grome,
And all my wede is bespreind with here blod isome,
And all my robe ifuled to here grete shome.
The day of th'ilke wreche leveth in my thought,
The yer of medes-yelding ne foryet ich nought.   15
Ich loked all aboute som helpinge mon,
Ich soughte all the route, bote help nas ther non.
It was mine owne strengthe that this bote wroughte,
Mine owne doughtinesse that help ther me broughte.
On Godes milsfolnesse ich wole bethenche me,   20
And herien him in alle thing that he yeldeth me.
Ich habbe itrodded the folk in wrethe and in grome,
Adreint all with shennesse, idrawe down with shome.'

*I have trodden them in wrath and in anger, and all my raiment is spattered
with their blood together, and my coat all fouled to their great shame. The
day of that very vengeance lives in my thought, I do not forget the time for paying
out rewards. I looked all round for someone to help, I searched all the company but
help was there none. It was my own strength that achieved this remedy, my own
valour that helped me there. On God's mercy I will reflect and praise him in all he
grants me. I have trodden the people in wrath and in anger, all drowned in
humiliation, dragged down with shame.'*

28

WILLIAM HEREBERT

The devout man prays to his relations

Thou wommon boute fere   earlier 14c.
Thine owne fader bere:
Gret wonder this was,
That on wommon was moder
To fader and hire brother,   5
So never other nas.

*Woman without compare, you bore your own father: a great wonder this was that
one woman was mother to her father and her brother, as no other ever was.*

Thou my suster and my moder,
And thy sone is my brother:
Who shulde thenne drede?
Whoso haveth the king to brother,   10
And ek the quene to moder,
Well aughte for to spede.

Dame!—suster and moder—
Say thy sone, my brother,
That is Domesmon,   15
That for thee that him bere
To me be debonere—
My robe he haveth upon.

Seththe he my robe tok,
Also ich finde in Bok,   20
He is to me ibounde:
And helpe he wole, ich wot,
For Love the chartre wrot,
And the enke orn of his wounde.

Ich take to witnessinge   25
The spere and the crowninge,
The nailes and the Rode:
That he that is so kunde
This ever haveth in munde,
That boughte ous with his blode.   30

You are my sister and my mother, and your son is my brother: who ought, then, to be afraid? Whoever has the king for brother and also the queen for mother ought indeed to succeed.

Lady!—sister and mother—speak to your son, my brother, who is the Judge, that, for you who bore him, he may be gentle to me—he has my coat (i.e. human nature).

Since he took my coat, as I find in the Scriptures, he is bound to me: and I know he will help, for Love wrote the charter, and the ink ran from his wounds.

I take as my evidence the spear and the crowning with thorns, the nails and the Cross, that he who is so benevolent and bought us with his blood has this constantly in mind.

When thou yeve him my wede,
Dame, help at the nede—
Ich wot thou might fol well:
That for no wreched gult
Ich be to helle ipult,   35
To thee ich make apel.

Now, Dame, ich thee beseche
At th'ilke day of wreche
Be by thy sones trone,
When sunne shall ben sought   40
In werk, in word, in thought,
And spek for me thou one.

When ich mot nede apere
For mine gultes here
Tofore the Domesmon,   45
Suster, be ther my fere,
And make him debonere
That my robe haveth upon.

For habbe ich thee and him,
That markes berth with him,   50
That charite him tok,
The woundes all blody,
The toknes of mercy,
Ase techeth Holy Bok,
Tharf me nothing drede: 55
Sathan shall nout spede,
With wrenches ne with crok.   Amen.

*When you gave him my raiment (i.e. since God became incarnate in your womb),
Lady, help in my need—I know you can full well: to you I appeal that I may not
be driven to hell for any wretched sin.*
*Now, Lady, I implore you to be by your son's throne on that very day of ven-
geance, when sin shall be sought out in work and word and thought, and, alone,
speak for me.*
*When I must needs appear for my sins on earth before the Judge, sister, be my
friend there and make him gentle who has my coat on.*
*For if I have you and him who bears the marks with him that love took, the
wounds all bloody, the tokens of mercy, as Holy Scripture teaches, I need fear
nothing: Satan shall have no success with tricks or guile. Amen.*

29

WILLIAM HEREBERT

A Palm-Sunday hymn

Wele, herying and worshipe be to Christ   earlier 14c.
    that dere ous boughte,
To wham gradden 'Osanna!' children clene
    of thoughte.

Thou art King of Israel and of Davides kunne,
Blessed King that comest till ous withoute wem of sunne.

All that is in Hevene thee herieth under on,   5
And all thine owne hondewerk and euch dedlich mon.

The folk of Giwes with bowes comen ayeinest thee,
And we with bedes and with song meketh ous to thee.

He kepten thee with worshiping, ayeinst thou shuldest deye,
And we singeth to thy worshipe, in trone that sittest heye.   10

Here wil and here mekinge thou nome tho to thonk;
Queme thee thenne, milsful King, oure offringe of this song.

1. *Glory, praise and honour.* 2. gradden, *cried aloud.* 3. Davides, *MS.* Davidpes; kunne, *family.* 4. *Blessed King who comes to us without stain of sin.* 5. herieth under on, *praises with one voice.* 6. *And all your own creation and every mortal man.* 7. *The people of the Jews with boughs (of palm) came to meet you.* 8. bedes, *prayers;* meketh, *humble.* 9. *They watched over you worshipfully, expecting you were to die.* 10. trone, *throne;* heye, *high.* 11. *Their intention and their homage you then graciously accepted.* 12. *May it please you, then, merciful King.*

30

I ought to weep

Whanne ic se on Rode   earlier 14c.
Jesu, my lemman,
And besiden him stonden
Marye and Johan,
And his rig iswongen,   5
And his side istungen,
For the luve of man;
Well ou ic to wepen,
And sinnes for to leten,
Yif ic of luve can,   10
Yif ic of luve can,
Yif ic of luve can.

1. ic, *I.* 2. lemman, *lover.* 5. rig, *back;* iswongen, *scourged.* 6. istungen, *pierced.* 8. ou, *ought.* 9. leten, *abandon.* 10, etc. Yif, *If;* can, *know.*

3 1

I am from Ireland

Ich am of Irlaunde,   earlier 14c.
And of the holy londe
Of Irlande.

Gode sire, pray ich thee,
For of sainte charite,   5
Come and daunce wit me
In Irlaunde.

1, 4. Ich, *I.* 4. thee, *MS.* 3e. 5. sainte, *holy.*

32

The Annunciation

Gabriel, fram Hevene King   earlier 14c.
Sent to the maide swete,
Broughte hire blisful tiding,
And faire he gan hire grete:
'Heil! be thu, full of grace aright,   5
For Godes sone, this Hevene light,
For mannes loven
Wile man becomen,
And taken
Fleas of the maiden bright,   10
Manken fre for to maken
Of senne and Devles might.'

Mildeliche him gan andsweren
The milde maiden thanne:
'Whiche wise sold ich beren   15
Child withuten manne?'
Th'angle seide, 'Ne dred thee nought!
Thurw th'Holy Gast shall ben iwrought
This ilche thing,
Wharof tiding   20
Ich bringe.
All manken wurth ibought
Thurw thy swete childinge,
And ut of pine ibrought.'

Whan the maiden understud,   25
And th'angles wordes herde,
Mildeliche, with milde mud,
To th'angle hie andswerde:

3, etc. hire, *her*, MS. þire (*and in several other instances* þ *for* h). 4. gan grete, *greeted.* 5. aright, *rightly.* 6. *this light of Heaven.* 7–8. *For love of man will become man.* 10, etc. Fleas, *Flesh.* 11, 22. Manken, *Mankind.* 12, 53. senne, *sin.* 13–19. *The gentle maiden then answered him gently:* 'In what way am I to bear a child without knowing a man?' *The angel said,* 'Have no fear! Through the Holy Ghost this same thing shall be done. 22. *All mankind shall be redeemed.* 23. childinge, *child-bearing.* 24. *And brought out of torment.* 27. mud, *heart.* 28. hie, *she.*

'Ur Lordes theumaiden, iwis,
Ich am, that her aboven is.   30
Anenttis me,
Fulfurthed be
Thy sawe,
That ich, sithen his wil is,
Maiden, withuten lawe,   35
Of moder have the blis.'

Th'angle went awey mid than
All ut of hire sight.
Hire womb arise gan
Thurw th'Holy Gastes might.   40
In hire was Christ beloken, anon,
Soth God, soth man, ine fleas and bon,
And of hir flcas
Iboren was
At time,   45
Wharthurw us cam god won:
He bought us ut of pine,
And let him for us slon.

Maiden, moder, makeles,
Of milche ful ibunde,   50
Bid for us him that thee ches,
At wham thu grace fundc,
That he forgive us senne and wrake,
And clene of evry gelt us make,
And Hevne blis,   55
Whan ure time is
To sterven,
Us give for thine sake,
Him so her for to serven
That he us to him take.   60

29–36. *I am, indeed, the handmaid of our Lord who is above. For my part, let your saying be fulfilled, that, since it is his will, I, being a maiden, against all laws have the happiness of being a mother.* 37. mid than, *with that.* 41. beloken, *enclosed.* 42. Soth, *True.* 43–8. *And when her time came was born of her flesh, whereby we received hope: he bought us out of torment and had himself slain for us.* 49. makeles, *without equal, mate.* 50. *Altogether possessed by mercy.* 51–2. *Pray for us to him who chose you, with whom you found favour.* 53. wrake, *retribution.* 54. gelt, *offence.* 57. sterven, *die.* 59. her, *here.*

33

The maiden lay in the wilds

Maiden in the mor lay,   earlier 14c.
In the mor lay;
Sevenight fulle,
Sevenight fulle,
Maiden in the mor lay;   5
In the mor lay,
Sevenightes fulle and a day.

Welle was hire mete.
What was hire mete?
The primerole and the—   10
The primerole and the—
Welle was hire mete.
What was hire mete?
The primerole and the violet.

Welle was hire dring.   15
What was hire dring?
The chelde water of the—
The chelde water of the—
Welle was hire dring.
What was hire dring?   20
The chelde water of the welle-spring.

Welle was hire bowr.
What was hire bowr?
The rede rose and the—
The rede rose and the—   25
Welle was hire bowr.
What was hire bowr?
The rede rose and the lilye flour.

1. mor, *moor, wilds.* 3, 7. *A whole week.* 8. Welle, *Good;* mete, *food.* 10. primerole, *primrose.* 15. dring, *drink.* 17. chelde, *cold.* 22. bowr, *abode. Last two stanzas: note 33.*

34

WILLIAM OF SHOREHAM (?)

A song to Mary

Marye, maide, milde and fre,   earlier 14c.
Chambre of the Trinite,
One while lest to me,
Ase ich thee grete with songe.
Thagh my fet unclene be,   5
My mes thou onderfonge.

Thou art Quene of Paradis,
Of Hevene, of erthe, of all that is;
Thou bere thane Kinge of bliss,
Withoute senne and sore.   10
Thou hast iright that was amis,
Iwonne that was ilore.

Thou art the colvere of Noe,
That broughte the braunche of olive tre
In tokne that pais sholde be   15
Betwexte God and manne.
Swete Levedy, help thou me
Whanne ich shall wende hanne.

Thou art the boshe of Sinai,
Thou art the righte Sarray;   20
Thou hast ibrought ous out of cry
Of calenge of the Fende;
Thou art Christes owene drury,
And of Davies kende.

1, etc. *Mary, maiden, gracious and noble.* 3. lest, *listen.* 4, etc. ich, *I.* 5. fet, *vessel.*
6. *Receive my dish.* 9, etc. thane, *the.* 10. *Without sin and pain (of labour).* 11–12. *You
have put right what was amiss, won what was lost.* 13. colvere, *dove.* 17, etc. Levedy,
Lady. 18. hanne, *hence.* 19. boshe, *bush.* 20. righte Sarray, *legitimate (wife), Sarah.*
21. cry, *calling distance.* 22. calenge, *claim? accusation? command.* 23. drury, *beloved,
(treasure).* 24. *And of David's stock.*

Thou art the slinge, thy sone the ston,   25
That Davy slange Golye upon;
Thou art the yerd all of Aaron,
Me dreye isegh springinde:
Witnesse at ham everychon
That wiste of thine childinge.   30

Thou art the temple Salomon;
In thee wondrede Gedeon;
Thou hast igladed Simeon
With thine swete offringe
In the temple, atte auterston,   35
With Jesus, Hevene Kinge.

Thou art Judith, that faire wif,
Thou hast abated all that strif;
Holofernes, with his knif,
His hevede thou him benome: 40
Thou hast isaved here lif
That to thee wille come.

Thou art Hester, that swete thinge,
And Asseuer, the riche kinge,
Thee hath ichose to his weddinge,   45
And quene he hath avonge;
For Mardocheus, thy derlinge,
Sire Aman was ihonge.

The prophete Ezekiel
In his boke it witnesseth wel,   50
Thou art the gate so stronge so stel
Ac evere ishet fram manne;
Thou arte the righte faire Rachel,
Fairest of alle wimman.

---

26. *That David slung at Goliath.* 27. yerd, *rod.* 28. *Which was seen putting forth a shoot while dry.* 29. *Take everyone of them as witness* (?). 30. *Who knew of your child-bearing.* 32. *Gideon wondered at you.* 33–6. *Luke ii, 22–35.* 35. atte auterston, *at the altar-stone.* 40. *You took his head away from him.* 41. here, *their.* 43. Hester, *Esther.* 44. *Ahasuerus the great king.* 45. Thee, *MS.* pey; ichose, *chosen.* 46. avonge, *taken.* 48. ihonge, *hanged.* 51. so . . . so, *as . . . as.* 52. *But ever shut against man.*

By righte tokninge thou art the hel   55
Of wan spellede Daniel;
Thou art Emaus, the riche castel,
That resteth alle werye;
Ine thee restede Emmanuel
Of wan ispeketh Isaye.   60

Ine thee is God become a child,
Ine thee is wreche become mild;
That unicorn that was so wild
Aleyd is of a cheaste;
Thou hast itamed and istild   65
With melke of thy breste.

Ine the Apocalyps, Sent John
Isegh ane wimman with sonne begon,
Thane mone all onder hire ton,
Icrowned with twel sterre.   70
Swil a levedy nas nevere non
With thane Fend to werre.

Ase the sonne taketh hire pas,
Withoute breche, thorghout that glas,
Thy maidenhod unwemmed it was   75
For bere of thine childe.
Now swete levedy of solas
To ous senfolle be thou milde.

Have, Levedy, this litel songe
That out of senfol herte spronge.   80
Ayens the Feend thou make me stronge,
And gif me thy wissinge,
And thagh ich habbe ido thee wrange,
Thou graunte me amendinge.

---

55. *Truly represented by the symbol (or) 'type' you are the hill of whom David told.*
60. *Isaiah vii, 14.* 62. wreche, *vengeance.* 64. *Is tamed by a chaste woman.* 65. istild, *subdued.* 66. melke, *milk.* 68. *Saw a woman clothed with the sun.* 69. *The moon under her toes;* mone, *MS.* mowe. 70. *Crowned with twelve stars.* 71. Swil, *Such.* 72. *To make war on the Fiend.* 73. pas, *way.* 74. breche, *breaking.* 75. unwemmed, *unspotted.* 76. *By bearing of your child.* 78. *Be gracious to us sinners.* 81. Ayens, *Against.* 82. wissinge, *guidance.* 83–4. *And though I have wronged you, grant I may improve.*

35

An adult lullaby

Lollay, lollay, little child, why wepestou so sore?   earlier 14c.
Nedes mostou wepe—it was iyarked thee yore
Ever to lib in sorow, and sich and mourne evere,
As thine eldren did er this, whil hi alives were.
Lollay, lollay, little child, child, lollay, lullow,   5
Into uncuth world icommen so ertou.

Bestes, and thos foules, the fisses in the flode,
And euch shef alives, imaked of bone and blode,
Whan hi commeth to the world, hi doth hamsilf sum gode,
All bot the wrech brol that is of Adames blode.   10
Lollay, lollay, little child, to car ertou bemette;
Thou nost noght this worldes wild before thee is isette.

Child, if betideth that thou shalt thrive and thee,
Thench thou wer ifostred up thy moder kne:
Ever hab mund in thy hert of thos thinges thre,   15
Whan thou commest, what thou art, and what shall com of
    thee.
Lollay, lollay, little child, child, lollay, lollay,
With sorow thou com into this world, with sorow shalt wend
    away.

Lollay, lollay, little child, why do you cry so hard? You must needs cry—it was ordained for you of old to live for ever in sorrow and to sigh and mourn for ever, as your elders did before this, while they were alive. Lollay, lollay, little child, child, lollay, lullow, you have come into an alien world.
Beasts and birds, the fish in the river, and every living creature, made of blood and bone, when they come into the world do themselves some good, all except the wretched child descended from Adam. Lollay, lollay, little child, you are destined for trouble; you do not know the wilderness of this world is set before you.
Child, if it happens that you thrive and prosper, think you were brought up upon your mother's knee: always remember in your heart those three things, whence you have come, what you are, and what shall come of you. Lollay, lollay, little child, child, lollay, lollay, with sorrow you came into this world, and with sorrow shall go away.

16. what (thou), *MS.* whan (thou).

Ne tristou to this world: it is thy ful fo.
The rich he maketh pouer, the pore rich also.   20
It turneth woe to wel, and ek wel to wo.
Ne trist no man to this world whil it turneth so.
Lollay, lollay, little child, the fote is in the whele:
Thou nost whoder turne, to wo other wele.

Child, thou ert a pilgrim in wikedness ibor: 25
Thou wandrest in this fals world—thou lok thee befor!
Deth shall come with a blast, ute of a well dim horre,
Adames kin dun to cast, himsilf hath ido befor.
Lollay, lollay, little child, so wo thee worp Adam,
In the lond of paradis, throgh wikedness of Satan.   30

Child, thou nert a pilgrim bot an uncuthe guest:
Thy dawes beth itold, thy jurneys beth icest.
Whoder thou shalt wend, north other est,
Deth thee shall betide with bitter bale in brest.
Lollay, lollay, little child, this wo Adam thee wroght,   35
Whan he of the apple ete and Eve it him betoght.

*Put no trust in this world: it is your deadly enemy. It makes the rich poor and the
poor rich as well. It turns pain to prosperity and also prosperity into pain. Let no
man trust in this world while it turns so. Lollay, lollay, little child, your foot is on
Fortune's wheel, and you do not know which way it will turn, to pain or pros-
perity.*
*Child, you are a pilgrim born in sin: you wander in this treacherous world—look
ahead! Death is bound to come out of a very dark door (?) with a gust to cast down
the kin of Adam as he has done before (?). Lollay, lollay, little child, so Adam
wove suffering for you in the land of paradise through Satan's wickedness.*
*Child, you are not a pilgrim but an alien guest: your days are numbered, your
travels planned. Which ever way you go, north or east, Death shall happen to you
with bitter misery in your breast. Lollay, lollay, little child, this suffering Adam
made for you when he ate the apple and Eve gave it to him.*

29. worp, *MS.* worþ.

36

RICHARD ROLLE

A song of love for Jesus

Now I write a sang of luve that thou shall delite in when thou ert luvand Jesu Christe

My sange es in sihting,   mid 14c.
My life es in langinge,
Till I thee se, my king,
So faire in thy shining,
So faire in thy fairehede.   5
Intil thy light me lede,
And in thy luve me fede.
In luve make me to spede,
That thou be ever my mede.
When will thou come,   10
Jesus, my joy,
And cover me of care,
And give me thee,
That I may se,
And have for evermare?   15
All my coveiting war comen
If I might till thee fare.
I will na thing bot anely thee
That all my will ware.
Jesu, my savioure,   20
Jesu, my comfortoure,
Of all my fairness flowre,
My helpe in my socoure,
When may I see thy towre?
When will thou me call?   25
Me langes to thy hall,
To se thee than all.

1. sihting, *sighing.* 2. langing, *love-longing.* 5. fairehede, *beauty.* 9. mede, *reward.* 12. *recover me from.* 15. And . . . mare, *so Bodleian MS. but this MS.* lif and euermare. 16. war(e), *would be;* comen, *achieved.* 17, etc. till, *to.* 19. will, *desire;* and 40. war(e), *were, might be.* 24. towre, *i.e. of Heaven.* 26. me langes to, *I long for.* 27, 34. than, *then.*

Thy luve lat it not fall.
My hert paintes the pall
That steds us in stall.   30
Now wax I pale and wan
For luve of my lemman.
Jesu, bath God and man,
Thy luve thou lerd me than
When I to thee fast ran;   35
Forthy now I luve can.
I sitt and sing of luve-langing
That in my breste es bredde.
Jesu, Jesu, Jesu,
When war I to thee ledde?   40
Full wele I wate
Thou sees my state:
In luve my thoght es stedde.
When I thee se
And dwell with thee   45
Than am I filde and fedde.
Jesu, thy luve es fest
And me to luve think best.
My hert, when may it brest
To come to thee, my rest?   50
Jesu, Jesu, Jesu,
Till thee it es that I morne,
For my life and my living.
When may I hethen torne?
Jesu, my dere and my drewry,   55
Delite ert thou to singe.
Jesu, my mirth and melody,
When will thou com, my king?
Jesu, my hele and my hony,
My quart and my comforting.   60
Jesu, I coveite for to dy

---

29 (?) *Is the reference to the painting of a device, perhaps a badge of Jesus* (?). 29–30.
Omitted Bodl. MSS. 30. *That is of help to us* (?). 31. wax, *grow.* 32. lemman, *lover.*
33. bath, *both.* 34. lerd, *taught.* 36. Forthy, *Therefore;* can, *know* (*how to*). 41. wate,
know. 43. stedde, *firmly established.* 47–8. *Jesu, your love is firmly fixed and it seems to
me best to love.* 49. brest, *break.* 52. morne, *lament.* 54. hethen, *hence.* 55. drewry,
beloved, treasure. 59, 78. hele, *healing.* 60. quart, (*source of*) *health.*

When it es thy paying.
Langing es in me lent
That my luve hase me sent:
All wa es fra me went   65
Sen that my hert es brent,
In Christe luve so swete,
That never I will lete,
Bot ever to luve I hete,
For luve my bale may bete,   70
And till his blis me bring,
And give me my yerning.
Jesu, my luve, my sweting,
Langing es in me light,
That bindes me day and night,   75
Till I it have in sight,
His face, so faire and bright.
Jesu, my hope, my hele,
My joy ever ilk a dele,
Thy luve, lat it noght kele,   80
That I thy luve may fele
And won with thee in wele.
Jesu, with thee I big and belde.
Lever me war to dy
Than all this worlde to welde,   85
And have it in maistry.
When will thou rew on me,
Jesu, that I might with thee be,
To luve and lok on thee?
My settle ordaine for me,   90
And set thou me tharin,
For then mon we never twin,
And I thy luve shall sing,
Thorow sight of thy shining,
In Heven withouten ending.   95
Amen.

62. paying, *pleasure.* 63. *Love-longing has come upon me.* 65. wa, *woe;* went, *gone, turned.* 66. Sen that, *Since;* brent, *set on fire.* 68. lete, *leave off.* 69. hete, *promise.* 70. bale, *ill;* bete, *cure.* 74. *has alighted upon me.* 79. ever . . . dele, *every single bit.* 80. kele, *cool.* 82. won, *dwell;* wele, *well-being.* 83. big, *dwell;* belde, *build.* 84. *I had rather die.* 85. welde, *rule, possess.* 86. *And have dominion over it.* 87. rew, *have pity.* 90. settle, *place (in Heaven).* 92. *For then shall we never part.*

37

Christ's tear breaks my heart

Lovely ter of lovely eiye,   mid 14c.
Why dostu me so wo?
Sorful ter of sorful eiye,
Thu brekst mine herte ato.

Thu sikest sore,   5
Thy sorwe is more
Than mannis muth may telle:
Thu singest of sorwe
Manken to borwe
Out of the pit of helle.   10

I prud and kene,
Thu meke and clene,
Withouten wo or wile.
Thu art ded for me,
And I live thoru thee,   15
So blissed be that while.

Thy moder seet
How wo thee beet,
And therfore yerne she yerte.
To hire thu speke   20
Hire sorwe to sleke:
Swet sute wan thine herte.

Thine herte is rent,
Thy body is bent
Upon the Rode Tree.   25
The weder is went,
The Devil is shent,
Christ, thoru the might of thee.

2. *Why do you cause me such sorrow.* 3. *Sorrowful.* 4. *In two.* 5. *You sigh heavily.* 9. *To ransom mankind.* 11. *I, proud and violent.* 13. wile, *guile.* 17. *sees.* 18. *What a plight you are in.* 19. yerne, *earnestly;* yerte, *MS.* ȝepte, *cried out.* 20. *Speak to her.* 21. sleke, *abate.* 22. sute, *MS.* suet, *petition;* wan, *won.* 26. *The weather is changed (?) the storm is past (?).* 27. shent, *destroyed, shamed.*

38

Jesus reassures his mother

Lullay, lullay, la, lullay,   mid 14c.
My dere moder, lullay.

As I lay upon a night,
Alone in my longing,
Me thoughte I saw a wonder sight,   5
A maiden child rocking.

The maiden wolde withouten song
Hire child aslepe bringe;
The child thoughte she ded him wrong,
And bad his moder singe.   10

'Sing now, moder,' seide that child,
'What me shall befalle
Hereafter whan I cum to eld,
So don modres alle.

'Ich a moder treuly,   15
That can hire credel kepe,
Is wone to lullen lovely
And singen hire child aslepe.

'Swete moder, fair and fre,
Sithen that it is so,   20
I preye thee that thu lulle me,
And sing sumwhat therto.'

'Swete son,' seide she,
'Wherof shuld I singe?
Wist I nevere yet more of thee   25
But Gabrieles gretinge.

5. *It seemed to me I saw a wonderful sight.* 9. ded, *MS.* de. 13. eld, *old age.* 14. So don, *As do.* 15. Ich a, *Every.* 16. *Who knows how to look after her cradle.* 17. wone, *wont.* 19. fre, *noble, generous.* 20, 56. Sithen that, *Since.* 25. Wist, *knew.*

'He grette me godly on his kne
And seide, "Heil! Marye,
Full of grace, God is with thee.
Beren thu shalt Messye."   30

'I wondred michil in my thought,
For man wold I right none.
"Marye," he seide, "drede thee nought:
Lat God of Hevene alone."

. . .

'I answerede blethely,   35
For his word me paiyede,
"Lo! Godis servant, her am I,
Be it as thu me seide."

'Ther, as he seide, I thee bare
On midwenter night,   40
In maidenhed, withouten care,
By grace of God almight.

'The shepperdis that wakkeden in the wolde
Herden a wonder mirthe
Of angles ther, as they tolde,   45
In time of thy birthe.

'Swete son, sikirly,
No more can I say;
And, if I coude, fawen wold I
To don all at thy pay.'   50

'Moder,' seide that swete thing,
'To singen I shall thee lere

27. *He greeted me courteously, kneeling down.* 30. Messye, *The Messiah.* 31. michil, *much;* thought, *mind.* 32. *For I would have no man at all.* 34. *Leave it to the God of Heaven.* 34, 35. *Three stanzas omitted.* 35. blethely, *gladly.* 36. paiyede, *pleased.* 41. *Being a virgin without doubt.* 43. wakkeden, *kept watch;* wolde, *open country.* 44. *Heard a wonderful rejoicing.* 45. angles, *angels;* ther, MS. þᵗ. 47. sikirly, *for certain.* 49. fawen, *gladly.* 50. all at, MS. at al; *do all to your liking.* 52. lere, *teach.*

What me fallet to suffring
And don whil I am here.'

. . .

'Allas! sone,' seide that may,   55
'Sithen that it is so,
Whorto shall I biden that day
To beren thee to this wo?'

'Moder,' he seide, 'tak it lighte,
For liven I shall ayeine,   60
And in thy kinde, thoru my might,
For elles I wroughte in veine.

'To my Fader I shall wende
In mine manhed to Hevene;
The Holy Ghost I shall thee sende,   65
With hise sondes sevene.

'I shall thee taken, whan time is,
To me at the laste,
To ben with me, moder, in blis:
All this, than, have I caste.   70

'All this werld demen I shall,
At the dom rising;
Swete moder, here is all
That I wile now sing.'

Certeinly this sighte I say,   75
This song I herde sing,
As I lay this Yolisday,
Alone in my longing.

53–4. *What it will be my lot to suffer and to do while I am here.* 54, 55. *Fifteen stanzas about Jesus' life and Passion omitted.* 55. may, *maiden.* 57. *Why must I live to see that day.* 59. lighte, *easily.* 60. ayeine, *again.* 61. kinde, *nature.* 62. wroughte, *acted.* 66. sondes, *gifts.* 70. than, *then;* caste, *arranged.* 71. demen, *judge.* 72. *At the resurrection (of all the dead) for judgement.* 75. say, *saw.* 77. Yolisday, *Christmas.*

39

A prayer to the Sacrament of the Altar

Jesu, Lord, welcom thou be,   mid or
In forme of bred as I thee see.   later 14c.
Jesu, for thine Holy Name,
Shild me today fro sinne and shame.
As thou were of a maide born,   5
Thou lat me never be forlorn.
Ne lat me never for noo sinne
Lese the joye that thou art inne.
Thou, rihtwise King of all thing,
Grant me Shrifte, Housil and good ending,   10
Riht beleve beforn my ded day,
And blisse with thee that leste shall ay.

6. *Don't ever let me be utterly lost.* 7. *Nor let me ever for any sin.* 8. Lese, *Lose.*
9. rihtwise, *righteous.* 10. Shrifte, *Absolution;* Housil, *Communion.* 11. ded, *death.*

40

A hymn to the Cross

Steddefast Crosse, inmong alle other,   14c.
Thou art a tree mikel of prise:
In brawnche and flore swilk another
I ne wot non in wode no ris.
Swete be the nalis, and swete be the tree,   5
And sweter be the birdin that hangis upon thee.

2. mikel of prise, *most precious.* 3. flore, *flower;* swilk, *such.* 4. *I know none in wood
or thicket.*

41

Jesus bids man remember

Men rent me on Rode   14c.
With wundes woliche wode;
All blet my blode:
Thenk, man, all it is thee to gode.

Thenk who thee first wroughte,   5
For what werk helle thou soughte;
Thenk who thee agein boughte:
Werk warly, faile me noughte.

Beheld my side,
My wundes sprede so wide;   10
Restless I ride:
Lok upon me—put fro thee pride.

My palefrey is of tre,
With nailes nailede thurh me.
Ne is more sorwe to se;   15
Certes, noon more no may be.

Under my gore
Ben wundes selcouthe sore.
Ler, man, my lore,
For my love sinne no more.   20

Fal nought for fonding:
That shall thee most turne to goode.
Mak stif withstonding:
Thenk well who me rente on the Rode.

1–2. *Men tore me savagely on the Cross with grievous wounds.* 3. blet, *bleeds.* 4. *thee to gode, for your good.* 6. werk, *act.* 7. agein boughte, *redeemed.* 8. *Behave wisely, fail me not.* 16. *Certainly, any more is impossible.* 17. *Under my clothes (skirt).* 18. *Are extremely painful wounds.* 19. Ler, *MS.* Der (?), *Learn.* 21. fonding, *temptation.* 22. That (*viz. resisting temptation*); (*for*) thee. 23. stif, *strong.* 24. *Consider well who* (*viz. every sinner every time he sins*) *tore me on the Cross.*

42

Jesus, my sweet lover

Jesu Christ, my lemmon swete,   mid or
That diyedest on the Rode Tree,   later 14c.
With all my might I thee beseche,
For thy woundes two and three,
That also faste mot thy love   5
Into mine herte fitched be
As was the spere into thine herte,
Whon thou soffredest deth for me.

1. lemmon, *lover*. 5. also, *as;* mot, *may.* 6. fitched, *fixed.*

43

All turns into yesterday

Whon men beth muriest at her mele,   mid or
With mete and drink to maken hem glade,   later
With worship and with worldly wele,   14c.
They ben so set they conne not sade.
They have no deinte for to dele   5
With thinges that ben devoutly made:
They wene her honour and here hele
Shall ever laste and never diffade.
But in her hertes I wolde they hade,
Whon they gon richest men on array,   10
How sone that God hem may degrade,
And sumtime thenk on yesterday.

1. beth, *are;* etc., her(e), *their.* 3. wele, *happiness.* 4. *They are so placed they cannot be serious.* 5. deinte, *fondness.* 7. *They think their dignity and their well-being.* 8. diffade, *fade.* 10. on, *in.* 11. sone, *soon;* etc., hem, *them.*

This day as leef we may be light,
With all the murthes that men may vise,
To revele with this birdes bright,   15
Uche mon gayest on his gise.
At the last it draweth to night,
That slep most make his maistrise.
Whon that he hath icud his might,
The morwe, he bosketh up to rise.   20
Then all draweth hem to fantasyse:
Wher he is becomen con no mon say.
And yif he wuste they were full wise,
For all is tornd to yesterday.

. . .

Socrates seith a word full wis: 25
It were well betere for to see
A mon that now parteth and dis
Then a feste of realte.
The feste wol make his flesh to ris,
And drawe his herte to vanite;   30
The body that on the bere lis
Sheweth the same that we shall be.
That ferful fit may no mon flee,
Ne with no wiles win it away:
Therfore among all jolite   35
Sumtime thenk on yesterday.

. . .

I have wist, sin I couthe meen,
That children hath by candle light
Her shadewe on the wal iseen,
And ronne therafter all the night.   40
Bisy aboute they han ben
To catchen it with all here might,

---

14. murthes, *joys;* vise, *devise.* 15. this, *these;* birdes, *girls.* 16. *Each man gayest in his dress.* 18–24. *So that sleep must show his power. When sleep has made his might known, the next day, he prepares to get up. Then all start speculating: where that day has gone no man can say. And if anyone knew, they would be very wise, for all is turned into yesterday.* 24, 25. *Five stanzas omitted.* 28. *Than a royal feast.* 31. bere, *bier.* 33. ferful fit, *terrifying experience.* 34. *Nor persuade it to go away by any cunning.* 36, 37. *Two stanzas omitted.* 37. *I have known since I could remember.*

And whon they catchen it best wolde wene,
Sannest it shet out of her sight.
The shadewe catchen they ne might,   45
For no lines that they couthe lay.
This shadewe I may likne aright
To this world and yesterday.

. . .

Well thou wost withouten faile
That deth hath manast thee to die,   50
But whon that he wol thee assaile
That wost thou not ne never may spye.
Yif thou wolt don by my counsaile,
With siker defence be ay redye,
For siker defence in this bataile   55
Is clene lif, parfit and trye.
Put thy trust in Godes mercye,
It is the beste at all assay.
And ever among thou thee en-nuye
Into this world and yesterday.   60

43. *And when they most expected to catch it.* 44. Sannest, *Quickest;* shet, *shoots.*
48, 49. *Two stanzas omitted.* 49, 52. wost, *knowest.* 50. manast, *threatened.* 54, 55. siker,
secure. 56. trye, *excellent.* 58. at all assay, *in every trial.* 59–60. *And, for the rest, be
weary of this world and yesterday* (?). *One stanza omitted at end.*

44

Mary suffers with her son

Why have ye no reuthe on my child?   mid 14c.
Have reuthe on me, full of murning.
Taket down on Rode my derworthy child,
Or prek me on Rode with my derling.

More pine ne may me ben don   5
Than laten me liven in sorwe and shame.
Als love me bindet to my sone,
So lat us deiyen bothen isame.

1, 2. reuthe, *pity.* 2. murning, *mourning.* 3. *Take down from the Cross my precious
child.* 4. prek, *impale.* 5. pine, *torment.* 7. Als, *As.* 8. *So let us die both together.*

45

A devout prayer of the Passion

In seyinge of this orisoun stinteth and bideth at every cros and thinketh whate ye have seide. For a more devout prayere fond I never of the Passioun, whoso wolde devoutly say itte.

Jesu, that hast me dere iboght,   mid or
Write thou gostly in my thoght,   later 14c.
That I mow with devocion
Thinke on thy dere Passion.
For thogh my hert be hard as stone   5
Yit maist thou gostly write theron
With naill and with spere kene,
And so shullen the lettres be sene.

Write in my hert with speches swete
Whan Judas, the traitour, can thee mete: 10
That traitour was ful of the Feende,
And yit thou caldest him thy frende.
Swete Jesu, how might thou soo
Cal him thy frend, so fel and foo?
Bot sethen thou spake so lovely   15
To him that was thine enemy,
How swete shulle thy speches be
To ham that hertely loven thee,
Whan they in Hevin with thee shall dwelle,
Iwis, ther may no tonge telle.   20

Write how thou were bounde sore
And drawen forth Pilate before;
And how swetly thou answard tho
To him that was thy fel foo.

stinteth, *stop;* bideth, *wait;* cros, *i.e. marks in margin at points for meditation. (I have not reproduced them here.)*
2. gostly, *spiritually.* 3, 111, 131. mow, *may.* 8, 17. shulle(n), *shall.* 10, 37. can, *did(st).* 14, 143. fel, *cruel;* foo, *hostile.* 15, 148. sethen, *since.* 18, 73. ham, *them.* 20, 59, 149. Iwis, *Indeed.* 23. tho, *then.*

Write how that fals enqueste   25
Cried ay withouten reste,
'Honge him on the Rode Tree,
For he will kinge of Jewes be.'

Write upon my hert boke
Thy faire and swete, lovely loke,   30
For shame of har hiddous crye
That wolden of thee have no mercy.

Write how whan the cros was forth broght,
And the naill of iron wroght,
How thou began to chever and quake: 35
Thine hert was woo thogh thou ne spake.

Write how downward thou can loke
Whan Jewes to thee the cros betoke:
Thou bare it forth with reuthly chere;
The teres ran down by thy lere.   40

Jesu, write in my hert depe
How that thou began to wepe
Tho thy bak was to the Rode bent,
With rogget naill thy handes rent.

Write the strokes with hameres stout,   45
With the blood renninge about;
How the naill stint at the bone
Whan thou were ful wo-begone.

Jesu, yit write in my hert
How bloode out of thy woundes stert;   50
And with that blode write thou so ofte
Mine hard hert, til it be softe.

Jesu, that art so miche of might,
Write in my hert that reuthful sight,
To loken on thy moder fre   55
When thou were honged on Rode Tree.

Write thy swete moderes woo
Whan sho saw thee to the deth goo:
Iwis, thogh I write all my live,
I sholde never hir woo discrive.   60

In mine hert ay mot it be,
That hard, knotty Rode Tree;
The naill and the spere also
That thou were with to deth do;
The crown, and the scourges grete   65
That thou were with so sore ibette;
Thy wepinge and thy woundes wide;
The blode that ran down by thy side;
The shame, the scorne, the grete despite,
The spottel that defouled thy face so white;   70
The eisel and the bitter galle
And other of thy peines alle:
For while I have ham in my thoght
The Devil, I hope, shall dere me noght.

Jesu, write this that I might knowe   75
How michel love to thee I owe:
For thogh that I wolde fro thee flee
Thou folwest ever to save me.

Jesu, whan I thinke on thee,
How thou were bound for love of me,   80
Wel owe I to wepe that stounde
That thou for me so sore were bounde.
Bot thou that bare upon thy handes
For my sinnes so bitter bandes,

---

53. miche, *great.* 55. *Looking at your gracious mother.* 58. sho, *she.* 60. discrive,
describe. 61. mot, *may.* 64. *With which you were done to death.* 71. eisel, *vinegar.*
74. dere, *harm.* 76, 94. miche(l), *much.* 81. owe, *ought;* stounde, *time.*

With love bandes bind thou so me   85
That I be never departed fro thee.

Jesu, that was with love so bounde,
That soffred for me dethes wounde,
At my deyinge so visite me,
And make the Fend away to flee.   90

Jesu, make me glad to be
Simple and pouer for love of thee,
And let me never, for more ne lasse,
Love good too miche, that sone shal passe.

Jesu, that art Kinge of life,   95
Tech my soule, that is thy wif,
To love best no thinge in londe
Bot thee, Jesu, hir dere housbonde.
For other blisse and other beaute,
Be it foule and sorow to see: 100
For other joy and other blisse,
Woo and sorow, forsoth, it is,
And lesteth bot a little while,
Mannis soule for to begyle.

Jesu, let me fele what joy it be   105
To suffere wo for love of thee;
How myry it is for to wepe;
How softe in hard clothes to slepe.
Lat Love now his bow bende
And love arowes to my hert send,   110
That it mow percen to the roote,
For suche woundes shold be my bote.
Whan I am lowe for thy love
Than am I moste at mine above:
Fastinge is feest, murninge is blis;   115
For thy love, povert is richesse.

86. be never, *so MSS. Bodl. 850 and Egerton 3245, but this MS. and Bodl. e. mus. 232,*
never be; departed, *parted.* 94. good, *possessions.* 97. in londe, *there is (vague formula).*
107. myry, *joyful.* 109. Lat, *Let.* 112, bote, *salvation.* 114. at mine above, *exalted.*

The hard here shold be more of pris
Than softe silk, or pelur, or bis.
Defaut, for thy love, is plente,
And fleishely lust wel loth shold be.   120
Whan I am with woo bestadde,
For thy love, than am I glad;
To suffre scornes and grete despite,
For love of thee, is my delite.

Jesu make me oo night to wake   125
And in my thoght thy name to take,
And whether the night be short or longe,
Of thee, Jesu, be ever my songe.
Let this prayere a chaine be
To draw thee down of thy se,   130
That I mow make thee dwellinge
In my hert at thy likinge.

Jesu, I pray thee forsake nat me,
Thogh I of sin gilty be:
For that thef that henge thee by,   135
Redily thou yaf him thy mercy.

Jesu, that art so corteisly,
Make me bold on thee to cry:
For wel I wot, without drede,
Thy mercy is more than my misdede.   140

Jesu, that art so lef and dere,
Hire and spede this pouer prayere.
For Poul, that was so fel and wode
To spil Cristen mennis blode,
To thee wold he no prayere make,   145
And thou woldest nat him forsake.
Than maist thou noght forsake me,
Sethen that I pray thus to thee.

---

117. here, *hair-shirt;* of pris, *valuable.* 118. pelur, *fur;* bis, *fine linen.* 119. Defaut, *Want.* 120. loth, *loathsome.* 121. bestadde, *beset.* 125. oo, *at.* 130. of, *from;* se, *throne.* 132. at, *to.* 136. yaf, *gave.* 137. corteisly, *gracious.* 139. wot, *know;* drede, *doubt.* 141. lef, *beloved.* 142. Hire, *Hear;* spede, *further.* 143. wode, *mad.* 148. to, *so other MSS. but this MS. omits.*

At my deyinge I hop, iwis,
Of thy presens I shall noght misse.   150
Jesu, make me than to rise
From deth to live, on such a wise
As thou rose up on Estre Day,
In joy and blisse to live aye.

                                        Amen.

46

Jesus to those who pass by

Ye that pasen by the weiye,   mid 14c.
Abidet a little stounde.
Beholdet, all my felawes,
Yef any me lik is founde.
To the Tre with nailes thre   5
Wol fast I hange bounde;
With a spere all thoru my side
To mine herte is mad a wounde.

2. *Stay a short while.* 4. Yef, *If.* 6. Wol, *Very.*

47

Jesus reproaches his people

My folk, now answere me,   mid 14c.
And sey what is my gilth.
What might I mor ha don for thee
That I ne have fulfilth?

2. gilth, *guilt.*

Out of Egypte I broughte thee,   5
Ther thu wer in thy wo:
And wickedliche thu nome me
Als I hadde ben thy fo.

Over all abouten I ledde thee,
And oforn thee I yede: 10
And no frenchipe fond I in thee
Whan that I hadde nede.

Fourty wenter I sente thee
Angeles mete fro Hevene:
And thu heng me on Rode Tre,   15
And greddest with loud stevene.

Heilsum water I sente thee
Out of the harde ston:
And eisil and galle thu sentest me—
Other yef thu me non.   20

The see I parted asunder for thee,
And ledde thee thoru wol wide:
And the herte blod to sen of me
Thu smettest me thoru the side.

Alle thy fon I slow for thee,   25
And made thee cout of name:
And thu heng me on Rode Tre,
And dedest me michil shame.

A kinges yerde I thee betok,
Till thu wer all beforn: 30
And thu heng me on Rode Tre
And corownedest me with a thorn.

I made thine enemies and thee
For to ben knowen asunder:
And on an hey hil thu henge me,   35
All the werld on me to wonder.

6. Ther, *Where.* 7. nome, *(you) took.* 10. *And before you I went.* 14. *Manna.* 15, etc.
heng(e), *(you) hanged.* 16. *And cried out with a loud voice.* 17. Heilsum, *Wholesome.*
19. eisil, *vinegar.* 20. yef, *(you) gave.* 22. wol, *very.* 23. sen, *see.* 25. fon, *enemies;* slow,
slew. 26. cout, *famous.* 28. michil, *much.* 29. *I granted you a king's sceptre.* 34. *To be
distinguished apart.* 35. hey, *high.*

48

The world an illusion

I wolde witen of sum wis wight,   mid or
Witterly, what this world were: later 14c.
It fareth as a foules flight,
Now is it henne, now is it here;
Ne be we never so muche of might,   5
Now be we on benche, now be we on bere;
And be we never so war and wight,
Now be we sek, now be we fere;
Now is on proud, withouten pere,
Now is the selve iset not by;   10
And whos wol alle thing hertly here,
This world fareth as a fantasy.

The sonnes cours, we may well kenne,
Ariseth est and geth down west;
The rivers into the see they renne,   15
And it is never the more, almest;
Windes rosheth her and henne,
In snow and rein is non arest.
Whon this wol stunte, who wot or whenne,
But only God, on grounde grest?   20
The erthe in on is ever prest,
Now bedropped, now all drye,
But uche gome glit forth as a gest:
This world fareth as a fantasy.

Kunredes come and kunredes gon,   25
As joineth generacions,
But alle hee passeth everichon,

1. witen, *know;* wight, *person.* 2. Witterly, *Assuredly.* 3, etc. fareth, *passes,
vanishes;* foules, *bird's.* 4, etc. henne, *hence.* 6. bere, *bier.* 7. war, *vigilant;* wight,
brave. 8. sek, *sick;* fere, *in good health.* 9. on, *one;* and 93, pere, *equal.* 10. *At the
next moment the same person enjoys no esteem.* 11. whos, *whoso;* hertly, *sincerely.*
12. fantasy, *illusion.* 13. kenne, *know.* 16. almest, *almost (a tag).* 18. arest, *end.*
19. stunte, *stop;* etc., wot, *knows.* 20. *greatest in the world (?).* 21. *The earth is always
ready (?).* 22. drye, MS. druyze. 23. *But each man glides away as a visitor.* 25. Kun-
redes, *Races.* 27, etc. he(e), *they;* everichon, *everyone.*

For all her preparacions.
Sum are foryete, clene as bon,
Among alle maner nacions: 30
So shull men thenken us nothing on,
That now han the ocupacions.
And alle thes disputacions
Ideliche all us ocupye,
For Christ maketh the creacions,   35
And this world fareth as a fantasy.

Whuch is mon who wot, and what,
Whether that he be ought or nought?
Of erthe and eir groweth up a gnat,
And so doth mon, whon all is sought.   40
Thaugh mon be waxen gret and fat,
Mon melteth awey so deth a mought:
Monnes might nis worth a mat,
But nuyeth himself and turneth to nought.
Who wot, save he that all hath wrought,   45
Wher mon becometh whon he shall die?
Who knoweth by dede oughte, bote
   by thought?
For this world fareth as a fantasy.

Dieth mon and beestes die,
And all is on ocasion;   50
And alle o deth bos bothe drye,
And han on incarnacion:
Save that men beth more sleighe,
All is o comparison.
Who wot yif monnes soule stighe,   55
And bestes soules sinketh down?

28, etc. her(e), *their.* 29–32. *Some are forgotten, clean as bone, among peoples of all kinds: in the same way men are bound not to think of us who now have the positions of power.* 34. Ideliche, *Uselessly.* 35. creacions, *created things.* 37. Whuch, *Of what sort?* 42. *Man melts away as a moth does.* 43. mat, *mat (?).* 44. nuyeth, *injures, vexes,* MS. nuyȝeþ. 47. *Who knows anything (of the future life) by experience, but only by speculation (?).* 50. *And all is one circumstance.* 51–2. bos, MS. hos; *And it behoves both to suffer the very same death and to have the same birth (?).* 53. beth, *are;* sleighe, *clever, wise.* 54. *All is of a likeness.* 55. yif, *if;* stighe, *ascends.*

Who knoweth beestes intencioun,
On her creatour how they crye?
Save only God that knoweth here soun,
For this world fareth as a fantasy.   60

Uche secte hopeth to be save,
Baldely, by here beleve,
And uch one upon God he crave—
Why shulde God with hem him greve?
Uch one trouweth that other rave,   65
But alle he cheoseth God for cheve;
And hope in God uch one they have,
And by here wit here worching preve.
Thus mony matters men don meve,
Sechen her wittes how and why;   70
But Godes mercy us alle biheve,
For this world fareth as a fantasy.
. . .

But leve we ure disputisoun,
And leve on him that all hath wrought:
We mowe not preve, by no resoun,   75
How he was born that all us bought;
But whol in ure intencioun
Worshipe we him in herte and thought,
For he may turne kindes upsedown,
That alle kindes made of nought.   80
Whon all ur bokes ben forth brought,
And all ur craft of clergye,
And all ur wittes ben thoroughout sought,
Yit we fareth as a fantasy.

Of fantasy is all ur fare,   85
Olde and yonge and alle ifere:

59. soun, *sound.* 62. Baldely, *Boldly.* 63–8. *And each one begs God earnestly—why should God bother himself with them? Each one believes the other is mad, but all choose God for lord; and each one hopes in God, and by (his) wit justifies what (he) does.* 69. don meve, *discuss.* 70. Sechen, *Search.* 71. *But God's mercy is necessary for us all.* 72, 73. *Two stanzas omitted.* 73. *But let us stop disputing.* 74. leve, *believe.* 75. mowe, *may.* 79. *For he can turn 'species upside down.* 82. *And all our professional learning.* 85. fare, *experience.* 86. ifere, *together.*

But make we murie and sle care,
And worshipe we God whil we ben here;
Spende ur good and litel spare,
And uche mon cheries otheres cheere.   90
Thenk how we comen hider all bare—
Ur wey-wending is in a were.
Prey we the Prince, that hath no pere,
Tak us whol to his mercy,
And kepe ur conscience clere,   95
For this world is but fantasy.

90. *And let each man consider the other's feelings.* 92. *Our departure is uncertain* (?).
One stanza omitted at end.

49

Crucified to the world

Gold and all this werdis win   mid 14c.
Is nought but Christis Rode:
I wolde be clad in Christis skin,
That ran so longe on blode,
And gon t' is herte and taken mine in,   5
Ther is a fulsum fode:
Than yef I little of kith or kin,
For ther is alle gode.

                                        Amen.

1. *werdis win,* world's joy. 5. *in,* dwelling. 6. *Where there is abundant food.* 7. *Then
would I care little for kith or kin.*

50

The Hours of the Passion

At the time of Matines, Lord, thu were itake,   mid 14c.
And of thine disciples sone were forsake.

130

The felle Jewes thee token in that iche stounde,
And ledden thee to Caiphas, thine handis harde ibounde.

We honuren thee, Christ, and blissen thee with vois,   5
For thu boutest this werd with thine Holy Crois.

At Prime, Lord, thu were ilad Pilat beforn,
And there wol fals witnesse on thee was iborn.
He smiten thee under the ere and seiden, 'Who was tat?'
Of hem thy faire face foule was bespat.   10

At Underne, Lord, they gunnen thee to crucifiye,
And clotheden thee in pourpre, in scoren and in enviye.
With wol kene thornes icorowned thu were,
And on thy sulder to thy peines thine Holy Crois thu bere.

At Midday, Lord, thu were nailed to the Rode,   15
Betwixen tweiye theves, ihanged all on blode.
For thy pine thu wexe athrist and seidest, 'Sicio'.
Galle and eisil they yeven thee to drinken tho.

At the heiye Non, Lord, thu toke thy leve
And into thy Fader hond the Holy Ghost thu yeve.   20
Longis, the knight, a sarp spere all to thine herte pithte.
The erde quakede and tremlede, the sunne les hire lithte.

Of the Rode he was idon at the time of Evesong;
Mildeliche and stille he suffrede all here wrong.
Swich a deth he underfong that us helpen may.   25
Allas! the crune of joiye under thornes lay.

At Cumplin time he was ibiriyed, and in a ston ipith,
Jesu Christe's swete body, and so seit Holy Writh,

3. *The cruel Jews took you at that very hour.* 6. *For by your Holy Cross you redeemed this world.* 8, 13. wol, *very.* 9. He, *They;* smiten, *smote.* 10. Of hem, *by them.* 11. gunnen, *began.* 14. sulder, *shoulder.* 17. pine, *suffering, torment;* wexe, *grew;* Sicio, *I thirst.* 18. eisil, *vinegar;* and 20. yeve(n), *gave;* tho, *then.* 19. heiye, *high.* 21. Longis, *note 166, l. 54;* sarp, *sharp;* pithte, *drove home.* 22. erde, *earth;* sunne lost its light. 23. *From the Cross he was taken.* 24. here, *their.* 25. Swich, *Such;* deth, MS. det3; underfong, *underwent.* 26. crune, *crown.* 27. *At Compline time he was buried and put in a tomb.* 28. seit, *says.*

Enoint with an oniment—and than was cumpliyed
That beforn of Jesu Christ was ilupropheciyed.   30

This iche holy orisoun of thy Passioun
I thenke to thee, Jesu Christ, with devocioun,
That thu that suffredest for me harde piningge
Be my solas and my confort at my last endingge.

                                                  Amen.

29. cumpliyed, *accomplished.* 31. iche, *same.* 32. thenke, *think.* 33. piningge,
suffering.

51

Undo your heart

I am Jesu that cum to fight   mid 14c.
Withouten sheld and spere:
Elles were thy deth idight,
Yif my fighting ne were.
Sithen I am comen and have thee brought   5
A blisful bote of bale,
Undo thin herte, tell me thy thought,
Thy sennes grete and smale.

3. idight, *appointed.* 4. Yif, *If.* 5. Sithen, *Since.* 6. *A blessed remedy for ill.* 8. sennes,
sins.

52

GEOFFREY CHAUCER

Welcome, Summer

Nowe welcome, Somor, with sonne softe,   later 14c.
That hast thes Wintres wedres overeshake,

1, etc. Somor, *Summer (probably including our Spring); Digby MS.* with thy sonne;
softe, *mild, balmy.* 2, etc. wedres, *storms;* overeshake, *shaken off.*

And drevine away the lange nightes blake.
Saint Valentine, that ert full hye alofte,
Thus singen smal fowles for thy sake.   5

Nowe welcome, Somor, with sonne softe,
That hast thes Wintres wedres overeshake.

Wele han they cause for to gladen ofte,
Sethe ech of hem recoverede hathe his make:
Full blisseful mowe they ben when they wake.   10

Nowe welcome, Somor, with sonne softe,
That hast thes Wintres wedres overeshake,
And drevine away the lange nightes blake.

3, 13. lange, *MS.* lage, *with* r *inserted in same hand above line between* a *and* g.
Digby MS. longe. *Line omitted St. John's MS.* 5. smal, *Digby and St. John's MSS.*
smale; fowles, *birds.* 8. gladen, *rejoice.* 9. Sethe, *Since;* make, *mate.* 10. mowe, *may;*
ben, *St. John's MS.* synge; *Digby MS.* Full blisfully they synge and endles ioy þei
make.

53

GEOFFREY CHAUCER

Ballade to Rosamund

Madame, ye ben of all beaute shrine,   later 14c.
As fer as cercled is the mapamounde,
For as the crystal glorious ye shine,
And like ruby ben your chekes rounde;
Therwith ye ben so mery and so jocounde,   5
That at a revel, whan that I see you dance,
It is an oinement unto my wounde,
Thogh ye to me ne do no daliance.

1, etc. ye ben, *you are.* 2. mapamounde, *map of world, world.* 5. mery, *pleasant;*
jocounde, *gay.* 8, etc. *Though you have no conversation with me, will not let me make
love to you.*

For thogh I wepe of teres full a tine,
Yet may that wo mine herte nat confounde.   10
Your semy voys, that ye so small out-twine,
Maketh my thoght in joy and bliss abounde.
So curtaisly I go, with love bounde,
That to myself I sey, in my penance,
'Suffiseth me to love you, Rosemounde,   15
Thogh ye to me ne do no daliance.'

Nas never pyk walwed in galantine
As I in love am walwed and iwounde:
For which, full ofte, I of myself divine
That I am trew Tristam the Secounde.   20
My love may not refreyde nor affounde;
I brenne ay in an amorouse plesance:
Do what you list, I will your thral be founde,
Thogh ye to me ne do no daliance.

9. tine, *tub (for brewing)*. 11. semy, *thin, tiny (?)*; voys, *voice*; small, *fine, soft*; out-twine, *twist out, utter*. 13. *So meekly I go, fettered with love.* 14. penance, *suffering*. 15. (*It*) suffiseth. 17. *There was never a pike was so immersed in sauce.* 21. refreyde, *grow cold*; affounde, *go numb with cold*. 22. brenne, *burn*; plesance, *state of pleasure*. 23. list, *like*.

54

GEOFFREY CHAUCER

A lady without paragon

Hide, Absolon, thy gilte tresses clere;   later 14c.
Ester, ley thou thy mekenesse all adown;
Hide, Jonathas, all thy frendly manere;
Penalopee, and Marcia Catoun,
Make of youre wifhode no comparisoun;   5
Hide ye youre beautes, Isoude and Heleine:
My lady cometh that all this may disteine.

1. gilte, *gilded, golden*; clere, *shining*. 5. wifhode, *womanhood*. 7, *etc.* disteine, *outshine*.

Thy faire body, lat it nat appere,
Lavine, and thou, Lucresse of Rome town;
And Polixene, that boghten love so dere,   10
And Cleopatre, with all thy passioun,
Hide ye your trouthe of love and your renown;
And thou, Tesbe, that hast of love suche peine:
My lady cometh that all this may disteine.

Hero, Dido, Laudomia, alle ifere,   15
And Phyllis, hanging for thy Demophoun,
And Canace, espied by thy chere,
Ysiphile, betraysed with Jasoun:
Maketh of your trouthe neither boost ne soun,
Nor Ypermystre or Adriane, ye tweine: 20
My lady cometh that all this may disteine.

The famous people mentioned are: Absalom, Esther, Jonathan, Penelope, Marcia (wife of Cato), Isolde, Helen, Lavinia, Lucretia, Polyxena, Cleopatra, Thisbe, Hero, Dido, Laodamia, Phyllis (and her Demophon), Canace, Hypsipyle (and Jason), Hypermnestra, Ariadne.
   12. trouthe of, faithfulness in. 15. alle ifere, all together. 17. disclosed by your appearance. 18. deceived by. 19. soun, sound.

55

GEOFFREY CHAUCER

Truth shall set you free

Fle fro the pres and dwelle with sothefastnesse;   later
Suffise thine owen thing, thei it be smal: 14c.
For horde hathe hate and climbing tikelnesse,
Pres hath envye and wele blent overal.
Savoure no more thanne thee behove shall;   5
Reule weel thyself, that other folk canst rede,
And trouthe shall deliver, it is no drede.

1–7. Flee from the (ambitious) throng (of the court) and live with truth; be content with what you have though it is little: for hoarding means hatred and climbing insecurity, the throng is envious and prosperity blinds completely. Take pleasure in no more than is necessary for you; you who are able to advise others, rule yourself properly and there is no doubt truth shall set (you) free.

Tempest thee nought al croked to redresse,
In trust of hire that torneth as a bal;
Myche wele stant in litel besinesse.   10
Bewar therfore to spurne ayeins an al;
Strive not as dothe the crocke with the wal;
Daunte thyself that dauntest otheres dede,
And trouthe shall deliver, it is no drede.

That thee is sent, receive in buxumnesse;   15
The wrestling for the worlde axeth a fal;
Here is non home, here nis but wildernesse;
Forthe! pilgrime, forthe! Forthe! beste, out of the stal.
Knowe thy contre, loke up, thonk God of al.
Holde the heye weye and lat thy ghost thee lede,   20
And trouthe shall deliver, it is no drede.

Therfore, thou Vache, leve thine olde wrechedenesse!
Unto the world leve now to be thral!
Crye him mercy, that of his hie godnesse
Made thee of nought; and, in especial,   25
Drawe unto him and pray in general
For thee, and eke for other, heveneliche mede,
And trouthe shall deliver, it is no drede.

8. Tempest, *Disturb.* 9. hire, i.e. *Fortune.* 10. Myche, *Much;* stant, *stands;* besinesse, *activity.* 11. *Take care, therefore, not to kick against the pricks.* 12. *Don't run your head against a brick wall.* 13. Daunte, *overcome.* 15. *That (which to) you;* in buxumnesse, *submissively.* 16. axeth, *asks (for).* 19. contre, *country.* 20. ghost, *spirit.* 27. eke, *also;* other, *others;* mede, *reward, (meadow? appropriate to a* vache = *cow).*

56

GEOFFREY CHAUCER

A song to his purse for the king

To you, my purse, and to noon other wight   later
Complain I, for ye be my lady dere.   14c.
I am so sory now that ye been light,

1. wight, *creature.* 3. light, *lacking weight, unchaste.*

For, certes, but if ye make me hevy chere,
Me were as leef be laid upon my bere!   5
For which unto your mercy thus I crye:
Beth hevy ayeine, or elles mot I die.

Now voucheth sauf this day, or it be night,
That I of you the blisful soun may here,
Or see your colour, like the sonne bright,   10
That of yellownesse hadde never pere.
Ye be my lif! Ye be mine hertis stere!
Quene of comfort, and of good companye!
Beth hevy ayeine, or elles mot I die.

Now, purse, that ben to me my lives light   15
And saviour, as down in this worlde here,
Oute of this towne helpe me thurgh your might,
Sin that ye wole nat bene my tresorere!
For I am shave as nye as is a frere.
But yet I pray unto your curtesye,   20
Beth hevy ayeine, or elles mot I die.

L'envoi de Chaucer

O! Conquerour of Brutes Albion,
Whiche that, by line and free eleccion,
Been verray kinge, this song to you I sende:
And ye, that mowen alle mine harme amende,   25
Have minde upon my supplicacion.

---

4. *For, certainly, unless you give me a 'heavy' welcome (such as a lover would not normally want!); but if, some MSS. but.* 5. *Me . . . leef, I should be as glad; bere, bier.* 7. mot, *may.* 8. or, *before.* 9. soun, *sound.* 11. pere, *equal.* 12. stere, *star.* 18. Sin that, *Since;* tresorere, *treasurer.* 19. shave . . . frere, *cropped of money as close as a religious is of hair.* 22. Conquerour, *Henry IV, who had deposed Richard II;* Brutes Albion, *the Britain of Brutus, from whom, according to the old chronicles, the British are descended (and Brutus, in his turn, from Aeneas).* 23. line, *lineal descent;* eleccion, *choice.* 24. verray, *true.* 25. mowen, *can.*

57

GEOFFREY CHAUCER (?)

Three roundels of love unreturned

ONE

Your yen two woll sle me sodenly!   later 14c.
I may the beaute of them not sustene,
So wondeth it thorowout my herte kene.
And, but your word woll helen hastely
My hertes wound, while that it is grene,   5

Your yen two woll sle me sodenly!
I may the beaute of them not sustene.

Upon my trouth, I sey you feithfully,
That ye ben of my liffe and deth the quene:
For with my deth the trouth shall be sene.   10

Your yen two woll sle me sodenly!
I may the beaute of them not sustene,
So wondeth it thorowout my herte kene.

TWO

So hath your beaute fro your herte chased
Pitee, that me n'availeth not to plaine,   15
For Danger halt your mercy in his chaine.
Giltless, my deth thus have ye me purchased!
I sey you soth, me nedeth not to feine.

So hath your beaute fro your herte chased
Pitee, that me n'availeth not to plaine.   20

1. yen two, *both MSS.* two yen; *but ll. 6–7 and 11–13 are abbreviated in MSS. to* Your yen; yen, *eyes.* 3. *So does the sharp wound go through my heart.* 4. but, *unless.* 5. grene, *fresh.* 8, 10. trouth, '*word*', *truth.* 15. that . . . plaine, *that there's no point in my complaining.* 16. Danger, *the power of a woman's disdainful or aloof self-possession over a man;* halt, *holds.* 18. soth, *truth.*

Alas! that Nature hath in you compassed
So grete beaute that no man may attaine
To mercy, though he sterve for the paine.

So hath your beaute fro your herte chased
Pitee, that me n'availeth not to plaine,   25
For Danger halt your mercy in his chaine.

THREE

Sin I fro Love escaped am so fat,
I never thenk to ben in his prison lene!
Sin I am free, I counte him not a bene!
He may answere, and sey this and that: 30
I do no fors, I speke right as I mene.

Sin I fro Love escaped am so fat,
I never thenk to ben in his prison lene!

Love hath my name istrike out of his slat,
And he is strike out of my bokes clene   35
For evermo—this is non other mene.

Sin I fro Love escaped am so fat,
I never thenk to ben in his prison lene!
Sin I am free, I counte him not a bene!

21. compassed, *contrived.* 23. sterve, *die.* 27, etc. Sin, *Since.* 28. in his prison,
Skeat suggests omitting in, *for* prison *can* = *prisoner.* 31. I . . . fors, *I don't care.* 34. *Love
has struck my name off his list.* 36. mene, *course.*

58

Love unlike love

Christ maketh to man a fair present—   later
His blody body with love brent.   14c.
That blisful body his lif hath lent

2. brent, *set on fire.* 3. lent, *given.*

For love of man that sinne hath blent.
O! love, love, what hast thou ment?   5
Me thinketh that love to wrathe is went.

Thy loveliche hondes love hath to-rent,
And thy lithe armes well streit itent.
Thy brest is baar, thy body is bent,
For wrong hath wonne and right is shent.   10

Thy milde boones love hath to-drawe:
The nailes, thy feet han all to-gnawe;
The Lord of love love hath now slawe—
Whane love is strong it hath no lawe.

His herte is rent,   15
His body is bent,
Upon the Roode Tree.
Wrong is went,
The devil is shent,
Christ, thurgh the might of thee.   20

For thee that herte is leid to wedde:
Swich was the love that herte us kedde,
That herte barst, that herte bledde,
That herte blood oure soules fedde.

That herte clefte for treuthe of love,   25
Therfore in him oon is trewe love.
For love of thee that herte is yove:
Kepe thou that herte and thou art above.

Love, love, where shalt thou wone?
Thy woningstede is thee binome: 30

4. blent, (*blinded*), *led astray?* 5. *What is the meaning of this?* 6. *It seems to me that love is turned into anger.* 7. to-rent, *torn in pieces.* 8. well . . . itent, *most tightly stretched.* 9, 16. bent, *arched (?) made fast (?).* 10, 19. shent, *shamed, ruined.* 11. milde, *gentle;* boones, *bones;* to-drawe, *pulled asunder.* 12. to-gnawe, *gnawed to pieces.* 13, 37. slawe, *slain.* 18. went, *gone.* 21. to wedde, *for a pledge.* 22. Swich, *Such;* kedde, *showed.* 23. barst, *broke.* 25. treuthe of, *faithfulness in (love).* 26. oon, *alone.* 27. yove, *given.* 28. above, (*in Heaven*). 29. wone, *dwell.* 30. *Thy dwelling place is taken from thee.*

For Christes herte, that was thine home,
He is deed—now hast thou none.
Love, love, why doist thou so?
Love, thou brekest mine herte a-two.

Love hath shewed his greet might,   35
For love hath maad of day the night.
Love hath slawe the King of Right,
And love hath ended the strong fight.

So inliche love was nevere non,
That witeth well Marye and Jon;   40
And also witen they, everychon,
That love with him is maad at on.

Love maketh, Christ, thine herte mine,
So maketh, love, mine herte thine.
Thanne shulde mine be trewe all time,   45
And love in love shall make it fine.

37. Right, *Righteousness.* 39. inliche, *heartfelt.* 40, 41. witeth, *know.* 41. everychon, *everyone.* 42. *That love and he (i.e. the King of Righteousness) are united.* 46. fine, *end.*

59

Friars' enormities

Of thes Frer Minours me thenkes moch wonder,   later
That waxen are thus hautein that somtime   14C.
   weren under:
Among men of Holy Chirch thay maken mochel
   blonder.
Now he that sites us above make ham sone to sonder.
With an O, and an I, thay praisen not Seint Poule,   5
Thay lyen on Seint Fraunceys, by my fader soule!

1. *It seems to me a most surprising thing about these Minorite or Franciscan Friars.*
2. waxen, *grown;* hautein, *haughty.* 3. mochel, *great;* blonder, *confusion.* 4. *May God who sits above us soon have them disperse.* 6, 16. lye(n) on, *tell lies about.*

First thay gabben on God, that all men may se,
When thay hangen him on hegh on a grene tre,
With leves and with blossemes that bright are of ble—
That was never Goddes son, by my leute!   10
With an O, and an I, men wenen that thay wede,
To carpe so of clergy—thay can not thair crede!

Thay have done him on a crois fer up in the skye,
And festned in him wyenges as he shuld flye:
This fals, feined belefe shall thay soure bye,   15
On that lovelich Lord so for to lie.
With an O, and an I, one said full still,
'Armachan destroy ham, if it is Goddes will.'

. . .

A cart was made all of fire as it shuld be:
A gray frer I sawe therinne that best liked me.   20
Wele I wote thay shall be brent, by my leaute!
God graunt me that grace that I may it se!
With an O, and an I, brent be thay all,
And all that helpes therto, faire mot befall.

Thay preche all of povert bot that love thay noght;   25
For gode mete to thair mouthe the town is thurgh soght;
Wide are thair wonninges and wonderfully wroght,
Murdre and whoredome full dere has it boght.
With an O, and an I, for sixe pens er thay faile,
Sle thy fadre and jape thy modre and thay will thee assoile! 30

---

7. gabben on, *scoff at.* 9. ble, *hue.* 10, 21. by my leute, *trust me.* 11. wenen, *think;* wede, *go mad.* 12. *To speak so about learning (when) they don't (even) know their creed (i.e. barest minimum).* 13. done, *put.* 14. festned, *fastened;* wyenges, *wings.* 15. soure bye, *pay for dearly.* 17. full still, *very quietly.* 18. Armachan, *Archbishop of Armagh, Richard Fitzralph (14c.) who preached against mendicant abuses.* 18, 19. *Two stanzas omitted.* 20. liked, *pleased.* 21. wote, *know;* and 23. brent, *burnt.* 24. therto, *to that end;* faire mot befall, *may good luck be (theirs).* 25. povert, *poverty.* 26. thurgh, *through.* 27. Wide, *Spacious;* wonninges, *dwellings.* 29. er, *before;* faile, *lack.* 30. jape, *seduce;* assoile, *absolve.*

60

The pointless pride of man

When Adam delf,   14c.?
And Eve span,
Spir, if thou will spede,
Whare was than
The pride of man   5
That now merres his mede?
Of erth and slame,
Als was Adam,
Maked to noyes and nede,
Ar we als he   10
Maked to be,
Whil we this lif shall lede.
With I and E,
Born ar we,
Als Salomon us hight,   15
To travel here,
Whils we ar fere,
Als fowls to the flight.

In worlde we ware
Cast for to care,   20
To we be broght to wende
Till wele or wa—
An of tha twa—
To won withouten ende.
Forthy, whils thou   25
May helpe thee now,
Amend thee and haf minde
When thou shall ga

1. delf. *dug.* 3. *For your advantage, ask.* 6. *That now stands in the way of his (heavenly) reward.* 7. slame, *slime.* 8, etc. Als, *As.* 9. noyes, *afflictions.* 15. hight, *promised.* 17. fere, *alive (in health).* 18. fowls, *birds.* 21. To, *Until.* 22. *To happiness or woe.* 23. *One of those two.* 24. won, *dwell.* 25, etc. Forthy, *Therefore.*

He bese thy fa
That ar was here thy frende.   30
With E and I,
I rede, forthy,
Thou think upon thies thre,
What we are,
And what we ware,   35
And what we shall be.

War thou als wise,
Praised in price,
Als was Salomon,
Fairer fode   40
Of bone and blode
Then was Absalon,
Strengthy and strang
To wreke thy wrang
Als ever was Sampson,   45
Thou ne might a day,
Na mare then thay,
Dede withstand allon.
With I and E,
Dede to thee   50
Shall com, als I thee kenne.
Thou ne wate
In what state,
How, ne whare, ne when.

Of erth aght   55
That thee was raght
Thou shall not have, I hete,
Bot seven fote
Therin to rote,
And thy windingshete.   60

---

29. *He will be your enemy.* 30. ar, *before.* 32. rede, *advise.* 38. price, *esteem.* 40. fode, *child.* 44. wreke, *avenge.* 48, etc. Dede, *Death.* 51. kenne, *teach.* 52. *You don't know.* 55. aght, *ought.* 56. *That was bestowed on you.* 57. hete, *promise.* 59. rote, *rot.*

Forthy gif
Whils thou may lif,
Or all gase that thou gete—
Thy gast fra God,
Thy godes olod,   65
Thy flesh fouled under fete.
With I and E,
Siker thou be
That thy secutours
Of thee ne will rek,   70
Bot skelk and skek
Full boldly in thy bowrs.

Of welth and wit
This shall be hitt,
In world that thou here wroght.   75
Reckon thou mon
And yelde reson
Of thing that thou here thoght.
May no falas
Help in this case,   80
Ne counsel getes thou noght;
Gift ne grace
Nane thare gase,
Bot brok als thou hase boght.
With I and E,   85
The Boke biddes thee,
Man, beware of thy werkes:
Terme of the yere
Hase thou nan here,
Thy mede bese ther thy merkes.   90

61–6. *Therefore, while you are still alive, give (what is due to God) before all goes which you may get—your spirit from God (to Hell), your possessions dispersed, and your flesh trampled under foot (in the grave).* 68, 104. *Siker, Certain.* 69. *secutours, executors.* 70. *Will not care about you.* 71. *But mock (?) skulk (?) and plunder.* 74. *hitt, verified.* 76–8. *You will have to settle your account and give reasons for what you thought here.* 79. *falas, sophism; MS. fals, Lincoln MS. fallace.* 82–4. *No gift or favour works there, but enjoy what you have bought.* 88. *Time of the year (?).* 90. *There your reward shall be your limits (?).*

What may this be
That I here se,
The fairehede of thy face?
Thy ble so bright,
Thy main, thy might,   95
Thy mouth that miry mas?
All mon als was
To powder passe,
To dede, when thou gase;
A grisely geste   100
Bese than thy breste
In armes til enbrase.
With I and E,
Siker thou be
Thare es nane, I thee hete,   105
Of all thy kith
Wald slepe thee with
A night under shete.

93. fairehede, *beauty.* 94. ble, *colour.* 95. main, *strength, virtue.* 96. miry mas, *rejoices.*
97. *All must as a torch of straw.* 100. geste, *guest.* 102. til, *to.* 105. es, *is;* hete, *promise.*

61

RICHARD OF CAISTRE

A hymn to Jesus

Jesu, Lorde, that madest me,   about 1400
And with thy blessed blode hast bought,
Foryeve that I have greved thee
In worde, werke, will and thought.

Jesu, for thy woundes smerte   5
Of body, fete and hondes too,

4, 9, 19, 24, 29. will, Christ, gode, me, for, *so Bodl. MSS. but this MS. omits.*
5. smerte, *severe.* 6. Of . . . too, *so Rawlinson MS. but this MS.* On fote and handys
too; too, *two.*

Make me meke and lowe in hert,
And thee to love as I shulde doo.

Jesu Christ, to thee I calle,
As thu art God full of might: 10
Kepe me clene that I ne falle
In fleshely sin as I have tight.

Jesu, grante me mine asking,
Perfite pacionis in my disese,
And never I mot doo that thing   15
That shulde in onything displese.

Jesu, that art Hevene King,
Sothfast bothe God and man also,
Yeve me grace of gode ending,
And hem that I am beholden to.   20

Jesu, for tho dulful teres
That thu gretest for my gilt,
Here and spede my preyores,
And spare me that I be not spilt.

Jesu, for hem I thee beseche   25
That wrathen thee in ony wise:
Withhold from hem the hande of wreche,
And lete hem leven in thy servise.

Jesu, joyful for to sen
Of all thy seintes everichone,   30
Comfort hem that carful ben,
And helpe hem that ar woo-begone.

---

7. lowe, *humble.* 12. tight, *frequently* (?) *resolved* (?). 14. pacionis, *patience;* disese, *trouble.* 15. mot, *may.* 18. Sothfast, *Truly.* 19. Yeve, *Give.* 20, 25, etc. hem, *them.* 21, 46. tho, *those.* 22. gretest, *(you) shed.* 23. spede, *further.* 24. spilt, *destroyed.* 25. I thee, *so Bodl. MSS. but this MS.* pat I. 26. wrathen, *anger.* 27. wreche, *vengeance.* 29–30. *Jesu, joyful sight for every one of your saints.* 31. carful, *full of sorrow, trouble.*

Jesu, kepe hem that ben goode,
And mende hem that han greved thee;
And sende men frutes of erdely foode   35
As eche man nedeth to his degre.

Jesu, that art, withoutein lese,
Almighty God in Trinite,
Cese thise werres and send us pees,
With lesting love and cherite.   40

Jesu, that art the ghostly stone
Of all Holy Cherche and erde,
Bringe thy foldes floke in one,
And reule hem rightly with on herde.

Jesu, for thy blessed blode,   45
Bringe tho saules into bliss
Of whom I have had ony goode,
And spare that they han done amiss.
                                    Amen.

33. kepe, *protect.* 34. mende, *reform.* 35, 42, erde(ly), *earth(ly).* 37. withoutein
lese, *undoubtedly.* 41. ghostly, *spiritual.* 43. *Unite the flock of your fold.* 44. on herde,
one shepherd. 46. *so Ashmole MS. but this MS. omits.*

62

Quia amore langueo

In a tabernacle of a toure,   about 1400
As I stode musing on the mone,
A crowned quene, most of honoure,
Apered in ghostly sight full sone.
She made compleint, thus, by her one: 5

1. tabernacle, *canopied niche (for an image);* toure, *tower.* 4. ghostly, *spiritual.* 5. by
her one, *on her own.*

'For mannes soule was wrapped in wo
I may nat leve mankinde alone,
Quia amore langueo.

'I longe for love of man, my brother,
I am his vokete to voide his vice;   10
I am his moder—I can none other—
Why shuld I my dere childe despice?
Yif he me wrathe in diverse wise,
Through fleshes freelte fall me fro,
Yet must we rewe him till he rise,   15
Quia amore langueo.

'I bid, I bide in grete longing;
I love, I loke when man woll crave;
I pleine for pite of peining;
Wolde he aske mercy, he shuld it have.   20
Say to me, soule, and I shall save,
Bid me, my childe, and I shall go:
Thou prayde me never but my son forgave,
Quia amore langueo.

'O! wreche in the worlde, I loke on thee,   25
I see thy trespass day by day,
With lechery ageins my chastite,
With pride agene my pore array.
My love abideth, thine is away,
My love thee calleth, thou stelest me fro.   30
Turne to me sinner, I thee pray,
Quia amore langueo.

'Moder of mercy I was for thee made:
Who nedeth it but thou alone?
To gete thee grace I am more glade   35
Than thou to aske it. Why wilt thou noon?

8, etc. *Because I languish for love.* 10. *I am his intercessor to annul his faults.* 12. despice, *despise.* 13, etc. Yif, *If;* wrathe, *anger.* 14. freelte, *frailty.* 15. rewe, *pity.* 17, 22. bid, *pray;* bide, *wait.* 18. loke, *look;* woll crave, *will ask.* 19. *I lament for pity at suffering.* 21. Say, *Speak.* 23. but . . . forgave, *without my son forgiving.* 25–32. *This stanza follows the next in Paris and Lambeth MSS.* 27. ageins, *against.* 36. noon, *none.*

When seid I nay, tell me, till oon?
Forsoth, never yet to frende ne foo.
When thou askest nought, than make I moone,
Quia amore langueo.   40

'I seke thee in wele and wrechednesse,
I seke thee in riches and poverte.
Thou, man, beholde where thy moder is:
Why lovest thou me nat, sith I love thee?
Sinful or sory, howevere thou be,   45
So welcome to me there ar no mo.
I am thy sister, right trust on me,
Quia amore langueo.

'My childe is outlawed for thy sinne,
Mankinde is bette for his trespass;   50
Yet pricketh mine hert that so ny my kinne
Shuld be disseased. Oh! sone, alas!
Thou art his brother, his moder I was,
Thou soked my pappe, thou loved man so,
Thou died for him, mine hert he has,   55
Quia amore langueo.

'Man, leve thy sinne, than, for my sake.
Why shulde I gif thee that thou nat wolde?
And yet, yif thou sinne, som prayere take,
Or trust in me as I have tolde.   60
Am nat I thy moder called?
Why shulde I flee thee? I love thee so:
I am thy frende; I helpe, beholde,
Quia amore langueo.

37. till oon, *to anyone.* 39. than make I moone, *then I complain.* 41–8. *This stanza omitted from Paris and Lambeth MSS.* 41. wele, *prosperity.* 44. sith, *since.* 46. mo, *more.* 50. *Paris and Lambeth MSS.:* Hys body was beten for thi trespas; bette, *beaten* (?). 51. pricketh, *grieves;* ny, *near.* 52. disseased, *distressed.* 53–5. *Paris and Lambeth MSS.,* My son is thi fadur, thi (his) modur y was / He sucked my pappe, he lufd the so / He dyed for the, my hert thou has. 57–64. *Lambeth MS. has two other stanzas instead of this one.* 57, 68. than, *then.* 58. that . . . wolde, *what you don't want.* 65–72. *Paris MS. omits this and the last stanza but includes the intermediate stanzas in reverse order. B.M. MS. has a different version of this and the next stanza and omits the last.*

'Now sone,' she saide, 'wilt thou sey nay,   65
Whan man wolde mende him of his mis?
Thou lete me never in veine yet pray.
Than, sinful man, see thou to this.
What day thou comest, welcome thou is.
This hundreth yere yif thou were me fro,   70
I take thee full faine, I clippe, I kiss,
Quia amore langueo.

'Now wol I sit and sey no more,
Leve, and loke with grete longing.
When a man woll calle, I wol restore: 75
I love to save him, he is mine offspring.
No wonder yif mine hert on him hing:
He was my neighbore, what may I do?
For him had I this worshipping,
And therefore amore langueo.   80

'Why was I crowned and made a quene?
Why was I called of mercy the welle?
Why shuld an erthly woman bene
So high in Heven above aungell?
For thee, mankinde, the truthe I tell.   85
Thou aske me helpe, and I shall do
That I was ordeined—kepe thee fro hell—
Quia amore langueo.

'Nowe man have minde on me for ever,
Loke on thy love thus languishing.   90
Late us never fro other dissever:
Mine helpe is thine owne, crepe under my wing.
Thy sister is a quene, thy brother is a king,
This heritage is tailed—sone come therto:
Take me for thy wife and lerne to sing,   95
Quia amore langueo.'

65. sey nay, *refuse.* 66. mis, *wrong-doing.* 70. *If you had stayed away from me a hundred years.* 71. clippe, *embrace.* 74. Leve, *Cease.* 77. hing, *hang.* 83. bene, *be.* 87. ordeined, *appointed.* 91. dissever, *separate.* 94. *This inheritance is for yourself and your heirs—come quickly into it.*

63

Jesus contrasts man and himself

Jesus doth him bimene,   about 1400
And speketh to sinful mon:
'Thy garland is of grenc,
Of floures many on;
Mine of sharpe thornes—   5
Mine hewe it maketh won.

'Thine hondes streite gloved,
White and clene kept;
Mine with nailes thorled,
On Rode, and eke my feet.   10

'Across thou berest thine armes,
Whan thou dauncest narewe.
To me hastou non awe,
But to worldes glorye.
Mine for thee on Rode   15
With the Jewes wode
With grete ropes todraw.

'Opene thou hast thy side,
Spayers longe and wide,
For veinglorye and pride,   20
And thy longe knif astrout—
Thou ert of the gay route:
Mine with spere sharpe
Istongen to the herte;
My body with scourges smerte   25
Beswongen all aboute.

1. *Jesus complains.* 4. *Of many flowers.* 6. won, *pale.* 7. streite, *tightly.* 9. thorled, *pierced.* 10. eke, *also.* 12. narewe, *closely, carefully.* 13. *You have no reverence for me.* 16. *By the mad Jews.* 17. todraw, *torn asunder.* 19. Spayers, (*fashionable*) Slits (*in clothing*). 21. astrout, *sticking out.* 22. route, *company.* 24. Istongen, *Stabbed.* 25. smerte, *painful.* 26. *Soundly beaten all over.*

'All that I tholede on Rode for thee
To me was shame and sorwe:
Well little thou lovest me,
And lasse thou thenkest on me,   30
An evene and eke amorwe.

'Swete brother, well might thou se
Thes peines stronge in Rode Tre
Have I tholed for love of thee.
They that have wrought it me   35
May singe, "Welawo".
Be thou kinde, pur charite,
Let thy sinne and love thou me:
Hevene blisse I shall yeve thee,
That lasteth ay and oo.'   40

27, 34. tholed(e), *suffered.* 29. Well, *Very.* 30. lasse, *less.* 31. *At any time of the day.*
37. *for love.* 38. Let, *Leave.* 39. yeve, *give.* 40. *That lasts for ever and ever.*

64

I have a noble cock

I have a gentle cock,   earlier 15c.
Croweth me day:
He doth me risen erly
My matins for to say.

I have a gentle cock,   5
Comen he is of gret:
His comb is of red coral,
His tail is of jet.

1, etc. noble, *well-bred.* 3. *He gets me up early.* 6. *He is come of distinguished family.*

I have a gentle cock,
Comen he is of kinde: 10
His comb is of red coral,
His tail is of inde.

His legges ben of asor,
So gentle and so smale;
His spores arn of silver whit   15
Into the wortewale.

His eynen arn of cristal,
Loken all in aumber:
And every night he percheth him
In mine ladye's chaumber.   20

10. *He is of good birth.* 11. coral, *MS. scorel.* 12. *indigo.* 13. *His legs are of azure.* 14. *slender.* 16. *Up to the root (of the spur).* 17. *eyes.* 18. *Set.*

65

A warning to those who serve lords

Bewar, squier, yeman, and page,   earlier 15c.
For servise is non heritage!

If thou serve a lord of prise,
Be not too boistous in thine servise:
Damne not thine soule in none wise,   5
For servise is non heritage.

Winteres wether, and wommanes thought,
And lordes love chaungeth oft:
This is the sothe, if it be sought,
For servise is non heritage.   10

Now thou art gret, tomorwe shall I,
As lordes chaungen here baly:

2, etc. heritage, *inheritance.* 3, 17. prise, *worth.* 4. boistous, *violent.* 9. sothe, *truth.* 12. here, *their;* baly, *bailiff, authority.*

In thine welthe werk sekirly,
For servise is non heritage.

Than serve we God in alle wise: 15
He shall us quiten our servise,
And yeven us yiftes most of prise,
Hevene to ben our heritage.

13. werk sekirly, *work for security.* 15. Than, *Then.* 16. quiten, *repay.* 17. yeven, *give.*

66

I sing of a maiden

I sing of a maiden   earlier 15c.
That is makeles:
King of alle kinges
To here sone she ches.

He cam also stille   5
Ther his moder was,
As dew in Aprille
That falleth on the grass.

He cam also stille
To his moderes bowr,   10
As dew in Aprille
That falleth on the flowr.

He cam also stille
Ther his moder lay,
As dew in Aprille   15
That falleth on the spray.

Moder and maiden
Was never non but she:
Well may swich a lady
Godes moder be.   20

2. makeles, *without equal, mate.* 4. *She chose for her son.* 5, etc. also, *as.* 19. swich, *such.*

67

Remember the Day of Judgment

Gay, gay, gay, gay, earlier 15c.
Think on dredful Domesday.

Every day thou might lere
To helpe thyself whil thou art here:
Whan thou art ded and leid on bere 5
Christ help thy soule, for thou ne may.

Think, man, on thy wittes five,
Do sum good whil thou art on live:
Go to Cherche and do thee shrive,
And bring thy soule in good array. 10

Think, man, on thy sinnes sevene,
Think how merye it is in Hevene:
Prey to God, with milde stevene,
He be thine help on Domesday.

Loke that thou non thing stere, 15
Ne non fals witnesse bere;
Think how Christ was stunge with spere
Whan he deyed on Good Friday.

Loke that thou ne sle non man,
Ne do non foly with non woman; 20
Think the blod fro Jesu ran,
Whan he deyed, withouten nay.

3. *learn.* 7. wittes, *senses.* 9. *make your confession.* 13. stevene, *voice.* 15. *See to it you do not worship (offer incense to) anything (but God).* 18, 22. deyed, *died.* 22. withouten nay, *no doubt about it.*

68

A song to John, Christ's friend

Prey for us the Prince of Pees,   earlier 15c.
Amice Christi, Johannes.

To thee now, Christes dere derling,
That were a maiden bothe eld and ying,
Mine herte is set to thee to sing,   5
Amice Christi, Johannes.

For thou were so clene a may
The prevites of Hevene forsothe thou say
Whan on Christes brest thou lay,
Amice Christi, Johannes.   10

Whan Christ beforn Pilat was brought
Thou, clene maiden, forsok him nought:
To deye with him was all thy thought,
Amice Christi, Johannes.

Christes moder was thee betake,   15
A maiden to ben a maidenes make:
Thou be oure helpe we be not forsake,
Amice Christi, Johannes.

1. (*to*) the. 2, etc. *Friend of Christ, John.* 4. (*You*) *who were a virgin all your life.*
5. set, *disposed.* 7. may, *virgin.* 8. prevites, *secrets;* say, (*you*) *saw.* 13. deye, *die.*
15. (*to*) *you committed.* 16. make, *mate, companion.* 17. (*that*) we.

69

I have a new garden

I have a newe garden,   earlier 15c.
And newe is begunne:
Swich another garden
Know I not under sunne.

In the middes of my garden   5
Is a peryr set,
And it wille non per bern
But a per Jenet.

The fairest maide of this town
Preyed me   10
For to griffen her a grif
Of mine pery tree.

Whan I hadde hem griffed,
Alle at her wille,
The win and the ale   15
She dede in fille.

And I griffed her
Right up in her home:
And by that day twenty wowkes
It was quik in her womb.   20

That day twelfus month
That maide I met:
She seid it was a per Robert
But non per Jonet!

3. *Such.* 6. *pear-tree.* 7. *bear no pear.* 8. *(early pear).* 11. *To graft her a shoot.* 13. *them.* 15–16. *She filled me up with wine and ale.* 18. home, *MS.* honde, *membrane* (? *emendation of Robbins*). 19. *weeks.* 24. Jonet, *last two letters cut off in MS.*

70

To the one I love most

A celuy que pluys eyme en mounde,   earlier 15c.
Of alle tho that I have founde
Carissima,
Saluz ottreye amour,
With grace and joye and alle honour,   5
Dulcissima.

Sachez bien, pleysant et beele,
That I am right in good heele,
Laus Christo!
Et moun amour doné vous ay,   10
And also thine owene night and day
Incisto.

Ma tresduce et tresamé,
Night and day for love of thee
Suspiro.   15
Soyez permenant et leal:
Love me so that I it fele
Requiro.

Jeo suy pour toy dolant et tryst;
Thou me peinest bothe day and night   20
Amore.
Mort ha tret tost sun espeye:
Love me well er I deye
Dolore.

To the one I love most in the world, most dear of all those that I have found, may love grant greetings, with grace and joy and all honour, most sweet lady.
Pleasing and beautiful (as you are), be assured that I am in good health, praise Heaven! And I have given you my love, and I preserve your own enshrined night and day.
My most sweet and most beloved, I sigh night and day for love of you. Be constant and faithful; I ask you to love me so that I feel it.
I grieve and am sad because of you; you hurt me day and night for love. Death has speedily drawn his sword: love me well before I die of grief.

Saches bien, par verité,   25
Yif I deye I clepe to thee,
Causantem;
Et par ceo jeo vous tres ser
Love me well withouten daunger,
Amantem.   30
. . .

Cest est ma volunté
That I mighte be with thee,
Ludendo.
Vostre amour en moun qoer
Brenneth hote as doth the fir,   35
Cressendo.
. . .

Jeo vous pry, par charité,
The wordes that here wreten be
Tenete,
And turne thine herte me toward.   40
O! à Dieu, que vous gard;
Valete!

Understand clearly that if I die I call to you, the cause; and because I serve you faithfully love me well who love you, and don't be aloof.

This is my desire, that I might be with you, dallying. Your love in my heart burns as hot as fire, increasing.

I beg you, for goodness' sake, lay hold of the words here written and turn your heart towards me. O! to God, that he may keep you; farewell!

30, 31. *One stanza omitted.* 36, 37. *Four stanzas omitted. Textual notes are in note 70.*

71

Adam lay in bondage

Adam lay ibounden,   earlier 15c.
Bounden in a bond:
Foure thousand winter

1. Adam (*i.e. mankind*). 2. bond (*of sin and death, and subject to Satan through the Fall*). 3. *According to one tradition the era of creation was about 4000 B.C.*

Thought he not too long.
And all was for an apple,   5
And apple that he tok,
As clerkes finden
Wreten in here book.

Ne hadde the apple take ben,
The apple taken ben,   10
Ne hadde never our Lady
A ben Hevene Quen.
Blissed be the time
That apple take was!
Therfore we moun singen,   15
'Deo gracias!'

7. clerkes, *the learned.* 8. here, *their.* 12. *Have been Queen of Heaven.* 15. moun, *may.*
16. *Thanks be to God.*

72

Trust only yourself

Alas! deceite that in truste is nowe,   earlier 15c.
Duble as Fortune, turning as a balle,
Brotylle at assay like the roten bowe:
Who trusteth to trust is redy for to falle.
Suche gyle is in trust almost overalle   5
That in pointe a man no frende finde shalle:
Wherfore, beware of trust, after my devise!
Trust to thyselfe, and lerne to be wise.

3. *Easily broken, when tried out, like the rotten bough.* 5. *everywhere.* 7. *if you want my advice. Initial letters all lines trimmed away in MS.*

73

Jankin, the clerical seducer

Kyrie, so kyrie,   earlier 15c.
Jankin singeth merye,
With Aleison.

As I went on Yol Day
In oure prosession,   5
Knew I joly Jankin
By his mery ton,
Kyrieleyson.

Jankin began the offis
On the Yol Day,   10
And yit me thinketh it dos me good
So merye gan he say,
'Kyrieleyson'.

Jankin red the Pistle
Full faire and full well,   15
And yit me thinketh it dos me good
As evere have I sel,
Kyrieleyson.

Jankin at the Sanctus
Craketh a merye note,   20
And yit me thinketh it dos me good—
I payed for his cote,
Kyrieleyson.

Jankin craketh notes
An hundered on a knot,   25

1, 3, 8, etc. Kyrie eleison, *Lord, have mercy (an early part of the Mass).* 4, 10.
Christmas day. 7. *voice.* 11, etc. *And yet it seems to me it does me good.* 12. *did.* 14.
Epistle. 17. *As I hope always to be fortunate.* 19, 29. Sanctus, Agnus, (*later parts of*
Mass). 20, 24. Utters, Trills. 25. *A hundred at a time.*

Fifteenth Century

And yit he hacketh hem smallere
Than wortes to the pot,
Kyrieleyson.

Jankin at the Agnus
Bereth the pax-brede: 30
He twinkled but said nowt,
And on my fot he trede,
Kyrieleyson.

Benedicamus Domino,
Christ fro shame me shilde: 35
Deo gracias, therto—
Alas! I go with childe,
Kyrieleyson.

26. *them.* 27. *vegetables.* 30. *Carries the article kissed during Mass in exchanging the kiss of peace.* 31. *Winked.* 34. *Let us bless the Lord.* 36. *Thanks be to God, as well.*

74

A new song of MARY

Of M A R Y   earlier 15c.
Sing I will a new song.

Of thes four letters purpose I,
Of M and A, R and Y.
They betoken maid Mary—   5
All our joy of her it sprong.

Withouten wem of her body,
M and A, R and Y,
Of her was borne a King, truly,
The Jewes dedin to deth with wrong.   10

7. wem, *stain.* 10. *Whom the Jews wrongly put to death.*

163

Upon the mounte of Calvary,
M and A, R and Y,
Ther they beten his bar body
With scorges that war sharp and long.

Our der Lady she stod him by,   15
M and A, R and Y,
And wept water full bitterly,
And teres of blod ever among.

18. among, *from time to time.*

75

I have a young sister

I have a yong suster,   earlier 15c.
Fer beyonden the se:
Many be the drowryes
That she sente me.

She sente me the cherye   5
Withouten ony ston;
And so she dede the dove
Withouten ony bon;

She sente me the brer
Withouten ony rinde;   10
She bad me love my lemman
Withoute longing.

How shuld ony cherye
Be withoute ston?
And how shuld ony dove   15
Ben withoute bon?

How shuld ony brer
Ben withoute rinde?
How shuld love mine lemman
Without longing?   20

3. *love-tokens.* 7. the, *not in MS.* 9. *briar.* 10. *branch.* 11. *lover.*

Whan the cherye was a flowr
Than hadde it non ston;
Whan the dove was an ey
Than hadde it non bon;

Whan the brer was onbred   25
Than hadde it non rinde;
Whan the maiden hath that she loveth
She is without longing.

23. *egg.* 25. *in the seed.*

76

THOMAS HOCCLEVE

A description of his ugly lady

Of my lady well me rejoise I may!   earlier
Hir golden forheed is full narw and smal;   15c.
Hir browes been lik to dim, reed coral;
And as the jeet hir yen glistren ay.

Hir bowgy cheekes been as softe as clay,   5
With large jowes and substancial.

Hir nose a pentice is that it ne shal
Reine in hir mouth thogh she uprightes lay.

Hir mouth is nothing scant with lippes gray;
Hir chin unnethe may be seen at al.   10

Hir comly body shape as a footbal,
And she singeth full like a papejay.

4. jeet, *jet* (*black*); yen, *eyes.* 5. bowgy, *baggy.* 6. jowes, *jaws.* 7. pentice, *over-hanging roof.* 8. uprightes, *face upward.* 10. unnethe, *scarcely.* 12. papejay, *parrot.* 9–12. *These lines are bracketed together in the MS. and it is indicated that the burden should follow all four. I have made these lines consist with 5–6 and 7–8.*

77

A lullaby of the Nativity

Lullay, my liking, my dere son,
  my sweting.
Lullay, my dere herte, my owen
  dere derling.

earlier
15c.

I saw a fair maiden
Sitten and sing:
She lulled a little child,   5
A swete lording.

That eche Lord is that
That made alle thing:
Of alle lordes he is Lord,
Of alle kinges, King.   10

Ther was mekil melody
At that childes berth:
Alle tho wern in Hevene blis
They made mekil merth.

Aungele bright they song that night,   15
And seiden to that child:
'Blissed be thou, and so be she,
That is bothe mek and mild.'

Prey we now to that child,
And to his moder dere,   20
Graunt hem his blissing,
That now maken chere.

1. liking, *beloved.* 7. eche, *eternal.* 11, 14. mekil, *much.* 13. *All those that were in the bliss of Heaven.* 18. mild, *gracious, gentle.* 21. hem, *them.*

78

Sing we Yule

Make we mirth earlier 15c.
For Christes birth,
And sing we Yole till Candlemess.

The first day of Yole have we in mind
How God was man born of our kind, 5
For he the bondes wold unbind
Of all our sinnes and wickedness.

The second day we sing of Stephen,
That stoned was and steyed up even
To God that he saw stond in Heven, 10
And crowned was for his prowess.

The third day longeth to Sent John,
That was Christes darling, derer non:
Whom he betok, whan he shuld gon,
His moder der for her clenness. 15

The fourth day of the children yong,
That Herowd to deth had do with wrong.
And Christ they coud non tell with tong,
But with their blod bar him witness.

The fifth day longeth to Sent Thomas, 20
That as a strong piller of bras
Held up the Chirch and slain he was,
For he stod with rightwesness.

The eighth day tok Jesu his name,
That saved mankind fro sin and shame, 25
And circumcised was for no blame
But for ensample of mekness.

5. kind, *nature.* 9. was, *so Sloane MS. but this MS. omits;* steyed up even, *ascended up direct.* 12. longeth, *belongs.* 14–15. *To whom, when he had to go, he entrusted his dear mother for her purity.* 17. do, *put.* 23. *righteousness.*

The twelfth day offered to him kinges three
Gold, myrrh and cence, thes giftes free:
For God and man and King was he,   30
Thus worshipped they his worthiness.

On the fourtieth day cam Mary mild
Unto the temple with her child
To shew her clen that never was filed,
And therwith endeth Christmes.   35

29. *incense;* free, *noble, generous.* 34. *defiled.*

79

See! here, my heart

O! Mankinde,   earlier 15c.
Have in thy minde
My Passion smert,
And thou shall finde
Me full kinde—   5
Lo! here my hert.

3. smert, *keen.*

80

A carol of Agincourt

Deo gracias, Anglia,   earlier 15c.
Redde pro victoria.

Oure kinge went forth to Normandy
With grace and might of chivalry.

1–2. *Return thanks to God, England, for victory.* 4. Chivalry, *cavalry.*

Ther God for him wrought mervelusly: 5
Wherfore Englonde may calle and cry.
'Deo gracias'.

He sette a sege, the sothe for to say,
To Harflu towne with ryal array:
That towne he wan and made affray   10
That Fraunce shall riwe till Domesday.
'Deo gracias'.

Than went oure kinge with alle his hoste
Thorwe Fraunce, for alle the Frenshe boste:
He spared, no drede, of lest ne moste,   15
Till he come to Agincourt coste.
'Deo gracias'.

Than, forsoth, that knight comely
In Agincourt feld he faught manly.
Thorw grace of God most mighty   20
He had bothe the felde and the victory.
'Deo gracias'.

There dukis and erlis, lorde and barone,
Were take and slaine, and that well sone,
And summe were ladde into Lundone   25
With joye and merthe and grete renone.
'Deo gracias'.

Now gracious God he save oure kinge,
His peple and alle his well-willinge:
Yef him gode life and gode ending,   30
That we with merth mowe safely singe,
'Deo gracias'.

7, etc. *Thanks be to God.* 8. sothe, *truth.* 9. with ryal array, *royally ordered.* 10. affray, *attack.* 11. riwe, *regret.* 15. *He spared, undoubtedly, neither great nor small.* 16. coste, *district.* 18. forsoth, *truly.* 28. (*may*) he. 29. well-willinge, *friends.* 30. Yef, *Give.* 31. mowe, *may.*

81

JOHN AUDELAY

In his utter wretchedness

Lady! helpe, Jesu! mercy,   earlier 15c.
Timor mortis conturbat me.

Dred of deth, sorow of sin,
Trobils my hert full grevisly:
My soule it nyth with my lust then—   5
Passio Christi conforta me.

Fore blindness is a hevy thing,
And to be def therwith only:
To lese my light and my hering—
Passio Christi conforta me.   10

And to lese my tast and my smelling,
And to be seke in my body,
Here have I lost all my liking—
Passio Christi conforta me.

Thus God he gives and takes away,   15
And as he will, so mot it be:
His name be blessed both night and day—
Passio Christi conforta me.

Here is a cause of gret morning:
Of myselfe nothing I see   20
Save filth, unclenness, vile stinking—
Passio Christi conforta me.

Into this world no more I broght,
No more I gete with me, trewly,

---

2. *The fear of death confounds me.* 5. *Then my soul is in conflict with (?) my desire.*
6. *Passion of Christ, be my strength.* 8. only, *particularly (?)* 9, 11. lese, *lose.* 12, 31.
seke, *sick.* 16, 28. mot, *must, may.* 24. gete, *shall take.*

Save good ded, word, will and thoght—   25
Passio Christi conforta me.

The five wondis of Jesu Christ
My medcine now mot thay be,
The Fyndis powere down to cast—
Passio Christi conforta me.   30

As I lay seke in my langure,
With sorow of hert and teere of ye,
This carol I made with gret doloure—
Passio Christi conforta me.

Oft with this prayere I me blest,   35
'In manus tuas, Domine,
Thou take my soule into thy rest.'
Passio Christi conforta me.

Mary! moder, merciful may,
Fore the joys thou hadest, Lady,   40
To thy Son fore me thou pray—
Passio Christi conforta me.

Lerne this lesson of blind Awdlay,
When bale is hyest, then bot may be:
Yif thou be nyd night or day,   45
Say, 'Passio Christi conforta me.'

27. wondis, *wounds.* 32. ye, *eye.* 36. *Into your hands, O Lord.* 39. may, *maiden.*
44. bale, *ill;* bot, *remedy.* 45. Yif, *If;* nyd, *in trouble.*

82

JOHN AUDELAY

Be true to your condition in life

It is the best, erely and late,   earlier 15c.
Uche mon kepe his owne state.

2. *That each man should keep his own position.*

171

In what order or what degree
Holy Cherche hath bound thee to
Kepe it welle, I counsel thee,   5
Desire thou never to go therfro,
I say algate.

A hye worship it is to thee
To kepe thy state and thy good name,
Lewd or lered, where-ere it be,   10
Elles God and mon thay woll thee blame,
I say algate.

Fore four obisions now shull ye here
That God hates ille in his sight,
A harde prest, a proud frere,   15
An old mon lechoure, a coward knight,
I say algate.

A prest shuld shew uche mon mekeness,
And leve in love and charity:
Throgh his grace and his goodness   20
Set all other in unity,
I say algate.

A frere shuld love all holiness,
Prayers, penans and poverty:
Religious men, Christ hem ches   25
To foresake pride and vainglory,
I say algate.

An old mon shuld kepe him chast,
And leve the sinne of lechory;
All wedded men shuld be stedfast,   30
And foresake the sin of avowtry,
I say algate.

---

7. *I say always, at all events.* 10. lewd or lered, *educated or not.* 13. obisions, *abuses* (?). 15, 23. frere, *friar.* 16. lechoure, *lecherous.* 19. leve, *live.* 25. hem ches, *chose them.* 29. leve, *leave.* 31. avowtry, *adultery.*

A knight shuld feght ayains falsness,
And shew his monhod and his might,
And maintene trouth and rightwisness,　　　35
And Holy Cherche and widowes right,
I say algate.

Here be all the foure estates
In Holy Cherche God hath ordent:
He bedes you kepe hem well algate,　　　40
Whosoever hem shomes he will be shent,
I say algate.

39. ordent, *ordained.* 40. bedes, *commands;* and 41. hem, *them.* 41. Whosoever
hem shomes, *MS.* Wos euer he chomys (*corrected from* be chomyd); shomes, *dis-*
honours; shent, *punished, destroyed.*

83

Despise the world

Why is the world beloved, that fals is and vein,　　　15c.
Sithen that hise welthes ben uncertein?

Also soone slideth his power away
As doith a brokil pot that freish is and gay.

Truste ye rather to letters writen in th'is　　　5
Than to this wretched world, that full of sinne is.

It is fals in his beheste and right disceiveable;
It hath begiled manye men, it is so unstable.

It is rather to beleve the waveringe wind
Than the chaungeable world, that maketh men so blind.　　　10

1. vein, *empty.* 2. Sithen that, *Since;* welthes, *blessings.* 3. Also, *As.* 4. brokil,
fragile. 5. th'is, *the ice.* 7. beheste, *promise.* 9. rather, *preferable* (?) *easier* (?); waver-
inge, *so Laud and Bodley MSS. but this MS.* wageringe.

Whether thou slepe othere wake thou shalt finde it fals,
Bothe in his bisynesses and in his lustes als.

Telle me where is Salamon, sumtime a kinge riche?
Or Sampson in his strenkethe, to whom was no man liche.

Or the fair man, Absolon, merveilous in chere?   15
Or the duke, Jonatas, a well-beloved fere?

Where is become Cesar, that lord was of al?
Or the riche man cloithd in purpur and in pal?

Telle me where is Tullius, in eloquence so swete?
Or Aristotle the philisophre with his wit so grete?   20

Where ben these worithy that weren here toforen?
Boithe kinges and bishopes her power is all loren.

All these grete princes with her power so hiye
Ben vanished away in twinkeling of an iye.

The joye of this wretched world is a short feeste: 25
It is likned to a shadewe that abideth leeste.

And yit it draweth man from Heveneriche blis,
And ofte time maketh him to sinne and do amis.

Thou that art but wormes mete, powder and dust,
To enhance thysilf in pride sette not thy lust.   30

For thou woost not today that thou shalt live tomorewe,
Therfore do thou evere weel, and thanne shalt thou not sorewe.

It were full joyful and swete lordship to have,
If so that lordship miyite a man fro deeth save.

11. othere, *MS. epere, or.* 12. *Both in work and play.* 13. riche, *great.* 14. liche,
like. 15. chere, *face.* 16. duke, *leader, ruler;* fere, *friend.* 18. *clothed in rich purple.*
20. wit, *mind.* 21. worithy, *distinguished men;* toforen, *before.* 22, 23. her, *their;* loren,
lost. 24. iye, *eye.* 27. *And yet it draws man from the bliss of the Kingdom of Heaven.*
30. enhance, *MS. enchaunce;* lust, '*heart*'. 31. woost, *knowest.* 34. If, *MS. it;*
miyite, *could.*

But, for as miche a man muste die at the laste,   35
It is no worship but a charge lordship to taste.

Calle nothing thine owen, therfore, that thou maist her lese:
That the world hath lent thee, eft he wolde it sese!

Sette thine herte in Heven above and thenke what joye is there,
And thus to despise the world I rede that thou lere.   40

35. miche, *much (as)*. 36. worship, *honour;* charge, *burden.* 37. lese, *lose.* 38. eft . . .
sese, *he intends to take it back.* 40. rede, *advise;* lere, *learn.*

84

Holly and Ivy

Nay! Ivy, nay!   15c.
It shall not be, iwis:
Let Holy have the maistry,
As the maner is.

Holy stond in the hall   5
Faire to behold:
Ivy stond without the dore—
She is full sore acold.

Holy and his mery men
They daunsen and they sing;   10
Ivy and her maidenes
They wepen and they wring.

Ivy hath a kibe—
She caght it with the colde.
So mot they all have ay   15
That with Ivy hold.

2. iwis, *indeed.* 3. *Let Holly be top-dog.* 4. maner, *custom.* 5, 7. stond, *stands.*
12. wring, *suffer.* 13. kibe, *chilblain.* 15. mot, *may.*

Holy hath beris
As rede as any rose:
The foster, the hunters
Kepe hem fro the doos.   20

Ivy hath beris
As blake as any slo:
Ther com the owle
And ete hem as she goo.

Holy hath birdes,   25
A full faire flok:
The nightingale, the poppinguy,
The gayntil laverok.

Gode Ivy, gode Ivy,
What birdes hast thou?   30
Non but the owlet
That creye, 'How! how!'

19. foster, *forester*. 20. hem, *them*. 27. poppinguy, *parrot* (?). 28. *The noble* (?) *gentle* (?) *lark*. 29. Gode Ivy, gode Ivy, *MS. Gode Iuy*.

85

A lyric from a play

First shepherd: Hail! King I thee call,   about 1450
Hail! most of might,
Hail! the worthest of all,
Hail! duke, hail! knight.
Of greatt and small   5
Thou art Lorde by right.
Hail! perpetual,
Hail! farest wight.
Here I offer—

1. Hail, *MS*. haill (*throughout*). 4. duke, *ruler, leader*. 8. wight, *creature*.

I pray thee to take,   10
If thou wold for my sake;
With this may thou lake—
This litill spruce cofer.

Second shepherd: Hail! litill tiny mop,
                Rewarder of mede.   15
                Hail! bot oone drop
                Of grace at my nede.
                Hail! litill milk sop,
                Hail! David sede,
                Of oure crede thou art crop.   20
                Hail! in god hede,
                This ball
                That thou wold rcsavc.
                Litill is that I have:
                This will I vouchesave   25
                To play thee withall.

Third shepherd: Hail! maker of man,
              Hail! sweting,
              Hail! so as I can,
              Hail! praty miting.   30
              I couche to thee than,
              For fain nere greting.
              Hail! Lórd, here I ordan,
              Now at oure meting,
              This botell: 35
              It is an old byworde,
              It is a good bourde,
              For to drink of a gourde—
              It holdes a mett potell.

---

12. lake, *play.* 13. spruse, *from Prussia,* (*made of spruce fir?*). 14. mop, (*term of endearment for a baby*). 15. mede, *reward.* 19. David sede, *descendant* (*by his mother*) *of David.* 20. crede, *belief;* crop, *crown, head.* 21. *with favourable regard.* 23. resave, *receive.* 30. *pretty little mite.* 31. couche, *bow;* than, *then.* 32. *For joy near weeping* (?) 33. ordan, *provide.* 37. bourde, *sport.* 39. mett, *meet, suitable;* potell, *pottle* (*a specific measure*).

Mary: He that all mightes may,   40
The Makere of Heven—
That is for to say
My son that I neven—
Rewarde you this day,
As he sett all on seven.   45
He graunt you for ay
His blis full even
Continuing.
He gif you good grace
Tell furth of this case.   50
He spede youre pace,
And graunt you good ending.

First shepherd: Farewell! fare Lorde,
With thy moder also.
Second shepherd: We shall this recorde   55
Where as we go.
Third shepherd: We mon all be restorde,
God graunt it be so.
First shepherd: Amen! to that worde.
Sing we therto   60
On hight,
To joy all sam,
With mirth and gam,
To the laude of this lam,
Sing we in sight.   65

43. neven, *speak of.* 45. *As he built all (things) in seven (days).* 46, 49, 51. *(May)*
He. 47. even, *straight, direct.* 57. mon, *may.* 61. *Loudly.* 62. sam, *together.* 64. laude,
praise.

86

A song in his lady's absence

Now wolde I faine sum merthes make   15c.
All only for my lady's sake

1. *Now I would gladly rejoice.*

When I her see:
But nowe I am so far fro her
It will not be.   5

Though I be far out of her sight
I am her man both day and night,
And so will be:
Therfore wolde as I love her
She loved me.   10

Whan she is mery than am I gladde,
Whan she is sory than am I sadde,
And cause is why:
For he leveth not that loved her
So well as I.   15

She seith that she hath sein it write
That seldin sein is sone forgeit.
It is not so:
For in good feith, save only her,
I love no moo.   20

Wherfor I pray both night and day
That she may cast alle car away
And leve in rest.
And evermore, wherever she be,
To love me best.   25

And I to her to be so trewe,
And never to chaung for no newe,
Unto my ende.
And that I may in her service
Ever to amend.   30

14, 23. leve(th), *live(s)*. 16. sein, *seen*. 17. *seldom seen is soon forgot*. 20. moo, *more*.
30. *Ever improve (my position)*.

87

Earth out of earth

Memento, homo, quod cinis es,   mid 15c.
Et in cenerem reverteris.

Erthe oute of erthe is wonderly wroghte.
Erthe hase geten one erthe a dignite of noghte.
Erthe upon erthe hase sett alle his thoghte,   5
How that erthe upon erthe may be heghe broghte.

Erthe upon erthe wolde be a kinge,
Bot howe erthe to erthe shall thinkes he no thinge.
When erthe bredes erthe and his rentes home bringe,
Thane shall erthe of erthe have full harde partinge.   10

Erthe upon erthe winnes castells and towrres:
Thane sayse erthe unto erthe, 'This es alle ourres.'
When erthe upon erthe hase bigged up his bowrres,
Thane shall erthe for erthe suffere sharpe scowrres.

Erthe gose upon erthe as molde upon molde: 15
He that gose upon erthe, gleterande as golde,
Like as erthe never more go to erthe sholde—
And yitt shall erthe unto erthe ga rathere than he wolde.

Now, why that erthe luves erthe, wondere me thinke,
Or why that erthe for erthe sholde other swete or
   swinke: 20
For when that erthe upon erthe es broghte within brinke,
Thane shall erthe of erthe have a foulle stinke.
Mors solvit omnia.

1–2. *Remember, O! man, that you are ashes, and into ashes you will return.* 4. *Earth has acquired on earth a high position from nothing.* 6. heghe, *high.* 8. shall (*go*). 9. his . . . bringe, *shall bring his tributes home.* 10, etc. Thane, *Then;* of, *from.* 13. bigged, *built.* 14. scowrres, *assaults, pains.* 15. molde . . . molde, *earth, so Bodleian MS. and most other versions, but this MS.* golde. 16. gleterande, *glittering.* 18. rathere, *sooner.* 19. *it seems to me a wonder.* 20. other swete, *either sweat;* swinke, *labour.* 21. brinke (*of the grave*). 23. *Death puts paid to all.*

88

CHARLES OF ORLEANS (?)

Come, Death—my lady is dead

For dedy liif, my livy deth I wite;   mid 15c.
For ese of paine, in paine of ese I die;
For lengthe of woo, woo lengteth me so lite
That quik I die and yet as ded live I.
Thus nigh, afer, I fele the fer is nigh,   5
Of thing certeine that I, uncerteine, seche,
Which is the Deth, sith Deth hath my lady.
O! woful wretche! O! wretche, lesse ones thy speche!

O! ghost formatt, yelde up thy breth att ones!
O! carcas faint, take from this liif thy flight!   10
O! bolled hert, forbrest thou with thy grones!
O! mested eyen, why faile ye not youre sight?
Sin Deth, alas! hath tane my lady bright,
And left this world without on to her leche,
To lete me live ye do me gret unright.   15
O! woful wretche! O! wretche, lesse ones thy speche!

What is this liif?— a liif or deth I lede?
Nay! certes, deth in liif is likliness.
For though I faine me port of lustihede,
Yet, inward, lo! it sleth me, my distress.   20
For from me fledde is joy and all gladness,
That I may say, in all this world so reche
As I is noon of paine and heviness.
O! woful wretche! O! wretche, lesse ones thy speche!

1. *For life like death my living death I know.* 3. *For length of woe, woe prolongs my life so little.* 4. quik, *alive.* 5. afer, *afar;* fer, *far.* 6. seche, *seek.* 7. sith, *since.* 8, etc. lesse, *lose;* ones, *once for all.* 9. ghost, *spirit;* formatt, *vanquished.* 10. carcas, *body.* 11. bolled, *swollen;* forbrest, *break utterly.* 12. *O! misted eyes.* 13. Sin, *Since.* 14. without . . . leche, *without anyone like her.* 15. unright, *injustice.* 18. certes, *for sure;* likliness, *what is likely.* 19. port of lustihede, *cheerful manner.* 20. sleth, *kills.* 22. reche, *rich.* 23. of, *in.*

Ther nis no thing sauf Deth, to do me day,   25
That may of me the wooful paines leche.
But wolde I day, alas! yet I ne may.
O! woful wretche! O! wretche, lesse ones thy speche!

25. *There is nothing save Death, to cause me to die.* 26. leche, *cure,* MS. eche *(there is no French version and the Cambridge MS. omits ll. 25–8).* 27. ne may, *cannot.*

89

CHARLES OF ORLEANS (?)

A mistress without compare

Sin that I have a nounparall maistress,   mid 15c.
The which hath whool my service and
   mine hert,
I shall be glad, for any greef or smert,
To serve hir in hir goodly lustiness:
For now I trust to have, doutless,   5
More joy then ther be stiches in my shert.

Sin that I have a nounparall maistress,
The which hath whool my service and mine hert.

Though, to envious, it be heviness
And sorow gret, to don hem prike and stert,   10
Yet, by my trouthe, when that I me advert,
Ther displesere it is my gret gladness.

Sin that I have a nounparall maistress,
The which hath whool my service and mine hert.

1. *Since I have a mistress without compare.* 4. lustiness, *youthful vigour.* 9. to (*the*) envious; heviness, *sadness.* 10. don . . . stert, *cause them to be provoked (prance).* 11. by my trouthe, *upon my word;* me advert, *reflect.*

90

CHARLES OF ORLEANS (?)

Confession of a stolen kiss

My ghostly fader, I me confess,   mid 15c.
First to God and then to you,
That at a window, wot ye how,
I stale a kosse of gret swetness,
Which don was out avisiness—   5
But it is doon, not undoon, now.

My ghostly fader, I me confess,
First to God and then to you.

But I restore it shall, doutless,
Agein, if so be that I mow;   10
And that to God I make a vow,
And elles I axe foryefness.

My ghostly fader, I me confesse,
First to God and then to you.

1. ghostly, *spiritual.* 3. wot ye, *you know.* 4. stale, *stole.* 5. out, *without;* avisiness, *deliberation.* 10. mow, *can.* 11. to, *not in MS.*

91

CHARLES OF ORLEANS (?)

Go, sad complaint

O! sely anker, that in thy celle   mid 15c.
Iclosed art with stoon and gost not out,
Thou maist ben gladder so for to dwelle
Then I with wanton wandring thus about,

1. sely, *fortunate, pious;* anker, *anchorite.* 4. wanton, *unrestrained.*

That have me piked, amonges the rout,   5
An endless woo withouten recomfort,
That of my poore liif I stonde in dout—
Go! dull complaint, my lady this report.

The anker hath no more him for to greve
Then sool, alone, upon the walles stare.   10
But, welaway! I stonde in more mischeef,
For he hath helthe, and I of helthe am bare.
And, more and more, when I come where ther are
Of faire folkes to se a goodly sort,
A thousandfold that doth encrese my care—   15
Go! dull complaint, my lady this report.

It doth me thinke, 'Yonder is faire of face—
But, what? More faire, yet, is my lady dere!
Yond on is small, and yonde streight sides has,
Her foot is lite, and she hath eyen clere—   20
But all ther stained my lady, were she here.'
Thus thinke I, lo! which doth me discomfort,
Not for the sight, but for I nare hir nere—
Go! dull complaint, my lady this report.

Wo worth them which that raft me hir presence!   25
Wo worth the time to I to hir resort!
Wo worth is me to be thus in absence!
Go! dull complaint, my lady this report.

---

5. piked, *chosen;* rout, *crowd.* 6. recomfort, *comfort.* 8, etc. dull, *sad.* 10. Then, *Than;* sool, *only.* 11. *But, alas, my misfortune is greater.* 14. sort, *company.* 17, 22. doth, *causes.* 19. on, *one;* small, *slender.* 20. lite, *small;* eyen, *eyes.* 21. *But my lady would put all those in the shade* (etc.). 23. nare hir nere, *was not near her.* 25–7. *Woe betide them who deprived me of her presence! Woe betide the time until I come to her! Wretched am I, to be thus away from her!*

92

A carol of St. George

Enfors we us with all our might   mid 15c.
To love Seint George, our Lady knight.

Worship of virtu is the mede,
And seweth him ay of right:
To worship George then have we nede,   5
Which is our soverein Lady's knight.

He keped the mad from dragon's dred,
And fraid all France and put to flight.
At Agincourt—the crownecle ye red—
The French him se formest in fight.   10

In his virtu he wol us lede
Againis the Fend, the ful wight,
And with his banner us oversprede,
If we him love with all oure might.

1. *Let us do our utmost.* 2. *Lady's.* 3. *Honour is the reward of virtue.* 4. seweth, *follows.*
7. keped, *saved;* mad, *maid.* 8. fraid, *made afraid.* 9. crownecle, *chronicle;* red, *read.*
11. virtu, *virtue, power.* 12. wight, *creature.*

93

Unkindness has killed me

Grevus is my sorow: 15c.
Both evene and morow
Unto myselfe alone
Thus do I make my mone,

That unkindness haith killed me   5
And put me to this paine.
Alas! what remedy
That I cannot refraine?

Whan other men doith sleipe
Thene do I sigh and weipe,   10
All ragius in my bed,
As one for paines neire ded.
That unkindness haith killed me
And put me to this paine,
Alas! what remedy   15
That I cannot refraine?

. . .

Wo worth trust untrusty!
Wo worth love unloved!
Wo worth hap unblamed!
Wo worth faut unnamed!   20
Thus unkindly to kill me
And put me to this paine,
Now! alas! what remedy
That I cannot refraine?

. . .

My last will here I make: 25
To God my soule I betake,
And my wreched body
As erth in a hole to lie.
For unkindness to kill me
And put me to this paine,   30
Alas! what remedy
That I cannot refraine?

O! harte, I thee bequeth
To him that is my deth.

---

11. ragius, *full of passion.* 16, 17. *One stanza omitted.* 17, etc. Wo worth, *Woe betide.* 19. *mishap.* 20. *fault.* 24, 25. *Three stanzas omitted.* 26. *commit.*

If that no harte haith he   35
My harte his shall be.
Though unkindness haith killed me
And put me to this paine,
Yet, if my body die,
My hert cannot refraine.   40

Placebo, dilexi—
Com, weipe this obsequye;
My mournares, dolfully,
Come weipe this psalmody.
For unkindness haith killed me   45
And put me to this paine:
Behold this wreched body
That your unkindness haith slaine.

Now I besich all ye,
Namely, that lovers be,   50
My love my deth forgive
And soffer him to live.
Though unkindness haith killed me
And put me to this paine,
Yet had I rether die   55
For his sake ons againe.

My tombe it shall be blewe
In tokene that I was trewe:
To bringe my love frome doute
It shall be written aboute: 60
'That unkindness haith killed me
And put me to this paine:
Behold this wreched body
That your unkindness haith slaine.'

41. *The first words of Vespers and Matins, respectively, of the Dead.* 50. *Especially.*
51. (*for*) my. *Two stanzas omitted at end.*

94

An epitaph

Alanus calvus   15c.(?)
Jacet hic sub marmore duro:
Utrum sit salvus
Non curavit necque curo.

Here lieth under this marble ston   5
Riche Alane, the balled man:
Whether he be safe or noght
I recke never for he ne roght.

6. balled, *bald.* 8. *I don't care because he never did.*

95

A second epitaph

All ye that passe by this holy place,   15c.
Both spiritual and temporal of every degre,
Remember yourselfe well during time and space:
I was as ye are nowe, and as I ye shall be.
Wherfore I beseche you, of youre benignite,   5
For the love of Jesu and his mother Mare,
For my soule to say a Pater Noster and an Ave.

2. *Both clergy and laity.* 4. as I, *MS.* I as.

JOHN LYDGATE

The duplicity of women

This worlde is full of variaunce   mid 15c.
In everything, who taketh hede:
That feith and trust and all constaunce
Exiled ben, this is no drede;
And, save oonly in womanhede,   5
I can see no sikernesse.
But, for all that, yet, as I rede,
Bewar alway of doublenesse.

Also these freshe somer floures,
White and rede, blew and grene,   10
Ben sodeinly with winter shoures
Made feint and fade, withoute wene:
That trust is noon, as ye may sene,
In nothing, nor no stedfastnesse,
Except in women, thus I mene.   15
Yet ay bewar of doublenesse.

The croked moone—this is no tale—
Som while is shene and bright of hewe,
And, after that, ful derk and pale,
And every monith chaungeth newe: 20
That whoso the verray sothe knewe,
Alle thinge is bilte on brotilnesse,
Save that women ay be trewe—
Yet ay bewar of doublenesse.
. . .

1. variaunce, *variableness.* 4. drede, *doubt.* 6, 62. sikernesse, *certainty, security.*
7. rede, *advise.* 8, etc. doublenesse, *duplicity.* 12. feint, *weak (sickly)*; fade, *withered, feeble*; wene, *doubt.* 17. croked, *crescent (?) treacherous (?)*; tale, *falsehood.* 18. shene, *shining.* 21. verray sothe, *real truth.* 22. brotilnesse, *frailty, instability.* 24, 25. *One stanza omitted.*

The see eke with his sterne wawes   25
Eche day floweth new agein,
And by concourse of his lawes
The ebbe followeth in certein;
After gret drought ther cometh a reine,
That, farewell! here, all stabelnesse,   30
Save that women be hool and pleine—
Yet ay bewar of doublenesse.

Fortune's whele gooth rounde about
A thousande times day and night,
Whos course stondeth ever in doute,   35
For to transmewe she is so light.
For which adverteth in your sight
The untrust of worldly fikelnesse,
Save women, which of kindely right
Ne have no tache of doublenesse.   40
. . .

Wherfore, whoso hem accuse
Of any double entencioun,
To speke, roune, outher to muse,
To pinche at her condicioun,
Alle is but fals collusioun,   45
I dar right welle the sothe expresse:
They have no bette proteccioun
But shroude hem under doublenesse.
. . .

Sampson had experience
That women weren full trew founde,   50
Whan Dalida, of innocence,
With sheres gan his hede to rounde.

25. eke, *also;* wawes, *waves.* 27. by concourse of, *in accordance with.* 30. That, *So that;* here all, *so B.M. Additional MS. 16165, but other two MSS.* al her. 31. hool, *loyal;* pleine, *open.* 35. stondeth . . . doute, *is always uncertain.* 36. transmewe, *change;* light, *ready, quick.* 37. adverteth, *take note of.* 39. kindely, *natural.* 40. tache, *spot.* 40, 41. *Two stanzas omitted.* 41, 48. hem, *them.* 43. roune, *whisper, talk;* outher, *or;* muse, *murmur, grumble.* 44. pinche at, *find fault with;* and 56. her, *their.* 45. collusioun, *deceit.* 46. sothe, *truth.* 47. bette, *better.* 48, 49. *One stanza omitted.* 51. of innocence, *innocently.* 52. *cut his hair with scissors.*

To speke also of Rosamounde,
And Cleopatra's feithfulnesse,
The stories pleinly will confounde   55
Men that apeche her doublenesse.
. . .

L'envoi.

O! ye women, which ben inclined,
By influence of youre nature,
To ben as pure as golde ifined,
In your trouthe for to endure   60
Arme yourselfe in stronge armure,
Leste men assaile youre sikernesse:
Sette on youre brest, yourself t'assure,
A mighty shelde of doublenesse.

56. apeche, *bring a charge against.* 56, 57. *One stanza omitted.* 60. trouthe, *faithfulness.*

97

JOHN LYDGATE

Transient as a rose

Lat no man booste of conning nor vertu,   mid 15c.
Of tresour, richesse, nor of sapience,
Of worldly support, for all cometh of Jesu:
Counsail, comfort, discrecioun and prudence,
Provisioun, forsight, and providence,   5
Like as the Lord of grace list dispoose;
Som man hath wisdom, som man hath elloquence—
All stant on chaung, like a midsomer roose.

Wholsom in smelling be the soote floures,
Full delitable, outward, to the sight;   10
The thorn is sharp, curyd with fresh coloures;

1, 27. conning, *knowledge.* 2. sapience, *wisdom.* 6, etc. list, *please(s)(d) (to).*
8. stant on chaung, *is transient.* 9. soote, *sweet.* 10. delitable, *delightful.* 11. curyd
covered.

All is nat gold that outward sheweth bright;
A stokfish boon in dirknesse yeveth a light,
Twen fair and foul, as God list dispoose,
A difference atwix day and night—   15
All stant on chaung like a midsomer roose.

. . .

All worldly thing braideth upon time:
The sonne chaungeth, so doth the pale moone;
The Aureat Noumbre, in calenderes set for Prime;
Fortune is double, doth favour for no boone,   20
And who that hath with that queen to doone
Contrariously she will his chaunce dispoose,
Who sitteth highest, moost like to falle soone—
All stant on chaung like a midsomer roose.

. . .

Wher is now David, the moost worthy king,   25
Of Juda and Israel moost famous and notable?
And wher is Salomon, moost soverein of conning,
Richest of bilding, of tresour incomparable?
Face of Absolon moost fair, moost amiable?
Rekne up echon, of trouthe make no gloose,   30
Rekne up Jonathas, of frenship immutable—
All stant on chaung like a midsomer roose.

. . .

Wher is Tullius with his sugred tonge?
Or Crisistomus with his goldene mouth?
The aureat ditees that be red and songe   35
Of Homerus in Grece, both north and south?
The tragedies, divers and uncouth,
Of moral Senek, the mysteries to uncloose?
By many example this mateer is full couth—
All stant on chaung like a midsomer roose.   40

. . .

---

13. yeveth, *gives (a light, presumably because phosphorescent)*. 14. Twen, *Between.*
16, 17. *Three stanzas omitted.* 17. braideth, *changes appearance.* 19. Aureat Noumbre,
*Golden Number, the number of the lunar cycle of nineteen years by which the date of
the movable feast of Easter is determined;* Prime = *the Golden Number.* 20. boone,
request. 24, 25. *Two stanzas omitted.* 30. echon, *each one; of . . . gloose, don't gloss over
the truth.* 32, 33. *One stanza omitted.* 35. ditees, *compositions.* 37. uncouth, *marvellous.*
39. full couth, *well-known.* 40, 41. *One stanza omitted.*

Put in a som all marcial policye,
Compleet in Afric and boundes of Cartage,
The Theban legioun, example of chevalrye,
At Rodamus River was expert ther corage,
Ten thousand knightes, born of high parage,   45
Ther martyrdom, rad in metre and proose,
Ther goldene crownes, maad in the hevenly stage,
Fresher than lilies or ony somer roose.

The remembraunce of every famous knight,
Ground considered, is bilt on rightwisnesse: 50
Race out ech quarel that is not bilt on right;
Withoute trouthe, what vaileth high noblesse?
Lawrer of martyrs, founded on hoolynesse—
Whit was maad red, their triumphes to discloose:
The whit lillye was ther chaast clennesse,   55
Ther bloody suffraunce was no somer roose.

It was the Roose of the bloody feeld,
Roose of Jericho that grew in Beedlem,
The five rooses portrayed in the sheeld,
Splayed in the baneer at Jerusalem: 60
The sonne was clips, and dirk in every rem,
Whan Christ Jesu five welles list uncloose
Toward Paradis, called the rede strem—
Of whos five woundes prent in your hert a roose.

44. expert, *proved.* 45. parage, *lineage.* 46. rad, *read, learned about.* 47. stage, *station, scaffold (the platform holding the actors of God and the heavenly beings at a medieval play?).* 49–50. *When the reason for the memory of every famous knight is considered, it is founded on righteousness.* 51. Race, *Root.* 52. vaileth, *avails;* noblesse, *nobility.* 53. Lawrer, *Laurel.* 54. Whit, = *clennesse* (55); red, = *blood* (56). 55. clennesse, *purity.* 56. *(because it had everlasting consequences).* 58. Beedlem, *Bethlehem, where Jesus was born.* 60. Splayed, *Displayed, so Huntington MS. but this MS.* splayned. 61. clips, *eclipsed;* dirk, *dark;* rem, *realm.* 64. prent, *print.*

98

A prayer to the Trinity

Almighty God, Fader of Hevene,   15c.
For Christes love that dyde on Rode,
I praye thee, Lorde, thou here my stevene,
And fulfill my will in gode.

Christ, thy Fader for me praye,   5
For hir love thou lighted inne,
He yeve me might, or that I die,
Me to amende of all my sinne.

The Holy Ghost, thou graunte me grace
With such werkes my lif to lede   10
That I may se God in his face
On Domesday, withouten drede.

Marye, thy sone for me thou praye,
He yeve me grace, or that I wende,
That I have, after I die,   15
The blisse of Hevene withouten ende.

Fader and Sone and Holy Ghost,
All one God and Persones three,
Almighty God of mightes most,
Lord, thou have mercy on me.   20

And on alle that mercy nede for charite.
Amen, par amore, Amen.

3. stevene, *voice.* 4. *And let my desire be fulfilled in good things.* 7. *That he give me power, before I die.* 12. *On the Day of Judgment for certain.* 22. par amore, *for love.*

99

Inordinate love

I shall say what inordinat love is: 15c.
The furiosite and wodness of minde,
A instinguible brenning fawting blis,
A gret hungre, insaciat to finde,
A dowcet ille, a ivell swetness blinde,   5
A right wonderfulle, sugred, swete errour,
Withoute labour rest, contrary to kinde,
Or withoute quiete to have huge labour.

2. *The insanity and frenzy of mind.* 3. *An inextinguishable burning that lacks happiness.*
4. finde (*what is hungered for*). 5. *A dulcet ill, an evil and blind sweetness.* 7. kinde,
nature.

100

Man exalted

Nowel! nowel! nowel!   about 1450
Nowel! nowel! nowel!

Out of your slepe arise and wake,
For God mankind nowe hath itake,
All of a maide without eny make,
Of all women she bereth the belle,   5
Nowel!

And thorwe a maide, faire and wis,
Now man is made of full grete pris:
Now angelis knelen to mannis servis;   10
And at this time all this befell,
Nowel!

4. mankind, *human nature;* itake, *taken.* 5. make, *equal, mate.* 6. *She excels all*
women. 8. thorwe, *through.* 9. pris, *worth.*

Now man is brighter than the sonne;
Now man in Heven on hie shall wone;
Blessed be God, this game is begonne,   15
And his moder Emperesse of helle,
Nowel!

That ever was thralle, now is he free;
That ever was smalle, now grete is she;
Now shall God deme bothe thee and me   20
Unto his blisse, if we do well,
Nowel!

Now man may to Heven wende,
Now Heven and erthe to him they bende:
He that was foo, now is oure frende.   25
This is no nay that I yowe telle,
Nowel!

Now blessed brother, graunte us grace
A Domesday to se thy face,
And in thy courte to have a place,   30
That we mow there singe, 'Nowel',
Nowel!

14. wone, *dwell.* 15. game, '*business*'. 20. deme, *judge.* 26. *What I tell you cannot be denied.* 29. A, *At.* 31. mow, *may.*

IOI

The Sacrament of the Altar

It semes white and is red;   about 1450
It is quike and semes dede;
It is fleshe and semes bred;
It is on and semes too;
It is God body and no mo.   5

1. white (*bread*); red (*flesh*). 4. on, *one*; too, *two* (*bread and wine?*). 5. mo, *more,* MS. more.

I02

Jesus comforts his mother

A baby is borne us blis to bring;   15c.
A maidden, I hard, 'Loullay', sing:
'Dere son, now leive thy wepping,
Thy fadere is the King of Blis.'

'Nay! dere modere, for you weppe I noght,   5
But for thinges that shall be wroght,
Or that I have mankind iboght.
Was ther never pain like it, iwis.'

'Pes! dere sone, say thou me not so.
Thou art my child, I have no mo.   10
Alas! that I shuld see this wo:
It were to me gret heivynis.'

'My hondes, modere, that ye now see,
Thay shall be nailled one a tree;
My feit, also, fastned shall be: 15
Full mony shall wepe that it shall see.'

'Alas! dere son, sorrow now is my happe
To see my child that soukes my pappe
So ruthfully taken out of my lappe.
It were to me gret heivynis.'   20

'Also, modere, ther shall a speire
My tendere hert all to-teire:
The blud shall kevere my body there.
Gret ruthe it shall be to see.'

'A! dere sone, that is a heivy cas.   25
When Gabrell knelled before my face

2. hard, *heard*. 7. Or that, *Before*. 8. iwis, *indeed*. 9, 29. Pes, *Peace*. 10. mo, *more*.
12, etc. heivynes, *grief*. 17. happe, *lot*. 19. ruthfully, *pitifully*. 22. to-teire, *tear to
pieces*. 23. kevere, *cover*. 24. ruthe, *pity*. 25. heivy cas, *sad plight*.

And said, "Heille! Lady, full of grace,"
He never told me noothing of this.'

'Dere modere, pes! nowe I you pray,
And take no sorrow for that I say,   30
But singe this song, "By, by, loullay,"
To drive away all heivynis.'

103

Tutivillus, the devil

Tutivillus, the devil of hell,   15c.
He writeth har names, sothe to tell,
Ad missam garulantes.

Better wer be at home for ay
Than her to serve the Devil to pay,   5
Sic vana famulantes.

Thes women that sitteth the church about,
Thay beth all of the Develis rowte,
Divina impedientes.

But thay be still he will hem quell,   10
With kene crokes draw hem to hell,
Ad puteum autem flentes.

For his love that you der boght
Hold you still and jangle noght,
Sed prece deponentes.   15

The bliss of Heven than may ye win.
God bring us all to his in,
'Amen, amen,' dicentes.

2. *their; truth.* 3. *Who chatter at Mass.* 5. *Than here to serve to the Devil's satisfaction.*
6. *Serving such vain things.* 8. *are; crowd.* 9. *Who impede the things of God.* 10. *Unless;*
and 14. *silent; and* 11. *them (destroy).* 11. *sharp hooks.* 12. *Wailing, however, into the pit.*
15. *But be such as put away those things in prayer (?); prece (?) MS. parte (?).* 17.
dwelling. 18. *Who say, 'Amen'.*

104

Mary, Queen of Heaven

The infinite power essenciall   15c.
Me thoght I sawe, verrement,
Proceding from his trone celestiall
To a dere damsell that was gent.
Songes melodious was in their tent   5
Of Angells, singing with gret solemnite,
Before a quene whiche was present.
Ecce virgo, radix Jesse.

Tota pulchra, to the lilly like.
She was set withe saphures celestiall.   10
The odour of hir mouthe aromatike
Did coumford the world universall.
Moche clerer she was then the crystall.
She is the flowre of all formosite,
Devoide of actes criminall.   15
Ecce virgo, radix Jesse.

Oleum effusum, to languentes medsine,
A 'Maria' by denominacioun,
Fulgent as the beame celestine,
Called unto hir coronacioun.   20
Phebus persplendent made his abdominacioun,
Devoiding all in tenebrosite,
For gret love of hir exaltacioun.
Ecce virgo, radix Jesse.

1. essenciall, *absolute* (?), *in the highest degree* (?). 2. verrement, *truly.* 3, 52. trone, *throne.* 4. gent, *noble, beautiful.* 5. tent, *attention.* 8. *Behold a virgin, root of Jesse* (?). 9. *All beautiful.* 14. formosite, *beauty.* 17. *Oil poured out, medicine to the sick.* 18. denominacioun, *name.* 19. celestine, *heavenly.* 21. persplendent, *gleaming very bright;* abdominacioun, *abdication* (?), MS. abhominacioun. 22. *Getting rid of all in darkness.*

Right diligent were the minstrells divine,   25
Trones and dominaciones for to expresse,
Angells, Archangells, dubbit in doctrine,
To ministre to that regall arrayed in richesse.
The Prince perpetuall spake to that Princesse,
Smiling in his suavite,   30
'Columba mea, the cloistre of clandnesse,
Ecce virgo, radix Jesse.

'Surge, true tabernacle of virginite,
Bothe mother and maiden inculpable,
Cum furthe of thy consanguinite   35
Unto glorye incomparable.'
Then kneled this orient and amiable
Before the Pellicane of perpetuete,
And he crowned that regient venerable.
Ecce virgo, radix Jesse.   40

By the spectable splendure of hir fulgent face
My sprete was raveshed and in my body sprent.
Inflamed was my hert with gret solace
Of the luciant, corruscall resplendent.
Then this curious cumpany, incontinent,   45
Withe the seraphinnes in their solemnite
Solemply sang this subsequent.
Ecce virgo, radix Jesse.

'O! Deifere delicate and doghter divine,
Mother of mercy and meiden mellefluous,   50
Devoide of disceite, dubbit in doctrine,
Trone of the Trinite, treite thou for us.
Us defende from the dongeon dolorous,
And bring to abide in blisse withe thee,
There to love our God most glorious.'   55
Ecce virgo, radix Jesse.

26–7. (*Ranks of angels*); and 51. dubbit in doctrine, *named in the Church's teaching.*
28. regall, *royal personage.* 30. suavite, *sweetness.* 31. *My dove, the cloister of purity.*
33. Surge, *Rise.* 34. inculpable, *without blame.* 35. *Come forth from your human family.*
37. orient, *precious (one).* 38. of perpetuete, *everlasting.* 39. regient, *ruler.* 41.
spectable, *worthy to be seen, visible.* 42. sprete, *spirit;* sprent, *leapt.* 44. *Of the shining,
gleaming, glittering one.* 45. curious, *choice;* incontinent, *straightway.* 49. Deifere,
God-bearer. 52. Trone, *Throne;* treite, *intercede.* 53. dongeon (*i.e. Hell*).

105

A love letter

Go! little bill, and do me recommende   15c.
Unto my lady with godely countenaunce.
For, trusty messenger, I thee sende,
Pray her that she make purviaunce:
For my love, thurgh here sufferaunce,   5
In her bosome desireth to reste,
Sith of all women I love here beste.

She is lilly of redolence,
Which only may do me plesure;
She is the rose of confidence,   10
Most comforting to my nature.
Unto that lady I me assure:
I will her love and never mo,
Go! little bill, and sey her so.

She resteth in my remembraunce   15
Day other night wherso I be.
It is my special daliaunce
For to remember her bewte.
She is imprinted in ich degre
With yftes of nature inexplicable,   20
And eke of grace incomparable.

The cause therfor if she will witt
Will I presume on sych a flowre,
Say of her, for it is iwritt,
She is the feirest paramour,   25

1. bill, *letter*. 3–4. *Because . . . I send you, pray (? you to pray?) her . . .* 4. purviaunce *provision*. 5. *With her permission*. 7, etc. Sith, *Since*. 8. redolence, *fragrance*. 12. me assure, *pledge myself*. 13. mo, *more*. 15. resteth, *MS*. rested. 17. daliaunce, (*amorous*) *delight*. 19, 26. (*in*) *each* (*respect*). 20. yftes, *gifts*. 21. eke, *also*. 22. witt, *know*. 23. *Why I will take advantage of such a flower*. 25. paramour, *lover*.

And to man in ich langour
Most soveraine mediatrice.
Therfore I love that flowre of price.

Her bewte wholy to descrive
Who is she that may suffice?   30
Forsoth, no clerk that is on live,
Sith she is only withouten vice,
Her flavour excedeth the flowr-de-lice;
Afore all flowres I have her chose,
Enterely in mine herte to close.   35

Her I beseche, sith I not fein,
But only put me in her grace,
That of me she not disdein,
Taking regarde at old trespace.
Sith mine intent in every place   40
Shall be to doe her obeisaunce,
And her to love saunce variaunce.

26. langour, *sad plight.* 28. of price, *Precious.* 31. clerk, *learned man.* 36. *I implore her, since I am not pretending.* 42. saunce, *without.*

106

Wofully araide

Wofully araide,   15C.
My blode, man,
For thee ran,
It may not be naide:
My body blo and wanne,   5
Wofully araide.

Beholde me, I pray thee, with all thine whole reson,
And be not hard-herted for this encheson,
That I for thy saule sake was slaine in good seson,

1. araide, *afflicted.* 4. naide, *denied.* 5. *black and blue.* 8. encheson, *cause.*

Beguiled and betraide by Judas' fals treson,   10
Unkindly intreted,
With sharp corde sore freted:
The Jues me threted,
They mowed, they spitted and despised me,
Condemned to deth as thu maiste se.   15

Thus naked am I nailed, O! man for thy sake.
I love thee, thenne love me. Why slepest thu? Awake!
Remember my tender hert-rote for thee brake,
With paines my vaines constrained to crake.
Thus was I defased,   20
Thus was my flesh rased,
And I to deth chased,
Like a lambe led unto sacrefise,
Slaine I was in most cruel wise.

Of sharp thorne I have worne a crowne on my hed.   25
So rubbed, so bobbed, so rufulle, so red;
Sore pained, sore strained, and for thy love ded,
Unfained, not demed, my blod for thee shed;
My fete and handes sore
With sturde nailes bore.   30
What might I suffer more
Then I have sufferde, man, for thee?
Com when thu wilt and welcome to me!

Dere brother, non other thing I desire
But geve me thy hert fre to rewarde mine hire.   35
I am he that made the erth, water and fire.
Sathanas that sloven, and right lothely sire,
Him have I overcaste,
In hell presoune bounde faste,
Wher ay his woo shall laste.   40
I have purvaide a place full clere
For mankinde, whom I have bought dere.

10. treson, *treachery.* 11. intreted, *treated.* 13. threted, *threatened, rebuked.* 14.
mowed, *made grimaces.* 19. crake, *crack.* 20. defased, *disfigured.* 21. rased, *scratched.*
22. chased, *hunted.* 26. bobbed, *beaten* (?) *insulted* (?) 28. *Actual not imagined, my* (etc.).
30. sturde, *cruel, strong* (?). 35. hire, *service* (*done for reward*) (?). 37. sloven, *knave;*
lothely, *hateful.* 41. purvaide, *provided;* clere, *bright.*

107

A short prayer to Mary

Blessed Mary, moder virginal,   mid 15c.
Integrate maiden, sterre of the see,
Have remembraunce at the day final
On thy poore servaunt now praying to thee.
Mirroure without spot, rede rose of Jerico,   5
Close garden of grace, hope in disparage,
Whan my soule the body parte fro,
Socoure it frome mine enmies' rage.

2. Integrate, *Perfect.* 6. Close, *Closed;* disparage, *despair.*

108

A night with a holy-water clerk

Alas! alas! the while,   about 1450
Thought I on no gile,
So have I god chance.
Alas! alas! the while,
That ever I coude dance.   5

Ladd I the dance a Midsomer Day:
I made smale trippes, soth for to say.
Jack, oure haly-water clerk, com by the way,
And he lokede me upon—he thought that it was gay.
Thought I on no gile.   10

Jack, oure haly-water clerk, the yonge strippeling,
For the chesone of me he com to the ring,

3. *As I hope for good luck.* 6. Ladd, *Led.* 7. *I took small steps, truth to tell.* 8. clerk, *cleric.* 9. MS.? 12. *Because of me he came to the circle of the dance* (pp. 35–6).

And he trippede on my to and made a twinkeling—
Ever he cam ner, he spared for no thinge.
Thought I on no gile.   15

Jack, I wot, preyede in my faire face:
He thought me full werly, so have I god grace.
As we turnden oure dance in a narw place
Jack bed me the mouth—a kussinge ther was.
Thought I on no gile.   20

Jack tho began to roune in mine ere,
'Loke that thou be privey and grante that thou thee bere
A peire whit gloves, I ha to thine were.'
'Gramercy! Jacke', that was mine answere.
Thought I on no gile.   25

Sone after evensong Jack me mette:
'Com hom after thy gloves that I thee bihette.'
Whan I to his chambre com, down he me sette—
From him might I nat go whan we were mette.
Thought I on no gile.   30

Shetes and chalones, I wot, a were ispredde:
Forsothe tho Jack and I wenten to bedde.
He prikede and he pransede, nolde he never linne.
It was the murgest night that ever I cam inne.
Thought I on no gile.   35

Whan Jack had don, tho he rong the bell:
All night ther he made me to dwelle.
Of itrewe we hadden iserved the reaggeth Devil of helle:
Of other smale burdes kep I nout to telle.
Thought I on no gile.   40

13. *he stepped on my toe and winked.* 16, 31. *wot, know.* 17. *He thought me entirely cautious, so may good luck be mine.* 19. *bed, offered.* 21, 36. *tho, then; roune, whisper.* 22–3. *See you are discreet and let yourself carry a pair of white gloves which I have for your wearing.* 24. *Thanks very much, Jack.* 27. *bihette, promised.* 29. *we, not in MS.* 31. *chalones, blankets; a, they.* 33. *nolde he never linne, he would not leave off.* 34. *murgest, jolliest.* 36. *rong the bell, = ?.* 38. *Of itrewe, Truly; reaggeth, shaggy (?).* 39. *Of other little games (?) I don't care to tell.*

The other day at prime I com hom, as I wene:
Met I my dame, copped and kene.
'Sey thou, stronge strumpet, whare hastu bene?
Thy tripping and thy dancing well it will be sene!'
Thought I on no gile.   45

Ever by on and by on my damme reched me clot,
Ever I ber it privey while that I mouth,
Till my gurdle aros, my wombe wax out.
Evil ispunne yern ever it wole out!
Thought I on no gile.   50

41. *Next day I came home at the first hour of daylight, I suppose.* 42. *I met my mistress* (?) *mother* (?), *bad-tempered and fierce.* 46. *From time to time my mistress* (?) *mother* (?) *gave me a clout.* 47. *I kept it secret as long as I could.* 49. *Badly spun yarn will always ravel.*

109

Farewell, this world

Farewell, this world! I take my leve for evere.   15C.
I am arrested to apere at Goddes face.
O! mightyful God, thu knowest that I had levere
Than all this world to have oone houre space
To make asithe for all my grete trespace.   5
My hert, alas! is brokene for that sorowe:
Sum are today that shall not be tomorowe.

This life, I see, is but a cheyre feire.
All thinges passene, and so most I, algate.
Today I sat full ryall in a cheire,   10
Till sotell deth knoked at my gate,

3. levere, *rather*. 5. asithe, *reparation*. 7. that, *so Balliol MS. but this MS. omits*. 8. cheyre feire, *cherry fair*. 9. algate, *in any case*. 10. ryall, (*royal*) *'grand'*. 11, 13. sotell, *insidious, cunning*.

And, onavised, he seid to me, 'Chek-mate'.
Lo! how sotell he maketh a devors,
And wormes to fede, he hath here leid my cors.
. . .

This feble world, so fals and so unstable,   15
Promoteth his lovers for a little while;
But, at the last, he yeveth hem a bable,
Whene his peinted trouth is torned into gile.
Experience causeth me the trouth to compile,
Thinking this, too late, alas, that I began,   20
For foly and hope disseiveth many a man.

Farewell! my frendes, the tide abideth no man.
I moste departe hens, and so shall ye.
But in this passage the beste song that I can
Is 'Requiem Eternam'. I pray God grant it me.   25
Whan I have ended all mine adversite
Graunte me in Paradise to have a mansion,
That shede his blode for my redempcion.
    Beati mortui qui in Domino moriuntur.
    Humiliatus sum vermis.   30

12. onavised, *without warning.* 14, 15. *One stanza omitted.* 17. yeveth, *gives;* hem,
them; bable, *toy.* 18. peinted, *feigned;* and 19. trouth, *faith, truth.* 18–21. trouth is
torned into gile, *and all that follows: so Balliol MS. but this MS. omits.* 19. compile,
tell, formulate. 20. this, *(the truth to compile).* 22–30. *Stanza supplied from Balliol
MS.* 25. '*Eternal rest*'. 29–30. *Blessed are the dead who die in the Lord. I am brought low
with the worms.*

I 10

Christ complains to sinners

With a garlande of thornes kene   *Superbia*   15c.
My hed was crowned, and that was sene;
The stremes of blode ran by my cheke:
Thou, proude man, lorne to be meke.

2. sene, *apparent.*

When thou art wroth and wolde take wreche,   *Ira*   5
Kepe well the lore that I thee teche:
Thoro my right hond the naile goth—
Forgif, therfore, and be not wroth.

With a spere, sharpe and grill,   *Invidia*
My hert was wounded with my will: 10
For luf of man, that was me dere,
Envious man, of luf thou lere.

Rise up, luste, out of thy bed,   *Accidia*
Think on my fete that ar forbled,
And harde nailed upon a tre: 15
Think on, man, this was for thee.

Thrugh my right hand the naile was drive: *Avaricia*
Thinke theron, if thou wilt live,
And worshipe God with almesdede,
That at thy deying Heven may be thy mede.   20

In alle my paines I sufferd on Rode   *Gula*
Man gave me drinke nothing gode:
Eisell and galle for to drinke—
Gloton, theron ever thou thinke.

Of a maiden I was borne   *Luxuria*   25
To save the folke that were forlorne:
Alle my body was beten for sin—
Lechore, therfor, I rede thee, blin.

I was beten for thy sake: *Jesus*
Sin thou leve and shrifte thou take,   30
Forsake thy sin and luf me;
Amende thee, and I forgif thee.

---

5. wreche, *revenge.* 9. grill, *cruel.* 10. will, *consent.* 12. lere, *learn.* 14. fete, *MS.* fote; forbled, *bleeding badly.* 19. almesdede, *giving alms.* 20. mede, *reward.* 23. Eisell, *Vinegar.* 26. forlorne, *utterly lost.* 28. rede, *advise;* blin, *leave off.* 30. shrifte, *absolution.*

III

An A.B.C. of devotion

Crosse of Jesu Christ be ever oure spede,   15c.
And kepe us from peril of sinnes and paine.
Blessed be that Lorde that on the Crosse dide blede,
Christ, God and man that for us was slaine:
Dede he was, and rose up againe.   5
Ever helpe us, Crosse, with him to arise
Fro deeth to life, and sinne to despise.

Gracious Crosse, now graunt us that grace
Him for to worship with all oure minde
In wordes, in werkes and in every place,   10
Kneling and kissing thee where we thee finde.
Late us be never to him unkinde,
Mercifully that made us to be men,
No more to kepe but his heestis ten.

O blissful Crosse, teche us all vertu   15
Plesing to God for oure salvacion,
Quenching alle vices in the name of Jesu,
Raunson paying for oure dampnacion.
Sende us such grace of conversacion
That we may stighe and glorified be,   20
Where Christ is King that died on Tree.

Christ that died on the holy Roode,
I pray thee, good Lorde, with all my might,
Sende us sume part of all thy goode
And kepe us from evil ever day and night,   25
Continuing thy mercy, saving all right.
Titulle of thy passion point us save,
As to thy Crosse reverence we may have.

1, 28. Crosse, *MS.* +; spede, *helper.* 12. *Let; ungrateful, undutiful.* 14. kepe, *care for; commandments.* 19. *behaviour.* 20. *ascend.* 26. *justice.* 27. *Appoint us safely what thy passion entitles* (*viz. Heaven*) (?).

112

Mary complains to other mothers

Of all wemen that ever were borne,   about 1450
That bere childer, abide and see
How my sone lyeth me beforne,
Upon my skirte, taken from the Tree.
Youre childer ye daunce upon youre knee,   5
With laghing, kissing and mery chere:
Beholde my childe, beholde wele me,
For now lyeth dedd my dere sone, dere.

O! woman, woman, wele is thee:
Thy childis capps thou castest upon.   10
Thou pikest his heere, beholdest his ble,
Thou wottest not wele when thou haste don.
But ever, alas, I make my mon,
To see my sonis hedd as it is here:
I prike out thornes by oon and oon,   15
For now lyeth dedd my dere sone, dere.

O! woman, a chaplet chosen thou has:
Thy childe to were it dose thee liking.
Thou pinnest it on—grete joye thou mas.
And I sitt with my sone sore weping.   20
His chaplet is thornes sore pricking.
His mouth I kisse with a careful chere.
I sitt weping and thou singing,
For now lyeth dedd my dere sone, dere.

O! wemen, loketh to me ageine,   25
That playe and kisse youre childer pappis.
To see my sone I have grete peine,

2. That, (You) who. 4. Upon my skirte, *In my lap.* 9. *you are well off.* 11. pikest, (you) *make trim;* ble, *face.* 12. wottest, *knowest.* 13. mon, *complaint.* 15. by oon and oon, *one by one.* 18. *Having your child wear it gives you pleasure.* 19. mas, *makest.* 22. careful, *sorrowful;* chere, *face.*

In his breste so grete a gappe is,
And on his body so many swappis.
With blody lippis I kisse him here.   30
Alas! full harde me thinkis my happis,
For now lyeth dedd my dere sone, dere.

O! woman, thou takest thy childe by the hand,
And seyste, 'Dere sone, gif me a stroke.'
My sonis handes ar so bledand   35
To loke on them me liste not to layke.
His handes he sufferd for thy sake
Thus to be bored with nailes sere.
When thou makes mirth gret sorows I make,
For now lyeth dedd my dere sone, dere.   40

Beholde! wemen, when that ye play,
And have youre childer on kne daunsand,
Ye fele ther fete, so fete ar thay,
And to youre sight full well likand.
But the most finger of mine hand   45
Thorow my sonis fete I may put here,
And pulle it out sore bledand,
For now lyeth dedd my dere son, dere.

Therfore, wemen, by town and strete,
Youre childer handes when ye beholde,   50
Ther breste, ther body, and ther fete,
God were on my sone to thinke, and ye wolde,
How care hath made my hert full colde,
To see my sone with naile and spere,
With scourge and thornes manifolde,   55
Wounded and dedd my dere sone, dere.

---

29. swappis, *blows.* 31. *my misfortunes seem to me most hard.* 36. *Looking at them I have no desire to play;* layke, *so MS. Ff. 5.48 but this MS.* laghe. 38. sere, *divers.* 42. daunsand, *so MS. Ff.5.48 but this MS.* dawnsyng. 43. so fete, *so comely.* 44. likand, *pleasing, so MS. Ff.5.48 but this MS.* lykyng. 45. most, *biggest.* 52. God, *Good* were (*it*); *and, if.* 53. hert full, *so MS. Ff.5.48 but this MS.* herte. *Four stanzas at the end are omitted.*

113

Besse Bunting

In Aprell and in May,   15c.
When hartes be all mery,
Besse Bunting, the millaris may,
Withe lippes so red as chery,
She cast in hir remembrance   5
To passe hir time in daliance
And to leve hir thought driery.
Right womanly arayd
In a peticote of whit,
She was nothing dismayd—   10
Hir countenance was full light.

3. *the miller's girl.* 4. so, *as.* 6. daliance, *dallying, making love.* 7. *And to leave her sad thoughts.* 9. peticote, *skirt.* 11. light, *happy.*

114

The spring under a thorn

At a springe wel under a thorn   15c.
Ther was bote of bale a litel here aforn.
Ther beside stant a maide,
Fulle of love ibounde:
Whoso wol seche true love,   5
In hir it shall be founde.

2. bote of bale, *remedy for ill;* aforn, *before.* 3. stant, *stands.* 4. ibounde, *bound.* 5. seche, *seek.*

115

Smoke-blackened smiths

Swarte-smeked smethes, smatered with smoke,   mid 15c.
Drive me to deth with den of here dintes:
Swich nois on nightes ne herd men never,
What knavene cry and clatering of knockes!
The cammede kongons cryen after 'Col! col!'   5
And blowen here bellewes that all here brain brestes.
'Huf, puf,' seith that on, 'Haf, paf,' that other.
They spitten and sprawlen and spellen many spelles,
They gnawen and gnacchen, they grones togidere,
And holden hem hote with here hard hamers.   10
Of a bole hide ben here barm-felles,
Here shankes ben shakeled for the fere-flunderes.
Hevy hameres they han that hard ben handled,
Stark strokes they striken on a steled stocke.
'Lus, bus, las, das,' rowten by rowe.   15
Swiche dolful a dreme the Devil it todrive!
The maister longeth a litil and lasheth a lesse,
Twineth hem twein and toucheth a treble.
'Tik, tak, hic, hac, tikct, takct, tik, tak,
Lus, bus, lus, das'. Swich lif they leden,   20
Alle clothemeres, Christ hem give sorwe!
May no man for brenwateres on night han his rest.

Smoke-blackened smiths, begrimed with smoke, drive me to death with the din of
their blows: such noise by night no man ever heard, what crying of workmen and
clattering of blows! The snub-nosed (? crooked?) changelings cry out for, 'Coal!
coal!' and blow their bellows fit to burst their brains. 'Huf, puf', says that one,
and 'Haf, paf', the other. They spit and sprawl and tell many tales, they gnaw
and gnash, they groan together, and keep themselves hot with their hard hammers.
Of a bull's hide are their leather aprons, their legs are protected against the fiery
sparks. Heavy hammers they have that are handled hard, strong blows they strike
on an anvil of steel. 'Lus, bus, las, das', they crash in turn. May the Devil put an
end to so miserable a racket. The master-smith lengthens a little piece of iron,
hammers a smaller piece, twists the two together and strikes a treble note (?)
Such a life they lead, all smiths who clothe horses in iron armour, may Heaven
punish them! For smiths who burn water (when they cool hot iron in it) no man
can sleep at night.

116

In honour of Christmas

Good day, good day,   about 1450
My lord, Sire Christemasse, good day!

Good day, Sire Christemasse our king,
For every man both olde and yinge
Is glad and blithe of your cominge: 5
Good day!

Godis sone, so moche of might,
Fram Heven to erthe down is light,
And borne is of a maide so bright:
Good day!   10

Heven and erthe and also helle,
And alle that ever in hem dwelle,
Of your cominge they beth full snelle:
Good day!

Of your cominge this clerkes finde   15
Ye come to save all mankinde,
And of here bales hem unbinde:
Good day!

Alle manner of merthes we wole make,
And solas to oure hertes take,   20
My semely lorde, for your sake:
Good day!

---

8. light, *descended.* 12, 17. hem, *them.* 13. *They are most keen about your coming.*
15. this clerkes, *these learned men.* 17. here bales, *their woes.*

117

A hymn of the Incarnation

Glad and blithe mote ye be,   about 1450
All that ever I here nowe se,
Alleluia!
Kinge of kingis, Lord of alle,
Borne he is in oxe stalle,   5
Res miranda.

The angel of consel now borne he is,
Of a maide full clene, iwis,
Sol de stella.
The sunne that ever shineth bright,   10
The sterre that ever yeveth his light,
Semper clara.

Right as the sterre bringth forth his beme,
So the maide here barn teme.
Pari forma.   15
Nother the sterre for his beme,
Nother the maide for here barne-teme
Fit corrupta.

The cedur of Liban that groweth so hie
Unto the hysope is made lie   20
Valle nostra.
Godis sone of Heven bright
Until a maide is he light,
Carne sumpta.

---

1. mote, *may.* 6. *Matter for wonder.* 7. *Counsellor spirit (i.e. 'Word' of God) now he is born.* 8. iwis, *indeed.* 9. *Sun from the star.* 11. yeveth, *gives.* 12. *Always bright.* 14. *So the maid brought forth her child.* 15. *Of like nature.* 17–18. *Nor was the maid corrupted by her child-bearing.* 20–1. *Is made to lie with the hyssop in our valley.* 23. *Upon a maid has he descended, alighted.* 24. *Having taken flesh.*

Isaye saide by prophecye.   25
The Synagoge hath it in memorye,
Yit never he lynneth maliciusly
Esse ceca.
If they leve not here prophetis,
Then lete hem leve hethen metris,   30
In sibyllinis versiculis
Hec predicta.

Unhappy Jewe, come thu nere,
Beleve ellis thine eldere.
Why wolt thu, wretch, idampned be?   35
Whomme techeth the letter—
Beholde the childe the better—
Him bare a maide-moder, Marye.

25. *Isaiah foretold (the Incarnation).* 26–8. *Synagogue (Jews of the Old Testament) remembers it but, wickedly, never ceases to be blind.* 29. *leve, believe; here, their.* 30–2. *Then let them believe heathen poems, what was prophecied in sibylline verses.* 33. *Unhappy, Unfortunate.* 34. *Or believe the Ancients (of your race).* 36–8. *Him whom the Scriptures show—behold that child better—him a maiden-mother, Mary, bore.*

118

The wells of Jesus wounds

Jesus woundes so wide   later 15c.
Ben welles of lif to the goode,
Namely the stronde of his side,
That ran full breme on the Rode.

Yif thee liste to drinke,   5
To fle fro the fendes of helle,
Bowe thu down to the brinke,
And mekely taste of the welle.

2. *Ben, Are.* 3. *Namely, Especially; stronde, stream.* 4. *breme, fiercely.* 5. *If you are inclined to drink.*

119

Bring us in good ale

Bring us in good ale, and bring us in good ale,   later 15c.
Fore our blessed Lady sak, bring us in good ale.

Bring us in no browne bred, fore that is mad of brane;
Nor bring us in no whit bred, fore therin is no game:
But bring us in good ale.   5

Bring us in no befe, for ther is many bones;
But bring us in good ale, for that goth downe at ones,
And bring us in good ale.

Bring us in no bacon, for that is passing fat;
But bring us in good ale, and give us inought of that,   10
And bring us in good ale.

Bring us in no mutton, for that is ofte lene;
Nor bring us in no tripes, for they be seldom clene:
But bring us in good ale.

Bring us in no egges, for ther ar many shelles;   15
But bring us in good ale, and give us nothing elles,
And bring us in good ale.

Bring us in no butter, for therin ar many heres;
Nor bring us in no pigges flesh, for that will mak us bores:
But bring us in good ale.   20

Bring us in no podinges, for therin is all gotes blod;
Nor bring us in no venison, for that is not for our good:
But bring us in good ale.

Bring us in no capon's flesh, for that is ofte der;
Nor bring us in no dokes flesh for they slobber in the mer: 25
But bring us in good ale.

3. *made of bran.* 18. *hairs.* 21. *(black) puddings; gotes blod, goat's blood,* MS. *godes good.* 22. *good,* MS. *blod.* 24. *der, expensive.* 25. *ducks'; mer, pond.*

120

The Nativity

Jesus, almighty King of Blis,   later 15c.
Assumpsit carnem virgine.

As Holy Kirke makes mind,
Intravit ventris thalamum,
Fro Heven to erthe, to save monkind,   5
Pater misit Filium.

Of Mary milde Christe wolde be borne,
Sine virili semine,
To save monkind that was forlorne
Prime parentis crimine.   10

To Mary come a messenger,
Ferens salutem homini:
She answerd him with milde chere,
'Ecce ancilla Domini.'

Mekely on thee the Holy Ghoste   15
Palacium intrans uteri:
Of all thing meknes is moste
In conspectu Altissimi.

When he was borne that made all thing,
Pastor, creator omnium,   20
Angelles they began to sing
'Veni, redemptor gencium.'

---

2. *Took flesh by the Virgin.* 4. *He entered the chamber of her womb.* 6. *The Father sent his Son.* 7, 13. *milde, gracious, gentle.* 8. *Without a man's seed.* 9. *forlorne, utterly lost.* 10. *By the offence of our first parent.* 12. *Bearing a salutation to man.* 13. *chere, demeanour, heart.* 14. *Behold the hand-maid of the Lord.* 15-16. *Meekly the Holy Ghost descended upon you, entering the palace of your womb.* 18. *In the sight of the Most High.* 20. *The shepherd and creator of all.* 22. *Come! redeemer of the people.*

Thre kinges come on goid twelfth day,
Stella mycante previa;
To seche that childe they toke tho way,   25
Portantes sibi munera.

A sterne forth ladde theis kinges all,
Inquirentes Dominum;
Lying in an asse stall
Invenerunt puerum.   30

For he was King of kinges heghe,
Rex primus aurum optulit;
And also Lorde and King full right,
Secundus rex thus protulit;

For he was God, Mon and King,   35
Myrra mortem retulit:
He us all to Heven bring,
Qui mortem Cruce voluit.

23. goid, *good;* twelfth day (*after Christmas day*). 24. *Led by a shining star.* 25. seche, *seek.* 26. *Carrying presents for him.* 27. sterne, *star.* 28. *Seeking for the Lord.* 30. *They found the boy.* 32. *The first king offered gold.* 34. *The second king brought forth incense.* 36. *Myrrh told his death.* 37. (*May*) he. 38. *Who willed his death on the Cross.*

121

Three things Jeame lacks

He that will be a lover in every wise,   later 15c.
He muste have thre thinges whiche Jeame lacketh:
The first is goodlihede at point devise,
The secunde is manere which manhoode maketh,
The thrid is goode that no woman hateth.   5
Marke well this—that lovers will be
Must nedes have oone of thes thre.

3. *The first is goodly appearance* (or) *character to perfection.* 4. manere, *good-breeding, moral character.* 5. *possessions.*

122

Subject to all pain

Yet wulde I nat the causer fared amisse,   later 15c.
For all the good that ever I had or shall.
Therfor I take mine aventure, iwisse,
As she that hath forsaken joyes all,
And to all paine is bothe sojet and thralle.   5
Lo! thus I stonde, withouten wordes moo,
All voide of joy and full of paine and woo.

Now ye that bathe in mirthe and plesaunce
Have minde on me that was sumtime in ease,
And had the world at mine owne ordinaunce,   10
Whiche now is turned into all disease.
Now glad were she, that Fortune so coude please,
That she might stonde in verry sicurnesse,
Never to fele the stroke of unkindnesse.

Departing is the grounde of displesaunce   15
Most in my heart of eny thing erthly.
I you ensure wholy in remembraunce,
Within myself, I thenke it verrily,
Whiche shall continu with me daily.
Sins that ye moste nedes departe me fro,   20
It is to me a verry dedly woo.

3. aventure, *fortune;* iwisse, *indeed.* 4. As she that, *Being a woman who.* 6. moo, *more.* 10. world, *MS.* worldyl; owne, *MS.* ovns (?); ordinaunce, *disposition.* 11. disease, *discomfort.* 13, etc. verry(ly), *true(ly);* sicurnesse, *security.* 15. departing, *parting, going away.* 17. I you ensure, *I make you safe (?) I promise you (vague formula).* 18. thenke, *think.* 20. moste, *must.*

123

What women are not

Of all creatures women be best,   later 15c.
Cuius contrarium verum est.

In every place ye may well see
That women be trewe as tirtill on tree,
Not liberal in langage but ever in secree,   5
And gret joye amonge them is for to be.

The stedfastnes of women will never be don,
So gentil, so curtes, they be everichon,
Meke as a lambe, still as a stone,
Croked nor crabbed find ye none.   10

Men be more cumbers a thousandfold,
And I mervail how they dare be so bold
Against women for to hold,
Seeing them so pascient, softe and cold.

For tell a woman all your counsaile   15
And she can kepe it wonderly well:
She had lever go quik to hell
Than to her neighbour she wold it tell.
. . .

Now say well by women or elles be still,
For they never displesed man by ther will: 20
To be angry or wroth they can no skill,
For I dare say they think non ill.

2. *Of which the contrary is the truth.* 4. tirtill, *turtle-dove.* 5. in secree, *MS.* in secrete, (they speak) *in secrecy.* 8. gentil, *well-bred, gentle;* curtes, *courteous, well-mannered;* everichon, *everyone.* 9, 19. still, *silent.* 10. *You find none twisted and perverse.* 11. cumbers, *troublesome.* 17, 25. lever, *rather.* 18, 19. *One stanza omitted.* 21. *They have no idea how to be angry.* 22. non, *no.*

Trow ye that women list to smater,
Or against ther husbondes for to clater?
Nay! they had lever fast, bred and water,   25
Then for to dele in suche a matter.

. . .

To the tavern they will not go,
Nor to the alehous never the mo,
For, God wot, ther hartes wold be wo
To spende ther husbondes money so.   30

23. *Is it your belief that women love chattering?* 26, 27. *One stanza omitted.* 28. mo,
more. 29. wot, *knows;* wo, *sorry. One stanza omitted at end.*

124

A cause for wonder

Blessed be that lady bright,   later 15c.
That bare a child of great might,
Withouten peine, as it was right,
Maid, mother, Mary.

Goddis sonne is borne: 5
His moder is a maid,
Both after and beforne,
As the prophecy said,
With ay.
A wonder thing it is to see   10
How maiden and moder one may be:
Was there never nonne but she,
Maid, moder, Mary.

The great Lord of Heaven
Our servant is become,   15
Thorow Gabriel's steven,

16. steven, *voice.*

Our kind have benome,
With ay.
A wonder thing it is to see
How lord and servant one may be: 20
Was there never nonne but he,
Born of maid Mary.

Two sons together they
Ought to shine bright:
So did that fayer lady,   25
Whan Jesu in her light,
With ay.
A wonder thing is fall,
The Lord that bought free and thrall
Is found in an ass's stall   30
By his moder Mary.

17. *He has taken our nature. Two stanzas omitted at end.*

125

Impossible to trust women

Whan netilles in winter bere roses rede,   later 15c.
And thornes bere figges naturally,
And bromes bere appilles in every mede,
And lorelles bere cheris in the croppes so hie,
And okes bere dates so plentuosly,   5
And lekes geve honey in ther superfluence—
Than put in a woman your trust and confidence.

Whan whiting walk in forestes, hartes for to chase;
And heringes in parkes hornes boldly blowe,
And flownders more-hennes in fennes enbrace,   10

1, etc. bere, *bear.* 4. croppes, *tops (of trees).* 6. superfluence, *superabundance.* 7, etc.
Than, *Then.*

And gornardes shote rolyons out of a crosse-bowe,
And grengese ride in hunting the wolf to overthrowe,
And sperlinges rone with speres in harness to defence—
Than put in a woman your trust and confidence.

Whan sparowes bild chirches and stepulles hie,   15
And wrennes cary sackes to the mille,
And curlews cary clothes horses for to drye,
And se-mewes bring butter to the market to sell,
And wod-doves were wod-knives theves to kill,
And griffons to goslinges don obedience—   20
Than put in a woman your trust and confidence.

Whan crabbes tak wodcokes in forestes and parkes,
And hares ben taken with swetness of snailes,
And camelles with ther here tak swalowes and perches,
And mice mowe corn with waveying of ther tailes,   25
Whan duckes of the dunghill sek the Blod of Hailes,
Whan shrewed wives to ther husbondes do non offence—
Than put in a woman your trust and confidence.

11. gornardes, *gurnards (fish)*; rolyons, *fish*. 12. grengese, *goslings*. 13. sperlinges
rone, *smelts run;* harness, *armour*. 19. *And wood-pigeons wear hunting-knives to kill
thieves.* 20. griffons, *vultures*. 24. here, *hair*. 26. Blod of Hailes, *alleged blood of Christ
preserved at Hailes Abbey in Gloucestershire*. 27. shrewed, *shrewish*.

126

Money is what matters

Man upon mold, whatsoever thou be,   later 15c.
I warn utterly thou gettest no degree,
Ne no worship abid with thee,
But thou have the peny redy to tak to.

If thou be a yeman, a gentleman wold be,   5
Into sum lordes cort than put thou thee:

1. mold, *earth*. 2. utterly, *plainly*. 4, etc. But, *Unless*. 5. yeman, *yeoman*.

Lok thou have spending, larg and plente,
And alway the peny redy to tak to.

If thou be a gentleman and wold be a squire,
Ridest out of cuntre as wild as eny fire: 10
I thee warn as my frend thou failest of thy desire
But thou have the peny redy to tak to.

If thou be a squire and wold be a knight,
And darest not in armur put thee in fight,
Than to the kinges cort hy thee full tight, 15
And lok thou have the peny redy to tak to.

If thou be a lettred man to ber estat in scole,
A pilion or taberd to wer in hete or cole,
Thee to besy therabout I hold thee but a fole,
But thou have the peny redy to tak to. 20

If thou be a bachelar and woldest ever thrive,
Prickest out of contre and bringest home a wife:
In much sorow and car ledest thou thy life,
But thou have the peny redy to tak to.

If thou be a marchant to buy or to sell, 25
And over all the countre woldest bere the bell,
I thee connsell as a frend at home to dwell,
But thou have the peny redy to tak to.

If thou be a yong man, in lust thy life to lace,
About chirch and market the bishop will thee chace: 30
And if thou mayst be get thou getes nouther grace,
But thou have the peny redy to tak to.

If thou have out to do with the law to plete,
At London at the parvis many on will thee rehete:
I warne thee com not ther but thy purse may swete, 35
And that thou have the peny redy to tak to.

15. hy . . . tight, *hasten quickly.* 16. *And see to it you.* 17. *to have a position in a place of learning.* 18. *A cap or short coat to wear in heat or cold.* 21–8. *Parts of lines damaged in MS.* 22. Prickest, *Ride fast.* 26. woldest . . . bell, *would be supreme.* 29. lust, *pleasure;* lace, *involve.* 31. *And should you be caught you will get no mercy, either.* 33. out, *ought;* plete, *plead.* 34. parvis, *place at St. Paul's where lawyers met; many a one will attack you.* 35. swete, *sweat.*

127

Remember the last things

Man, hef in mind and mend thy mis,   later 15c.
Whil thou are heir in lif livand,
And think apone this warldis blis,
Sa oftsyis is variand.
For Fortonis wheill is ay turnand,   5
Whil to weil and whil to wa,
Whil oup, whil downe, I onderstand—
Memor esto novissima.

Thou seis thy sampil everilk day,
And thou tak heid, withouten les,   10
How sone that thou may pas away:
For bald Hector and Achilles,
And Alexander the proud in pres,
Hes tane thare leif, and mony ma,
That Ded hes drawene onetil his des—   15
Memor esto novissima.

Thidder thou com, nakit and bair,
As bannyst man of kith and kine:
So thee behuvis hine to fair,
For all the riches thou ma wine.   20
Is na defens, be craft na gine,
That ma defend thee fra thy fa,
Bot cherite be thee within—
Memor esto novissima.

1, 39. *Man, remember to correct your faults.* 2. heir, *here;* livand, *living.* 4. (*Which*) *is so often changing.* 6. Whil, *At one (another) time.* 8. *Remember the last things.* 9. sampil, *example.* 10. And, *If;* withouten les, *believe me.* 12, 26. bald(ast), bold(*est*). 13. Alexander, *MS.* alex; pres, *battle.* 14. *Have taken their leave, and many more.* 15. Ded, *Death;* onto his seat. 18. *Like one banished from kith and kin.* 19. hine, *hence;* and 41. fair, *go.* 20, 22. ma, *can.* 21. (*There*) is; be, *by;* gine, *device.* 22. fa, *foe.* 23. Bot, *Unless.*

This day thocht thou were hail and feir,   25
As berne baldast, ore king with crowne,
The morne thou may be brocht one beir,
For all thy castalis, towre and towne:
Thay may nocht all mak thy ransone
Fra Ded becumin that is so thra: 30
Thou art his pra, but radempsione—
Memor esto novissima.

When thou art ded and laid in laime,
And thy ribbis ar thy ruf tre,
Thou art than brocht to thy lang haime: 35
Adew, all warldis dignite!
Than is too lait, forsucht, think me,
When wormis gnawis thee to and fra.
Now mind thy mis in all degre—
Memor esto novissima.   40

Sen it is sa that thou man fair,
And knawis nocht the wayis richt
Out of this warld, withouten mare,
Whether to Hel or Hevene so bricht,
Thou pray to hime, most is of micht,   45
That he thee fra the devillis ta,
And shild thee fra the Fendis plicht—
Memor esto novissima.

25. thocht, *though; healthy and handsome.* 26. berne, *knight.* 27. *In the morning;* beir, *bier.* 29–30. *Not all these may bring about your ransom from Death that is so fierce.* 31. *You are his prey unless redeemed.* 33. laime, *loam.* 34. *And your ribs form the roof of your house.* 37. *It is too late, then, in truth, it seems to me.* 38. gnawis, *MS.* gawys. 41. Sen, *Since;* man, *must.* 43. mare, *more (ado).* 46. ta, *take.* 47. shild, *shield;* plicht, *peril.*

128

In praise of Ivy

Ivy, chefe of trees it is,
Veni, coronaberis.

later 15c.

The most worthye she is in towne—
He that seith other do amiss—
And worthy to ber the crowne.
Veni, coronaberis.

5

Ivy is soft and mek of spech,
Ageinst all bale she is bliss.
Well is he that may her rech.
Veni, coronaberis.

10

Ivy is green with colour bright,
Of all trees best she is,
And that I preve well now be right.
Veni, coronaberis.

Ivy bereth beris black.
God graunt us all his bliss,
For there shall we nothing lack.
Veni, coronaberis.

15

2, etc. *Come, you shall be crowned.* 3. in towne, *alive.* 4. *does amiss.* 8. *She is the source of all blessedness as opposed to misery.* 9. *attain.* 13. *prove.*

129

JAMES RYMAN

Now the Most High is born

Angelus inquit pastoribus,   later 15c.
'Nunc natus est Altissimus.'

Upon a night an aungell bright
Pastoribus apparuit,
And anone right, thurgh Goddes might,   5
Lux magna illis claruit:
For love of us
(Scripture seith thus)
Nunc natus est Altissimus.

And of that light that was so bright   10
Hii valde timuerunt;
A signe of blis to us it is,
Hec lux quam hii viderunt:
For love of us
(Scripture seith thus)   15
Nunc natus est Altissimus.

'Drede ye nothing, grete joy I bringe,
Quod erit omni populo,
Forwhy to you Christe is borne nowe,
Testante evangelio.'   20
For love of us
(Scripture seith thus)
Nunc natus est Altissimus.

'With good Joseph and Mary milde
Positum in presepio   25
Ye shall finde that hevenly childe

1–2. *The angel said to the shepherds, 'Now the Most High is born'.* 4. *Appeared to the shepherds.* 5. anone right, *straightway.* 6. *A great light shone upon them.* 11. *They were exceedingly afraid.* 13. *This light which they saw.* 18. *Which shall be for all men.* 19. Forwhy, *Because.* 20. *As the Gospel witnesses.* 24. milde, *gracious.* 25. *Placed in a crib.*

Qui celi preest solio.'
For love of us
(Scripture seith thus)
Nunc natus est Altissimus.   30

The aungell songe thoo with many moo,
'Gloria, in altissimis!
In erthe be peas to man also
Et gaudium sit angelis.'
For love of us   35
(Scripture seith thus)
Nunc natus est Altissimus.

The shepeherdes ran to Bedleme than
Et invenerunt puerum,
The whiche is perfecte God and man   40
Atque Salvator omnium.
For love of us
(Scripture seith thus)
Nunc natus est Altissimus.

When in suche wise founde him they had   45
Ut dictum est per angelum,
Ayene they came, being full glad,
Magnificantes Dominum.
For love of us
(Scripture seith thus)   50
Nunc natus est Altissimus.

Nowe lete us singe with angelis,
'Gloria, in altissimis!'
That we may come unto that blis
Ubi partus est virginis,   55
For love of us
(Scripture seith thus)
Nunc natus est Altissimus.

27. *Who rules from the throne of Heaven.* 31. thoo, *then;* moo, *more.* 32, 53. *Glory in the most high places.* 34. *And joy be among the angels.* 38. than, *then.* 39. *And found the boy.* 41. *And Saviour of all.* 46. *As was said by the angel.* 47. Ayene, *Back.* 48. *Praising the Lord.* 55. *Where the child of the Virgin is.*

130

JAMES RYMAN

Farewell! Advent

Farewele! Advent, Christemas is come,   later 15c.
Farewele! fro us both alle and some.

With paciens thou hast us fed,
And made us go hungrye to bed;
For lak of mete we were nighe ded—   5
Farewele fro us both alle and some.

While thou haste be within oure house
We ete no puddinges ne no souse,
But stinking fishe not worthe a louse—
Farewele fro us both alle and some.   10

There was no freshe fishe, ferre ne nere,
Salt fishe and salmon was too dere:
And thus we have had hevy chere—
Farewele fro us both alle and some.

Thou hast us fedde with plaices thin,   15
Nothing on them but bone and skin;
Therfore oure love thou shalt not win—
Farewele fro us both alle and some.

With muskilles gaping afture the mone
Thou hast us fedde at night and none   20
But ones a wike, and that too sone—
Farewele fro us both alle and some.

Oure brede was browne, oure ale was thin,
Oure brede was musty in the bin,
Oure ale soure or we did begin—   25
Farewele fro us both alle and some.

2, etc. fro, *from;* both . . . some, *one and all.* 3. paciens, *patience.* 8. souse, *pickled pork.* 19. muskilles, *mussels;* mone, *moon.* 20. none, *noon.* 21. wike, *week.* 25. or, *before.*

Thou art of grete ingratitude
Good mete fro us for to exclude:
Thou art not kinde but verey rude—
Farewele fro us both alle and some.   30

. . .

This time of Christes feest natall
We will be mery, grete and small,
And thou shalt goo oute of this hall—
Farewele fro us both alle and some.

Advent is gone, Christemas is come,   35
Be we mery now, alle and some!
He is not wise that will be dume
In ortu Regis omnium.

30, 31. *Seven stanzas omitted.* 31. feest natall, *birthday.* 38. *At the birth of the King of all.*

131

ROBERT HENRYSON

Cresseid's complaint against Fortune

O! sop of sorrow, sonkin into cair.   later 15c.
O! cative Creisseid, for now and ever mair
Gane is thy joy and all thy mirth in eird.
Of all bliithness now art thou blaiknit bair.
Thair is na salve may saif thee of thy sair.   5
Fell is thy fortoun, wickit is thy weird,
Thy blis is baneist and thy baill on breird.
Under the eirth God gif I gravin wer,
Quhair nane of Grece nor yit of Troy micht heir'd.

O! (woman) steeped in sorrow (morsel dipped in liquid), plunged in care, O! wretched Cresseid, for now and for ever your joy and all your pleasure on earth is gone. Now you are stripped bare (made pale) of all happiness. There is no medicine that can save you from your sickness. Cruel is your fortune, disastrous is your fate, your bliss is banished and your misery newly-sprung. Would that I were buried under the earth where none of Greece and none of Troy might hear it.

Quhair is thy chalmer, wantounlye besene? 10
With burely bed and bankouris browderit bene,
Spicis and wine to thy collatioun,
The cowpis all of gold and silver shene,
The sweit meitis servit in plaittis clene,
With saipheron sals of ane gud sessoun. 15
Thy gay garmentis with mony gudely goun,
Thy plesand lawn, pinnit with goldin prene—
All is areir, thy greit royal renoun!

Quhair is thy garding with thir greissis gay?
And freshe flowris quhilk the Quene Floray 20
Had paintit plesandly in everye pane,
Quhair thou was wont full merilye in May
To walk and tak the dew be it was day,
And heir the merle and mawis mony ane,
With ladyis fair in carrolling to gane, 25
And se the royal rinkis in thair array,
In garmentis gay, garnishit on everye grane.

Thy greit, triumphand fame and hie honour,
Quhair thou was callit of eirdlye wichtis flour,
All is decayit, thy weird is welterit so. 30
Thy hie estait is turnit in darkness dour.

Where is your chamber, luxuriously furnished? with bed finely made and chair-covers, handsomely embroidered, spices and wine as your refreshment, the cups all of gold and shining silver, the sweet-meats served on clean plates with saffron sauce that seasons well. Your gay garments with many a fine gown, your pleasing lawn, pinned with a golden brooch, your great regal renown—all now is past!
Where is your garden with its gay plants, and fresh flowers which Queen Flora (Roman goddess of spring and flowers) had pleasantly coloured in every flower-bed, where it was your custom to walk and enjoy the fresh morning as soon as it was day, and to hear the blackbird and many a thrush, and to go dancing (?) and singing carols with fair ladies, and to see the royal knights in their turn-out, in gay garments adorned with every colour?
Your great, triumphant fame and high repute, whereby you were known as the flower of earthly creatures, all is decayed, your fate has been so tossed about. Your high condition is turned into grim darkness.

This lipper ludge tak for thy burelye bour,
And for thy bed tak now ane bunche of stro;
For waillit wine and meitis thou had tho
Tak mowlit breid, peirrye and ceder sour.   35
Bot cop and clapper, now is all ago.

My cleir voice and courtlye carrolling,
Quhair I was wont with ladyis for to sing,
Is rawk as ruik full hiddeous hoir and hace.
My plesand port, all utheris precelling.   40
Of lustiness I was hald maist conding.
Now is deformit the figour of my face:
To luik on it na leid now liking hes.
Sowpit in syte, I say with sair siching,
Ludgeit amang the lipper leid, allace!   45

O! ladyis fair of Troy and Grece attend
My miserye quhilk nane may comprehend,
My frivoll fortoun, my infelicitye,
My greit mischeif quhilk na man can amend.
Be war in time—approchis neir the end—   50
And in your mind ane mirrour mak of me:
As I am now, peradventure that ye,
For all your micht, may cum to that same end,
Or ellis war, gif ony war may be.

Take this lepers' home for your finely-made chamber, and for your bed take now a bunch of straw; for choice wine and foods, which you then had, take mouldy bread, perry and sour cider. Except for cup and clapper (by which a leper begged and warned of his approach) now all is gone.

My clear voice and courtly carolling, when (?) with which (?) it was my custom to sing with ladies, is raucous as a rook, hideous, harsh and hoarse. My pleasing carriage, surpassing all others, while in youthful vigour I was held of greatest worth, is gone. Now the appearance of my face is deformed: no one takes any pleasure now in looking at it. Sunk in sorrow, I say, sorely sighing, and lodged among the leper folk, alas!

O! fair ladies of Troy and Greece give heed to my misery which none may understand, my worthless fortune, my unhappiness, my great distress which no one can amend. Beware in time—the end draws near—and in your mind make of me an example: you, for all your strength, as I am now, to that same end may come, or else to worse, if any worse can be (? or else watch out, if any defence is possible?).

Nocht is your fairness bot ane faiding flour!　　　　55
Nocht is your famous laud and hie honour
Bot wind inflat in uther mennis eiris!
Your roising reid to rotting sall retour:
Exempill mak of me in your memour,
Quhilk of sic thingis wofull witness beiris.　　　　60
All welth in eird away as wind it weiris!
Be war thairfoir, approchis neir the hour.
Fortoun is fikkill, quhen scho beginnis and steiris.

Your beauty is but a fading flower! Your resounding praise and high repute are only wind in other men's ears! Your rosy red shall revert to rottenness: make me in your memory an example, for I am sad evidence of such things. All earth's well-being fades away like the wind! Beware, therefore, the hour draws near. Fortune is fickle when she begins to rule.

132

Mock medicine

For a man that is almost blind,　　　　later 15c.
Lat him go barhed all day agein the wind,
Till the sonne be set.
At even wrap him in a cloke
And put him in a hous full of smoke,　　　　5
And loke that every hol be well shet.

And when his eyen begine to rope,
Fill hem full of brimstone and sope,
And hill him well and warm:
And if he see not by the next mone,　　　　10
As well at midnight as at none,
I shall lese my right arm!

2. barhed, *bare-headed;* agein, *against,* out in, MS. agey. 7. *eyes;* rope, *water.* 8. them. 9. *cover.* 10. *moon.* 12. *lose.*

133

Mary is with child

Nowel! nowel! nowel!   later 15c.
Sing we with mirth!
Christ is come well
With us to dwell,
By his most noble birth.   5

Under a tree
In sporting me,
Alone by a wod-side,
I hard a maid
That swetly said,   10
'I am with child this tide.

'Graciously
Conceived have I
The Son of God so swete:
His gracious will   15
I put me till,
As moder him to kepe.

'Both night and day
I will him pray,
And her his lawes taught,   20
And every dell
His trewe gospell
In his apostles fraught.

'This ghostly case
Doth me embrace,   25
Without despite or mock;

8. wod, *wood.* 11. this tide, *at this time.* 12. Graciously, *Through God's grace.* 16.
till, *to.* 17. kepe, *care for.* 20. her, *hear.* 21. every dell, *wholly.* 23. fraught, *loaded* (?)
carried (?). 24. ghostly, *spiritual;* case, *act* (?) *destiny* (?). 25. embrace, *surround pro-*
tectively, comfort.

With my derling,
"Lullay," to sing,
And lovely him to rock.

'Without distress   30
In grete lightness
I am both night and day.
This hevenly fod
In his childhod
Shall daily with me play.   35

'Soone must I sing
With rejoicing,
For the time is all ronne
That I shall child,
All undefil'd,   40
The King of Heven's Sonne.'

31. lightness (*of heart*). 33. fod, *child*. 39. child, *give birth to*.

134

Men only pretend

Whatso men sayn,   later 15c.
Love is no pain
To them, certain,
But varians:
For they constrain   5
Ther hertes to fein,
Ther mouthes to plain,
Ther displesauns.

Which is, indede,
But feined drede,   10
So God me spede,
And doubleness:

4. *Without variation.* 7. plain, *utter.* 8. *Their discontent.* 10. *But feigned anxiety.* 11. *So help me God.*

Ther othes to bede,
Ther lives to lede,
And profer mede—   15
Newfangleness!

For, when they pray,
Ye shall have nay,
Whatso they say—
Beware for shame!   20
For every day
They waite ther pray
Wherso they may,
And make but game.

Then, semeth me,   25
Ye may well se
They be so fre
In every place,
It were pite
But they shold be   30
Begeled, parde,
Withouten grace.

13. bede, *offer.* 15. profer, *MS.* profereth; mede, *reward.* 16. *Liking for the new*
(*lover*). 22. *They wait for their prey.* 30–1. *If they were not beguiled, God knows.*

135

Against women

Looke well about, ye that lovers be: later 15c.
Lat nat youre lustes leede you to dotage.
Be nat enamered on all thing that ye see:
Sampson the fort, and Salomon the sage,
Deceived were for all theire gret corage.   5
Men deme it right that they see with ey—
Beware! therfore: the blind eteth many a fly.

2. *Don't let your desires lead you into dotage.* 4. fort, *strong.* 5. corage, *spirit.*

I mene of wemen, for all theire cheres queint—
Trust hem nat too moche, theire trouth is but geason.
The feirest outward full well can they peint;   10
Theire stedfastness endureth but a season,
For they feine frendliness and worchen treson.
And for they ar chaungeabill naturally,
Beware! therfore: the blind eteth many a fly.

What wight onlive trusteth in theire cheres   15
Shall have at last his guerdon and his mede,
For wemen can shave nerer then rasours or sheres.
All is nat gold that shineth—men take hede.
Theire gall is hid under a sugred wede.
It is full queint theire fantasy to aspy—   20
Beware! therfore: the blind eteth many a fly.

Though all the world do his besy cure
To make wemen stond in stabilness,
It woll nat be; it is again nature—
The world is do when they lak doubilness!   25
For they can laugh and love nat, this is express.
To trust on them it is but fantasy.
Beware! therfore: the blind eteth many a fly.

Wemen of kinde have condicions three:
The furst is they be full of deceit;   30
To spinne also is theire propurte;
And wemen have a wonderfull conceit,
For they can wepe oft and all is a sleit,
And when they list the teere is in the ey—
Beware! therfore: the blind eteth many a fly.   35

---

8. cheres queint, *pretty looks.* 9. *Don't trust them too much, they have only a little integrity.* 12. *and act treacherously.* 15. *What living creature trusts in their looks.* 16. mede, *reward.* 19. wede, *covering (garment).* 20. *It is very wise to watch out for their caprice.* 22. *Though everyone applies himself diligently.* 24. again, *contrary to.* 26. express, *definite.* 27. fantasy, *illusion.* 29. of kinde, *by nature;* condicions, *characteristics.* 32. conceit, *cleverness.* 33. a sleit, *MS.* asceyte, *B.M. MS.* a sleight, *Trinity MS. 0.9.38,* dysceyte, *trick.* 34. And, *this MS. and B.M. MS.* And ever; list, *please.*

In sothe to say, though all the erthe so wan
Were parchemine smothe, white and scribabill,
And the gret see, that called is the occian,
Were torned into inke, blacker then is sabill,
Every stik a penne, iche man a scrivener abill,   40
They coude not writen wimmenes treiterye—
Beware! therfore: the blind eteth many a fly.

36. sothe, *truth;* wan, dark. 41. *So Trinity MS. 0.9.38, but this MS.* Nat cowde
then wryte womans trechery; treiterye, *treachery.*

136

Peace

Pees maketh plente;   later 15c.
Plente maketh pride;
Pride maketh plee;
Plee maketh povert;
Povert maketh pees.   5

3. plee, *lawsuit.*

137

A lover left alone

Continuaunce   later 15c.
Of remembraunce,
Withoute ending,
Doth me penaunce
And grete grevaunce,   5
For your partinge.

4. *Causes me pain.*

Fifteenth Century

So depe ye be
Gravene, parde,
Within mine hert,
That afore me   10
Ever I you see,
In thought covert.

Though I ne plain
My woful pain,
But bere it still,   15
It were in vain
To say again
Fortune's will.

8. *Engraved, God knows.* 13. *Though I do not utter.* 17. *To speak against.*

138

Welcome! our Messiah

Hey! now, now, now,   later 15c.

Swet Jesus
Is cum to us,
This good tim of Christmas.
Wherfor with praise   5
Sing we always,
'Welcum, our Messias'.

The God Almight,
And King of light,
Whose powr is over all,   10
Give us, of grace,
For to purchase
His realme celestial.

12. purchase, *gain.*

Wher his angels
And archangels   15
Do sing incessantly,
His principates
And potestates
Maketh gret harmony.

The cherubins   20
And seraphins,
With ther tunikes mery,
The trones all,
Most musical,
Sing the hevenly Kery.   25

The vertues clere
Ther tunes bere,
Ther quere for to repair;
Whose song to hold
Was manifold   30
Of dominacions fair.

With one accord
Serve we that Lord
With laudes and oraison,
The which hath sent,   35
By good assent,
To us his only Son.

14–31. *Names of the nine orders of angels.* 22. tunikes, *tunes* (?). 25. Kery, *Kyrie Kleison* (*Lord have mercy: from the Mass*). 26. clere, *shining.* 28. *To adorn* (?) *strengthen* (?) *their choir.* 29–31. *The song sung by the fair Dominations was diverse.* 34. *With praises and prayer. Fifteen stanzas omitted at the end.*

139

A! mercy, Fortune

A! mercy, Fortune, have pitee on me,   later 15c.
And thinke that thu hast done gretely amisse
To parte asondre them whiche ought to be
Alwey in on. Why hast thu doo thus?
Have I offended thee? I? Nay! iwisse.   5
Then turne thy whele and be my frende again,
And send me joy where I am nowe in pain.

And thinke what sorowe is the departing
Of two trewe hertes loving feithfully.
For parting is the most soroughfull thinge,   10
To mine entent, that ever yet knewe I.
Therfore I pray to thee right hertely
To turne thy whele and be my frende again,
And sende me joy where I am nowe in pain.

For, till we mete, I dare well say, for trouth,   15
That I shall never be in ease of herte.
Wherfor I pray you to have of me sume routh,
And release me of all my paines smerte,
Now, sith thu woste it is nat my deserte.
Then turne thy whele and be my frende again,   20
And sende me joy where I am nowe in pain.

---

4. in on, *united*. 5. iwisse, *indeed*. 8. departing, *parting, going away*. 11. To mine entent, *in my opinion* . 17. routh, *pity*. 18. smerte, *severe*. 19. *since you know it is not what I deserve.*

140

A grotesque love-letter

To my trew love and able—   later 15c.
As the wedir cock he is stable—
This letter to him be delivered.

Unto you, most froward, this letter I write
Which hath caused me so longe in despaire.   5
The goodlinesse of your persone is esye to endite,
For he leveth nat that can youre persone appaire,
So comly best shapen, of feture most faire,
Most fresh of contenaunce, even as an owle
Is best and most favored of ony oder fowle.   10

Youre manly visage, shortly to declare,
Your forehed, mouth and nose so flatte,
In short conclusion best likened to an hare,
Of alle living thinges, save only a catte.
More wold I sey if I wist what.   15
That swete visage full ofte is beshrewed
Whan I remember of som bawd so lewd.

The proporcion of your body comende welle
    me aught,
Fro the shuldre down, behinde and beforn.
If alle the peintours in a land togeder were soght   20
A worse coude they not portrey, thogh alle they
    had it sworn.
Kepe welle your pacience, thogh I sende you
    a scorne!
Your garmentes upon you full gayly they hinge,
As it were an olde gose had a broke winge.

6. endite, *express.* 7. *lives;* appaire, *depreciate.* 10. *any other bird.* 13. *Put briefly, best compared to a hare.* 15. wist, *knew.* 16. beshrewed, *cursed.* 22. scorne, *insult.* 24. *goose.*

Your thighes misgrowen, youre shankes mich worse,   25
Whoso beholde youre knees so croked,
As ich of hem bad oder Christes curse,
So go they outward; youre hammes ben hoked;
Such a peire chaumbes I never on loked;
So ungoodly youre heles ye lifte,   30
And youre feet ben croked, with evil thrifte.

Who might have the love of so swete a wight
She might be right glad that ever was she born.
She that onis wold in a dark night
Renne for your love, till she had caught a thorn,   35
I wolde her no more harme but hanged on the morn,
That hath two good eyen and ichese here suche a make
Or onis wold lift up here hole for youre sake!

    Youre swete love with blody nailes,
    Whiche fedeth mo lice than quailes.   40

25. misgrowen, *misshapen;* shankes, *lower legs.* 27. *As if each of them swore at the other.* 28. *your legs are bandy.* 29. *pair of buttocks* (? *N.E.D. s.v. Jamb, 3*), *legs* (?). 31. thrifte, *luck.* 32. wight, *person.* 34, 38. onis, *once.* 35. (?). 37. eyen, *eyes;* ichese, *chose;* make, *mate;* and 38. here, *her.* 40. mo, *more.*

141

Go! heart, hurt with adversity

Go! hert, hurt with adversite,   15c.
And let my lady thy wondis see,
And say hir this, as I say thee,
'Farwell! my joy, and welcom paine,
Till I see my lady againe.'

2. *wounds.*

142

The one I love is gone away

My lefe is faren in a lond—   about 1500
Alas! why is she so?
And I am so sore bound
I may nat com her to.
She hath my hert in hold,   5
Where-ever she ride or go,
With trew love a thousandfold.

1. *The one I love is gone away.* 5. in hold, *imprisoned.*

143

WILLIAM DUNBAR

Sweet rose of virtue

Sweit rois of vertew and of gentilnes,   later 15c.,
Delitsum lilye of everye lustines,   earlier 16c.
Richest in bontye and in bewtye cleir,
And everye vertew that is held most deir—
Except, onlye, that ye ar mercyles.   5

Into your garthe, this day, I did persew:
Thair saw I flowres that freshe wer of hew;
Baith white and reid moist lusty wer to seine,
And halsum herbes upone stalkes grene—
Yit leif nor flowr find could I nane of rew.   10

1, 4. vertew, *virtue, power;* and 12. gentil(nes), *mild(ness), good-breeding.* 2. everye lustines, *all youthful vigour.* 3. bontye, *bounty, goodness;* cleir, *bright, distinguished.* 4. held most, *not in MS.* 6. garthe, *garden;* persew, *go.* 8. Baith, *Both;* lusty, *pleasant, joyful;* seine, *see.* 9. halsum, *wholesome;* and 12. herbe(s), *plant(s), herb(s).*

I dout that Merche with his caild blastes keine
Hes slane this gentill herbe that I of mene,
Whois petewous deithe dois to my hart sic pane
That I wald mak to plant his rute agane,
So confortand his leves unto me bene.   15

11. dout, *fear;* caild, *cold.* 12. mene, *complain,* 13. sic, *such.* 14. mak, *compose poetry.*
15. confortand, *comforting.*

144

WILLIAM DUNBAR

A hymn to Mary

Haile! sterne superne. Haile! in eterne,   later 15c.,
In Godis sicht to shine.   earlier 16c.
Lucerne in derne for to discerne
Be glory and grace divine.
Hodiern, modern, sempitern,   5
Angelicall regine,
Our tern inferne for to dispern,
Helpe! rialest rosine.
Ave! Maria, gracia plena,
Haile! freshe floure feminine,   10
Yerne us, guberne, virgin matern,
Of reuth baith rute and rine.
. . .
Emprice of pris, imperatrice,
Bricht, polist, precious stane,
Victrice of vice, hie genetrice   15

1, 22. sterne, *star;* superne, *on high;* eterne, *eternity.* 3. Lucerne, *Lamp;* derne, *darkness;* discerne, *perceive.* 4. Be, *by.* 5. Hodiern, *Of today;* modern, *now existing;* sempitern, *everlasting.* 6. regine, *queen.* 7. tern, *vicissitude;* inferne, *below;* dispern, *drive away.* 8, 29. rial(est), *(most) royal;* rosine, *rose.* 9, etc. Hail! *Mary, full of grace.* 11. Yerne, *Desire;* guberne, *govern;* matern, *maternal.* 12. reuth, *pity;* baith, *both;* rute, *root;* rine, *rind.* 12, 13. *Four stanzas omitted.* 13. Emprice, *Sovereign;* of pris, *excellent;* imperatrice, *empress.* 14. polist, *polished.* 15. Victrice, *(Female) conqueror;* and 27. hie, *high;* genetrice, *mother.*

Of Jesu, Lord soveraine,
Our wis pavis fra enemis
Agane the Feindis traine,
Oratrice, mediatrice, salvatrice,
To God gret suffragane.   20
Ave! Maria, gracia plena,
Haile! sterne meridiane,
Spice, flowr delice of paradise,
That baire the glorius graine.

Imperiall wall, place palestrall   25
Of peirless pulcritude,
Triumphale hall, hie trone regall
Of Godis celsitude,
Hospitall riall, the Lord of all
Thy closet did include,   30
Bricht ball crystall, ros virginall,
Fulfillit of angel fude.
Ave! Maria, gracia plena,
Thy birth has, with his blude,
Fra fall mortall, originall,   35
Us raunsound on the Rude.

17. pavis, *shield.* 19. Oratrice, (*Female*) *petitioner.* 20. suffragane. *co-adjutor.* 22. meridiane, *mid-day.* 23. flowr delice = *fleur-de-lis,* (*heraldic*) *lily.* 24. graine, *seed (i.e. Jesus).* 25. palestrall, *palatial.* 27. trone, *throne.* 28. celsitude, *majesty.* 29. *Royal lodging.* 30. closet, *chamber.* 32. *Filled full with angels' food (i.e. Jesus).* 34. birth, *child.*

145

WILLIAM DUNBAR

The man of valour to his fair lady

In secreit place, this hindir nicht,   later 15c.,
I hard ane beirne say till ane bricht,   earlier 16c.
'My huny, my hart, my hoip, my heill,
I have bene lang your luifar leill,

1. hindir, *last.* 2. *I heard a man (of valour) say to a fair lady.* 3. heill, *health.* 4. *I have long been your loyal lover.*

And can of you get confort nane.   5
How lang will ye with danger deill?
Ye brek my hart, my bony ane.'

His bony beird was kemmit and croppit,
Bot all with cale it was bedroppit,
And he wes townishe, peirt and gukit.   10
He clappit fast, he kist and chukkit,
As with the glaikis he were ovirgane,
Yit be his feirris he wald have fukkit!
Ye brek my hart, my bony ane.

Quod he, 'My hairt, sweit as the hunye,   15
Sen that I borne wes of my minnye
I nevir wowit weycht bot you.
My wambe is of your lufe sa fow
That as ane gaist I glour and grane,
I trimble sa, ye will not trow—   20
Ye brek my hart my bony ane.'

'Tehe!' quod sho, and gaif ane gawfe,
'Be still my tuchan and my calfe,
My new spanit howffing fra the sowk,
And all the blithnes of my bowk.   25
My sweit swanking, saif you allane,
Na leid I luiffit all this owk,
Full leif is me your graceles gane.'

Quod he, 'My claver and my curldodie,
My huny soppis, my sweit possodie,   30
Be not oure-bosteous to your Billie,

---

6. danger, *aloofness, power of woman's superior detachment;* deill, *act, have to do with.*
8. kemmit, *combed.* 9. cale, *broth.* 10. *And he was of town (as distinct from court), lively
and foolish.* 11. clappit, *caressed.* 12. *As if he were overcome by sexual desire.* 13. be his
feirris, *by his conduct.* 16. Sen that, *Since;* minnye, *mother.* 17. weycht, *creature.* 18.
fow, *full.* 19. gaist, *ghost;* glour, *stare;* grane, *groan.* 20. trow, *believe.* 22. gawfe,
guffaw. 23. tuchan, *stuffed calf's skin (to encourage cow to give milk).* 24. *My new-weaned
little suckling lout.* 25. bowk, *body.* 26. swanking, *fine fellow.* 27. *I loved no man all
week.* 28. *Most dear to me is your ugly face.* 29. *My clover and my plantain.* 30. *My
honey drink, my sweet sheep's head broth.* 31. oure-bosteous, *over-rough.*

Be warme-hairtit and not ill-willie.
Your heilis, whit as whalis bane,
Garris riis on loft my whillylillie—
Ye brek my hart my bony ane.   35

. . .

He gaiff to hir ane apill rubye.
Quod sho, 'Gramercye, my sweit cowhubye!'
And thay tway to ane play began
Whilk men dois call 'the dery dan,'
Whill that thair mirthis met baithe in ane.   40
'Wo! is me,' quod sho, 'whair will ye, man?
Best now I luif that graceles gane.'

32. ill-willie, *so Advocates MS. but this MS.* ewill wille. 33. heilis, *neck* (?), *heels* (?). 34. Garris riis, *Makes rise;* whillylillie, *penis: so Advocates MS. but this MS.* quhillelille. 35, 36. *Three stanzas omitted.* 37. cowhubye, *weak character.* 39. Whilk, *Which.* 40. mirthis, *pleasures;* baithe, *both.*

146

WILLIAM DUNBAR

The fear of death confounds me

I that in heill wes, and gladnes,   later 15c.,
Am trublit now with gret seiknes,   earlier 16c.
And feblit with infermite.
Timor mortis conturbat me.

Our plesance heir is all vaneglory;   5
This fals warld is bot transitory;
The flesh is brukle the Fend is sle.
Timor mortis conturbat me.

The stait of man dois change and vary,
Now sound, now seik, now blith, now sary,   10
Now dansand mery, now like to dee.
Timor mortis conturbat me.

1. heill, *health.* 4. *The fear of death confounds me.* 5. plesance, *pleasure;* etc. heir, *here (in this world).* 7. brukle, *frail;* sle, *wily.* 11. dee, *die.*

No stait in erd heir standis sickir:
As with the wind wavis the wickir,
Wavis this warldis vanite.   15
Timor mortis conturbat me.

On to the ded gois all estatis,
Princis, prelotis, and potestatis,
Baith riche and pur of all degre.
Timor mortis conturbat me.   20

He takis the knightis into feild,
Anarmit under helme and sheild:
Victour he is at all melle.
Timor mortis conturbat me.

That strang, unmerciful tyrand   25
Tak one the moderis breist sowkand
The bab, full of benignite.
Timor mortis conturbat me.

He takis the campion in the stour,
The capitane closit in the tour,   30
The lady in bour, full of bewte,
Timor mortis conturbat me.

He sparis no lord for his piscence,
Na clerk for his intelligence:
His awful strak may no man fle.   35
Timor mortis conturbat me.

Art magicianis and astrologgis,
Rethoris, logicianis and theologgis,
Thame helpis no conclusionis sle.
Timor mortis conturbat me.   40

In medicine the most practicianis,
Lechis, surrigianis and physicianis,

---

13. erd, *earth;* sickir, *secure.* 14. wickir, *branch.* 17, etc. ded(e), *death.* 18. potestatis, *powers.* 19. Baith, *Both;* pur, *poor.* 21. into, *in.* 22. Anarmit, *Armed.* 23. at all melle, *in every fight.* 26. Tak one, *Takes on;* sowkand, *sucking.* 27. benignite, *gentleness.* 29. campion, *champion;* stour, *conflict.* 33. piscence, *power.* 34. clerk, *scholar.* 35. strak, *stroke.* 37. *Those practising the art of magic and astrologers.* 38. Rethoris, *Rhetoricians.* 39. *No subtle conclusions can help them.* 41. most, *greatest.* 42. *Leeches, surgeons.*

Thameself fra ded may not supple.
Timor mortis conturbat me.

I se that makaris amang the laif   45
Playis heir ther pageant, syne gois to graif:
Sparit is nought ther faculte.
Timor mortis conturbat me.

He has done petuously devour
The noble Chaucer, of makaris flour,   50
The Monk of Bery and Gower all thre.
Timor mortis conturbat me.
. . .

In Dunfermeline he has done roune
With Maister Robert Henrisoun;
Sir Johne the Ros enbrast has he.   55
Timor mortis conturbat me.

And he has now tane last of aw
Gud, gentil Stobo and Quintyne Shaw,
Of wham all wichtis has pete.
Timor mortis conturbat me.   60

Gud Maister Walter Kennedy
In point of dede lyis veraly:
Gret reuth it wer that so suld be.
Timor mortis conturbat me.

Sen he has all my brether tane,   65
He will nought lat me lif alane:
On forse I man his nixt pray be.
Timor mortis conturbat me.

Sen for the ded remeid is none,
Best is that we for dede dispone,   70
Eftir our ded, that lif may we.
Timor mortis conturbat me.

---

43. supple, *deliver.* 45, 50. makaris, *poets;* laif, *rest.* 46. syne . . . graif, *then go to the grave.* 47. faculte, *profession, art.* 49. *Tragically, he has devoured.* 51. Monk of Bery, *John Lydgate;* Gower, *contemporary of Chaucer's and writer of long poems in Latin, French and English.* 52–3. *Seven stanzas omitted lamenting dead Scottish poets.* 53. done roune, *talked.* 54. Henrisoun, *Robert Henryson.* 55–61. *Scottish poets.* 55. enbrast, *embraced.* 58. gentil, *gentle, noble.* 59. wichtis, *people;* pete, *pity.* 63. reuth, *pity.* 65, 69. Sen, *Since.* 67. *Of necessity I must be his next prey.* 69. remeid, *remedy.* 70. dispone, *make ready.*

147

WILLIAM DUNBAR

A hymn of the Resurrection

Done is a battell on the dragon blak!   later 15c.,
Our campioun, Christ, confoundit hes his force;   earlier 16c.
The yettis of hell ar brokin with a crak;
The signe triumphall rasit is of the Croce;
The divillis trimmillis with hiddous voce;   5
The saulis ar borrowit and to the blis can go:
Christ with his blud our ransonis dois indoce.
Surrexit Dominus de sepulchro.

Dungin is the deidly dragon, Lucifer,
The crewall serpent with the mortall stang,   10
The auld, kene tegir with his teith on char,
Whilk in a wait hes line for us so lang,
Thinking to grip us in his clows strang:
The mercifull Lord wald nocht that it wer so—
He maid him for to felye of that fang.   15
Surrexit Dominus de sepulchro.

He for our saik that sufferit to be slane,
And lik a lamb in sacrifice wes dicht,
Is lik a lione rissin up agane,
And as gyane raxit him on hicht.   20
Sprungin is Aurora radius and bricht;
On loft is gone the glorius Appollo;
The blisfull day depairtit fro the nicht.
Surrexit Dominus de sepulchro.

2. campioun, *champion.* 3. yettis, *gates.* 5. divillis, *devils;* trimmillis, *tremble; read
with stresses as shown, eliding the two unstressed syllables.* 6. Saulis, *souls;* borrowit,
ransomed; read with stresses as shown and on and; *elide unstressed syllables.* 7. indoce,
endorse. 8. *The Lord has risen from the tomb.* 9. Dungin, *Overcome.* 10. stang, *sting.* 11.
auld, *old;* tegir, *tiger;* on char, *open.* 12. Whilk, *Which.* 15. *He caused him to have no
success in that capture.* 18. dicht, *used.* 20. gyane, *giant;* raxit, *stretches.* 20, 25. on hicht,
up(wards). 21. radius, *radiant.* 23. depairtit, *departed* (?) *separated* (?).

The grit victour agane is rissin on hicht,   25
That for our querrell to the deth wes woundit;
The sone that wox all paill now shinis bricht,
And, dirknes clerit, our faith is now refoundit;
The knell of mercy fra the Hevin is soundit;
The Christin ar deliverit of thair wo;   30
The Jowis and thair errour ar confoundit.
Surrexit Dominus de sepulchro.

The fo is chasit, the battell is done ceis;
The presone brokin, the jevellouris fleit and flemit;
The weir is gon, confermit is the peis;   35
The fetteris lowsit and the dungeoun temit;
The ransoun maid, the presoneris redemit;
The feild is win, ourcumin is the fo,
Dispulit of the tresur that he yemit.
Surrexit Dominus de sepulchro.   40

25. grit, *great.* 26. querrell, *cause.* 27. wox, *grew.* 31. Jowis, *Jews.* 33. done ceis, *brought to an end.* 34. *The prison broken open, the gaolers scared and driven away.* 35. weir, *war.* 36. temit, *emptied.* 39. yemit, *guarded.*

148

Most sovereign lady

Most soveren lady, comfort of care,   about 1500
A next in my hert, most in my minde,
Right welth and cause of my welefare,
Gentle trulove, special and kinde,
Eey pinacle, pight with stidfasteness,   5
Right tristy, and truth of my salace,
Ever well-springinge stillatorye of sweteness,
Tresore full dere, gronded with grace.

2. A, *Always;* next, *nearest.* 5. Eey, *High;* pight, *fixed fast.* 6. tristy, *trustful, trustworthy;* truth, *promise* (?); salace, *consolation.* 7. stillatorye, *still* (noun). 8. dere, *Robbins reads* bare; gronded with, *founded in.*

149

Wishing my death

Alone walking,   about 1500
In thought pleining
And sore sighing,
All desolate,
Me remembring   5
Of my living,
My deth wishing
Bothe erly and late.

Infortunate
Is so my fate   10
That—wote ye whate?—
Oute of mesure
My life I hate.
Thus desperate
In suche pore estate   15
Do I endure.

Of other cure
Am I nat sure.
Thus to endure
Is hard certain.   20
Suche is my ure
I you ensure:
What creature
May have more pain?

My trouth so plein   25
Is take in vein,
And gret disdein
In remembraunce.

2. *complaining.* 11. *Do you know what?* 21. ure, *custom.* 25. *My fidelity so manifest* (?) *complete* (?).

Yet I full feine
Wold me compleine   30
Me to absteine
From this penaunce.

But in substaunce
Noon allegeaunce
Of my grevaunce   35
Can I nat finde.
Right so my chaunce
With displesaunce
Doth me avaunce—
And thus an ende.   40

31-2. *To keep myself from this suffering.* 34. *alleviation.* 37. chaunce, *fate.* 38. *displeasure.*

150

Christ calls man home

Com home againe!   about 1500
Com home againe!
Mine owene swet hart, com home againe!
Ye are gone astray
Out of youer way,   5
Therefore, com home againe!

Mankend I cale
Which lyeth in thrale:
For love I mad thee fre.
To pay the det,   10
The prise was gret,
From hell that I ransomed thee.

8. thrale, *MS.* frale.

My blod so red
For thee was shed,
The prise it is not smale.   15
Remembre welle
What I thee tell,
And com whan I thee cale.

   . . .

Therefore refreine
And torne againe   20
And leve thine owene intent,
The which it is
Contrare, iwis,
Unto my commaundment.

Thou standest in dout   25
And sekest about
Where that thou mayst me se:
Idoules be set,
Mony for to get,
Which is made of stone and tre.   30

I am no stoke,
Nor no paincted bloke,
Nor mad by no mannes hand:
Bot I am he
That shall los thee   35
From Satan the Phinnes bonde.

18, 19. *Two stanzas omitted, one incomplete.* 22–3. *Which is, indeed, contrary.* 28–30.
Idols, made of stone and wood, are placed to get money. 31. *log.* 32. *painted block.* 33. *made.*
35. *loose.* 36. *Fiend's.*

151

She saw me in church

Go! little bill, and command me hertely   about 1500
Unto her that I call my trulof and lady,
By this same tru tokeninge,
That sho see me in a kirk on a Friday in a morning,
With a sper-hawk on my hand,   5
And my mone did by her stand,
And an old womon sete her by,
That little cold of curtesy;
And oft on her sho did smile
To loke on me for a while.   10
And yet by this, another token,
To the kirk she comme with a gentilwomon:
Even behind the kirk dore
Thay kneled bothe on the flore,
And fast thay did pitter-patter—   15
I hope thay said matins togeder!
Yet ones or twyes, at the lest,
Sho did on me her ee kest,
Then went I forthe prevely
And hailsed on thaym curtesly.   20
By alle the tokens, truly,
Command me to her hertely!

1. bill, *letter;* and 22, command, *commend.* 4. sho see, *she saw.* 5. sper-hawk, *sparrow-hawk.* 6. mone, *companion* (?) 8. *Who did not know much of how the 'well-bred' behave (particularly as between the sexes).* 9. her, *(the old woman).* 13. Even, *Right.* 18. *cast her eye.* 20. *greeted them courteously (see l. 8).*

152

STEPHEN HAWES

A pair of wings

See   about 1500
Me   (kinde
Be
Againe
My paine   (in minde   5
Retaine
My swete bloode
On the Roode   (my brother
Dide thee good
My face right redde   10
Mine armes spredde   (thinke none other
My woundes bledde
Beholde thou my side
Wounded so right wide   (all for thine owne sake
Bledinge sore that tide   15
Thus for thee I smerted
Why arte thou harde-herted   (and thy sweringe aslake
Be by me converted
Tere me now no more
My woundes are sore   (and come to my grace   20
Leve sweringe therfore
I am redy
To graunte mercy   (for thy trespace
To thee truely
Come now nere   25
My frende dere   (before me
And appere
I so
In wo   (see see
Dide go   30
I
Crye   (thee
Hy

15. tide, *time.* 17. aslake, *abate.* 19. tere, *tear.* 33. Hy, *hasten.*

153

Too much sex

Burgeis, thou haste so blowen atte the cole,   about
That alle thy rode is from thine face agoon,   1500
And haste do so many shotte and istoole,
That fleesh upon thy carkeis is there noon:
There is nought lefte but empty skinne and bone.   5
Thou were a trewe swinkere, atte the fulle,
But nowe thy chaumbre toukes been, echon,
Peesed and fleedde, and of her laboure dulle.

Thy warderer, that was wonte for to be
Mighty and sadde and grene in his laboure,   10
So wery is of superfluite
He wolle no more be none ratoure.
Himselfe he is thy verrey accusoure,
For so sayne they that knowe his impotence
As welle as ye, my maister reveloure.   15
Nowe been ye apte to lye in continence!

Thy pilers of thine body in apparence
Been sufficiaunt to utwarde juggement,
But they been feint and weike in existence,
For that her stuffe iwastede is and spente.   20
And yette thou haste a desirous talente
For to fullefille that that wol not be.
For love of God, be nat impaciente,
But what that I shalle say, nowe herken me.

1. *Citizen, you have so fanned the flames of passion.* 2. rode, *ruddy colour.* 3. shotte, MS. doo shotte, *issue;* istoole, *discharge of faeces.* 6. swinkere, *labourer (at sex).* 7. *But your bed-room thrusting swords are, each one.* 8. Peesed, *Stilled;* fleedde, *fled (?); etc.,* her, *their.* 9. warderer, *truncheon.* 10. sadde, *strong;* grene, *vital.* 12. ratoure, *lecher.* 17. pilers, *testicles (?).* 19. existence, *fact.* 21. talente, *appetite. Four stanzas omitted at end commending patience since it is previous excess that has had these unpleasant physical results.*

154

I must go walk the wood

I must go walke the woed so wild   about 1500
And wander here and there
In dred and dedly fere,
For where I trusted I am begild,
And all for one.   5

Thus am I banished from my blis
By craft and false pretens,
Fautless, without offens,
As of return no certen is,
And all for fer of one.   10

My bed shall be under the grenwod tree,
A tuft of brakes under my hed,
As one from joyc were fled.
Thus from my lif day by day I flee,
And all for one.   15

The ronning stremes shall be my drinke,
Acorns shall be my fode:
Nothing may do me good,
But when of your bewty I do think,
And all for love of one.   20

9. *certainty.* 14. lif, *beloved, source of my life.* 19. of, *not in MS.* 20. *Line difficult to read in photostat of MS.*

155

Jesu! send us peace

Jesu! for thy mercy endelesse,   about 1500
Save thy pepill and sende us pesse.

Jesu! for thy wondes fife,
Save fro sheding Christain blode;
Sese alle grete trobill of malice and strife,   5
And of oure neybores sende us tidinges gode.

Blessed Jesu!
Blessed Jesu!

156

The lily-white rose

This day day dawes,   about 1500
This gentil day day dawes,
This gentil day dawes,
And I must home gone.
This gentil day dawes,   5
This day day dawes,
This gentil day dawes,
And we must home gone.

In a glorius garden grene
Sawe I sitting a comly quene   10
Among the floures that fresh bene.

1, etc. dawes, *dawns.*

She gaderd a floure and set betwene.
The lily-whighte rose me thought I sawe,
The lily-whighte rose me thought I sawe,
And ever she sang: 15

In that garden be floures of hewe,
The gelofir gent that she well knewe;
The floure-de-luce she did on rewe,
And said, 'The white rose is most trewe
This garden to rule by rightwis lawe.'   20
The lily-whighte rose me thought I sawe,
And ever she sang:

12. set, *sat;* betwene, *in the midst.* 16. hewe, *colour.* 17. gelofir, *gillyflower;* gent, *pretty.* 18. floure-de-luce, *fleur-de-lis;* did on rewe, *had pity on.* 20. rightwis, *righteous, rightful.*

157

THOMAS PHILLIPPS (?)

I love a flower

'I love, I love, and whom love ye?'   about 1500
'I love a flowre of fresh beaute.'
'I love another as well as ye.'
'Than shall be proved here, anon,
If we three can agre in on.'   5

'I love a flowre of swete odour.'
'Magerome gentil, or lavendour?
Columbine, goldes of swete flavour?'
'Nay! nay! let be:
Is non of them   10
That liketh me.'

4, 45. Than, *Then.* 5, 46. in on, *together.* 8. goldes, *marigolds.* 11, etc. liketh, *pleases.*

'There is a flowre whereso he be,
And shall not yet be named for me.'
'Primeros, violet or fresh daisy?'
'He pass them all   15
In his degree,
That best liketh me.'

'On that I love most enterly.'
'Gelofyr gentil, or rosemary?
Camamill, borage or savery?'   20
'Nay! certenly,
Here is not he
That pleseth me.'

'I chese a floure, freshest of face.'
'What is his name that thou chosen has?   25
The rose I suppose?—thine hart unbrace!'
'That same is he,
In hart so fre,
That best liketh me.'

'The rose it is a ryall flour.'   30
'The red or the white?—shewe his colour!'
'Both be full swete and of like savour:
All on they be
That day to se,
It liketh well me.'   35

'I love the rose, both red and white.'
'Is that your pure perfite appetite?'
'To here talke of them is my delite.'
'Joyed may we be
Oure prince to se,   40
And roses thre.

  'Nowe have we loved, and love will we,
  This faire, fresh floure, full of beaute.'
  'Most worthy it is, as thinketh me.'
  'Than may be proved here, anon,   45
  That we three be agrede in on.'

13. for me, *so far as I am concerned.* 16. degree, *manner.* 18. On, *One.* 19. Gelofyr,
Gillyflower. 24. chese, *choose.* 26. *open your heart.* 28. fre, *noble, generous.* 33. *The same
thing they are.*

158

A friar complains

Alas! what shul we freres do,   about 1500
Now lewed men cun Holy Writ?
Alle aboute where I go
They aposen me of it.

Then wondreth me that it is so,   5
How lewed men cun alle wit.
Sertely, we be undo
But if we mo amende it.

I trowe the devil brought it aboute,
To write the Gospel in Englishe,   10
For lewed men ben nowe so stout
That they yeven us neither fleshe ne fishe.

When I come into a shope
For to say, 'In principio,'
They bidenc me, 'Go forth, lewed "Pope",'   15
And worche and win my silver so.

If I say it longeth not
For prestes to worche whether they go,
They leggen for them Holy Writ,
And seyn that Seint Polle did so.   20

Than they loken on my nabite
And seyn, 'Forsothe, withouten othes,
Whether it be russet, black or white,
It is worthe alle oure weringe clothes!'

I seye I bidde not for me   25
Bot for them that have none:

2, etc. lewed, *lay;* cun, *know.* 4. *They confront me with hard questions about it.* 5.
wondreth me, *I wonder.* 6. cun . . . wit, *can know all.* 9. trowe, *believe.* 12. yeven, *give.*
15. lewed, *ignorant, wicked.* 16, 18. worche, *work.* 17. *If I say it is not right.* 18.
whether, *whithersoever.* 19. leggen, *cite.* 21. nabite, *habit.* 24. oure weringe clothes,
clothes we wear. 25. bidde, *beg, not in MS.*

They seyn, 'Thou havest to or thre!
Yeven them that nedeth therof one.'

Thus oure disceites bene aspiede,
In this maner, and many moo,   30
Fewe men bedden us abide,
But hey fast, that we were go.

If it go forthe in this maner
It wole doen us miche gile.
Men shul finde unnethe a frere   35
In Englonde within a while.

28. Yeven, *Give (to)*. 29. bene, *are*. 30. moo, *more*. 31–2. *Few men bid us stay but (rather) hurry up and be off.* 34. *It will cause us great harm (be treacherous to us) (?)*. 35. unnethe a, *scarcely one*.

159

JOHN SKELTON

Unfriendly Fortune

Go! piteous hart, rased with dedly wo,   later 15c.,
Persed with pain, bleding with wondes smart,   earlier 16c.
Bewaile thy fortune with vaines wan and blo.
O! Fortune, unfrendly, Fortune, unkinde thou art!
To be so cruel and so overthwart,   5
To suffer me so carefull to endure,
That wher I love best I dare not discure.

One ther is, and ever one shall be,
For whose sake my hart is sore diseased:
For whose love, welcom! disease to me—   10
I am content so all partis be pleased.
Yet, and God wold, I wold my paine were eased:
But Fortune enforseth me so carefully to endure,
That where I love best I dare not discure.

1. rased, *gashed*. 2. wondes smart, *grievous wounds*. 3. vaines, *veins*; wan and blo, *black and blue*. 5. overthwart, *perverse*. 6, 13. carefull(y), *full of sorrow*. 7. discure, *reveal (love)*. 9, 10. disease(d), *trouble(d)*. 12. and, *if*.

160

JOHN SKELTON

The sleeper hood-winked

With, 'Lullay! lullay!' like a childe   later 15c.,
Thou slepest too long, thou art begilde!   earlier 16c.

'My darling dere, my daisy floure,
Let me', quod he, 'ly in your lap.'
'Ly still', quod she, 'my paramoure,   5
Ly still, hardely, and take a nap.'
His hed was hevy, such was his hap!
All drowsy, dreming, drownd in slepe,
That of his love he toke no kepe.

With, 'Ba! ba! ba!' and, 'bas! bas! bas!'   10
She cherished him both cheke and chin,
That he wist never where he was,
He had forgoten all dedely sin.
He wanted wit her love to win!
He trusted her payment and lost all his pray,   15
She left him sleping and stale away.

The rivers rowth, the waters wan,
She spared not to wete her fete.
She waded over, she found a man
That halsed her hartely and kist her swete.   20
Thus after her cold she cought a hete!
'My lefe,' she said, 'rowteth in his bed.
Iwis, he hath an hevy hed!'

4. quod, *said.* 5. paramoure, *sweetheart.* 6. hardely, *by all means.* 7. hap, *luck.* 9. kepe, *notice.* 12. wist, *knew.* 14. wanted, *lacked.* 15. pray, *prey.* 17. rowth, *rough;* wan, *dark.* 20. halsed, *greeted, embraced.* 22. lefe, *beloved;* rowteth, *snores.* 23, 30. Iwis, *Indeed.*

What dremest thou, drunchard, drowsy pate,
Thy lust and liking is from thee gone!   25
Thou blinkerd blowboll, thou wakest too late!
Behold! thou lyeste, luggard, alone.
Well may thou sigh, well may thou grone,
To dele with her so cowardly.
Iwis, powle-hachet, she blered thine I!   30

25. lust, *pleasure.* 26. blinkerd, '*short-sighted*'; blowboll, (*blow-bowl*), *heavy drinker.*
27. luggard, *sluggard.* 30. *Indeed, pole-axe* (?), *she hoodwinked you.*

161

JOHN SKELTON

To Mistress Margaret Tilney

I you assure,   earlier 16c.
Full well I know
My besy cure
To you I owe,
Humbly and low   5
Commendinge me
To youre bounte.
    As Machareus,
Faire Canace,
So I, iwis,   10
Endevoure me
Your name to se
It be enrolde
Written with golde.
    Phedra ye may   15
Well represent,
Intentive, ay,
And diligent,
No time mispent.
Wherfore delight   20

3. diligent *duty.* 10. So I, *indeed.* 17. Assiduous *always.*

I have to write
  Of Margarite,
Perle orient,
Lode sterre of light.
Moche relucent,   25
Madame, regent
I may you call
Of vertuows all.

23. *Precious pearl.* 24. Lode, *editions* Lede; lode sterre, *guiding star, shining example.*
25. *Much refulgent.* 28. *Of all virtues.*

162

Rise with the Lamb of Innocence

Thou that in prayeres hes bene lent,   16c.
In prayeres and in abstinence,
For thy trespasses penitent,
Confessed and cleine of all offence,
Ris with the Lambe of Innocence,   5
To den that did the dragoun drif.
This day with hie magnificence
The Lord is rissen fra deth to life.

The sign triumpant of the Croce
Shew to confound the Feindes feid.   10
And when he feihtes with maist force
With confessioun hald down his heid.
Ris with thy ransomer fra dede
And thee of all thy sinnes shrive:
Thou rew apoun his woundes reid,   15
That for thee deid and rais on life.

1. lent, *devoted.* 6. *Who drove (Satan) the dragon to his den (in Hell).* 10. feid,
hostility. 11. feihtes, *fights.* 13. dede, *death.* 14. shrive, *absolve.* 15. *Have pity on his red
wounds.*

And thou that art in hert so dour,
That noght for his gret passioun growes,
Behald thy meik, sweit Salviour,
Thee to embrace how that he bowes;   20
See how he mertyred wes with Jowes,
And how he stud for thee in strif.
Hes he thy luve, all he allowes,
That for thee deid and rais on life.

And thou that art in errour dirked,   25
Follow thy Lord—the way is plane—
And of his futsteppes be noght irked,
That tuke thy gidschip with sic pane.
When thou goes wrang, returne agane,
And with thy ransomer revive: 30
Lang in sin thou ly not plane,
Bot ris with him fra ded to life.

O! man, that wes in sin despared,
Tak now gude hope and have contritioun,
For thou, that rebel wes declared,   35
Hes of thy realmes restitutioun.
Now blinded is thy inhibitioun
With the blud of Christes woundes five,
And seilled agane is thy remissioun,
To ris with him fra ded to life.   40

17. dour, *hard, stubborn.* 18. *(You) who feel no horror at his great suffering.* 21.
with, *by.* 22. stud, *stood.* 23. *If he has your love.* 25. dirked, *made blind, in the dark.* 27.
And be not dismayed at (following in) his footsteps. 28. gidschip, *guidance;* sic, *such;*
pane, *MS.* pyne. 30. revive, *Advocates MS.* revife, *this MS.* rewis. 31. *(do)* thou;
plane, *entirely (?) openly (?).* 33. despared, *in despair.* 35. thou, *not in MS.* 37. blinded,
hidden, covered; inhibitioun, *(from entering Heaven).* 39. seilled, *sealed.*

163

Distant as the Duchess of Savoy

O! mestress, why   earlier 16c.
Outecaste am I
All utterly
From your pleasaunce?
Sithe ye and I   5
Or this, truly,
Familiarly
Have had pastaunce.

And, lovingly,
Ye wolde apply   10
Thy company
To my comforte:
But now, truly,
Unlovingly,
Ye do deny   15
Me to resorte.

And me to see
As strange ye be
As thowe that ye
Shuld nowe deny,   20
Or else possess
That nobleness
To be Dochess
Of grete Savoy.

But sithe that ye   25
So strange will be
As toward me,
And will not medill,

---

4. *From your pleasure.* 5, 25. sithe, *since.* 6. Or, *before.* 8. *Have had diversion.* 11. Thy, *MS.* My. 18, 26. strange, *distant.* 28. *And will not meddle, have sexual intercourse.*

I truste, percase,
To finde some grace   30
To have free chaise,
And spede as well.

29. percase, *as may chance.* 31. chaise, *hunting (i.e. enjoyment of another woman).*

164

The Corpus Christi carol

Lully, lulley, lully, lulley,   earlier 16c.
The fawcon hath born my mak away.

He bare him up, he bare him down,
He bare him into an orchard brown.

In that orchard ther was an hall,   5
That was hanged with purpill and pall.

And in that hall ther was a bed:
It was hanged with gold so red.

And in that bed ther lythe a knight,
His woundes bleding day and night.   10

By that bedes side ther kneleth a may,
And she wepeth both night and day.

And by that bedes side ther stondeth a ston,
'Corpus Christi' wreten theron.

2. fawcon, *falcon;* mak, *mate.* 6. purpill and pall, *rich purple cloth.* 11. may, *maiden.*
14. *'The Body of Christ'.*

165

O! mistress mine

O! maistres mine, till you I me commend,   earlier
Alhaill my hairt sen that ye haif in cure,   16c.
For, but your grace, my life is neir the end.
Now lat me nocht in danger me endure.
Of liif, lik luve, suppois I be sure,   5
Whay wat na God may me sum succur send?
Than for your luve why wald ye I forfure?
O! maistres mine, till you I me commend.

The wintir nicht ane hour I may nocht sleip,
For thocht of you bot tumland to and fro.   10
Methink ye ar into my armis, sweit,
And, when I walkin, ye ar so far me fro!
Allace! allace! than walkinnis my wo,
Than wary I the time that I you kend.
War nocht gud hoip, my hairt wald birst in two!   15
O! maistres mine, till you I me commend.

Sen ye ar ane that hes my hairt, alhaill,
Without fenyeing I may it nocht genstand:
Ye ar the bontye, bliss of all my baill,
Baith life and deth standis into your hand.   20
Sen that I am sair bundin in your band,
That nicht or day I wait nocht whair to wend,
Lat me anis say that I your freindship fand—
O! maistres mine, till you I me commend.

1, etc. till, to. 2, 17. Alhaill, entirely; etc. sen (that), since; cure, care. 3. but, without. 4, 23. lat, let. 5–6. Suppose I am sure of my life (only as much) as of love, who knows (whether) God may not. . . . 7, etc. Than, Then; forfure, perish. 12, 13. walkin(nis), waken(s). 14. wary, curse; kend, came to know. 15. War, Were (there). 18. genstand, resist. 19. bontye, virtue; baill, ill. 20. into, in; and 21. MS. hand, l. 21, band, l. 20; band, bond (of love). 22. wait, know. 23. anis, once; fand, found.

166

The Passion of Jesus

Compatience perses, reuth and marcy stoundes 16c.
In middis my hert, and thirles throw the vanes.
Thy deid, Jesu, thy petuous, cruel woundes,
Thy grim passion, gret tormentes, grevous panes,
Ingraved sadlye in my spreit remanes.   5
Sen me of nought thou hes bought with thy blude,
My ene, for doloure, woful teres ranes,
When that I see thee haled on the Rude.

In Simon lepros hous of Bathany
Thy feit anointed Mary Magdalen   10
With precius balme and nardus-spikardy.
Sho passed fra time, hir sinnes wer forgeven.
Thy fleshe and blude in breid and wine betwen
Gaif thy disciples, and lawlye woshe thair feit.
Thy manheid dred thy passioun to sustene,   15
When that thou prayed on Monte Oliveit.

To gide the Jowes come Judas Scariot
And kist thee Christ—all the disciples fled.
To ane wraiched man, Caiphas, and Pilot,
Bund as ane theif, so wes thou harled and led,   20
Till Herod had, in purpor habit cled.
For hethin, halsed, blasphemed with mony blaw,
Beft at ane pillar, blaikned and forbled,
At Locostratus whair thay leid the law.

---

1. *Compassion pierces, pity and mercy stab with pain.* 2. thirles, *pierces.* 3. deid, *death;*
petuous, *pitiful.* 5. sadlye, *deeply;* spreit, *spirit.* 6. Sen, *MS.* se, *Since.* 7, etc. ene, *eyes;*
ranes, *shed.* 8. haled, *hauled.* 11. spikardy, *MS.* specatyve. 12. Sho, *She.* 13. betwen,
jointly. 15. dred, *feared.* 19. *To a wretched man (called) Caiaphas, and (also to) Pilate.*
20. harled, *dragged.* 21. *Brought to Herod, dressed in purple.* 22. hethin, *scorn;* halsed,
greeted, embraced; blaw, *blow of the fist.* 23. *Beaten at a pillar, made pale and weak with
loss of blood.* 24. leid, *expounded (?) presented (?).*

Cuttes for thy cot thay keist, was never sewed;   25
Out-throw thy hernis the crown of thorn thay applied;
Vailland thine ene, into thy visage spitted,
And for derisioun, 'King of Jowes', thay cried.
That night thy name Sanct Peter thris denied.
Drowned in dule mirk was thy mind, Mary.   30
To wonder on, throw Jerusalem thou hied
To see thy awin sone, that thou fostered, de.

Ruffed on Croce thir wordes did repeit,
'Scicio'. Right sone thay served thee with gall.
Sharpe wes the speir, the nales lang and gret,   35
Thy ribbes racked, thy face ourespitted all.
To Golgatha, Godis sone celestiall,
Thy Croce with force thou bure with cure and heit.
Thy tender hid and fleshe virginall
Werry forwreght, in watter, blude and sweit.   40

Throw Maryis saule the swerd of dolour thrist,
When that thou said, 'Se thair thy sone, woman,'
Commending hir to John the Evangelist.
Sharp, bludy teres hir crystal ene out ran.
Swolled wer thy siddes, for scurges bla and wan,   45
Naiked and paill, ded on the Croce thou hang.
Thy vanes bursen, thy senowes shorn, than,
Crowned with thorne, for scorne, two theves amang.

My woful hert is baith rejosed and sade,
Thy corps, Lorde Jesu Christ, when I behalde.   50
Of my redempcioun I am baith blyth and glaid;
Seand thy panes, sorelye weip I walde.
Cryand, 'Hely', thy gaistlye spreit thou yalde
To Longus' hande: thy blude ran in ane rest;
Thy woful moder swoned, stif and calde,   55
When thou inclined with, 'Consummatum est'.

25. (which) was. 26. Out-throw, *Right through;* hernis, *brains.* 27. Vailland, *Blind-folding.* 30. dule mirk, *gloomy darkness* (?) *dark grief* (?). 31. *Cause for wonder* (?); hied, *hastened.* 32. awin, *own;* and 62. de, *die.* 33. Ruffed, *Nailed;* thir, *these.* 34. Scicio, '*I thirst*'. 38. bure, *bore;* cure, *trouble;* heit, *heat.* 39. hid, *skin.* 40. Werry forwreght, *Exhausted with toil.* 45. for, *through;* bla and wan, *black and blue.* 47. bursen, *burst;* senowes shorn, *sinews cut* (?); than, *then.* 52. Seand, *Seeing.* 53. 'Hely', '*Eloi*'; gaistlye, *devout;* spreit, *spirit.* 54. rest, *place for lance to rest* (?).

Dirk wes the sone fra the sext hour to nine.
Montanes trimbled, hilles shuke and roches claif.
Centurio said, 'Thou art Goddis sone divine.'
Joseph decurio spiced thee in thy graif   60
With myr and must, most vertuis and suaif.
Thay gert thee de and forgaif Berrabas.
My saule with sanctes, Salviour resaif,
Sen that thy Passioun purged my trespas.

60. decurio, (*Vulgate, Luke xxiii, 50*) *the councillor.* 61. must, *musk;* vertuis, *effective;* suaif, *sweet.* 62. gert, *caused.* 63. resaif, *receive.* 64. Sen that, *Since.*

167

Fill the bowl, butler!

How! butler, how!   earlier 16c.
Bevis à tout!
Fill the boll, gentill butler,
And let the cup rought!

Gentill butler, bell ami,   5
Fill the boll by the eye,
That we may drink by and by.
With, how! butler, how! Bevis à tout!
Fill the boll, butler, and let the cup rought.

Here is mete for us all,   10
Both for gret and for small,
I trow we must the butler call.
With, how! butler, how! Bevis à tout!
Fill the boll, butler, and let the cup rought.

2. Bevis à tout, *Drink to all.* 3, 5. gentill, *noble.* 4. rought, *go round.* 5. bell ami, *good friend.* 6. by the eye, *abundantly* (?) *immediately* (?). 7. by and by, *straightway.* 12, etc. trow, *believe.*

I am so dry I cannot spek,   15
I am nigh choked with my mete!
I trow the butler be aslepe!
With, how! butler, how! Bevis à tout!
Fill the boll, butler, and let the cup rought.

Butler! butler! fill the boll,   20
Or elles I beshrewe thy noll!
I trow we must the bell toll.
With, how! butler, how! Bevis à tout!
Fill the boll, butler, and let the cup rought.

If the butler's name be Water   25
I wold he were a galow-claper,
But if he bring us drink the rather.
With, how! butler, how! Bevis à tout!
Fill the boll, butler, and let the cup rought.

21. *Or else a curse on your head.* 26. galow-claper, *gallows bird.* 27. But if, *Unless;* rather, *sooner.*

168

Now is the time of Christmas

Make we mery bothe more and lasse,   earlier
For now is the time of Christimas.   16c.

Let no man cum into this hall,
Grome, page, nor yet marshall,
But that sum sport he bring withall,   5
For now is the time of Christmas.

1. *high and low.* 4. (*Servants and officers of the household*). 5, 8. sport, *entertainment.*

If that he say he cannot sing
Sum oder sport then let him bring
That it may please at this festing,
For now is the time of Christmas.   10

If he say he can nought do,
Then for my love aske him no mo,
But to the stockes then let him go,
For now is the time of Christmas.

11. *do nothing.* 12. *more.*

169

The boar's head carol

Caput apri refero,   earlier 16c.
Resonens laudes Domino.

The bores hed in hondes I bring,
With garlondes gay and birdes singing:
I pray you all, helpe me to sing,   5
Qui estis in convivio.

The boris hede I understond
Is cheff service in all this lond:
Whersoever it may be fond
Servitur cum sinapio.   10

The bores hede, I dare well say,
Anon, after the twelfth day,
He taketh his leve and goth away,
Exivit tunc de patria.

1–2. *I bring back the boar's head, sounding praises to the Lord.* 6. *Who are at this banquet.* 8. *service, course.* 10. *It is served with mustard.* 14. *Then he has left the country.*

170

Fearful death

Alas, my hart will brek in three: earlier 16c.
Terribilis mors conturbat me.

Illa iuventus, that is so nise,
Me deduxit into vain devise:
Infirmus sum, I may not rise.   5
Terribilis mors conturbat me.

Dum iuvenis fui, litill I dred,
Sed semper in sinne I ete my bred,
Iam ductus sum into my bed.   10
Terribilis mors conturbat me.

Corpus migrat in my soule;
Respicit demon in his rowle—
Desiderat ipse to have his tolle.
Terribilis mors conturbat me.

Christus se ipsum, whan he shuld die,   15
Patri suo his manhode did crye:
'Respice me, Pater, that is so hye.'
Terribilis mors conturbat me.

Queso iam the Trinite
Duc me from this vanite   20
In celum, ther is joy with thee.
Terribilis mors conturbat me.

2, etc. *Fearful death confounds me.* 3. *Youth that is so foolish.* 4. *Led me into empty pleasure.* 5. *Infirm I am.* 7. *While I was young.* 8. *But ever.* 9. *Already I am led.* 11. *My body parts from my soul.* 12. *The demon looks in his roll.* 13. *He wants to.* 15. *Christ himself.* 16. *To his Father.* 17. *Look on me, Father.* 19. *Now I entreat.* 20. *Lead me.* 21. *To Heaven (where) ther.*

171

Holly against Ivy

Nay! nay! Ivy,   earlier 16c.
It may not be, iwis:
For Holy must have the mastry,
As the maner is.

Holy bereth beris,   5
Beris rede inough:
The thristilcok, the popingay
Daunce in every bough.
Welaway! sory Ivy,
What fowles hast thou?   10
But the sory owlet,
That singeth 'How! how!'

Ivy bereth beris
As black as any slo:
Ther commeth the woode-colver   15
And fedeth her of tho.
She lifteth up her taill,
And she cackes or she go:
She wold not for a hundred poundes
Serve Holy so.   20

Holy with his mery men
They can daunce in hall:
Ivy and her gentil women
Cannot daunce at all,
But like a meiny of bullockes   25
In a waterfall,
Or on a hot somer's day
Whan they be mad all.

2. *indeed.* 3. *be top-dog.* 4. *custom.* 6. *Really red berries.* 7. *cock thrush, the parrot* (?).
10. *birds.* 14. slo, MS. sho. 15. *wood-pigeon.* 16. *on them.* 18. *And she leaves droppings
before she goes.* 19. a hundred poundes, MS. C libra. 23, 31. *well-bred, gentle.* 25. *herd.*

Holy and his mery men
Sitt in cheires of gold: 30
Ivy and her gentil women
Sitt without in fold,
With a paire of kibed
Heles caught with cold—
So wold I that every man had   35
That with Ivy will hold!

32. *Sit outside on the ground* (?) *in the yard* (?). 33. kibed, *having chilblains.*

172

Wit wonders

A god and yet a man,   16c.
A maide and yet a mother:
Wit wonders what wit can
Conceave this or the other.

A god and can he die?   5
A dead man, can he live?
What wit can well replye?
What reason reason give?

God, Truth itselfe, doth teach it.
Man's wit senkis too far under   10
By reason's power to reach it:
Beleeve and leave to wonder.

10. senkis, *sinks.* 12. *Have faith and stop puzzling.*

173

Waking alone

In a goodly night, as in my bede I laye,   earlier 16c.
Pleasantlye sleping, this dreme I hade:
To me ther came a creature, brighter than the day,
Whiche comforted my sprites that were afore full sadde.
To beholde hur person, God knowes my hart was glade,   5
For hur swete visage, like Venus gold it shone;
To speke to hur I was right sore aferde,
But, when I waked, ther was I alone.

Then when she sawe that I lay soo still,
Full softely she drew unto my beddes side;   10
She bade me showe hur what was my will,
And my request it shuld not be denied.
With that she kist me—but, and I shulde have be dede,
I coude not speke, my sprites were soo ferre gone;
For verrey shame my face awey I wryede,   15
But, when I awoke, ther was but I alone.

Then speke I, goodly woordes to hur said:
'I beseche your noblenes on me to have some grace.
To aproche to your presence I was sumwhat aferde;
That causes me now to turn awey my face.'   20
'Nay, sir,' quod she, 'as touching this case,
I perdone you, my owne dere harte, anon.'
With that I toke hur softely, and swetly did hur basse,
But, when I awoke, ther was but I alone.

Then said she to me, 'O my dere harte,   25
May I content in any wise your minde?'
'Ye, God knowes,' said I, 'through loves darte
My harte forever to have ye do me binde.

13. and, *if.* 15. wryede, *turned.* 23, 37. basse(d), *kiss(ed).*

You be my comforth—I have you most in minde.
Have on me petye and lett me not this mone.' 30
'Leve', said she, 'this mourning; I will not be unkind.'
But, when I awoke, ther was but I alone.

I prayed hur hartely that she wolde come to bede.
She said she was content to doo me pleasure.
I know not wheder I was alive or dede, 35
So glad I was to have that goodly treasure.
I kissed hur, I bassed hur, out of all measure.
The more I kissede hur, the more hur bewty shone.
To serve hur, to please hur, that time I did me dever,
But, when I awoke, ther was but I alone. 40

Suche goodly sportes all night endured I
Unto the morow, that day cam to springe.
Soo glade I was of my dreme, verely,
That in my slepe loude I begane to singe.
And when I awoke, by Heven Kinge, 45
I wente after hur, and she was gone;
I had nothing but my pilowe in my armes lying,
For, when I awoke, ther was but I alone.

30. this mone, *complain of this.* 39. I . . . dever, *I endeavoured.*

174

Women are worthy

I am as light as any roe earlier 16c.
To preise women wher that I go.

To onpreise women it were a shame,
For a woman was thy dame:
Our Blessed Lady bereth the name 5
Of all women wher that they go.

1. light, *nimble, swift.* 4. dame, *mother, lady.*

A woman is a worthy thing:
They do the washe and do the wringe;
'Lullay, lullay,' she dothe thee singe,
And yet she hath but care and woe.   10

A woman is a worthy wight:
She serveth a man both daye and night;
Therto she putteth all her might,
And yet she hathe but care and woe.

8. *They do the washing and wringing* (?). *They wash for you and wring for you* (?). 9. *to* (?) *for* (?) *thee*. 11. *wight, creature*.

175

The magician and the baron's daughter

Draw me nere,   earlier 16c.
Draw me nere,
Draw me nere,
The joly juggelere.

Here beside dwelleth   5
A riche baron's doughter:
She wold have no man
That for her love had sought her—
So nise she was.

She wold have no man   10
That was made of molde,
But if he had a mouth of gold
To kisse her whan she wold—
So dangerus she was.

4. juggelere, *magician, conjuror*. 9. nise, *fastidious*. 10–11. man . . . molde, *mortal man*. 12. But if, *unless*. 14. dangerus, *haughty, difficult to please*.

Thereof hard a joly juggeler   15
That laid was on the grene,
And at this lady's wordes,
Iwis, he had gret tene—
An-angred he was.

He juggeled to him a well good stede   20
Of an old hors bone,
A sadill and a bridill both,
And set himself thereon—
A juggeler he was.

He priked and praunsed both   25
Before that lady's gate:
She wend he had ben an angel
Was come for her sake—
A pricker he was.

He priked and praunsed   30
Before that lady's bowr:
She wend he had ben an angel
Come from Heven towre—
A praunser he was.

Four and twenty knightes   35
Lade him into the hall,
And as many squires
His hors to the stall,
And gaff him mete.

They gaff him ottes,   40
And also hay;
He was an old shrew
And held his hed away—
He wold not ete.

15. hard, *heard.* 18. Iwis, *Indeed;* tene, *vexation.* 25. *rode fast and pranced (also used of the sex act, e.g. no. 108 l. 33).* 27, 32. wend, *thought;* had, *not in MS.* 33. Heven towre, *tower of Heaven (traditional symbol).* 44. *(because he was a magic horse.)*

The day began to passe,   45
The night began to come:
To bed was brought
The faire gentellwoman,
And the juggeler also.

The night began to passe,   50
The day began to springe,
All the birdes of her bowr
They began to singe—
And the cokoo also.

Where be ye my mery maidens   55
That ye come not me to?
The joly windows of my bowr
Look that you undo
That I may see;

For I have in mine armes   60
A duke or elles an erle.
But whan she looked him upon
He was a blere-eyed chorle—
'Alas,' she said.

She lade him to an hill   65
And hanged shuld he be:
He juggeled himself to a mele pok,
The dust fell in her eye—
Begiled she was.

God and our Lady,   70
And swete Seint Johan,
Send every giglot of this town
Such another leman,
Even as he was!

54. cokoo, *cuckoo, cuckold.* 67. mele pok, *meal-bag.* 72. giglot, *wanton.* 73. leman, *lover.*

176

A last will and testament

Terram terra tegat; Demon peccata resumat;   earlier
  Mundus res habeat; spiritus alta petat.   16c.

Terram terra tegat.

Four pointes, my will, or I hence departe,
Reason me moveth to make as I maye.   5
First to the erthe I bequeth his parte:
My wretched carein is but foule claye.
Like than to like, erthe in erthe to laye:
Sith it is according, by it I woll abide,
As for the first parte of my will, that erthe erth hide.   10

Demon peccata resumat.

Mine horrible sinnes that so sore me binde
With weight me oppresse, that lyen so manifold,
So many in numbre, so sondry in kinde.
The Fende, by his instaunce, to them made me bold.   15
From him they come, to him I yolde wolde.
Wherfore the second parte of my will is thus,
That the Fende receive all my sinnes as his.

Mundus res habeat.

Whate availeth goodes, am I ones dede and roten?   20
Them all and some I leve, peny and pounde,
Truely or untruely, some I trowe misgoten,
Though I wot not of whome, howe, nor in whate grounde.
The worldes they been, them in the worlde I founde:
And therfore the thirde parte is of my wille,   25
All my worldly goodes let the worlde have still.

1. *Let earth hide earth; let the Devil take back my sins.* 2. *Let the world have my goods; let my spirit seek high Heaven.* 4. or, *before.* 7. carein, *corpse.* 8, 28. than, *then.* 9. Sith, *Since;* according, *fitting.* 15. instaunce, *instigation.* 16. *to him I would yield (them).* 20. once I am. 22. trowe, *suppose; ill-gotten.* 23. wot, *know.*

Spiritus alta petat.

Nowe for the fourth pointe and than have I doo.
Nedefull for the soule me thinketh to provide,
Hence muste I nedes, but whother shall I goo?   30
I doute my demerittes which weyen on every side.
But Goddes mercy shall I truste to be my guide,
Under whose liecens yet, while I maye breth,
Unto Heven on high my soule I bequeth.

29. me thinketh, *it seems to me.* 31. doute, *fear.* 33. liecens, *permission.*

177

A cheerful welcome

What cher? Gud cher, gud cher, gud cher.   earlier
Be mery and glad this gud New Yere!   16c.

'Lift up your hartes and be glad
In Christes birth,' the angel bad.
'Say eche to oder, if any be sade,   5
"What cher?"'

Now the King of Heven his birth hath take
Joy and mirth we ought to make:
Say eche to oder, for his sake,
'What cher?'   10

I tell you all, with hart so free,
Right welcum ye be to me!
Be glad and mery for charite—
'What cher?'

The gudman of this place, in fere,   15
You to be mery he prayth you here,
And with gud hert he doth to you say,
'What cher?'

11. free, *open, generous.* 15. in fere, *together (with me).*

178

The scholar complains

Hay! hay! by this day,   earlier 16c.
What availeth it me though I say, nay?

I wold fain be a clarke,
But yet it is a strange werke:
The birchen twigges be so sharpe,   5
It maketh me have a faint harte.
What availeth it me though I say, nay?

On Monday in the morning whan I shall rise,
At six of the clok, it is the gise
To go to skole without avise—   10
I had lever go twenty mile twise.
What availeth it me though I say, nay?

My master loketh as he were madde:
'Wher hast thou be, thou sory ladde?'
'Milked duckes, my moder badde.'   15
It was no mervaile though I were sadde!
What availeth it me though I say, nay?

My master pepered my ars with well good spede:
It was worse than finkill sede.
He wold not leve till it did blede—   20
Mich sorow have he for his dede!
What availeth it me though I say, nay?

I wold my master were a watt,
And my boke a wild catt,
And a brase of grehoundes in his toppe—   25
I wold be glade for to see that!
What availeth it me though I say, nay?

3. clarke, *scholar.* 4. strange, *alien, difficult.* 10. avise, *arguing.* 11. lever, *rather.* 15.
My mother made me milk the ducks (!). 19. *It was sharper than fennel sauce.* 21. Mich,
Much. 23. watt, *hare.* 25. toppe, *hair.*

I wold my master were an hare,
And all his bokes houndes were,
And I myself a joly hontere;   30
To blow my horn I wold not spare,
For if he were dede I wold not care!
What availeth it me though I say, nay?

179

A little hymn to Mary

Haill! Quene of Heven and steren of blis,   16c.
Sen that thy sone thy fader is,
How suld he ony thing thee warn,
And thou his mother and he thy barne?

Haill! freshe fontane that springes new,   5
The rute and crope of all vertue.
Thou polist gem without offence,
Thou bair the Lambe of Innocence.

1. steren, *star.* 2. Sen that, *Since.* 3. suld, *should;* warn, *deny.* 4. barne, *child.* 7. polist, *polished.*

180

KING HENRY VIII (?)

Love ever green

Grene groweth the holy,   about 1515
So doth the ivy.
Thow winter blastes blow never so hye,
Grene growth the holy.

3. Thow, *Though.*

As the holy growth grene   5
And never chaungeth hew,
So I am, ever hath bene,
Unto my lady trew.

As the holy growth grene
With ivy all alone,   10
When floweres cannot be sene
And grenewode leves be gone,

Now unto my lady
Promise to her I make,
Frome all other only   15
To her I me betake.

Adew! mine owne lady,
Adew! my speciall,
Who hath my hart, trewly,
Be suere, and ever shall.   20

181

Western wind

Westron winde, when will thou blow,   earlier
The smalle raine downe can raine?   16c.
Christ if my love were in my armes,
And I in my bed againe.

182

WILLIAM CORNISH (?)

Pleasure it is

Pleasure it is   earlier 16c.
To here, iwis,
The birds sing;
The dere in the dale,
The shepe in the vale,   5
The corne springing.
God's purveaunce
For sustenaunce
It is for man:
Then we always   10
To him give praise,
And thank him than,
And thank him than.

2. iwis, *indeed.* 7. purveaunce, *providence, provision.*

183

The Coventry carol

Lully, lulla, thou little tiny child, 1534? 1591?
By, by, lully, lullay, thou little tiny child,
By, by, lully, lullay!

O! sisters too,
How may we do   5
For to preserve, this day,
This pore yongling
For whom we do singe,
'By, by, lully, lullay'?

4. too, *two.*

Herod, the king,   10
In his raging,
Charged he hath, this day,
His men of might
In his owne sight
All yonge children to slay.   15

That, wo is me,
Pore child, for thee,
And ever morne and may;
For thy parting
Nether say nor singe,   20
'By, by, lully, lullay.'

18. may, *transcript of Sharp*, say.

184

THOMAS WYATT

No! indeed

What no, perdy, ye may be sure!   earlier 16c.
Think not to make me to your lure,
With wordes and chere so contrarying,
Swete and soure contrewaing—
Too much it were still to endure!   5
Trouth is trayed where craft is in ure.
But though ye have had my hertes cure,
Trow ye I dote withoute ending?
What no, perdy!

Though that with pain I do procure   10
For to forgett that ons was pure,
Within my hert shall still that thing,
Unstable, unsure, and wavering,
Be in my minde withoute recure?
What no, perdy!   15

1, etc. perdy, *indeed.* 2. *Think not to have me at your beck and call* (*the* lure *is a device used by falconers to recall their hawks to them*). 3. chere, *manner;* contrarying, *contrary.* 6. trayed. *betrayed, grieved* (?); ure, *use.* 7. cure, *care.* 8. Trow, *Believe.* 14. recure, *remedy.*

185

THOMAS WYATT

My lute and I

At moost mischief   earlier 16c.
I suffre grief,
For of relief
Sins I have none,
My lute and I,   5
Continually,
Shall us apply
To sigh and mone.

Nought may prevail
To wepe or wail: 10
Pitye doeth fail
In you, alas!
Morning or mone,
Complaint or none,
It is all one,   15
As in this case.

For crueltye,
Moost that can be,
Hath soverainte
Within your hert;   20
Which maketh bare
All my welfare:
Nought do you care
How sore I smart.

No tigre's hert   25
Is so pervert
Withoute desert
To wreke his ire:

1. *In the greatest distress.* 4. Sins, *Since.*

And you me kill
For my good will—   30
Lo! how I spill
For my desire.

There is no love
That can ye move,
And I can prove   35
None othre way:
Therefore I must
Restrain my lust,
Banishe my trust
And welth away.   40

Thus in mischief
I suffre grief,
For of relief
Sins I have none,
My lute and I,   45
Continually,
Shall us apply
To sigh and mone.

31. spill, *perish.* 38. *desire.* 40. welth, *wellbeing.* 41. Thus, *so Devonshire MS. but this MS.* For in myschief *and ll. 42–8 omitted.*

186

THOMAS WYATT

What does this mean?

What menethe this? When I lye alone   earlier
I tosse, I turne, I sighe, I grone;   16c.
My bed me semes as hard as stone:
What menes this?

I sighe, I plaine continually;   5
The clothes that on my bed do lie
Always, methinks, they lie awry:
What menes this?

In slumbers oft for fere I quake,
For hete and cold I burne and shake,   10
For lake of slepe my hede dothe ake:
What menes this?

A morninges then when I do rise
I torne unto my wonted gise,
All day after muse and devise: 15
What menes this?

And if perchance by me there passe
She unto whome I sue for grace,
The cold blood forsakethe my face:
What menethe this?   20

But if I sitte nere her by
With loud voice my hart dothe cry,
And yet my mouthe is dome and dry:
What menes this?

To aske for helpe no hart I have,   25
My tong dothe faile what I shuld crave;
Yet inwardly I rage and rave:
What menes this?

Thus have I passed many a yere
And many a day, tho nought appere,   30
But most of that that most I fere:
What menes this?

187

THOMAS WYATT

What once I was

Ons in your grace I knowe I was,   earlier 16c.
Even as well as now is he;
Tho Fortune so hath torned my case
That I am downe and he full hye—
Yet ons I was.   5

Ons I was he that did you please
So well that nothing did I dobte,
And tho that nowe ye thinke it ease
To take him in and throw me out—
Yet ons I was.   10

Ons I was he in tims past
That as your owne ye did retaine:
And tho ye have me nowe out cast,
Shoing untruthe in you to raigne,
Yet ons I was.   15

Ons I was he that knit the knot
The whiche ye swore not to unknit,
And tho ye faine it now forgot,
In usinge your newfangled wit,
Yet ons I was.   20

Ons I was he to whome ye said,
'Welcomm! my joy, my whole delight.'
And tho ye ar nowe well apayd
Of me, your owne, to clame ye quit—
Yet ons I was.   25

11. tims: *MS.* time (?)—*last letter difficult to read.* 14. untruthe, *unfaithfulness.* 23. apayd, *content.* 24. quit, *rid.*

Ons I was he to whome ye spake,
'Have here my hart! It is thy owne.'
And tho thes wordes ye now forsake,
Saying therof my part is none,
Yet ons I was.   30

Ons I was he before reherst,
And nowe am he that nedes must die.
And tho I die, yet, at the lest,
In your remembrance let it lie
That ons I was.   35

31. reherst, *mentioned.*

Chronological Table
Further Reading
Abbreviations
Notes
Appendix
Index of First Lines

Chronological Table

Twelfth Century

1096: Crusades begin
About 1100: William of Aquitaine, first of the troubadours
1100–35: Henry I
1090–1153: St. Bernard
1135–54: Stephen
1154–89: Henry II
1170: Archbishop Thomas Becket murdered
1189–99: Richard I
By 1200: University of Oxford founded

Thirteenth Century

1199–1216: John
1181/2–1226: St. Francis
1215: Magna Carta
1216–72: Henry III
1225?–74: St. Thomas Aquinas
About 1235: *Roman de la Rose* begun
1270: Crusades end
1272–1307: Edward I
1297: Wallace wins at Stirling

Fourteenth Century

1265–1321: Dante
1307–27: Edward II
1314: Bruce wins at Bannockburn

1313?–75: Boccaccio
1327–77: Edward III
1346: French defeated at Crécy
1348–79: Black Death
1329?–84 John Wycliffe
1377–99: Richard II

Fifteenth Century

1399–1413: Henry IV
1413–22: Henry V
1415: French defeated at Agincourt
1422–61: Henry VI (died 1471)
1431: St. Joan of Arc dies
1455: Wars of Roses begin
1461–83: Edward IV
1469/70: Malory finished *Morte Darthur*
1483–5: Richard III
1485: Battle of Bosworth
1485–1509: Henry VII

Sixteenth Century

1466?–1536: Erasmus
1474–1533: Ariosto
1509–47: Henry VIII
1529: Fall of Wolsey
1548: English Prayer Book
1552?: Edmund Spenser born
1557: Tottel's Miscellany
1564: Shakespeare born

Further Reading

There are bibliographies in the volumes of the *Oxford History of English Literature* and in the *Cambridge Bibliography of English Literature*. These will give full guidance, and work on particular points should be sought in them. The books listed here are only a first selection and they only supplement those critical works and editions that are mentioned incidentally in this anthology and are not repeated here. Full details of the principal editions are given under 'Abbreviations' and are self-explanatory.

E. K. Chambers, 'The carol and fifteenth-century lyric' in *English literature at the close of the middle ages* (Oxford, 1945).

A. K. Moore, *The secular lyric in middle English* (University of Kentucky Press: Lexington, 1951).

J. Speirs, 'Carols and other songs and lyrics' in *Medieval English poetry: the Non-Chaucerian tradition* (London, 1957).

C. S. Lewis, variously in *English literature in the sixteenth century* (Oxford, 1954).

F. J. E. Raby, *History of Christian-Latin poetry from the beginning to the close of the middle ages* (Oxford, 1927).

— *History of secular Latin poetry in the middle ages* (Oxford, 1934/1957), 2 vols.

H. J. Chaytor, *Troubadours and England* (Cambridge, 1923).

Abbreviations

Adam: Adam of St. Victor, *The liturgical poetry*, ed. D. S. Wrangham (London, 1881), 3 vols.

B.M.: British Museum, London.

Bodl.: Bodleian Library, Oxford. (The number in brackets after the manuscript is that in the Summary Catalogue.)

St. Bonaventura: St. Bonaventura, *Opera omnia* (Paris, 1864–71), 15 vols.

c.: century.

C.B. *13c.*: *English lyrics of the thirteenth century*, ed. C. Brown (Oxford, 1932).

C.B. *14c.*: *Religious lyrics of the fourteenth century*, ed. C. Brown, 2nd edn. revised G. V. Smithers (Oxford, 1952).

C.B. *15c.*: *Religious lyrics of the fifteenth century*, ed. C. Brown (Oxford, 1939).

Camb. (Univ. Lib.): Cambridge (University Library).

Charters of Christ: M. C. Spalding, *The Middle English Charters of Christ* (Bryn Mawr: Pennsylvania, 1914).

Chaucer: *The works of Geoffrey Chaucer*, ed. F. N. Robinson, 2nd edn. (Boston, 1957).

Child: F. J. Child's *English and Scottish popular ballads*, ed. H. C. Sargent and G. L. Kittredge (London, n.d.).

col(s).: column(s).

Daniel: *Thesaurus hymnologicus*, ed. H. A. Daniel (Leipzig, 1855–6), 5 vols. in 2.

Dreves: *Analecta hymnica Medii Aevi*, ed. G. M. Dreves (Leipzig, 1886 etc.; Frankfurt, 1961), 50 vols.

E.E.L.: *Early English lyrics, amorous, divine, moral and trivial*, ed. E. K. Chambers and F. Sidgwick (London, 1907).

E.E.T.S. (E.S.) (O.S.): *Early English Text Society* (Extra Series) (Original Series).

E.M.E.T.: *Early Middle English texts*, ed. B. Dickins and R. M. Wilson (Cambridge, 1951).

ed.: edited by.

edn.: edition.

Abbreviations

f(f). . . . a(b).: folio(s) or 'page(s)' of a manuscript, the letter *a* or *b* after the number indicating whether on the front or the back.

Greene: *The early English carols*, ed. R. L. Greene (Oxford, 1935).

Greene, *Selection: A selection of English carols*, ed. R. L. Greene (Oxford, 1962).

Harley: *The Harley lyrics: the Middle English lyrics of MS. Harley 2253*, ed. G. L. Brook (Manchester, 1948).

Hours of B.V.M.: 'The Hours of the Blessed Virgin Mary' in *The Prymer or Lay Folk's Prayer Book*, ed. H. Littlehales, *E.E.T.S. O.S. 105 and 109* (1895 and 1897).

Index: *The Index of Middle English Verse*, ed. C. Brown and R. H. Robbins (New York, 1943).

J.E.G.P.: Journal of English and Germanic philology.

John: John of Hoveden, *Poems*, ed. F. J. E. Raby (Surtees Society, 1939).

l(l).: line(s).

Lydgate: J. Lydgate, *Minor poems*, part ii, ed. H. N. MacCracken, *E.E.T.S. O.S. 192* (1934).

M.L.N.: Modern language notes.

M.L.R.: Modern language review.

M.P.: Modern philology.

Meditations: Meditations on the Life and Passion of Christ, ed. C. d'Evelyn, *E.E.T.S. O.S. 158* (1921).

Mone: *Lateinische hymnen des Mittelalters*, ed. F. J. Mone (Freiburg, 1853–5), 3 vols.

MS(S).: Manuscript(s). When *MS.* occurs alone it refers to the first of the manuscripts listed as providing the text of a poem.

N. and Q.: Notes and Queries.

p(p).: page(s).

P.L.: Patrologia Latina, ed. J. P. Migne, 221 vols.

P.M.L.A.: Publications of the Modern Language Association of America.

P.Q.: Philological quarterly.

Patterson: F. A. Patterson, *The Middle English penitential lyric* (New York, 1911).

R.E.S.: Review of English studies.

R.H.R.: R. H. Robbins.

R.H.R. *Christmas carols: Early English Christmas carols*, ed. R. H. Robbins (New York and London, 1961).

R.H.R. *Sec. Lyrs.: Secular lyrics of the XIVth and XVth centuries*, ed. R. H. Robbins (Oxford, 1952).

Abbreviations

R.H.R. *Hist. poems: Historical poems of the fourteenth and fifteenth centuries*, ed. R. H. Robbins (New York, 1959).

S.P.: *Studies in Philology.*

S.T.C.: *Short Title Catalogue of books printed in England, Scotland and Ireland, and of English books printed abroad, 1475–1640*, compiled A. W. Pollard and G. R. Redgrave (London, 1926/1946).

S.T.S.: *Scottish Text Society.*

Sarum Breviary: *Breviarium ad usum insignis ecclesiae Sarum*, ed. F. Procter and C. Wordsworth (Cambridge, 1879–86), 3 vols.

Sarum Missal: *The Sarum Missal*, ed. J. W. Legg (Oxford, 1916).

Sisam: *Fourteenth century verse and prose*, ed. K. Sisam (Oxford, 1921 and frequently since).

Speculum: Speculum: a journal of mediaeval studies.

Stevens, *Carols.: Musica Britannica, iv, Mediaeval Carols*, ed. J. Stevens (London, 1952).

Stevens, *Early Tudor Court*: J. Stevens, *Music and poetry in the early Tudor court* (London, 1961).

Wyatt: *Collected poems of Sir Thomas Wyatt*, ed. K. Muir (London, 1949).

Notes

Poem 1. In his early days a sort of pedlar and pilgrim, Godric became a hermit at Finchale, near Durham, where he died in 1170. Three brief sets of verses are attributed to him. A contemporary Latin life reports that Saint Godric said the Blessed Virgin appeared to him and taught him words and music, also in MS., saying that she would come to his aid as soon as he called her by this song. The second verse, omitted by four of the MSS., contains traditional imagery though there is some doubt about its meaning: Mary, to whom l. 5 is addressed, is the chamber of Christ (pp. 17–18, 20–2), a pure maiden and a mother, and is figured as a flower (Appendix under *Lily* and *Rose*); but the syntax of l. 6 is difficult and the address may be changed to Christ, the flower born of Mary, in which case *clenhad* means, in all likelihood, 'a pure offspring' (Appendix under *Rods of Jesse* and *Aaron*). Though most verses seem to contain four stresses, variously distributed, and so may resemble the native alliterative verse (pp. 28, 34 and e.g. no. 15), there is no alliteration. It has been argued that Latin hymns were Godric's model, but there is certainly no particular hymn like his and his rhythm needs much pinching and pulling to prove anything of a likeness. It may be he writes in a native popular tradition about which very little is known.

Index 2988. B.M. MS. Royal 5.F.vii, f.85a. Ed. J. Hall in *Selections from early middle English, 1130–1250*, p. 5, no. 2; J. Zupitza, 'Cantus Beati Godrici', *Englische Studien*, xi (1888), pp. 401–32; J. W. Rankin, 'The hymns of St. Godric', *P.M.L.A.*, xxxviii (1923), pp. 699–711.

Poem 2. In nos. 2, 3 and 4 the inner world of the poet's mood is expressed in relation to the outer world of nature which is presented in concrete detail. Syntax is simple and a great part of the poem is left unsaid. All three are accompanied by music, but it is not the music of simple, rustic folk (pp. 27–8).

The music: New Oxford history of music, ii: Early medieval music up to 1300, ed. Dom A. Hughes (London, 1954); Giraldus Cambrensis

(12c.) reports there was a long tradition of singing in many parts in Wales and in two parts in England, north of the Humber: *Descriptio Cambriae*, ed. J. F. Dimock (Rolls Series, 1868), p. 189. *This poem is written* on a sheet that has been later bound up as a fly-leaf in another MS.

Index 2163. Bodl. MS. Rawlinson G. 22(14755), f.1b. C.B. *13c.*, p. 14, no. 7; *E.E.L.*, p. 3, no. 1; *E.M.E.T.*, p. 118, no. 25.

Poem 3. The rhythm of nos. 2, 3 and 4 readily finds itself in the read-ing: that of this poem, in particular, enacts the joy of spring. A sort of round, or *rota*, as it is called, it has Latin instructions for sing-ing it and it may be a learned adaptation of a popular tune.

The MS. is a commonplace book that belonged to Reading Abbey and contains, as well as much else, other musical pieces in Latin or French. *The Latin instructions* for singing this poem may have been necessary because the type of song was unusual, and the possibility of such elaborate music so early has been disputed: according to Hughes (note 2) the *pes* (ll. 1–2), sung by two voices, accompanies the singing of the other words, the form of which is 'that of an infinite canon at the unison for four voices'. Latin words which accompany it do not fit the music very well and they are probably a later attempt to adapt the secular work for religious uses.

Index 3223. B.M. MS. Harley 978, f.11b. C.B. *13c.*, p. 13, no. 6; *E.E.L.*, p. 4, no. 2; *E.M.E.T.*, p. 118, no. 24.

Poem 4. This is a two-part song (note 2), found among legal matter and lists of names and dates.

Index 864. Bodl. MS. Douce 139 (21713), f.5a. C.B. *13c.*, p. 14, no. 8; *E.E.L.*, p. 5, no. 3; *E.M.E.T.*, p. 119, no. 26.

Poem 5. A macaronic poem (p. 44) of Mary (pp. 17–18, 20–4 and Appendix) with a superbly gay movement (pp. 37–8).

Index 2645. B.M. MS. Egerton 613, f.2a. C.B. *13c.*, p. 26, no. 17B; *E.E.L.*, pp. 92–3, no. 46; Greene, pp. 141–2, no. 191 Ba; Patterson, pp. 96–8.

Poem 6. Quoted in a prose work where it is connected with the Virgin's committal to St. John by the dying Lord. She is said to use the words of the *Song of Songs* (i, 6): 'Look not upon me, because I am black, because the sun hath looked upon me,' and these lines by 'an Englishman' then follow. They may be part of a longer poem, the rest of which is now lost, or they may have been composed for use at this place in the long treatise. The sun going down may be a reference to the darkness in which Christ suffered (*Luke* xxiii, 44–5) whilst it is also a common figure of the dying Lord. The 'blackness' of Mary's face probably represents her sorrow. For the devotional tradition in which this poem stands see pp. 22, 38, 40.

Quoted in a prose work: St. Edmund's *Speculum Ecclesiae* (early 13c.). *Blackness of face:* Philippus de Harveng in his Commentary on the *Song of Songs* (*P.L.*, cciii, cols. 224ff.) explains that Mary is black because she is suffering; *Sun setting a figure of Christ's dying*: poem in B.M. MS. Additional 22283, f.1a: . . . the sonne to reste goinge/Was the deth of Hevene kinge.

Index 2320. Bodl. MS. Arch.Selden, supra 74 (3462), f.55b. C.B. *13c.*, p. 1, no. 1.

Poem 7. This poem denounces those who supported King Henry III against the barons, led by Earl Simon. In particular it deplores Richard, Earl of Cornwall, Henry's brother and King of the Germans (l. 4), Earl Warenne, Hugh Bigod and Edward, Henry's son. Wallingford was Richard's own castle and Windsor the King's. The battle referred to took place near Lewes and Richard was forced to retreat into a windmill (l. 14). The poem was, presumably, written between the defeat of Richard at this battle in 1264 and the death of Earl Simon in 1265.

Index 3155. B.M. MS. Harley 2253, f.58b. C.B. *13c.*, p. 131, no. 72.

Poem 8. A classic example of verses in contempt of the world (p. 40). The particular instance of the 'Ubi sunt' motif (note 83, no. 97 and no. 131) in the first three stanzas probably derives ultimately from the apocryphal *Book of Baruch*, iii, 16–19 (though more immediately, perhaps, from a 13c. Latin work ascribed to St. Bernard), and the image in l. 43 from *Ephesians* vi, 16. That the Christian life is a war against evil (ll. 31–48) is a commonplace (see *Job* vii, 1 and *II Corinthians* vii, 5). The examples of that Heaven (l. 19) which the great enjoy in this world are concrete and compelling. In four of the six MSS. these verses are certainly what they probably were in the original, an integral part of the 'Sayings of St. Bernard', a longer poem in the same stanza form. The purpose of the poem is clearly devotional, to move the penitent heart to confidence in God's power to endure a life of suffering, to overcome sin and eschew vanity, and to expect the promises of Heaven (pp. 22, 38).

Latin work ascribed to St. Bernard: 'Meditationes piissimae de conditione humana', *P.L.*, clxxxiv, col. 491. *Part of* '*Sayings of St. Bernard*': J. E. Cross, '*The Sayings of St. Bernard* and *Ubi scount qui ante nos fuerount*', *R.E.S.* N.S. ix (1958), 1–7.

Index 3310. Bodl. MS. Digby 86 (1687), f.126b. C.B. *13c.*, p. 85, no. 48; *E.E.L.*, pp. 163–5, no. 90; *E.M.E.T.*, pp. 127–8, no. 35.

Poem 9. A sort of *chanson d'aventure* (p. 43), this poem begins with two stanzas of a lover's complaint made of the commonplaces of love poetry (e.g. l. 1: l. 1, no. 88; ll. 9–10: l. 42, no. 25). This complaint opens quite a vigorous dialogue, probably in colloquial idiom and without pretensions to rhetorical high-style (compare nos. 25, 88, 53; pp. 26–7). In the MS. the poem is written in four-line stanzas of septenaries, or seven-stress lines.

Index 2236. B.M. MS. Harley 2253, f.80b. *Harley*, p. 62, no. 24; *E.E.L.*, pp. 12–4, no. 7; C.B. *13c.*, pp. 152–4, no. 85; *E.M.E.T.*, pp. 121–2, no. 29.

Poem 10. Much the same as no. 9 with respect to style. In the first stanza the association of love and spring, when the world grows green again, is traditional, and so are the images in ll. 6 and 24 (pp. 15–16, 44–5). The formula in l. 12 suggests a connection with a scandalous episode in the late 12c. reported by Gerald of Wales (p. 30), in which there occurs the same formula though not necessarily the same song. The use of this formula may, then, suggest that no. 10 is in a tradition of popular verse. In the MS. the poem is written in four-line stanzas of septenaries, or seven-stress lines. Some other Harley lyrics (p. 32) also have a difference of structure in the last stanza.

Giraldus Cambrensis, *Gemma Ecclesiastica*, ed. J. S. Brewer (Rolls Series, 1862), p. 120.

Index 4037. B.M. MS. Harley 2253, f.80b. *Harley*, p. 63, no. 25; *E.E.L.*, pp. 10–11, no. 6; C.B. *13c.*, p. 154, no. 86.

Poem 11. A poem of Mary (pp. 17–18, 20–2).

ll. 13–14: compare 'Salve Regina': '. . . advocata nostra, illos tuos misericordes oculos ad nos converte.'

Notes

Index 1836. Trinity Coll. Camb. MS. B.14.39 (323) f.42b. C.B. *13c.*, p. 42, no. 27.

Poem 12. A poem of Mary (pp. 17, 20, 24, 37) in which, as so often, with the traditional images and titles of the Virgin (Appendix) and the language of devotions are mixed the idea of the devotee as her 'knight' or 'man' (ll. 16 and 22) who is caught in the bonds of love (l. 35) and understands her love in secular terms as *derne* (l. 45). This is one of the earliest poems with music: it is for two voices (note 2).

Language of devotions etc.: compare l. 1 with 'Blessed art thou among women', frequently occurring in Hours B.V.M. and compare ll. 51–2 with Hours B.V.M., p. 2: Matins, Hymn, The cloistre of Marie berith him whom the erthe, watris and hevenes worshipen etc.

Index 708. Corpus Christi Coll. Oxford MS. 59, f. 113b. C.B. *13c.*, p. 116, no. 60.

Poem 13. The first stanza of no. 13 is, characteristically, made of the same commonplaces as there are in the first two stanzas of no. 10 together with the further conventional 'I am in her power'. The description of the beloved is the traditional ideal, the poet's sufferings are those of countless others (p. 44), and the eloquent comparison in l. 30 is found, e.g., in C.B. *13c.*, no. 51, l. 151. But this is a poem of delightful freshness and melody. In particular, the burden or refrain sings itself, and, though there is need to feel for the rhythm at many points, because some word-endings were still pronounced at this time and must be given their value to do the line justice, the rhythm of the entire poem is lyrical. The stanza form, in particular, contributes to this by the five lines with like rime in each, and by the speed of what were probably felt to be octosyllabic lines. There is much alliteration. The MS. indicates that the burden or refrain should be repeated after each stanza but there is no indication that the poem should begin with it, as in a carol (p. 36).

Index 515. B.M. MS. Harley 2253, f.63b. *Harley*, p. 33, no. 4; *E.E.L.*, pp. 6–7, no. 4; Sisam, pp. 165–6; C.B. *13c.*, p. 138, no. 77.

Poem 14. The stanza form is elaborate; there is much alliteration and several formulas from the tradition of alliterative verse, e.g. *stark ne stour* in l. 4 and *briht in bour* in l. 5 (pp. 32–3, 34–5 and note 15).

Notes

Some other Harley lyrics (p. 32) also have a difference of structure in the last stanza. This poem has one or two characteristics of a *chanson d'aventure* (p. 43), e.g. in ll. 11 and 12, and, though it is a religious lyric, the opening line is similar to that of some French secular lyrics (pp. 20–1, 24; Patterson, p. 33), whilst the same image is used in ll. 30 and 35 as in no. 10, l. 24.

Index 2359. B.M. MS. Harley 2253, f.80a. *Harley*, p. 60, no. 23; *E.E.L.*, pp. 97–9, no. 48; C.B. *14c.*, pp. 11–12, no. 10.

Poem 15. The stanza form is elaborate and the rhythm is that of native alliterative verse (p. 34) with four stresses in every line, each of which falls into two halves in which the stresses are variously distributed. According to widespread tradition the man in the moon was a thief carrying a bundle of thorns he had stolen (ll. 23–4 and below). In this poem his theft appears to be connected with his making a hedge, and he has been caught by the hedge-keeper and has had to give him a security against payment of a fine. This is, to the best of my knowledge, not only novel as a subject for a poem but also as part of the man-in-the-moon story, and I know no other instance of the means proposed in ll. 25–32 for helping him out of his difficulties though what is proposed is not perfectly clear. (Are the hedge-keeper and the bailiff the same man? or is money to be stolen from the hedge-keeper while he is drunk, to redeem the security which he has already passed to the bailiff?) It may be that no. 15 is not only a window on common village life about 1300, reminding of scenes in *Piers Plowman* or in Bruegel at a later date, but also different from many other medieval poems in being unconventional. The vigour and colour of its homely English may be compared with that of, say, Dunbar's Scottish, and it may not be insignificant that Dunbar, too, sometimes used the native alliterative verse.

See R. J. Menner, 'The man in the moon and hedging.' *J.E.G.P.*, xlviii (1949), pp. 1–14. The legend is related to the man who was stoned to death for gathering sticks on the Sabbath in *Numbers* xv, 32–6.

Index 2066. B.M. MS. Harley 2253, f.114b. *Harley*, p. 69, no. 30; C.B. *13c.*, pp. 160–1, no. 89; *E.M.E.T.*, pp. 123–4, no. 31.

Poem 16. This poem, in the address of the soul to the body, and no. 17, in its catalogue of the physical signs of dying, resemble an earlier, 12c. poem, and this, in its turn, sermons in Latin and, more especially, in Old English. Preachers in England before the Norman Conquest frequently made their theme a contemplation of death, and these poems are in their tradition (pp. 40–1). For the conflict between soul and body see, e.g., *Galatians* v, 17. It became a convention for the one to address the other.

Address of soul to body and physical signs of dying: see 'Worcester Fragments' in, e.g., *Selections from Early Middle English*, ed. J. Hall (Oxford, 1920); in vol. ii, pp. 232–4, are sources and analogues. A 13c. example is in Jesus Coll. Oxf. MS. 29, ed. R. Morris *E.E.T.S. O.S.* 49 (1872), pp. 173 ff. *Connection with Old English:* see E. K. Heningham, 'Old English precursors of *The Worcester Fragments*', *P.M.L.A.*, lv (1940), pp. 291–307.

Index 2336. Trinity Coll., Camb. MS. B.14.39(323), f.27a. C.B. *13c.*, p. 31, no. 20.

Poem 17. See note 16.

l. 9. riset = falls(?) see Kemp Malone, *E.L.H.*, ii (1935), p. 63. *l. 21*: 'The rof . . . schal ligge o thine chinne', C.B. *13c.*, no. 29B, l. 78; 14c./15c.: Dreves xxxiii, p. 262: 'Quando domi summitas super nasum iacet.'

Index 3998. Trinity Coll., Camb. MS. B.1.45(43), f.73b. C.B. *13c.*, p. 130, no. 71.

Poem 18. The earliest recorded English ballad or ballad-like poem (p. 45). It is known only through a written version and no oral and no later version exists. No more ballads were recorded until 15c. and then only a few: most are of 16c. and later. There is characteristic ellipsis in that there is no account of Judas' going to Jerusalem between ll. 6 and 7 nor of his sleeping between ll. 14 and 15: the essential moments are spot-lit, sparely and intensely. There is characteristic repetition in l. 5 and, in ll. 20–4, repetition with variation.

Index 1649. Trinity Coll. Camb. MS. B.14.39(323), f.34a. C.B. *13c.*, p. 38, no. 25; Child, p. 41, no. 23; Sisam, pp. 168–9.

Poem 19. A very good but rather exceptional poem in that it is one of the few extant and complete secular lyrics of this early date that is not in the Harley collection (p. 32) and in that it is one of the earliest recorded unmistakably in carol form (p. 35). It is a *chanson d'aventure* and closely parallels a particular poem in French (p. 43).

Notes

Index 360. Lincoln's Inn MS. Hale 135, f.138b. Greene, p. 305, no. 450; Sisam, p. 163; C.B. *13c.*, pp. 119–20, no. 62.

Poem 20. The five joys of Mary made a common medieval theme though the number of joys was sometimes greater. The introduction is in the manner of a *chanson d'aventure* (p. 43), and expresses the poet's longing (l. 16) for the holy maiden in terms that could be found in a secular love lyric (pp. 20–1, 24 and compare, e.g. no. 14).

Index 359. B.M. MS. Harley 2253, f.81b. *Harley,* pp. 65–6, no. 27; C.B. *14c.*, pp. 13–14, no. 11.

Poem 21. The conventions of love (pp. 44–5) warm to life at several points and particularly in the concrete image in the last stanza which remains specially attractive even when we have acknowledged the obvious charm of the birds and the prettiness of what is a conventional idea. This is a Harley lyric (p. 32) with much alliteration and a demanding stanza form which is apparently varied in stanzas 6 and 9. Because of this irregularity it has been suggested that the scribe wrote the stanzas in the wrong sequence, inventing the last two lines of stanza 6 for the sake of continuity, and that the stanzas should be re-ordered with the last stanza as a burden, as in a carol (p. 35), and the others 7, 8, 1, 2, 3, 4, 5, 6. A variation in the last stanza of a Harley lyric is not, however, uncommon (note 10).

Re-ordering stanzas: S. H. L. Degginger, "'A wayle whyt ase whalles bon"—reconstructed', *J.E.G.P.*, liii (1954), pp. 84–90.

Index 105. B.M. MS. Harley 2253, f.67a. *Harley,* p. 40, no. 9.

Poem 22. This fine poem presents the course of the Passion to the eye of the devout imagination to affect the heart (pp. 22, 37–8, 40). It is restrained and has a plain dignity. In predominantly three-stress lines and an elaborate stanza, it moves with ease and assurance.

Index 1365. B.M. Harley MS. 2253, f.80a. *Harley,* pp. 59–60, no. 22; C.B. *13c.*, p. 122, no. 64.

Poem 23. In many respects a typical Harley lyric (p. 32) with elaborate stanza and abundance of alliteration. The nakedness of the poet's feeling in ll. 34–6 and the actual earthiness as well as sexual frankness of the two images in ll. 31–3 are outstanding, though they focus and develop the conventional connection between the natural

world, here multifariously described, and the poet's inner life
(pp. 15, 20, 44).

Index 1861. B.M. MS. Harley 2253, f.71b. *Harley*, p. 43, no. 11;
E.E.L., pp. 8–9, no. 5; Sisam, pp. 164–5; C.B. *13c.*, pp. 145–6, no.
81.

Poem 24. This poem resembles, in some respects, the 13c. Latin
hymn, 'Stabat mater dolorosa', which has been associated with an
Italian hymn on the Passion by Jacopone, the Franciscan, containing
dialogue. The devotional tradition in which this poem stands is
considered on pp. 22, 37–8, 40. In two versions, no. 24 is found with
musical notation and it may be that it was sung dramatically in
church: there is some evidence that Latin complaints of the Virgin
were so sung on the Continent. It may, thus, be an instance of how
English drama grew, in part, from developments in the performance
of the Church's liturgy, in this case, of the liturgy of Passiontide
(compare nos. 85, 183).

ll. 31–6 have this place in the Digby and Royal MSS. but are
found between stanzas 2 and 3 in the Harley MS. They do not
occur in the St. John's MS.: that version of the poem ends in the
middle of stanza 5. *Dramatic Latin complaints* of the Virgin: K.
Young, *The Drama of the Medieval Church* (Oxford, 1933), vol. i,
pp. 496 ff.

Index 3211. B.M. MS. Harley 2253, f. 79a; Bodl. MS. Digby 86
(1687), f. 127a; St. John's Coll. Camb. MS. 111, f.106b; B.M. MS.
Royal 12.e.1, f.193a. *Harley*, pp. 56–7, no. 20; C.B. *13c.*, pp. 87–91,
203–4, no. 49.

Poem 25. The burden of this poem in the form of a carol (p. 35) may
well be that of a popular song: its character—in rhythm, imagery
and directness—is quite different from that of the rest of the poem.
In the MS. it precedes the first stanza and follows the first two.
ll. 5–36 are very bad, because merely and uncreatively and repeti-
tively conventional. The precious gems and flowers in ll. 29–36 are
little more than a list, glittering dully with the sort of rhetoric that
was used also of the Blessed Virgin (pp. 20–1). The lady's goodness
resembles coral only in that coral is a conventional instance of excel-
lence, as a lily is, or a lady. The physical beauty of coral, or of a lily
or a lady, is scarcely present, if at all. And what can be the propriety
of comparing cheeks to a lantern in the darkness (ll. 21–2)? The

figure of anaphora (the repetition of 'For hire love') in the last
stanza instead of building up an effect, flattens it utterly (pp. 25–6,
32–4). The psychological allegory in ll. 37–60, however, is much
better. Allegorical objectification of the intricacies and intangi-
bilities of a passionate relationship and of the inner life involved was
at the heart of the love tradition: the classic instance is in the *Roman
de la Rose* of 13c. (compare no. 143). In the last stanza, as in l. 53,
hire love is the poet's 'love of her', for there is no mention of his
mistress's attitude and it cannot, therefore, be 'her love (for him)'.
The implication is that she is conventionally aloof and unresponsive.
But she has him so in her power that all his feelings are hers (l. 40),
and his sighing and grief are therefore called her knights (l. 41) (no.
9, ll. 9–10). This is a Harley lyric (pp. 32–3) in which the conven-
tions of the love tradition (pp. 44–5) are used without much imagina-
tion (p. 20). But for a more approving account of the poem see
L. Spitzer, '*Explication de texte* applied to three great Middle English
poems', *Archivum Linguisticum*, iii (1951), pp. 1–22. Spitzer thinks
it significant that the poem has ten stanzas, for that is the 'perfect
number'.

Index 1395. B.M. MS. Harley 2253, f.72b. *Harley*, p. 48, no. 14;
C.B. *13c.*, pp. 148–50, no. 83; Greene, pp. 299–300, no. 440; *E.M.E.T.*,
pp. 119–21, no. 28.

Poem 26. This poem laments the death of King Edward I in 1307, and
was, presumably, written about then. It is like a French poem in the
same metre. The stanza form, that of Chaucer's *Monk's Tale* (p.
26), is very common. The minstrel begins by arresting his audience's
attention (no. 7), and continues in no great or very moving vein
but simply and directly. The Pope's brief words in l. 31 are quite
touching. The commendations of the dead king in stanza 2 are
entirely conventional: of any noble knight any poet would say he
was *trewest, war and wis* and *ber the pris* (Chaucer's Knight in ll. 6–7
of *General Prologue to Canterbury Tales* and Duke Theseus in ll. 5–7
of *Knight's Tale*).

Index 205. B.M. MS. Harley 2253, f.73a. R.H.R. *Hist. Poems*,
p. 21, no. 5.

Poem 27. This is a paraphrase of *Isaiah* lxiii, 1–7, which is part of a
lesson in one of the masses of Holy Week (pp. 17, 20). In ll. 1–6 the
element of 'strength' and 'might' in the prophet's first verse is

abstracted and developed into the traditional image of the Christ fighting the battle of redemption (nos. 41 and 51) and the irrelevant references to Edom and Bozrah are omitted (p. 23). Thereafter the prophet's words are followed closely (except that in ll. 20–4 his verses 6 and 7 are reversed) and interpreted in terms of the emphasis defined in the first lines, so that there is no suggestion here of the interpretation, common a century later, in terms of the mystic wine-press of the Cross, which extracted Jesus' blood for sinners to wash in.

Isaiah, lxiii, 1–7: see *Sarum Missal*, p. 100. *Mystic wine-press*: see E. Mâle, *L'art réligieux de la fin du moyen âge en France* (Paris, 1931), pp. 117–22.

Index 3906. B.M. (once Phillips 8336) Additional MS. 46919, f.210a. C.B. *14c.*, p. 28, no. 25.

Poem 28. (pp. 17, 20.) The character of this poem is considered on p. 22. The 'gret wonder' elaborated in the first two stanzas, the 'robe' of human nature taken by Christ in stanza 3, and, in ll. 23–4, the image of Christ's Passion as a charter written in Christ's own blood and bequeathing Heaven to man are all common topics.

gret wonder: see Mone, i, p. 59, no. 43: Verum est, mirum est,/ Nihil mirabilius,/Propriae filiae/Pater fit filius; i, p. 62, no. 47: Mater haec est filia,/Pater hic est natus; ii, p. 343, no. 548: Summi sponsa creatoris,/Soror, dos et filia,/Parens patris, nata prolis,/Virginum primaria; John, p. 241: O mira creatura,/Tam magna, tam pusilla,/Mater et virgo pura,/ Regina et ancilla,/Amica, sponsa, filia,/Et soror creatoris. *Robe:* see 5c.: Eucherius, *P.L.*, l, col. 733: 'Vestimentum Filii Dei aliquando caro ejus quae a divinitate assumpta est a divinis libris figuraliter accipitur, de quo indumento carnis Isaias vaticinans ait': (*Isaiah* lxiii, 1, and therefore see no. 27); 12c.?: Pseudo-Rabanus, *P.L.*, cxii, cols. 1075–6: 'Vestimentum est humanitas Christi' (*Revelation* xix, 16); 'Vestis est caro Christi' (*Revelation* xix, 13); Henryson, 'The Bludy Serk'; *Piers Plowman* B xviii, 22–3 identifies Piers' *armes* and *humana natura*. *The chartre:* see M. C. Spalding, *The Middle English Charters of Christ* (Bryn Mawr: Pennsylvania, 1914); from at least the early 14c. this image is further developed into the figure of Christ's own crucified body as the document, overwritten with his wounds; 13c.: Jacopone da Todi's *lauda* ci: E nelle tue sante mano ce scrivisti/Per noi salvare e darce lo tuo regno (In your holy hands you wrote in order to save us and give us your kingdom).

Index 3700. B.M. (once Phillipps 8336) Additional MS. 46919, f.206b. C.B. *14c.*, p. 18, no. 16.

Poem 29. (See p. 22.) A translation of the Latin hymn (p. 39) by Bishop Theodulph of the 8c. and 9c., familiar today as the 'All glory laud and honour' of J. M. Neale, and sung in the Palm-Sunday procession (p. 36 and see *Sarum Missal*, p. 96 and Daniel, i, pp. 215–16).

Index 3872. B.M. Additional (once Phillips 8336) MS. 46919, f.205b. C.B. *14c.*, pp. 16–17, no. 14.

Poem 30. Short and poignant, this poem calls up in the mind of the devotee some essentials of the scene of the Passion and then turns the pity stirred into self-rebuke and renewed love (pp. 22, 38).

Index 3964. B.M. MS. Royal 12 E, i, f.194b. C.B. *13c.*, p. 62, no. 35B.

Poem 31. This fragment may be part of a carol (p. 35). In the MS. it is written continuously, like prose, but, set out as it has been here, it has the characteristic stanza form and burden (no. 33). It has a magic that tantalizes partly because the poem is incomplete but also because, in this rare relic of a popular tradition (pp. 30–2), it is to Ireland that the strange woman beckons, the land of the saints (l. 2).

Index 1008. Bodl. MS. Rawlinson D. 913 (13679), Item 1. R.H.R. *Sec. Lyrs*, p. 11, no. 15; Sisam, p. 166.

Poem 32. A fair paraphrase of 'Angelus ad virginem', the Latin hymn sung by Nicholas, the *clerk*, in Chaucer's *Miller's Tale* (no. 52 in the *Oxford Book of Carols*). This Latin poem precedes no. 32 in the MS. and has music to which the English could quite happily be sung, so nearly has its rhythm been matched (p. 39).

Index 888. B.M. Arundel MS. 248, f.154a. C.B. *13c.*, p. 75, no. 44.

Poem 33. Despite the opinion of the Bishop of Ossory that this poem was unsuitable for his clergy to sing (p. 31) it has been argued that it is to be interpreted in the allegorical terms used, for example, in the Marian poems and explained in the Appendix, so that the moor is the wilderness of the world before Christ's coming, the well God's grace, the maiden Mary, and so on. But comparison of most obviously religious poems with no. 33 will show little but the sort of differences that associate it rather with nos. 66 and 114 (without necessarily excluding, altogether, association with religion); in particular, the repetitiveness, the advance through small increments, the incantation and the questioning which suggest popular origins (pp. 19, 30).

Interpretation as a poem in the tradition of the learned: (for) D. W. Robertson, 'Historical criticism', in *English Institute essays: 1950* (New York and London, 1951); (against) E. T. Donaldson, 'Patristic exegesis in the criticism of medieval literature,' in *Critical approaches to medieval literature* (New York, 1960). *Connection with Bishop of Ossory:* see R. L. Greene, '"The maid of the moor" in the *Red Book of Ossory*,' *Speculum*, xxvii (1952), pp. 504–6. *Last two stanzas:* on the narrow strip of parchment in which this poem is preserved the last stanzas have been abbreviated and are expanded here on the pattern of the first two.

Index 3891. Bodl. MS. Rawlinson D. 913(13679), Item I. R.H.R. *Sec. Lyrs.*, p. 12, no. 18; Sisam, p. 167.

Poem 34. It is uncertain whether this poem is by William of Shoreham, vicar of Chart, in Kent. It is made of allegorical figures and conventional titles for Mary and these are explained in general on p. 17 and in detail in the Appendix. I do not know, however, why the Blessed Virgin is the 'Castle of Emmaus' in ll. 57–8. The poetic nature and quality of the poem is considered on pp. 20–2.

In the unique MS. three poems are ascribed to William of Shoreham, but this one is associated instead with Robert Grosseteste, 13c. Bishop of Lincoln. Perhaps William translated it from Grosseteste's Latin.

Index 2107. B.M. Additional MS. 17376, f.204b. C.B. *14c.*, p. 46, no. 32; ed. M. Konrath, *E.E.T.S.* E.S. 86 (1902), pp. 127–9, no. 6.

Poem 35. A poem in contempt of the world (p. 40). It has a novel beginning of pungent irony: the first line is that of a normal lullaby which intends to go on to reassure the baby and prettily disarm its apprehension, but the second line alters direction entirely so that the poem becomes an adult lullaby assuring the baby that it has every reason to weep as it will soon discover! It is the earliest known lullaby poem (p. 40) though its ironic opening might suggest that the form was common before the beginning of the 14c. even if not recorded. In stanza 4, and particularly in l. 23, the work of the Goddess Fortune is implied, and the images in ll. 25 and 31 are traditional as are the three considerations of l. 16.

X 321

ll. 25 and 31: man a pilgrim in an alien land: Psalm xxxix, 12; *Hebrews* xiii, 14; xi, 13–16; *I Peter* iii, 11; and compare nos. 48, l. 23; 55, ll. 17–20; pseudo-Augustine, 'Liber meditationum', *P.L.*, xl, col. 915: peregrinamur a te etc. *l. 16, Whan thou commest* etc.: 12c.: Alanus de Insulis, *P.L.*, ccx, col. 580; Quid fecisti nasciturus, / Quid sis praesens, quid futurus, / Diligenter inspice; 12c.?: 'De cognitione humanae conditionis', *P.L.*, clxxxiv, col. 490: Attende, homo, quid fuisti ante ortum, et quid es ab ortu usque ad occasum, atque quid eris post hanc vitam.

Index 2025. B.M. MS. Harley 913, f.32a. C.B. *14c.*, p. 35, no. 28; *E.E.L.*, pp. 166–8, no. 91.

Poem 36. The devotional tradition in which this poem is written is considered on pp. 22, 40, and Rolle's life and place in the tradition on p. 38. This poem is from a brief epistle known as the 'Ego dormio' and dedicated to a nun whom Rolle says he will bring 'to his bed, that has made thee and boght thee, Christe, the King sonn of Heven'. The sensuousness of the love-longing (ll. 2 and 37) is not peculiar to Rolle: like other medieval religious poets he uses terms and phrases found also in secular poetry (e.g. ll. 31–2, 55, 59— with which latter compare, no. 145, l. 3—pp. 20–1, 24), and the standard text in commending the devout use of the Name of Jesus (e.g. ll. 20, 21, 39), 'Thy name is as ointment poured forth' (*Song of Songs* i, 3), itself contains a strikingly sensuous image; moreover, mystical writers in general sometimes use sensuous imagery to express what they regard as spiritual experience, and the sighing, the light, the feeding, the burning and feeling of love (ll. 1, 6, 7, 46, 66, 81) are typical of them. See also, however, below.

Thy name is as ointment: St. Bernard, 'Sermones in Cantica', *P.L.*, clxxxiii, cols. 843 ff.: 'Qualiter nomen Jesus est medicina salubris fidelibus Christianis in omnibus adversis' . . . *Oleum effusum nomen tuum. Sensuous religious imagery:* in his 'Form of Living', *English writings*, ed. H. E. Allen (Oxford, 1931), p. 118, Rolle tells Margaret the anchorite that 'contemplacion es a wonderful joy of Goddes luve, . . . that wonderful loving es in the saule, and for abundance of joy and swettenes it ascendes intil the mouth, swa that the hert and the tonge, acordes in ane, and body and sawle joyes in God livand'; see also Rolle's *Incendium Amoris*, trans. R. Misyn, *E.E.T.S.* O.S. 106 (1896), p. 31: 'Godis luve in heet, songe and swet-nes standis' etc. and chaps. xiv–xv generally.

Notes

Index 2270. Camb. Univ. Lib. MS. Dd. 5.64. III, f. 28a; Bodl. MS. (Vernon) Eng. poet. a.1 (3938), f.338b; etc. Richard Rolle, *English Writings*, ed. H. E. Allen (Oxford, 1931), pp. 70–2.

Poem 37. A carol (p. 35) of which the burden is addressed to a tear in Christ's eye and the stanzas to Christ himself. The last stanza is used in no. 58. The devotional background is considered on pp. 22, 38.

Index 3691. Nat. Lib. of Scotland MS. Advocates 18.7.21, f.124b. C.B. *14c.*, p. 87, no. 69; Greene, p. 193, no. 271.

Poem 38. A carol with the form of a *chanson d'aventure* (p. 43) and one of the earliest examples of a lullaby of the Child Jesus (p. 40). In stanza 2 the homely detail of the mother's hope that her child will go off to sleep without her having to sing is typical: it comes of the devout making real to themselves in meditation the episodes of our redemption (pp. 22, 23, 29, 35–6, 38). The *longing* of ll. 2 and 78 is that of the devotee for Christ (no. 36). In ll. 65–6 the seven gifts of the Holy Spirit are traditional (*Isaiah* xi, 2–3 and E. Mâle, *L'art réligieux du XIIIe siècle en France* (Paris, 1931), pp. 171 and 175).

Index 352. Nat. Lib. of Scotland MS. Advocates 18.7.21, f.3b. C.B. *14c.*, p. 70, no. 56; Greene, pp. 103–5, no. 149 and compare R.H.R. *Christmas carols*, p. 73, no. 27.

Poem 39. Addressed to Jesus in the Blessed Sacrament, probably for particular use in the Mass when the devotee can see the Elements, raised by the celebrant above his head.

Index 1729. B.M. (*once* Gurney) MS. Egerton 3245, f.189b. R.H.R., 'Popular prayers in Middle English verse', *M.P.*, xxxvi (1939), p. 337. R.H.R., 'The Gurney series of religious lyrics', *P.M.L.A.*, liv (1939), p. 369.

Poem 40. This is a translation of one stanza from the great hymn of Venantius Fortunatus (6c.), 'Pange, lingua, gloriosi' (Daniel i, pp. 163–4). The stanza translated—'Crux fidelis inter omnes'—was sometimes sung on its own and several times repeated between the other stanzas in the rites of Good Friday at the Adoration of the Cross.

Index 3212. Merton Coll. Oxf. MS. B.1.6. (248), f. 167a. C.B. *14c.*, p. 55, no. 40.

Notes

Poem 41. A complaint of Christ (p. 40). The image of Christ riding upon the Tree is very striking. It is traditional (the poem occurs in a preaching MS. of the Dominican friars): compare *Meditations*, ll. 1589–1604: The hors that thou onne ridest / Thou thorlest not with spores his sides. / Bright armure hast thou non (etc.); Crucifixion play in Towneley Cycle (*E.E.T.S.* E.S. lxxi (1897/1952), p. 261): let see / How we can horse oure kinge so free; see notes 27 and 51. There may be a connection with some verses of Philippe of Grève: see note 46.

Index 2150. B.M. MS. Harley 2316, f.25a. C.B. *14c.*, p. 67, no. 51.

Poem 42. Compactly made, this poem concludes neatly with a conceit. The devotional tradition is considered on pp. 22, 28, 38.

Index 1684. Bodl. MS. (Vernon) Eng. Poet. a.1 (3938), f.114b and f.300a. C.B. *14c.*, p. 68, no. 52.

Poem 43. A poem in contempt of the world (p. 40). The development of the figure of the 'shadow', though itself conventional (see no. 83, l. 26), is excellent and exceptional. Such a homely picture better achieves the moralist's intention than hundreds of lines of bald moralizing and dead lists of conventional *exempla*. The semi-refrain is also poignantly concrete. The wise words attributed to Socrates that begin at l. 25 are like those in *Ecclesiastes* vii, 2. The long stanza as well as the moral content is typical of a number of poems in this, the 'Vernon' MS. (no. 48 and p. 28).

Index 3996. Bodl. MS. (Vernon) Eng. poet. a.1 (3938), f.408a. C.B. *14c.*, p. 143, no. 101.

Poem 44. A poignantly brief complaint of Mary (pp. 23, 29, 40).

Index 4159. Nat. Lib. of Scotland MS. Advocates 18.7.21, f.24a. C.B. *14c.*, p. 81, no. 60.

Poem 45. A popular 'meditation' found in ten MSS. For the devotional tradition in which it is written see p. 22. It is in two parts. In the first, up to l. 74, Jesus is asked to write his Passion in the devotee's heart. Successive stages of the Passion are incised by the repeated, 'write', and their human pathos is drawn out boldly and tenderly but without sentimentality. ll. 13–20 are exceptional since, in this part of the meditation, there are no other reflections on the points of the Passion as they are held in the mind, each concluded in a stanza of four lines. The image of writing on the heart is common. At l. 75 there is a transition to the second part of the meditation which is punctuated by appeals to 'Jesu' and is a plea for his aid and a consideration of the love the devotee owes to him. The images in ll. 109–12 and 77–8 are also common. This poem derives from the 14c. English poem now known as the *Meditations on the life and Passion of Christ*, which, in its turn, derives from John of Hoveden's 13c. Latin *Philomena*. Not only is no. 45 briefer, but attention is concentrated on the Passion and the appeal of the devotee is made more direct.

'*Meditation*': so called in Egerton MS. 3245. *Writing on the heart: Jeremiah* xvii, 1; *II Corinthians* iii, 3; pseudo-Augustine, 'Liber meditationum', *P.L.*, xl, col. 931: Scribe digito tuo in pectore meo dulcem memoriam tui melliflui nominis, etc.; *Meditations* ll. 1350 ff. *Softening the heart: Ezekiel* xi, 19; pseudo-Augustine, 'Liber meditationum', *P.L.*, xl, col. 929: Rogo itaque te, Domine . . . mollifica cor meum durum et lapideum, saxeum et ferreum etc. *ll. 109–12, wounding by love*: pseudo-Augustine, 'Liber meditationum', *P.L.*, xl, col. 935: Tu sagitta electa, etc., . . . confige cor meum jaculo tui amoris: ut dicat tibi anima mea, 'Charitate tua vulnerata sum'; Rolle, 'Meditation on the Passion' in *English writings*, ed. H. E. Allen (Oxford, 1931), pp. 23–4: woundes of reuthe is al my desir, peine and compassioun of my Lord Jesu Christ; St. Bonaventura, 'Stimuli amoris', xii, p. 3: vulnere amoris tui. *ll. 77–8, hound of heaven*: see no. 62, ll. 41–2; second part 'Quia Amore' in *E.E.L.*, p. 151, l. 12; *C.B. 13c.*, no. 54, ll. 11–15; St. Augustine, 'Sermo li', *P.L.*, xxxviii, col. 333: Non enim tantum amatores venatorum, sed etiam ipsos venatores venatus est ad salutem; Jacopone da Todi's *lauda* xxvi: Figlio, non gir pur fugenno! / Tanto t'ho gito encalzanno. (Oh! son, stop flying from me. / I have travelled so long pursuing you.) *ll. 129–30, prayer as a chain*: (?) Homer, *Iliad*, viii, 19–22. *Derivation from 'Meditations'*: see C. D'Evelyn, '"Meditations on the life and passion of Christ": a note on its literary relationships', in *Essays and studies in honor of Carleton Browne* (New York and London, 1940), pp. 79–90. *Derivation from 'Philomena'*: see F. J. E. Raby, 'A middle English paraphrase', *M.L.R.*, xxx (1935), pp. 339–43.

Index 1761. Longleat MSS. 29, f.147a; 30, f.49a; Bodl. MS. 850 (2604), f.90a; e.Mus. 232 (3657), f.62a; B.M. Additional (Wheatley) MS. 39574, f.1a; (once Gurney) Egerton 3245, f.185b; Huntington MS. HM 142, f.45a; etc. C.B. *14c.*, p. 114, no. 91.

Poem 46. A complaint of Christ (p. 40), this poem grows from a verse of *Lamentations* paraphrased in ll. 1–4, which was part of a lesson in the Good Friday services. (See pp. 23, 29.)

Lamentations i, 12: *Sarum Breviary*, col. dcclxxxvii: O! vos omnes qui transitis per viam, attendite et videte si est dolor sicut dolor meus. Spoken originally by Jerusalem, these words are used in the service as if spoken by Christ. *There may be a connection* with some verses of Philippe de Grève, Chancellor of Paris in early 13c., in Mone, i, p. 172: Homo, vide, quid pro te patior, / Ad te clamo, qui pro te morior, / Vide clavos, quibus confodior, / Per quinque plagas nunc aperior. These Latin lines precede an English version in two 14c. MSS.

Index 4263. Nat. Lib. of Scotland MS. Advocates 18.7.21, f.125b. C.B. *14c.*, p. 90, no. 74.

Poem 47. A complaint of Christ (p. 40), which is basically a paraphrase of the Reproaches of Christ sung at the Adoration of the Cross in the Good Friday rites. (See pp. 23, 29.)

Reproaches begin 'Popule meus, quid feci tibi?' God reminds his people—Israel, under the old dispensation, and the Church, under the new—how he saved them from the Egyptians and led them towards the Promised Land (*Exodus* xii–xvii); but, in contrast with his mercy, they have sent him to the Cross.

Index 2240. Nat. Lib. of Scotland MS. Advocates 18.7.21, f.125a. C.B. *14c.*, pp. 88–9, no. 72.

Poem 48. A poem in contempt of the world (p. 40), in several places reflecting *Ecclesiastes* (that book of the Old Testament which itself has as theme, 'Vanity of vanities, saith the Preacher, . . . all is vanity') and, in ll. 3–4, the apocryphal *Wisdom of Solomon* (v, 11). The inclusion of religious controversy (ll. 61–72) among the instances of wordly vanity is an interesting and early variation on the central theme. See note 43.

Ecclesiastes i, 5–7 in ll. 13–17; i, 4 in ll. 25–6; iii, 18–20 in ll. 49–60.

Index 1402. Bodl. MS. (Vernon) Eng. Poet. a.1 (3938), f.409a. C.B. *14c.*, p. 160, no. 106.

Poem 49. The central images of this devotional poem, for the tradition of which see p. 22, are startling to most modern readers, and that of being clad in Christ's skin is very odd from any point of view: but they are basically traditional. (See pp. 23, 29, 38.)

Images traditional: e.g. 15c.: 'Salutatio ad latus Domini', Mone, i, p. 166, no. 126, especially: Plaga rubens aperire / Fac cor meum te sentire / Sive me in te transire, / Vellem totus introire, / Pulsanti pande pauperi. / . . . O quam dulcis sapor iste / Qui te gustat, Jesu Christe, / Tuo victus a dulcore / Mori posset prae amore / Te unum amans unice.

Index 1002. Nat. Lib. of Scotland MS. Advocates 18.7.21, f.124b. C.B. *14c.*, p. 88, no. 71.

Poem 50. This is a paraphrase of a Latin poem and an instance of a very common type, the Hours of the Passion based upon the sequence of the canonical hours, or services of the Church at regular times by day and night—Matins, in the early hours of the morning, Prime, at sunrise, the first hour of the day, Undern, at, say, nine, Sext, at, say, mid-day, Nones, at, say, three, Evensong, in the evening, and Compline at the last hour before bed. It may be this poem was used by the probable Franciscan, Friar John Grimestone (in whose commonplace book it is preserved) as a public devotion, the response (ll. 5–6) being said by the congregation after common meditation on each scene as the friar pronounced the stanzas (pp. 23, 29).

Latin Hours of the Passion: Daniel i, p. 337; and also in other vernaculars: Mone, i, pp. 106–30. In his *Speculum Ecclesiae* (13c.) St. Edmund had written a plan for meditation on the scenes of the Passion in which the divisions were by these Hours.

Index 441. Nat. Lib. of Scotland MS. Advocates 18.7.21, f.2b. C.B. *14c.*, p. 69, no. 55.

Poem 51. A poem to encourage penitence which is rather like a complaint of Christ (see p. 40). It represents Christ as the champion against man's foes, Satan and Death (no. 27 and note 41; pp. 23, 29).

Christ the champion: Meditations, ll. 1585 ff.: Writ now, love, that King of Might / In red armure is shape to fight; / Withouten stedes and hors of pris / He hath overcomon his enemys; Christ jousts against Satan on the cross in *Piers Plowman,* B xviii and xix, wearing Piers' armour, *humana natura* (note 28); W. Gaffney, 'The allegory of the Christ Knight in *Piers Plowman*', *P.M.L.A.,* xlvi (1931), 155–68; R. Woolf, 'The theme of Christ the lover-knight in medieval English literature', *R.E.S.,* N.S., xiii (1962), 1–16.

Notes

Index 1274. Nat. Lib. of Scotland MS. Advocates 18.7.21, f.119b. C.B. *14c.*, p. 82, no. 63.

Poem 52. This is a *roundel* (p. 43), as Chaucer calls it, sung to a *note*, or tune, that 'imaked was in Fraunce', by select birds in honour of the Goddess Nature at the end of their debate about a question of love in the *Parlement of Fowles,* which was almost certainly for public delivery on St. Valentine's Day (l. 4). The return of Spring and the revival of love in that season (l. 9) are conventional elements (p. 15) but the *lange nightes blake* is an instance of that indefinable and inimitable characteristic of medieval English poetry which one calls weakly, its 'freshness' or 'immediacy' (pp. 26–7, 30–4).

Index 2375. Camb. Univ. Lib. MS. Gg.4.27, Ia, f.490b; St. John's Coll. Oxf. MS. LVII, f.226a (lines 4, 5, 8, 9, 10 only); Bodl. MS. Digby 181 (1782), f.51b (lines 1, 2, 3, 4, 5, 9, 10 only). Chaucer, p. 318.

Poem 53. A ballade (p. 43). The first stanza is finely magniloquent (pp. 25, 32). Its images and rhetorical figures are conventional. Here are *exclamatio* (l. 1), *translatio* (ll. 1 and 7), *imago* (ll. 3 and 4) and a sort of *expolitio* (ll. 3 and 4), what we should call, apostrophe, metaphor, simile and amplification-by-variation. They come naturally and with assured ease. We cannot be absolutely certain of the tone of the first four lines of the last stanza. What is most likely is that this is a poem of mixed tone and that Chaucer presents himself not only as nobly eloquent, as in the first stanza, burning with constant passion and devotion though for no reward, but also, in this stanza, as a little ridiculous, a fish swamped in sentiment, a rueful version of that Tristram who was the ideal lover.

Difficulty in determining tone?: Theseus in *Knight's Tale,* narrator in *Franklin's Tale,* Pandarus and Criseyde in *Troilus and Criseyde* call in question some of the sentimental excesses of refined love (pp. 44–5) so that an ironic attitude in the final stanza is consistent with attitudes Chaucer realized elsewhere. Though Criseyde in love compares herself with a fish in *Troilus and Criseyde,* iv, ll. 764–6, and in iii, l. 35 Venus is said to know why people fall in love, 'As why this fish, and naught that, comth to were', (and though the Christian soul is commonly represented as a fish caught by Christ), the 'fish' image in no. 53 differs from these serious uses in that the fish in no. 53 is cooked and served up in sauce! However, M. D. Legge in *French Studies,* iv (1950), pp. 50–4, comments on toothache as a comparison for love in, for example, Jehan Renart, without intended incongruity; and what is thought comic varies from age to age. There are other passages in Chaucer the tone of which is uncertain. What, for example, is the tone of *Canterbury Tales*, F. 1016–18, *Troilus and Criseyde*, ii, 904–6, iii, 185–6, 617–21, 1256–7, etc.? It is not impossible that these are poetically imperfect and that Chaucer was exceptionally insensitive to their bathos. Compare, however, these lines of a poem on f.4b of B.M. Additional MS. (Wheatley) 39574: Haile bote of bale, blissed quene, / To sight so semely is noon sene; / Lady of aungels, quene of Heven, / Emprice of helle is that I mene.

Index 2031. Bodl. MS. Rawlinson Poet. 163 (14655), f.114a. Chaucer, p. 533.

Poem 54. A ballade (p. 43), in rime-royal stanzas, in which the poet is superbly sure of himself and the lines are not only melodious but dignified and resonant with a heavier incidence of stresses than in nos. 53 or 55 (pp. 25, 32). The confident tone struck by the vocatives and imperatives is sustained through a succession of distinguished names and examples paralleled in the poems of contemporary Frenchmen. It is a *song in preysinge* of the lady, Alceste, as she is led by the God of Love and seen in a dream which the poet had one May and described in the Prologue to the *Legend of Good Women*.

Index 100. Bodl. MS. Fairfax 16 (3896), f.86a. Chaucer, p. 488.

Poem 55. A ballade (p. 43), in rime-royal stanzas, of which the *envoi* occurs in only one MS. so that it may have been written later. I have taken *Vache* in l. 22 to be the name of the man to whom the *envoi* is addressed. Here the philosophical Chaucer reworks in verse traditional sentiments and images. Some are Scriptural, some very like those to be found in the *Consolation of Philosophy* of Boethius (p. 41) and l. 10, e.g., is a proverb.

Traditional sentiments and images: compare generally Gower, *Confessio Amantis*, v, 7735 ff.; l. 7: *John* viii, 32; l. 9, Fortune, p. 41; l. 11: *Acts* ix, 5?; ll. 17–20: note 35; l. 10 proverb: see M. P. Tilley, *A dictionary of the proverbs in English* (1950). B 751.

Index 809. B.M. Additional MS. 10340, f.41a. Chaucer, p. 536.

Poem 56. A ballade (p. 43). The *envoi* has been added later to alter an original complaint to his purse into a complaint to King Henry IV. Chaucer plays cleverly with the implications of identifying his beloved purse with the beloved lady of the love tradition (pp. 44–5; e.g. ll. 3, 4, etc.). The 'saviour' of l. 16 and the 'light of my life', in l. 15, may be straight Christian references and may be related to the friar of l. 19, or they may be felt, rather, through long use, to be formulas from love literature, though originally borrowed from Christianity.

Index 3787. Bodl. MS. Fairfax 16 (3896), f.193a. Chaucer, p.539.

Poem 57. A triple roundel (p. 43) with several parallels of detail in French, and it would be unwise to regard either the humour or the colloquial vigour of the final roundel as peculiarly Chaucerian. On the other hand, though Chaucer's name is nowhere attached to this poem, manuscript context as well as style make it almost certainly his. Refined love and its allegorical expression: pp. 44–5, no. 25, ll. 37–60.

French parallels: l. 27 compare Duc de Berry's 'Puiz qu'a Amours suis si gras eschapé.'

Index 4282. Magdalene Coll. Camb. MS. Pepys 2006, p. 390; B.M. Additional MS. 38179, II, f.51a. Chaucer, p. 542; *E.E.L.*, p. 23, no. 13.

Poem 58. Such an apostrophe to love and the vision of love as both harsh and beneficent is not new, nor is the deliberately startling exploration of the paradoxes of the Atonement and of the apparently contradictory attributes of God, his Righteousness and his Love, which makes this poem at first difficult for the unfamiliar reader to grasp, but which, in reality, draws out the fundamental and mysterious Christian truths (p. 22, nos. 28, 62). The central paradox is stated formally and in readily intelligible terms in ll. 13–14, and it may help to read the poem with them clearly in mind. ll. 15–20 comprise a stanza, alien in form and borrowed from another poem (no. 37), which, set at the transition from the statement of the theme to the drawing out of its significance, is itself a statement of the same theme, but simply and without paradox. This poem has some elements in common with secular love lyrics (ll. 14, 43–4, 46; p. 20).

Love: 13c.: John, 'Canticum Amoris', p. 214: Amor nudat amictu vestium / Vestientem vernale lilium; / . . . Amor, nosti quem sic expolias? / Flos est vigens, fundens fragrancias, / Fons felices donans delicias, / Et mel mentes demulcens anxias; p. 226: Amor, regem si possis vincere, / Cuius regnum non potest ruere, / Ne mireris, cum tibi libere / Se festinat confestim subdere; in the poem, derived from

John of Hoveden's *Philomena*, 14c.: *Meditations*, ll. 787–94: Love now taketh a wonder way, / He maketh that lif is dethes pray; / He wirketh al right as he wil, / And whatso he doth, al it is skil. / Than it is right and al resoun / So to do tho king adoun, / And the servant to make a king: / Now is this a wonder thing; ll. 1821–2: love is fers and wol not spare / Til he have mad his body bare (etc.); ll. 1881–98: ȝaf us ensample also / For love of him to suffre wo. / Love, thou hast bounden the King / That is Lord over alle thing, / And send him to us hider adoun / To dwelle with us in oure prisoun. / It semeth thou art more of might / Than is Jesu the King of right. / To dispute that wole I not dwelle, / Any sortain ther-of to telle. / But this wot I wel forsothe / On substaunce they ben bothe; . . . For the bok seith that God is love / That cam adoun fram Hevene above; 13c.: Jacopone da Todi's *laude* lxxxiii and xc. *Wondering exploration of the paradoxes* of man's redemption: compare pseudo-Augustine, 'Liber meditationum', *P.L.*, xl, col. 906: Dei in passione Christi mira dispositio . . . O mirabilis censurae conditio, et ineffabilis mysterii dispositio! Peccat iniquus et punitur justus (etc.).

Index 611. Glasgow Univ. Lib. Hunterian Museum MS. V.8.15, f.34a; C.B. *14c.*, p. 113, no. 90.

Poem 59. Founded in 13c. by St. Francis, who gave himself to a life of heroic poverty and compassion, by 14c. the Friars Minor had gained a reputation for the opposite. They were often satirized. This poem is puzzling. l. 19 may refer to the playing by Franciscans in miracle plays, where, say, Elijah was represented in a fiery chariot, and ll. 8–9 may refer to a representation of Christ nailed to the Tree of Life, conventional symbol of his redemptive death, painted on the wall of a church. The 'O and I' refrain, or something like it, is not uncommon but its significance is uncertain.

Index 2663. B.M. MS. Cotton Cleopatra B, ii, f.64b. R.H.R. *Hist. poems*, p. 163, no. 66.

Poem 60. In contempt of the world (p. 40). The telling reflection at the beginning, the grisly reminder at the end, the three considerations in ll. 34–6, the image of the bird's flight in ll. 14–18 (derived from *Wisdom of Solomon* v, 11), the examples in ll. 37–45 of the wise, beautiful and strong, and the 'E and I' refrain (the significance of which is unknown) are all typically common. This poem is one of a group of lyrics in the Cambridge MS. which may be by Richard

Rolle (p. 38): they end with the uncertain words, 'Expliciunt cantica divini amoris secundum Ricardum Hampole'. But the Lincoln MS. does not mention his name.

Index 3921. Camb. Univ. Lib. Dd. 5.64, III, f.35b; Lincoln Cath. Lib. MS. 91, f.213a. C.B. *14c.*, p. 96, no. 81; *Richard Rolle*, ed. C. Horstman (London, 1895), i, p. 73.

Poem 61. The most popular of medieval devotional poems occurs in at least eighteen MSS. A Latin rubric calls it a 'prayer' by 'Richard de Caistre, at one time vicar of St. Stephen's, Norwich', who died in 1420. But six of the stanzas are found, for example, in two, probably earlier, 14c. versions, and four in another, and none is ascribed to Richard. He may well have expanded and re-arranged an already popular poem.

l. 41: *spiritual stone: Matthew* xxi, 42; *Isaiah* xxviii, 16; *I Peter* ii, 6–7.

Index 1727. B.M. MS. Harley Charter 58.C.14; Bodl. MS. Barlow 33 (6488), f.57b; Ashmole 751 (8193), f.142a; Rawlinson liturgical e.3 (15799), f.123b; Trinity Coll. Camb. MS. B.14.19 (305), f.162b; etc. C.B. *15c.*, p. 98, no. 64; Patterson, pp. 129–31.

Poem 62. This fine complaint of Mary (p. 40), with likenesses to a *chanson d'aventure* (p. 43), had wide currency. What difficulty there may be for the modern reader (and it would seem, from the variant readings, may also have been for contemporary scribes) in grasping to whom and about whom Mary is speaking is resolved when it is understood that Mary is traditionally both the Mother of God and the Mother of Man (see ll. 61, 43, 33, 11–16, in that order). But, further, Mary identifies her *childe*, Jesus, and *mankinde* in ll. 49–50 because on the Cross Christ suffers for the sins of all mankind and in Christ human nature is taken into the Godhead; and, in ll. 53–5, she does not so much turn from Jesus to man and from man to Jesus and address each separately, but both together, because both are one through the Incarnation (see l. 76 where Mary calls *man* expressly her *offspring*). Characteristically (pp. 17, 22) the refrain is from *Song of Songs* (ii, 5 and v, 8) and it is the warm and tender, human love evoked by the poem in the devout reader (p. 38), and the intimacy of family relationship which is pressed so closely home (compare no. 28) that accounts for the final appeal in l. 95 that the devotee should take Mary as his wife.

The poem has rhetorical elements, *anaphora* (beginning successive phrases with the same words, ll. 10 and 11), and a sort of *paronomasia* (or modification in the sound of a word producing close resemblance in ll. 17 and 18). But, more generally, the poet is confident and ample, varying an idea, for example, in ll. 21 and 22, and, with the addition of antithesis, in ll. 29 and 30, and freely arguing with the reader in ll. 33–8. The legal and theological image in ll. 93–4 is in all respects exact. This is, generally, characteristic of the entire poem in which sentiment is not only evoked but controlled (pp. 22, 38).

Chanson d'aventure?: the 'vision' (l. 4) with which the poet is blessed as he looks in the moonlight at a niche, presumably containing an image of Mary, could be seen as a variant in the *chanson d'aventure* form that was, anyway, characteristically varied. *Mary the Mother of God and Man:* St. Anselm, *Orationes*, lii, *P.L.* clviii, cols. 957–8: O domina, . . . parens es salutis et salvatorum . . . Mater Dei est mater nostra . . . Si enim tu domina es mater ejus, nonne et alii filii tui sunt fratres ejus? . . . Magne Domine, tu noster major frater, magna domina, tu nostra melior mater. *Wide currency:* 6 MSS.: a related poem in which it is Christ who languishes follows it in early 15c. Lambeth MS. and one other, later 15c., MS. only.

Index 1460. Bodl. MS. Douce 322 (21896), f.8b; Ashmole 59 (6943), f.66a; Bibliothèque Nationale, Paris, MS. Anglais 41 (ed. S. Segawa, 1934), f.3b; B.M. Additional MS. 37049, f.25b; Lambeth MS. 853, p. 4; etc. C.B. *14c.*, p. 234, no. 132.

Poem 63. A complaint of Christ (p. 40). The poignant contrasts which Christ draws between his agony and man's vanity resemble others in Latin and English prose works of the 13c. and 14c. but the method itself, albeit as a meditation on the Passion, and not spoken by Christ, goes back to 11c.

Meditations ascribed to St. Augustine: 11c.?: *Liber Meditationum, P.L.,* xl, col. 906: Ego superbivi, tu humiliaris; ego tumui, tu attenuaris; ego inobediens exstiti, tu obediens scelus inobedientiae luis . . . ego delector cibo, tu laboras patibulo; ego fruor deliciis, tu laniaris clavis; ego pomi dulcedinem, tu fellis gustas amaritudinem; mihi ridens congaudet Eva, tibi plorans compatitur Maria (etc.); *Legenda Aurea,* 'on the Passion': 13c.: tu homo es et habes sertum de floribus et ego Deus et habeo coronam de spinis, tu habes chirothecas in manibus et ego habeo clavos defixos, tu in albis vestibus tripudias et ego pro te derisus fui ab Herode in veste alba, tu tripudias cum pedibus et ego laboravi cum meis pedibus, tu in choreis brachia extendis in modum crucis in gaudium et ego ea in cruce extensa habui in opprobrium, ego in cruce dolui et tu in cruce exsultas, tu habes latus apertum et pectus in signum vanae gloriae et ego latus effossum habui pro te (etc.): quoted B. D. Brown, 'The source of a 14c. lyric,' *M.L.N.*, xl (1925); 14c.: *Mirk's Festial*, ed. T. Erbe, *E.E.T.S.* E.S. 96 (1905), p. 113, 'Passion Sunday Homily': Saint Barnard in Christis person makith gret waymentacion . . .: 'Thow man for vanite singist and rowtes and I for thee crye and wepe; thou hast on thy hed a garland of flowres, and I for thee on my hed suffir a wrethe of stinking thornes; . . . whit gloves . . . blody hondis; . . . thine armes sprad on brode leding carallis . . . mine armes sprad on the tre' (etc.).

Index 1699. Bodl. MS. 416 (2315), f.106a. C.B. *14c.*, p. 225, no. 126.

Poem 64. Both Chaucer's description of the cock in the *Nun's Priest's Tale* and that here, which is very like it, may reflect a popular tradition. May this, also, be reflected in the Nursery rhyme, 'Goosey, goosey gander'? This heraldic and enamelled cockerel, noble by nature and by birth, aristocratically slender and perched by night in my lady's chamber, is intangibly significant (compare nos. 69 and 75).

Resemblance to cock in 'Nun's Priest's Tale': both have red coral combs, azure legs, white spurs and parts as black as jet; both are *gentle*. '*Goosey, goosey gander*' in *The Oxford Dictionary of Nursery Rhymes*, ed. I. and P. Opie (Oxford, 1951), p. 191, no. 190. This rhyme includes the words 'in my lady's chamber', and the earliest record of it does not include the last four lines of the rhyme, as generally known, with their reference to the old man.

Index 1299. B.M. MS. Sloane 2593, f.10b. R.H.R. *Sec. Lyrs*, p. 41, no. 46; *E.E.L.*, p. 249, no. 148.

Poem 65. A robust carol on a very common proverbial theme (l. 2), conventionally varied throughout with bluff vigour and neatly turned in the last line.

Index 1433. B.M. MS. Sloane 2593, f.8a. Greene, p. 255, no. 381; *E.E.L.*, p. 185, no. 104.

Poem 66. This poem is considered in detail on pp. 14–19, 23.

Discussions of the poem: J. Speirs, *Medieval English poetry* (London 1957), pp. 67–9; B. C. Raw, 'As dew in Aprille', *M.L.R.*, lv (1960), pp. 411–14; S. Manning, 'I syng of a myden', *P.M.L.A.*, lxxv (1960), pp. 8–12. *13c. poem:* C.B. *13c.* p. 55, no. 31. *Stillness as that of Christmas night: Sarum Missal*, p. 34: Introit of Mass of Sunday in Octave of Christmas (*Wisdom* xviii, 14–15), Dum medium silentium tenerent omnia, et nox in suo cursu medium iter haberet, omnipotens Sermo tuus, Domine, de celis a regalibus sedibus venit. *Stillness as freedom from concupiscence:* Amadeus of Lausanne, 'De Maria Virginea Matre', *P. L.*, clxxxviii, cols. 1316–17: Ita imber veniens de ultra super coelestes aquas, descendit in gremium Virginis sine humano opere, absque motu concupiscentiae, salva integritate et claustris virgineis obseratis leniter infusus est, tranquille susceptus, incarnatus ineffabiliter. *April and the new age of man's redemption:* Adam, Abbot of Persena, 'Mariale': *P.L.* ccxi, col. 709: Quando Florem istum Virga nostra producit, ver nostrum incipit, hiems pertransit, imber abit. . . . Unde, cum aperiatur terra, et germinet Salvatorem, primum mensem anni mundum renovantis ad gratiam, quemdam Aprilem possumus appellare. Aprilis enim . . . huic mysterio congruit, quod haec solemnitas tempore veris, et octavo Kalend. Aprilis celebratur.

Index 1367. B.M. MS. Sloane 2593, f.10b. C.B. *15c.*, p. 119, no. 81; *E.E.L.*, p. 107, no. 54.

Poem 67. A carol in contempt of the world (pp. 35, 40). It may be that the first line of the burden, which is here, presumably, addressed to the foolishly gay, oblivious of his ultimate destiny, was taken from some secular song and that this religious carol was written to its tune.

Index 739. B.M. MS. Sloane 2593, f.4b. Greene, p. 225, no. 329; *E.E.L.*, p. 180, no. 100.

Poem 68. A carol (p. 35) of which six copies are known (more than of any other), several with music for two or three voices. Even if in the learned tradition, it would have required no abstruse exposition, for l. 16 was a commonplace and so was l. 8: *John* xiii, 23; *Altenglische Legenden*, ed. C. Horstmann (1881), p. 35: ll. 17–18, and ll. 72–5, a buke he wrate/Of hevinly sightes, that he gun se/Whils that he slepid in Cristes kne./That buke 'Apocolips' es cald.

Index 3776. Trinity Coll. Camb. MS. O.3.58 (1230) recto. Greene, p. 66, no. 103 Aa; Stevens, *Carols*, p. 10, no. 13.

Poem 69. The point of this poem is that the child which the 'fairest maid' bears has one, Robert, as its father and is not the result of the particular grafting operation involving the *jenet*, or 'early', pear of the poet. There is rough play on this name and the poet's, which is, presumably, John. The power of the poem lies also in the obliqueness of the image of the garden and the pear which is probably to be associated with the tradition of popular poetry. Compare this poem with nos. 64 and 75. All are from the same MS. (p. 29), occur nowhere else, begin with the same formula (that of a nursery rhyme), have the same stanza form and the same mature rhythm, flexible and unhesitant.

Popular tradition: the carpenter's young wife, in Chaucer's *Miller's Tale*, who has an affair with the *clerk* Nicholas, was 'more blisful on to see/Than is the newe pere-jonette tree.'

Index 1302. B.M. MS. Sloane 2593, f.11b. R.H.R. *Sec. Lyrs.*, p. 15, no. 21.

Poem 70. A macaronic poem of love (pp. 44–5).

l. 4. ottreye, MS. *od treye:* (= Old French, *otreyer* from Latin *auctoricare) emendation of L. Spitzer in *M.L.N.*, lxvii (1952), pp. 150–5, and, independently and privately, of J. Linskill of the University of Liverpool for whose help with this poem I am specially grateful; *l. 12, incisto*, MS. *in cisto* (*incistare = to enshrine) see Spitzer; *l. 22, ha tret*, MS. *hatt3; l. 28, tres ser*, MS. *treser:* emendation of J. Linskill.

Index 16. Camb. Univ. Lib. MS. Gg.4.27, Pt Ia, f.10b. *E.E.L.*, p. 15, no. 8.

Poem 71. This poem is discussed on pp. 21–3.

Index 117. B.M. MS. Sloane 2593, f.11a. C.B. *15c.*, p. 120, no. 83; *E.E.L.*, p. 102, no. 50.

Poem 72. Whereas the earlier lines reflect something of the tradition of contempt for the world (pp. 40–1), this poem concludes with a brand of practical advice that does not. It is scribbled on the flyleaf of a collection of Lives of the Saints.

Index 145. Bodl. MS. Laud Misc. 108 (1486), f.238b (flysheet). R.H.R. *Sec. Lyrs.*, p. 100, no. 108.

Poem 73. A carol (p. 35). Poems about cleric's love affairs are not uncommon and Jankin seems to have been the typical name. The heart of this poem is the delicate incongruity of the indelicate

Notes

situation, the unexpected transposing of Holy Mass and sexual attraction, typified by the play on the name of the woman, Alison, and the Greek words of appeal to God, *Kyrie eleison* (l. 3). The brief cry in l. 37 followed by the last repetition of the impudent refrain line makes a perfect ending. (See p. 42.)

Name 'Jankin': see *An Old English Miscellany*, ed. R. Morris, E.E.T.S., O.S., xlix (1872), p. 188; theos prude maidenes/That luvieth Janekin; Chaucer, *Wife of Bath's Prologue*, D628: This joly clerk, Jankin, that was so hende/Hath wedded me.

Index 377. B.M. MS. Sloane 2593, f.34a. Greene, p. 309, no. 457; R.H.R. *Sec. Lyrs.*, p. 21, no. 27; *E.E.L.*, pp. 220–1, no. 127.

Poem 74. A carol of Mary in which her tears of blood (l. 18) reflect the later medieval tendency to make her grief at a son's death a Passion parallel in every detail with his (pp. 35–6, 38, 40).

Index 1650. Bodl. MS. Eng. Poet. e.1 (29734), f.25a. Greene, p. 135, no. 180A.

Poem 75. A present-day nursery rhyme is a variant of this poem which resembles the ballad of 'Captain Wedderburn's Courtship' in that it poses riddles in connection with love (compare nos. 64 and 69, and see p. 29).

Nursery rhyme: The Oxford Dictionary of Nursery Rhymes, ed. I. and P. Opie (Oxford, 1951), pp. 386–8, no. 478. 'Captain Wedderburn's Courtship' is in Child, pp. 83–6, no. 46.

Index 1303. B.M. MS. Sloane 2593, f.11a. R.H.R. *Sec. Lyrs.*, p. 40, no. 45.

Poem 76. Crude and shocking, this is an exceptional poem among the chiefly didactic poems of Hoccleve, clerk in the office of the Privy Seal about 1378–1425, and a gay bachelor who eventually married, was short of money, and, for a time, mad.

Index 2640. Huntington (once Gollancz) MS. HM. 744, f.52b. R.H.R. *Sec. Lyrs.*, p. 223, no. 210; *Hoccleve's Works*, II, *The minor poems in the Ashburnham MS.*, ed. I. Gollancz, *E.E.T.S.* E.S. 73 (1925), pp. 37–8.

Poem 77. A carol and lullaby of the Child Jesus (pp. 35, 40).

Index 1351. B.M. MS. Sloane 2593, f.32a. Greene, p. 98, no. 143; *E.E.L.*, p. 131, no. 69.

Y

Poem 78. A carol, a form which became largely associated with Christmas only in the later middle ages (p. 35). That Christian Feast took into itself the pagan fertility rites of Yule (l. 3) with its holly and mistletoe, conspicuously fruitful in mid-winter, its burning log which brought in the new fire, and its ceremonial wassail-bowl. Ecclesiastically, the Feast extended until Candlemas, the Feast of the Purification on 2 February, and included the feast-days of St. Stephen, the first martyr (*Acts* vii, 55 ff.), St. John the Evangelist, the Holy Innocents, St. Thomas Becket (murdered by knights of King Henry II in 1170), the Circumcision and the Epiphany (for ll. 28–31 see note 120). Celebrations, especially in the large households, were therefore extensive, elaborate and whole-hearted. A Lord of Misrule might preside not only to organize but to see that everybody contributed to the merriment under penalty of a forfeit. No. 168 may have been used by such a Master of Ceremonies.

Index 3343. Bodl. MS. Eng. Poet. e.1 (29734), f.22a. Greene, p. 7, no. 8a.

Poem 79. Accompanied by pictures representing their subjects, nos. 79 and 152 are, in one way, rather like the 'emblem' verses of 17c. No. 79 is written to the right of the face of a naked Christ, crudely dotted with wounds and presenting to a religious kneeling in prayer a heart as tall as Christ, with a gaping wound in its centre and numerous drops of blood springing from it. There are comparable, though longer, poems from MSS. of 16c. in *Devotional pieces in verse and prose* ed. J. A. W. Bennett (Scottish Text Society, 1955 for 1948–9) and from the same MS. as no. 79 in C.B. *15c.* (pp. 168–9, no. 108). J. Evans, in *Pattern, a study of ornament in Western Europe, from 1180 to 1900* (Oxford, 1931), mentions on p. 152 of vol. i a William Billyng who wrote verses between 1400 and 1430 to illustrate devices of the Five Wounds of Christ, suitable for embroidery.

Index 2507. B.M. Additional MS. 37049, f.24a. T. W. Ross, 'Five fifteenth-century "emblem" verses from Brit. Mus. Addit. MS. 37049', *Speculum*, xxxii (1957), p. 276.

Poem 80. The Agincourt carol. The battle took place in 1415.

Index 2716. Bodl. MS. Arch. Selden B.26 (3340), f.17b. R.H.R. *Hist. Poems*, p. 91, no. 32; Greene, p. 289, no. 426; Stevens, *Carols*, p. 6, no. 8.

Notes

Poem 81. There are many medieval poems on the fear of death like this carol (no. 146), but Audelay unusually confines the 'Timor mortis' to the burden and, for all that the instances of old age are conventional (ll. 11–12, 20–1), this is a personal poem. Exceptional among medieval poets in that he often mentions his own name and blindness, John Audelay (first half 15c.) was a chantry priest of Lord Strange in Shropshire and probably spent his last days in Haghmond Abbey, a house of Augustinian Canons. (See pp. 35–6.)

Audelay's fifty-five poems are in one MS. Some twenty-five are carols. l. 6 is from the prayer, 'Anima Christi sanctifica me' and l. 44 is a proverb.

Index 693. Bodl. MS. Douce 302 (21876), ff.30b and 32a. Greene, p. 247, no. 369; ed. E. K. Whiting, *E.E.T.S.*, O.S. 184 (1931), pp. 211–12, no. 51.

Poem 82. The particular list of the four estates (l. 38) in this carol differs from all others, though two of the estates are usual, namely the knight and the priest. The third is normally the labourer. Impropriety or 'unnaturalness' was highly significant to the medieval mind. (Note 81.)

Index 1588. Bodl. MS. Douce 302 (21876), f.29b. Greene, p. 235, no. 347; ed. E. K. Whiting, *E.E.T.S.* O.S. 184 (1931), pp. 195–7, no. 40.

Poem 83. A free translation of the Latin 'Cur mundus militat', probably of the 11c. or 12c., a classic expression of the theme of contempt of the world (p. 40 and note 8, no. 97 and no. 131). The words 'Ubi sunt', which, in the Latin, start the section beginning at l. 13, have become a title for this very common and conventional form of complaint. The names from the Old Testament and the Ancient World of Greece and Rome (*Tullius* in l. 19 is Cicero) are typical examples of the great who have passed away.

Cur mundus militat: variously ascribed: text in *Daniel,* ii, pp. 379–380 and *P.L.,* clxxxiv, cols. 1313–16. There are differences between these Latin versions and between them and the English. The last four lines as printed here, and as found in Latin versions, occur in the MSS. between ll. 28 and 29. Other instances of *De Contemptu Mundi* in Latin in Mone, i, pp. 395–7, no. 288; p. 415, no. 299. *l. 26: life like a shadow: Ecclesiastes* vi, 12; viii, 13; apocryphal *Book of Wisdom* v, 9.

Index 4160. Trinity Coll. Camb. MS. B.15.39 (181), f.169b; Bodl. MSS. Laud Misc. 23 (655), f.112b; 220 (2103), f.106a; Ashmole 59 (6943), f.83a; B.M. Additional MS. 37788, f.81b; Huntington Lib. MS. HM 744, f.13a; (etc.) C.B. *14c.*, p. 237, no. 134.

Poem 84. Holly and ivy are common in English folk-songs and the identification of holly with the male and ivy with the female is common in folk-customs (Greene, pp. xcvii–ciii). Their contention is the battle of the sexes. Both have particular importance in the Christmas Feast (note 78). The birds mentioned are also related to folk beliefs (the owl was associated with ivy and with sex antagonism, and could be an object of derision) and in ll. 18 and 22 the primary colours and the similes drawn are characteristic of popular poetry. I have broken the longer lines in which this poem is recorded into two. This is a carol (p. 35).

Index 1226. B.M. MS. Harley 5396, f.275b. Greene, p. 93, no. 136A.

Poem 85. There are non-dramatic examples in Latin and English of this form, characterized by the reiterated 'Hail' or '*Salve*' or '*Ave*', but this poem, addressed to the Christ Child, is from the first of two religious plays of the Shepherds and of the Nativity in the Towneley MS. which records a cycle of plays probably performed annually at Wakefield. Such plays often contain such lyrics. This poem is in the stanza form usually associated with the work of the Wakefield Master, as he is called nowadays.

Latin and English non-dramatic examples: Mone, i, pp. 156–8; no. 120; *Minor poems of the Vernon MS.* I, ed. C. Horstmann, *E.E.T.S.* O.S. 98 (1892), pp. 24–5. *Relationship lyrics and plays:* see G. C. Taylor, 'Relation of the English Corpus Christi Play to the M.E. Religious Lyric', *M.P.*, v (1907), pp. 1–38. In the Towneley Crucifixion and Resurrection plays there are also incorporated complaints of Christ, and in the Crucifixion play a complaint of Mary (p. 40). It has been argued that the Passion plays may have developed from this form of lyric, but there is no certain evidence that this is true in the case of the elaborate plays in these late cycles. It may well be that the vividness of such dramatic representations of the Passion inspired in this type of lyric a warmer life.

Huntington Lib.,Towneley MS. First 'Shepherds' Play' in *Towneley Plays*, ed. G. England, *E.E.T.S.* E.S. lxxi (1897/1952), pp. 114–16.

Notes

Poem 86. This love poem is accompanied by music.

Index 2381. Bodl. MS. Ashmole 191 (6668), f.191a. R.H.R. *Sec. Lyrs*, p. 159, no. 171; *E.E.L.*, pp. 32–3, no. 18.

Poem 87. One version or another of this poem was extremely popular particularly in 15c. but also for several centuries later when it was quite a popular tombstone inscription (p. 40). There are one or two Latin versions but it is probably English in origin, the earliest known (though very brief) example being among the Harley lyrics (pp. 32–33 and compare nos. 16 and 17). The ingenuity of the play on 'earth' is integral to the poetic meaning. The Latin words at the beginning are, of course, not a burden but only a heading.

Index 704. Lincoln Cathedral Lib. MS. Thornton, f.279a. *E.E.L.*, p. 171, no. 94; ed. H. M. R. Murray, *E.E.T.S.* O.S. 141 (1911).

Poem 88. It is more likely than not that nos. 88–91 were the work of Charles of Orleans who was captured at Agincourt at the age of twenty-one and held prisoner in England from 1415 until 1440. They belong to a sequence of love poems. No. 88 is a ballade (p. 43) and elaborately rhetorical, using these figures: *exclamatio*, the apostrophe of ll. 8, 9, etc.; *interrogatio*, the rhetorical question of l. 17, which may, perhaps, be *ratiocinatio*, self-questioning; *conduplicatio*, the repetition of 'wreche' to stir pity in the last line of each stanza; *interpretatio* or *expolitio*, amplifying by variation in, say, the first stanza, the variations being in the form of *commutatio*, in that two contrasted thoughts are connected neatly in each line by transposing the words in each half line. The effect of all this is dignity, elegance and the evocation of controlled feeling (pp. 25, 32). The paradoxical nature of love is a commonplace (note 99; p. 44; and below).

Authorship uncertain: there is in French a sequence of love poems which is very like that in English and undoubtedly by Charles, but it is uncertain which came first. It often looks as if it was the French. However, the B.M. MS. contains some seventy-seven poems, including nos. 88, 90 and 91, which have no French equivalents and there are English poems among the French in the French MS. This was Charles's own and is in his own hand. Steele argues that the relationship between French and English is not one of translation but 'rather of rehandling identical themes and thoughts', for there are differences of sentiment and style. *Love paradoxical:* e.g. 12c.: Alanus de Insulis, 'De planctu naturae', *P.L.*, ccx, col. 455: Pax odio, fraudique fides, spes juncta timori,/Est amor, et mistus cum ratione furor/. . . satiata fames . . . Dulce malum . . . Mors vivens, moriens vita, etc., etc.

Index 816. B.M. MS. Harley 682, f.40b; Camb. Univ. Lib. Additional MS. 2585. *English poems of Charles of Orleans*, ed. R. Steele, *E.E.T.S.* O.S. 215 (1941), p. 71, Ballade 60; R.H.R., 'Some Charles d'Orleans fragments', *M.L.N.*, lxvi (1951), pp. 504–5.

Poem 89. A decasyllabic roundel of love (pp. 43–5) in which the octo-syllabic l. 5 is a not uncommon variation. The homely image of l. 6, which is not in the French equivalent (note 88), gives warmth and substance to the joy. Used several times by this poet, it is, to the best of my knowledge, peculiar to him (no. 88 and p. 27).

Index 3142. B.M. MS. Harley 682, f.63a; Camb. Univ. Lib. Additional MS. 2585. *English poems of Charles of Orleans*, ed. R. Steele, *E.E.T.S.* O.S. 215 (1941), p. 107, Roundel 5; R.H.R. 'Some Charles d'Orleans fragments', *M.L.N.*, lxvi (1951), p. 505.

Poem 90. One of some dozen roundels (p. 43) in octosyllabics, it moves with appropriate glibness. Nos. 88–91 all adopt the attitudes of the typical 'refined' lover (p. 44). The lover as a penitent making his confession is not uncommon but the wit of this poem is excep-tionally subtle. That the theft of the kiss was unpremeditated (l. 5) would, in moral theology, reduce the gravity of the sin, and it would be a natural requirement for absolution that the stolen object should be returned (l. 9).

Index 2243. B.M. MS. Harley 682, f.88b. R.H.R. *Sec. Lyrs*, p. 183, no. 185; *E.E.L.*, p. 31, no. 17; *English poems of Charles of Orleans*, ed. R. Steele, *E.E.T.S.* O.S. 215 (1941), Roundel 57, p. 133.

Poem 91. Basically decasyllabic, nos. 88, 89 and 91 are all rhyth-mically ambitious and stumble only occasionally, e.g. in the first stanza of this poem. No. 91 is rhetorical (note 88 and pp. 25, 33): e.g. in ll. 25–7 is the figure of *anaphora*, the same word beginning successive lines. The invigorating, brief question and answer of stanza three is also characteristic.

Index 2550. B.M. MS. Harley 682, f.133a. *English poems of Charles of Orleans*, ed. R. Steele, *E.E.T.S.* O.S. 215 (1941), Ballade 97, p. 194.

Poem 92. A carol with music in a manuscript which has only recently

Notes

come to light and been edited. St. George is reported to have appeared above the field of Agincourt (ll. 8–10). (p. 35.)

B.M. MS. Egerton 3307, f.63b. Stevens, *Carols*, p. 49, no. 60.

Poem 93. A love poem (p. 44) the rhythm of which reminds somewhat of Skeltonics. The 'refrain' is varied and cleverly built-in. There are characteristically 'rhetorical' elements, e.g. *anaphora* in ll. 17–20 (compare no. 91) and *exclamatio* in l. 33.

Index 1018. B.M. MS. Sloane 1584, f.85a. R.H.R. *Sec. Lyrs*, p. 214, no. 206.

Poem 94. Index 1207. B.M. MS. Harley 665, f.295a. R.H.R. *Sec. Lyrs*, p. 118, no. 124.

Poem 95. '*As I ye shall be*' is a commonplace dating from at least late Roman times and variously spoken by Death, a skeleton, etc.: D. Gray, 'A Middle English epitaph', *N. & Q.* N.S. viii (1961), 135.

Index 237. Trinity Coll. Camb. MS. B.15.31 (366), flyleaf. R.H.R. *Sec. Lyrs*, p. 119, no. 126.

Poem 96. That stanzas are almost all interchangeable in this poem and no. 97 supports the surgery done on them. They are ballades (p. 40) rhythmically slack (pp. 34–5) and often verbally and syntactically so: in no. 96 'this is no drede' and 'as I rede' are fill-up formulas (though by no means peculiar to Lydgate) and in ll. 43 and 44 there is no poetic gain in the flaccid multiplication of similar verbs. Both poems show a remarkable facility for shapeless rambling and for the multiplication of conventional examples of a conventional theme, which is the basic rhetorical device. In ll. 49–56 of no. 96 there is some difficulty in discovering the tone. Presumably the reference to Delilah is nicely ironic, but the references to Rosamounde and Cleopatra are less certain.

Dalida: Delilah, *Judges* xvi, 4 ff. *Rosamounde*: traditionally the mistress of King Henry II but also, traditionally, utterly loyal to him and poisoned by his wife, Eleanor. *Cleopatra*: in the *Legend of Good Women*, Chaucer praises Cleopatra as faithful and one of Love's martyrs, and so do all the other English writers up to 1568 listed by F. L. Utley in his *Crooked Rib* (Columbus: Ohio, 1944). But, if Plutarch's *Lives* were known to Chaucer and Lydgate they found there a Cleopatra who 'betrayed' Antony by fleeing in the sea-battle and who had had other lovers before him. Perhaps Lydgate has loosely cited three examples of women who were generally deplored in an anti-feminist tradition and has not chosen those who were, in particular, unfaithful to their lovers.

Index 3656. Bodl. MS. Fairfax 16 (3896), f. 199a; B.M. MS. Harley 7578, f.17b; B.M. Additional MS. 16165, f.252a. *Chaucerian and other pieces*, ed. W. W. Skeat (1897), no. 13, pp. 291–4; *The Minor Poems of John Lydgate*, ed. H. N. MacCracken, *E.E.T.S.* O.S. 192 (1934), pp. 438–42.

Poem 97. ll. 12–15, 41–8 and 57–61 are articulated with characteristic uncertainty (note 96). The refrain (like l. 29 of no. 96) is probably proverbial. In the last two stanzas the exciting and poignant (and, to my knowledge, original) play on the rose as a token of decay, of martyrdom and of Jesus is, nevertheless, with traditional religious allegory. (See pp. 26, 34, 40, 43 and notes 8, 83.)

ll. 8, etc., rose as symbol of mortality: Poésies populaires latines du moyen âge, ed. E. du Méril (Paris, 1847), p. 108: Vita mundi, res morbosa,/Magis fragilis quam rosa . . .; Alanus de Insulis, *P.L.* ccx, col. 579: Nostrum statum pingit rosa/. . . Quae dum primo mane floret,/Defloratus flos effloret/Vespertino senio. *l. 33, Tullius:* Cicero, Roman law-court orator, famous as author of books on rhetoric. *l. 34, Chrysostom*, Bishop of Constantinople, famous as preacher. *l. 36, Homer*, Greek epic poet. *l. 38, Seneca*, Roman moral philosopher and tragedian. *ll. 41–8:* traditionally, a legion of Christians from the Thebaid, or Upper Nile, were martyred under the Emperor Maximian in 3c. Gaul for refusing to sacrifice. *l. 57, bloody feeld:* the Crucifixion, see nos. 27 and 51. *l. 58, Roose of Jericho:* see Appendix, 'Rose', but here Wisdom = Christ. *l. 59, five rooses:* e.g. Pseudo-St. Bernard, 'Vitis mystica seu tractatus de Passione Domini', *P.L.* clxxxiv, col. 715: Vide totum corpus, sicubi rosae sanguineae florem non invenias. Inspice manum unam et alteram, si florem rosae invenias in utraque. Inspice pedem et unum et alterum: numquid non rosei? Inspice lateris aperturam, quia nec illa caret rosa, quamvis ipsa subrubea sit propter mixturam aquae. *ll. 59–60, sheeld . . . baneer: Meditations*, ll. 699 ff.; 15c.: *Tretise of Love*, ed. J. H. Fisher, *E.E.T.S.* O.S. 225 (1951), pp. 12–13, based on 14c. version of *Ancren Riwle*, ed. J. Påhlsson (Lund, 1918), p. 184, which says: Jesus . . . His shilde that covered the godhede was his blessed body that was spred upon the harde crosse. Ther appered he as a shilde in his armes with his

Notes

handes streined and persed and his feete nailed down, as summe men sey, the tone upon the tother; see notes 27 and 51. *l. 62, welles:* note 114.

Index 1865. B.M. MS. Harley 2255, f.3b; Huntington (once Phillipps 8299), MS. HM 140, f.87b; (etc.). *The Minor Poems of John Lydgate,* ed. H. N. MacCracken, *E.E.T.S.* O.S. 192 (1934), pp. 780–785.

Poem 98. Poems addressed to the Trinity are uncommon (p. 40) but see C.B. *13c.* pp. 114–16, no. 59. Mary has almost as great a place as any of the three Persons in a somewhat earlier poem of 14c. (C.B. *14c.,* no. 93).

Index 241. B.M. MS. Harley 2406, f.8b. C.B. *15c.,* p. 79, no. 50.

Poem 99. A Latin version, found also elsewhere and which it translates, accompanies this poem: the Latin refers the traditional disadvantages of love simply to *amor,* but this poem ascribes them to *intemperate,* as distinguished from *lawful,* love. The paradoxes of love are commonplaces (p. 44 and note 88).

Latin version: see also note to no. 9 in C.B. *13c.*; preceding no. 99 are these Latin lines: Dicam quid sit Amor: Amor est insania mentis/ Ardor inextinctus, insaciata fames/Dulce malum, mala dulcedo, dulcissimus error/Absque labore quies, absque quiete labor (cf. Alanus de Insulis, note 88). *The English translation adds* (led by the exigencies of rime?), as well as *inordinat, fawting blis, blinde, contrary to kinde. Inordinat love:* see, e.g., Malory, ed. E. Vinaver (Oxford, 1947), pp. 896–7: Launcelot has loved Gwenyver 'unmesurably'; pp. 1093–1094: Elayne has loved Launcelot 'oute of mesure' (R. T. Davies, 'Malory's "vertuouse love",' *S.P.,* liii (1956), 459–69); Alanus de Insulis, 'De planctu naturae', *P.L.,* ccx, 456: Non enim originalem Cupidinis naturam in honestate, redarguo, si circumscribatur frenis modestiae, si habenis temperantiae castigetur . . . Quoniam omnis excessus, temperatae mediocritatis incessum disturbat, etc. *Traditional disadvantages of love:* see Ovid's *Artis Amatoriae,* i, 729–42, etc. and *Remedia Amoris*; the third book of Andreas Capellanus' *De Amore Libri Tres*; and Criseyde herself in Chaucer's *Troilus and Criseyde,* ii, 771–805.

Index 1359. Copenhagen: Kongelige Bibliotek Thott 110, 4to., f.163a. C.B. *15c.,* p. 287, no. 187.

Poem 100. A carol accompanied by music for three voices. Wonder at the exaltation of man by the taking of his manhood into the Godhead in the Incarnation is traditional (note 28). (p. 35.)

Index 2733. Bodl. MS. Arch. Selden B.26 (3340), f.14b. Greene, p. 21, no. 30; *E.E.L.*, p. 115, no. 59; and compare R.H.R. *Christmas Carols*, pp. 18–19, no. 4.

Poem 101 uses, for teaching purposes, the charm and memorability of a riddle, to which form the paradoxes and numerical precision of medieval religion readily lent themselves.

Index 1640. B.M. MS. Royal 17.A.xvi, f.27b. R.H.R., 'Popular prayers in Middle English verse', *M.P.*, xxxvi (1939), p. 344.

Poem 102. A lullaby of the Child Jesus (p. 40) with the stanzas of which alternate stanzas of the Latin hymn 'Christe qui lux es et dies', an unparalleled arrangement to my knowledge, and without any indication of how it was to be read or performed. The homely complaint of ll. 25–8 is most poignant.

Index 22. Nat. Lib. of Wales MS. Brogyntyn (Porkington) 10, f.201a. C.B. *15c.*, p. 1, no. 1; Greene, pp. 112–13, no. 152.

Poem 103. A macaronic poem (p. 44) about a devil of great fame at this time who had a part in Miracle and Morality Plays. His function was to collect the words skipped and mumbled during Church services and register them against the offender. Clerical wit (p. 42) invented him and he is a European figure, often referred to in sermons, by the time of this poem something like two centuries old; here he is specially interested in chattering women.

Index 3812. Bodl. MS. Douce 104 (21678), f.112b. C.B. *15c.*, p. 277, no. 179.

Poem 104. A poem of Mary (pp. 17, 20) in the aureate style (pp. 25–26), attempting lofty dignity and glittering splendour and to be compared with no. 144 and C.B. *15c.*, pp. 80–1, no. 51, which is probably by the same poet.

l. 38, *Pellicane* = Christ, since both wounded themselves to save others with their blood: E. Mâle, *L'art réligieux au XIII siècle* (Paris, 1910), p. 57.

Index 3391. B.M. Additional MS. 20059, f.99a. C.B. *15c.*, pp. 67–69, no. 38.

Poem 105. This poem, in the form of a love-letter, is probably addressed to Mary but may be to a mistress (pp. 20, 24). Another poem, however, which is addressed to Mary, has the first two lines of its last stanza almost identical with the first two lines of the first stanza here.

Index 927. Bodl. MS. Douce 326 (21900), f.14a. C.B. *15c.*, p. 75, no. 46.

Poem 106. A complaint of Christ which has, on little evidence, been ascribed to John Skelton (p. 40). When the complaint opens out in stanzas two and three the expansion tends to the flaccid and naïve, while the occasional internal rimes and alliterative linking, which might have stiffened the poem, in fact weaken it further. Rubrics at beginning and end promise periods of pardon from purgatory to those who say this prayer. There may be a connection with some lines of Philippe de Grève (note 46).

Ascribed to Skelton: Dyce included a version of this poem in his edition of Skelton in 1843. There were two grounds for this: one copy of the poem, on the flyleaf of a book once belonging to Richard Heber, concludes with a unique stanza and a last stanza with many unique lines, and it ends 'Explicit qd. Skelton;' Skelton, in talking about his own compositions in 'The Garland of Laurel', mentions 'Wofully arayd and shamefully betrayd'. But the other three MS. versions of this poem do not ascribe it to Skelton and there is no printed text; while the words 'and shamefully betrayd' do not occur in this poem, and there is no need, anyway, to assume that a reference to what is the first line of a burden is a reference also to the rest of what might be a poem which adopted it but was independently composed.

Index 497. B.M. MS. Harley 4012, f.109a; B.M. Additional MS. 5465, f.63b and f.73b; etc. C.B. *15c.*, p. 156, no. 103.

Poem 107. Poems of this kind and the Marian imagery are considered on pp. 17, 20 and in the Appendix.

Index 534. Bodl. MS. Douce 1 (21575), f.77a. C.B. *15c.*, p. 73, no. 44.

Poem 108. A carol of clerical seduction with a burden that may be that of a popular song. The poem is probably, like no. 73, the work of a cleric. Its detail is vivid, strong and homely, the kissing in a convenient corner, the seduction through a pair of white gloves, her mistress's abuse of the girl as she comes home with the milk. As in the ballads and as in many a sophisticated medieval romance, dialogue is natural and has a major place.

Index 1849. Gonville and Caius Coll. Camb. MS. 383, p. 41. Greene, p. 307, no. 453; R.H.R. *Sec. Lyrs*, p. 22, no. 28.

Poem 109. A robust poem of death without sentimentality and with much less attention than in many such to the physical nastiness of decay. Its confident and noble tone derives partly from its assured interjections and inversions, and from its rhythm (e.g. the enjambement of ll. 3–5 and the placing at the beginning of l. 14 of 'And wormes to fede'). Its dramatic dignity is exceptional but its content entirely traditional (pp. 40–1 and below) and the last stanza was often used separately as an epitaph in the later 15c.

ll. 3–5: compare: (ascribed to St. Bernard) 'Meditationes de cognitione humanae conditionis', *P.L.*, clxxxiv, col. 488: Veniunt enim angeli assumere illam (etc. . . . But he says) 'Date mihi vel unius horae spatium'. *l. 8 cherry fair:* C.B. *14c.*, p. 199, no. 117, l. 85 and Greene, p. 249, no. 371. *Chess and death:* 13c./14c.: *Gesta Romanorum*, ed. H. Oesterley (Berlin, 1872), chap. 166; G. R. Owst, *Preaching in Medieval England* (Cambridge, 1926), p. 326; chess and a husband's catching his wife out: Chaucer, *Troilus and Criseyde*, ii, 754. *Epitaph:* D. Gray, 'A Middle English epitaph', *N. & Q.* N.S. viii (1961), 132–5.

Index 769. Trinity Coll. Camb. MS. O.2.53 (1157), f.67a; Balliol Coll. Oxf. MS. 354, f.199a. C.B. *15c.*, p. 236, no. 149.

Poem 110. A complaint of Christ (p. 40) in which the traditional contrasts between Christ's agony and man's vanity (see no. 63) are systematically drawn with reference to the seven mortal sins, each of which is listed opposite the appropriate stanza.

Index 4185 and 4200. Camb. Univ. Lib. MS. Ff.5.48, f.43b. *Cambridge M.E. Lyrics*, ed. H. A. Person, p. 10, no. 8; C.B. *14c.*, pp. 227–8, no. 127.

Poem 111. The initial letters of successive lines form the alphabet. The alphabet was learned in the middle ages from a horn book, an inscribed sheet mounted on wood and faced with horn. At the beginning, e.g., stood a cross, and at the end might be an 'etc.'

(ll. 25–6: *And C*), a 'tittle' (*Titulle*, in another sense, l. 27, or one of a group of three dots), and other punctuation marks, including a 'point' (l. 27). In l. 21 'U' 'V' and 'W' are represented by one letter, and in l. 23 'Y' by 'I', as was often the scribal custom. In l. 22 the *Ch* of *Christ* represents the Greek 'X' and in l. 24 'S' represents 'Z' as it could be in another dialect. There were somewhat similar poems in Latin and earlier examples in English of 14c.

Poems in Latin of which the initial letter of each four-line stanza forms the alphabet: 8c.: Mone, i, pp. 447–9, no. 314; 9c.: Mone, i, pp. 387–90, no. 285. *Horn books:* A. W. Tuer, *History of the Horn-Book* (London, 1897). *An earlier English example* cited: C.B. *15c.*, p. 324, no. 101.

Index 664. Bodl. MS. Rawlinson B.408 (11755), f.3a. C.B. *15c.*, p. 149, no. 101.

Poem 112. A complaint of Mary (p. 40), this poem is found in two MSS. with the addition of a *chanson d'aventure* introduction (p. 43). In this introduction the poet tells how, kneeling the other day in church to hear mass, he saw a *pite*, that is, a pieta, or representation of Mary holding the dead Jesus, newly taken from the Cross, in her lap: then the poem continues as here. Such moving representations in painting and sculpture are found increasingly from the last years of 14c. (pp. 38, 41).

Pietas: E. Mâle, *L'art réligieux de la fin du moyen âge en France* (Paris, 1931), pp. 126 ff. *Chanson d'aventure* introduction: these versions are printed in H. E. Sandison, *The 'chanson d'aventure' in Middle English* (1913), pp. 104 ff.

Index 2619. Camb. Univ. MS. Ff.2.38, f.55b; Ff.5.48, f.73a; (etc.) C.B. *15c.*, p. 13, no. 7.

Poem 113. Besse Bunting is a most appropriate name for the girl in no. 113 since a 'bunting' was a pet bird (no. 21, l. 52) and 'to bunt' was to sift meal. The rhymes (and perhaps the sense) suggest that a line is missing between ll. 5 and 6. That Miss Bunting should go out in the Spring and that her lips should be like cherries is traditional but few poems could be more suggestive in their freshness and delightful incompletion.

Index 1470. Bodl. MS. Laud Misc. 609 (754), f.170b. P. J. Frankis, 'Two minor French lyric forms in English', *Neuphilologische Mitteilungen*, lx (1959), p. 70.

Notes

Poem 114. The healing and holy well, the thorn and the maiden who stands beside, have a mysterious resonance that suggests their connection with popular lore rather than with the tradition of the learned (pp. 19, 24). But the lines occur in the midst of Latin and with reference to 'confession': the crucified Christ and his wounds were, in the lore of the Church, commonly represented by the image of a well from which flow mercy and salvation (no. 118 and see Appendix, 'Well'), while the 'thorn' may be the crown of thorns and the maid, Mary.

Well (of salvation): Meditations, ll. 647 ff.: (addresses the parts of Christ's crucified body) Heil be thou, breste, veine of pite,/Flour of Hevene, welle of bounte./Whoso hath grace of anything/He dringeth of that welle-spring./ . . . Thou welle flowing from Hevon above,/Mak me drink thorw migth of love./ . . . Thou herte, ful of love gret,/ My drye herte make it wet,/ And on drope of love-liking/ Let me have of thy welle-spring; Greene, no. 123A, p. 79: Ther is a blossom sprong of a thorn / To save mankind that was forlorne,/As the prophettis said beforne/Deo patri sit gloria./Ther sprong a well at Maris fote,/That torned all this world to bote;/Of her toke Jesu flesshe and blod./From that well ther strake a strem;/Out of Egypt into Bedlem/God, thorowgh his highness torned it again./ . . . (but I do not know what all the references in this poem mean.)

Index 420. Magdalen Coll. Oxf. MS. 60, f.214a. C.B. *14c.*, p. 229, no. 130.

Poem 115. A singular poem in the tradition of native alliterative verse, evincing all its vigour and solidity, its conspicuous verbs and its stress and clash of consonants (no. 15). There are, characteristically, several compound words, for example, in ll. 21 and 22, which convey pictures in miniature and are found nowhere else. Detail is select and concrete, and drawn from eye and ear. The scene and the style remind of *Piers Plowman* and no. 15, but I know no other description quite like this. It must be direct from experience. (p. 34.)

Index 3227. B.M. MS. Arundel 292, f.71b. R.H.R. *Sec. Lyrs,* p. 106, no. 118; Sisam, pp. 169–70.

Poem 116. A carol with music for two voices (p. 35).

Index 1004. Bodl. MS. Arch. Selden B.26 (3340), f.8a. Greene, p. 5, no. 5; *E.E.L.*, p. 233, no. 135; R.H.R. *Christmas Carols*, pp. 16–17, no. 3.

Poem 117. A translation of the Latin 'prose' or 'sequence', 'Laeta-bundus', attributed to St. Bernard and sung in the Mass of Christmas day (p. 39). (A prose or sequence is a species of hymn sung in the Mass between Epistle and Gospel.) Except in the last stanza the rhythm and form approximate quite closely to that of the Latin. The Latin lines are precisely those found at these points in the original.

Sequence in *P.L.*, clxxxiv, cols. 1327–8; *Sarum Missal*, p. 481. *ll. 19–20:* see *I Kings* iv, 33 and pseudo-Rabanus, 'Allegoriae in Sacram Scripturam', *P.L.*, cxii, col. 891. *ll. 31–2:* Sibyls were supposed to have foretold Christ's coming.

Index 909. Bodl. MS. Arch. Selden B.26 (3340), f.19b. C.B. *15c.*, p. 113, no. 77B; Greene, pp. lxxviii–lxxix.

Poem 118. The wounds of Jesus as the wells of life are common (no. 114) but the serenity of this poem is remarkable and to this the development of the image in the last stanza contributes through the contrast of *bowe* and *mekely* with fleeing and fiends, and through the concrete picture of one bowing down to the *brinke* of the spring, suggesting temperate refreshment and pastoral satisfaction. Presumably the poet has here in mind the soul thirsting for God, 'As the hart panteth after the water brooks', in Psalm 42.

Index 1787. B.M. Arundel MS. 286, f.3a. C.B. *15c.*, p. 149, no. 100.

Poem 119. A drinking song (p. 42) in carol form (p. 35).

Index 549. Bodl. MS. Eng. poet. e.1 (29734), f.41b. R.H.R. *Sec. Lyrs*, p. 9, no. 13; *E.E.L.*, pp. 222–3, no. 128; Greene, p. 285, no. 422A.

Poem 120. A macaronic carol (pp. 35, 44) incorporating lines from services in Latin, e.g. ll. 8, 20, 22, all of which are from Christmas services. The gifts of the three Kings are traditionally differentiated, gold for the Child as King (with power), incense for him as God (and priest), and myrrh for him as Man (dead and buried, for myrrh was used to embalm) as we are told in a response in Matins of the Epiphany (*Sarum Breviary*, I, cccxxiv).

Index 340. Nat. Lib. of Scotland MS. Advocates 19.3.1, f.59a. C.B. *15c.*, p. 123, no. 86; *E.E.L.*; pp. 134–5, no. 72; Greene, pp. 16–18, no. 23.

Poem 121. Was it Jeame, Jeame's beloved, or another who wrote this?

From a collection of medical treatises and recipes for medicines, assembled variously through 14c. and 15c. and among several other short pieces in different hands.

Index 1170. B.M. MS. Royal 18.A. vi, f.22a. K. G. Wilson, 'Five fugitive pieces of fifteenth-century secular verse,' *M.L.N.*, lxix (1954), p. 22.

Poem 122. A ballade in rime royal and decasyllabic lines with quite a strong rhythm (pp. 27, 43). It is one of the love poems found only in a MS. that may, Robbins argues, have belonged to the Finderns, 'one of the leading county families' of Southern Derbyshire, and which was written by various people between 1450 and 1550. Several women signed their names in it, and one may have written this poem (p. 29).

Camb. Univ. Lib. MS. Ff.1.6, f.153b. R.H.R., 'The Findern Anthology', *P.M.L.A.*, lxix (1954), p. 638.

Poem 123. A carol which is an ironic satire on women (pp. 35, 42). If the burden which reverses the tenor of the stanzas seems a little heavy-handed, the device was commonly used and presumably, therefore, popular, particularly, it may be guessed, if the women present could not understand the Latin.

Index 1485. Balliol Coll. Oxf. MS. 354, f.250a; Bodl. MS. Eng. poet. e.1 (29734), f.55b. R.H.R. *Sec. Lyrs.*, p. 35, no. 38; Greene, p. 265, no. 399a.

Poem 124. A carol of the nativity full of traditional elements such as the two suns of ll. 23–4 (pp. 35–6 and Appendix, 'Two lights'), and the paradoxes summed up as 'a wonder thing' (p. 22).

Index 998. Bodl. MS. Eng. poet. e.1 (29734), f.52b. Greene, p. 29, no. 44; *E.E.L.*, pp. 136–7, no. 73.

Poem 125. Less a satire on women than a series of delightful grotesques such as abound in the sculpture, woodwork and drawing of the time: it is like looking along a row of misericords. Their organization, roughly speaking, is by plants in the first stanza, creatures of the water in the second, of the air in the third, and of the land in the last. The form is an extended ballade in rime royal (p. 43).

Index 3999. Balliol Coll. Oxf. MS. 354, f.250b; Bodl. MS. Eng. poet. e.1 (29734), f.43b (seven stanzas including these four); B.M.

printed book IB 55242 (Trevisa's *Bartholomaeus Anglicus*) back fly-leaf. R.H.R. *Sec. Lyrs*, p. 103, no. 114; Greene, p. 269, no. 402b.

Poem 126. While written in a tradition of satire against simony and corruption in Church and Law (e.g. ll. 29–36), this poem characteristically reflects changing social and economic conditions in that, e.g. there is no need, now, to be a soldier to be a knight, and in that wealth can determine rank. Such topics, however, are found in Chaucer's poetry and *Piers Plowman* some century before and money had been commonly personified as Penny or Sir Penny from 12c. or 13c.

Index 2082. Bodl. MS. Eng. poet. e.1 (29734), f.26b. R.H.R. *Sec. Lyrs*, p. 55, no. 59.

Poem 127. A poem in contempt of the world, plumb in the mainstream of a well-developed tradition (p. 40). Hector, Achilles and Alexander are, of course, instances of greatness in the Ancient World.

Index 2057. Edinburgh Univ. Lib. MS. 205 (Laing 149), f.87a. C.B. *15c.*, p. 246, no. 156.

Poem 128. The Latin line is from the *Song of Songs* (iv, 8) and is used, for example, of the Blessed Virgin in a carol by James Ryman (Greene, p. 187, no. 262). A 15c. carol (Greene, pp. 95–6, no. 139) gives a pious significance to the letters I(esus) V(ife = Wife = Mary) E(mmanuel), and so sanctifies the traditional subject (no. 84): the same may be the purpose of this poem in which the ivy may be identified with the Blessed Virgin of whom the expression in l. 8 was often used, though it was as commonly used in secular love poetry (pp. 20, 24).

Index 3438. Bodl. MS. Eng. poet. e.1 (29734), f.54a. R.H.R. *Sec. Lyrs*, p. 46, no. 52; *E.E.L.*, p. 236, no. 138; Greene, p. 95, no. 138.

Poem 129. A clever macaronic poem, exceptional among Ryman's many dull poems, a number of which are translations of Latin hymns. He was a Franciscan (pp. 23, 31, 35). There are several tunes in rough notation in the MS.

There are 166 pieces in this MS., containing Ryman's name and the date 1492, of which 119 are carols, i.e. a quarter of all those known up to 1550.

Index 3837. Camb. Univ. Lib. MS. Ee.1.12, f.33a. Greene, p. 47, no. 75.

Poem 130. This is so unlike Ryman's other poems in sentiment, tone and colour, that one might doubt his authorship (note 129). Christmas and Lent were often impersonated and so, perhaps, was Advent. Perhaps the departure of the season of fasting that precedes Christmas was celebrated by singing this song against Advent while ejecting its impersonator.

Index 4197. Camb. Univ. Lib. MS. Ee.1.12, f.58b. Greene, p. 4, no. 3.

Poem 131. Cresseid's 'complaint' against misfortune in the *Testament of Cresseid* has Henryson's (p. 34) characteristic warmth and homeliness in predominant native Scottish and a typical measure of alliteration. This, and such a line as the first, might suggest the influence of native alliterative verse (pp. 34–5, nos. 15 and 115) for l. 1 reads itself as a four-stress line, divided in the middle into two halves, as do many other lines. On the other hand it has ten syllables and is no less a 'standard' English line than one of Shakespeare's or Keats'. l. 18 has five stresses and a resonance that is a measure of Henryson's rhythmic assurance. l. 45 does not divide in the middle at all and l. 46 does not naturally divide into two but into three, and is, anyway, continuous with the next line. Cresseid's complaint is one of the finest formal poems in 'high' style in this anthology (pp. 25, 33). In these stanzas, nobly built, the figures used give distinction with appropriate ornament and also move feeling with dignity: there are here forms of *exclamatio* (ll. 1 and 2); *interrogatio* (ll. 10 and 19); *expolitio* (in the varied illustrations of what has passed away); *interpretatio* (in the replacing of words in the first half of l. 6 by words of the same meaning in the second); *translatio* (or metaphor, in l. 1). The question, 'Quhair is' relates the poem to others in Latin, French and English which have 'Ubi sunt' for their theme and form (notes 8 and 83, and no. 97), and the dominance of Fortune and Cresseid's begging her listeners to see in her sad case an example of their own (*mirrour*, l. 51, *exempill*, l. 59) relate it to the long, deep tradition of didactic art throughout the European Middle Ages (pp. 40–1). Whereas, then, it has certain virtues which are Henryson's and Scottish, this is not a provincial or personal poem.

Cresseid's complaint is distinguished from the body of the poem, which is in rime royal, by its stanza form. Having had to leave her lover, the Prince Troilus, Cresseid had given her love to Diomeid. But when he had 'had all his appetite' he abandoned her, and in her degradation she returned to her father's house where, having blasphemed the gods by blaming them for her 'misfortune', she was punished by them with leprosy.

The Testament of Cresseid, printed H. Charteris, Edinburgh (1593): B.M. printed book C.21.c.14. *The poems of Robert Henryson*, ed. H. H. Wood (Edinburgh and London, 1933), pp. 119–21.

Poem 132. This mock medical receipt is uncommonly like many a serious one.

Index 813. Bodl. MS. Eng. poet. e.1 (29734), f.21b. R.H.R. *Sec. Lyrs*, p. 102, no. 113.

Poem 133. A carol and a *chanson d'aventure* (pp. 35, 43), a form which occurs in English with religious content as early as secular. Greene has suggested, however, that this is like those lyrics in French and English in which a woman laments being pregnant and that this is a religious imitation of a secular lyric, for the maid of this poem is the Mother of God. Might not the first stanza have belonged to such a poem as no. 73 or no. 108? In the MS. the heading is 'A song upon "Now must I sing, etc."' and perhaps 'Now must I sing' was a secular song.

Index 3822. Bodl. MS. Eng. poet. e.1 (29734), f.47b. Greene, p. 186, no. 261.

Poem 134. The rhythmic shape of this poem is common (e.g. nos. 149 and 185) and probably taken from medieval Latin poetry: lines of two stresses and four syllables are grouped in stanzas in which the sense and sound is closed and there are only two rhymes, the second of these, connecting the middle and last lines, breaking those that have the first rhyme into couplets or triplets. It is a rhythm which, because it can make for economy and astringency of statement, happily conveys the laconic or bitter (no. 185). This is a poem from the Findern MS. (note 122).

Rhythmic shape: compare Mone, ii, pp. 396–7, no. 582: Jesse proles,/ Quibus doles,/ Leva moles/ Scelerum,/ Mater solis,/ Carens dolis,/Lux in polis/Siderum./etc.

Index 3917. Camb. Univ. Lib. MS. Ff.1.6, f.56a. R.H.R., 'The Findern Anthology', *P.M.L.A.*, lxix (1954), p. 632.

Poem 135. A direct satire on women (p. 42). The three characteristics of women in l. 29 are traditional, the image in the last stanza, which is fully rounded out and seizes the imagination, is common in a number of languages, and the line repeated at the end of each stanza is the first recorded instance of a proverb. Rhythm: pp. 34–5.

Traditional characteristics l. 29: the Latin 'Fallere, flere, nere tria sunt haec in muliere' (with variations) accompanies this stanza in one MS., and, in several of Chaucer's MSS., the Wife of Bath's 'Deceite, weping, spinning God hath give/To wommen kindely' (*Canterbury Tales*, D 401–2). *Image in last stanza:* see I. Linn, 'If all the sky were parchment', *P.M.L.A.*, liii (1938), pp. 951–70.

Index 1944. Trinity Coll. Camb. MS. R.3.19 (599), f.207a; O.9.38 (1450), f.28a; B.M. MS. Harley 2251, f.149b. *Chaucerian & other pieces*, ed. W. W. Skeat (1897), pp. 295–6; R.H.R. *Sec. Lyrs*, p. 224, no. 211.

Poem 136. A popular tag found in thirteen MSS. (incl. 'Findern', note 122).

Index 2742. Camb. Univ. Lib. MS. Ff.1.6, f.53b. R.H.R. *Sec. Lyrs*, p. 81, no. 84.

Poem 137. A unique love poem from the Findern MS. (note 122) with the rhythmic pattern of no. 134.

Index 657. Camb. Univ. Lib. MS. Ff.1.6, f.138b. R.H.R., 'The Findern Anthology', *P.M.L.A.*, lxix (1954), p. 636.

Poem 138. The burden must be that of the secular song which gave its tune to this carol which is headed in the MS. 'A song in the tune of "And I were a maid, etc.".' It was probably the lament of an abandoned girl.

Index 3235. Bodl. MS. Eng. poet. e.1 (29734), f.45b. Greene, p. 58, no. 93.

Poem 139. A ballade in rime royal from the Findern MS. (note 122) and addressed to Fortune (p. 40). Ten syllables seem to be intended in every line, but only the last two lines of each stanza have a clear rhythm.

Index 12. Camb. Univ. Lib. MS. Ff.1.6, f.178a. C.B. *15c.*, p. 262, no. 170.

Notes

Poem 140. A grotesquely improper love-letter (p. 27) abusing the conventions of the epistle and of rhetorical praise for the beloved and concluding the preposterous venture in the last two lines by the supposedly female writer insulting herself also. It may belong to a tradition of abusive writing, that of the 'flyting', in which the point was to be as offensive as possible (nos. 105, 151).

Index 3832. Bodl. MS. Rawlinson poet. 36 (14530), f.3b. R.H.R. *Sec. Lyrs*, p. 219, no. 208.

Poem 141. Accompanied by music for three voices.

Index 925. Bodl. MS. Ashmole 191 (6668), f. 192b. R.H.R. *Sec. Lyrs*, p. 150, no. 155.

Poem 142. Presumably the song the cock and hen sang in Chaucer's *Nonnes Preestes Tale* (B.4069).

Index 2254. Trinity Coll. Camb. MS. R.3.19 (599), f.154a. R.H.R. *Sec. Lyrs*, p. 152, no. 160.

Poem 143. This is an accomplished lyric of 'refined' love (p. 44), both elegant and fresh, and given both unity and movement by a simple plot, neatly turned in the last three lines. As in the 13c. *Roman de la Rose*, from which stems the chief tradition in which this poem is written, the poet seeks the love of the woman, the Rose, in the Garden (l. 6) of the Rose, where Dunbar represents other features of the love relationship allegorically by plants, for example, rue or pity (l. 10). Dunbar: p. 34.

Magdalene Coll. Camb. (Maitland) MS. Pepys 2553, p. 320. *The poems of William Dunbar*, ed. W. M. Mackenzie (1932), p. 99, no. 49; ed. J. Kinsley (1958), p. 21, no. 9.

Poem 144. An accomplished and classic example of the aureate (pp. 25–6): *superna, hodierna, regina*, have been only slightly trimmed into the forms used in this poem and can never have been meant to fit into Scottish. To the effect of Latin resonance and splendour the internal rhymes also contribute. For the traditional images (e.g. *wall* in l. 25) see Appendix. Dunbar: p. 34.

l. 32, Angels' food: St. Bruno, 'Expositio Psalmorum', *P.L.*, cxlii, col. 294 glosses *Psalm* lxxviii, 25: 'Panis ergo angelorum bene dicitur Christus, quia videlicet ipsius laude pascuntur: verum hic

357

panis, in coelo replet angelos, nos pascit in terris.' See, also, St.
Augustine, 'De Libero Arbitrio', *P.L.*, xxxii, col. 1286.

Lady Talbot de Malahide (in B.M.): Asloan MS. (f.303a) ed.
W. A. Craigie, vol. 2, *S.T.S.* (1923–5). *The poems of William Dunbar*,
ed. W. M. Mackenzie (1932), pp. 160–2, no. 82; ed. J. Kinsley
(1958), pp. 8–9, no. 4.

Poem 145. A grotesquely comic *chanson d'aventure* (p. 43): the
complaint of the lover, to whom is applied the heroic word *beirne*,
insists on his long, unrewarded service and laments the woman's
danger (pp. 44–5); but he is foul in appearance and sexually aroused
and this is no 'refined' love dialogue which exploits with such
characteristic relish and plenitude the resources of the native tongue
(pp. 26, 34).

Magdalene Coll. Camb. (Maitland) MS. Pepys 2553, pp. 308 and
311; Nat. Lib. of Scotland (Bannatyne) MS. Advocates 1.1.6, f.103b.
The poems of William Dunbar, ed. W. M. Mackenzie (1932), pp. 53–5,
no. 28; ed. J. Kinsley (1958), pp. 40–2, no. 13.

Poem 146. A dramatic meditation on death (pp. 40–1) comparable
with the visual representations of the Dance of Death. The Latin
refrain (no. 170) is from the Office for the Dead (*Sarum Breviary*, II,
278). Dunbar: p. 34.

Printed Chepman & Myllar 1508 (?), ed. G. Stevenson, *S.T.S.*
(1918); Magdalene Coll. Camb. (Maitland) MS. Pepys 2553, p. 189.
The poems of William Dunbar, ed. W. M. Mackenzie (1932), pp. 20–3,
no. 7; ed. J. Kinsley, pp. 61–4, no. 23.

Poem 147. In this fine poem, powerfully controlled but quite unself-
conscious, celebrating Christ as risen champion over death and hell
(nos. 27, 41 and 51), the vernacular, into which a few Romance
elements have been completely assimilated, achieves, without any
affectation, a natural sublimity, the grandeur of the refrain line trans-
posed into Scottish (pp. 26, 34). Whereas Dunbar's poetry can be in
the nature of a bizarre *tour de force*, it is in such a poem as this that he
truly follows the central genius of Chaucer and is unrivalled until the
great Elizabethans. There are many traditional images. If not to be
regarded as a sort of ballade (p. 43), no. 147 has, in its long, closed
stanzas, linked by a refrain, some of the virtues of one. The assurance
of the rhythm needs no more comment than does that of Chaucer,

Shakespeare or Pope, for, with one or two exceptions, to an ear used to their lines, every line speaks itself.

Traditional images: ll. 9–10, serpent with mortall stang: Revelation xx, 2–3: the dragon, the old serpent, which is the Devil; *l. 11, tegir with his teith on char:* St. Peter Damian, *P.L.,* cxlv, col. 775; Et quid hic tigris, nisi diabolus debet intelligi? *l. 18, lamb in sacrifice: Revelation* v, 6: a Lamb standing as though it had been slain; *l. 19, lik a lione: Revelation* v, 5: the Lion . . . hath overcome; *l. 21, Sprungin is Aurora:* Alanus de Insulis, 'Liber in distinctionibus dictionum theologicalium', *P.L.,* ccx, col. 714: *Aurora,* Dicitur Christus, unde in hymno: 'Aurora totus prodeat'; quia, sicut sol materialis mundum illuminat, ita spiritualis sol, scilicet Christus, sanctam Ecclesiam; *Revelation* xxii, 16: I, Jesus . . . the bright, the morning star; *l. 22, Appollo, l. 27, sone: Sarum Breviary,* I, lxxxi: antiphon in Vespers of Second Sunday in Advent: Orietur sicut sol Salvator mundi.

Nat. Lib. of Scotland, Advocates MS. 1.1.6, f.35a. *The poems of William Dunbar,* ed. W. M. Mackenzie (1932), pp. 159–60, no. 81; ed. J. Kinsley (1958), pp. 7–8, no. 3.

Poem 148. Acrostics were popular and this, in which the initial letters of the lines spell 'Margaret', is passable; but it is not ambitious since it is no more than an assortment of conventional variations on the theme of the 'lady beloved' (pp. 34, 44). This poem is from the Newton MS. (p. 29) and, like no. 151, is ascribed by Robbins and the Bodleian Library's accessions list to the compiler, Humfrey Newton, himself. But I don't see on what certain grounds.

Index 2217. Bodl. (*once* Capesthorne) MS. Lat. misc. c.66, f.93b. R.H.R., 'The poems of Humfrey Newton, Esquire', *P.M.L.A.,* lxv (1950), p. 266.

Poem 149. A love poem in a common verse form (note 134 and pp. 44–5). An interesting variation is the linking of stanzas by using as dominant rhyme in each the subordinate rhyme of the one before.

Index 267. Trinity Coll. Camb. MS. R.3.19 (599), f.160a. R.H.R. *Sec. Lyrs,* p. 162, no. 173; *E.E.L.,* pp. 27–8, no. 15.

Poem 150. The burden of this carol is quite probably secular and it is Greene's opinion that this religious poem was sung to a well-known secular tune, Christ complaining to the erring soul with the same music as a lover to his wandering sweetheart. But Greene is unable to find the secular song and no reference is made to one in the MS. Reforming zeal is reflected in the last two stanzas. (pp. 35–6.)

Index 2086. B.M. MS. Royal 17.B.xliii, f.184a. Greene, p. 192, no. 270.

Poem 151. Poems in the form of a letter are common in 15c. but this poet has the same sort of reverence for rhythmic form as for the woman addressed: he will play with both just so much as it pleases him. In this, and the sort of episode which he makes visually real, he is like his contemporary, Skelton. The poem is from the Newton MS. (p. 29 and no. 148).

Index 926. Bodl. (*once* Capesthorne) MS. Lat. misc. c.66, f.94a. R.H.R. 'The poems of Humfrey Newton, Esquire', *P.M.L.A.*, lxv (1950), p. 271; R.H.R. *Sec. Lyrs*, p. 195, no. 194.

Poem 152. This poem, shaped like a pair of wings, is the first known in English to copy the pattern poems of the *Greek Anthology*. Stephen Hawes travelled in France where poets were already shaping poems like eggs and wings. The words after the brackets in the second line of each triplet represent the second of the pair of wings, so that there are three poems in one, each self-contained in form and, to all intents and purposes, in sense, viz. the words before or after the brackets, read separately, or all the words read together. A block, inset for the first nine lines, depicts Christ and the symbols of his Passion: 'See me . . .' (note 79). This poem is set in a longer poem, *The Conversion of Swerers*, made otherwise of forty-six rime-royal stanzas. Hawes was an officer of the household of Henry VII.

Printed by Johan Butler (n.d.: 1530?): unique copy in Huntington Library; first edition by Wynkyn de Worde (1509); etc. *The Conversion of Swerers.* (Reprinted for the Abbotsford Club: Edinburgh, 1865); M. Church, 'The first English pattern poems,' *P.M.L.A.*, lxi (1946), pp. 636–50.

Poem 153. The practical morality of this poem, of which the more didactic stanzas are omitted, does not necessarily mark it out as of the later middle ages. Its earthiness, appropriately vulgar, links it with the fabliaux tradition, in which Chaucer's Miller's and Reeve's Tales are written, and in the learned tradition it was quite customary to dissuade from attachment to things of the flesh by listing nasty physical facts (note 16). On the other hand there is no mention of God and it

is because lechery is physically inconvenient and not because it is sin-
ful that it is condemned. No. 153 is not only plain-spoken but work-
manlike and the verse is easy-moving.

Index 551. B.M. MS. Harley 7578, f.16a. R.H.R. 'A warning
against lechery', *P.Q.*, xxxv (1956), p. 93.

Poem 154. This love poem has much in common with a poem
ascribed to Wyatt, and may be either a song which he adapted for
his own purposes or a partial version of his. The association of un-
satisfied love with the savage life in the woods is traditional (e.g.
no. 9, ll. 61–2) and, though there is a certain artificial feel about them
here, the wild woods, greenwood tree, running stream and acorns
may associate the poem with such others as, say, no. 33 (pp. 44–5).

Poem ascribed to Wyatt: see *Unpublished poems of Sir Thomas Wyatt
and his circle*, ed. K. Muir (Liverpool, 1961).

Index 1333. Huntington (*once* Ellesmere) MS. EL 1160, f.11b.
R.H.R. *Sec. Lyrs.*, p. 14, no. 20.

Poem 155. A carol (despite its one stanza) and set to music for two or
three voices (pp. 29, 35).

Index 1710. B.M. Additional MS. 5665, f.44b. R.H.R. *Hist. poems*,
p. 242, no. 100; Greene, p. 296, no. 435; Stevens, p. 102, no. 112.

Poem 156. A carol for three voices, this poem may have an earlier,
probably popular or minstrel, tune as burden, though elaborated in
this setting. It has been suggested that it may have been an *aube* or *alba*,
or lovers' parting at dawn, but the evidence is inconclusive. Cer-
tainly the burden has no apparent connection with the sense of the
verses. The celebration of the white rose suggests that the poem may
be in honour of Elizabeth of York who married Henry VII in 1486
(l. 10) and the flower references in stanza two may all be to heraldic
national emblems.

Index 1450. B.M. Additional MS. 5465, f.108b. R.H.R. *Hist.
Poems*, p. 93, no. 34; Greene, p. 294, no. 432; Stevens, *Early Tudor
Court*, pp. 381–2, no. F 45.

Poem 157. With music for three voices by Sir Thomas Phillipps who is
otherwise unknown. The words may also be by him, and probably
refer to the reconciliation of the houses of York and Lancaster, the

white and red roses, by the marriage of 1486; there may be a reference to the birth of Prince Arthur in l. 40.

Index 1327. B.M. Additional MS. 5465, f.40b. R.H.R. *Hist. Poems*, p. 94, no. 35; Greene, p. 295, no. 433; *E.E.L.*, p. 72, no. 34; Stevens, *Early Tudor Court*, pp. 364–5, no. F 27.

Poem 158. Spoken by a sad friar who cannot see why he is disliked. Criticism of the friars became, in 14c., to all intents and purposes, a commonplace or conventional theme and the same points were repeatedly satirized (no. 59).

l. 2, Holy Writ: English translations of the Scriptures, associated with the Lollards and Wycliffe, had appeared in the 1380's. *l. 14, In principio:* 'In the beginning': the opening words of St. John's gospel seem often to have been used with a sort of magic significance, especially by friars (cf. Chaucer's friar in *General Prologue to Canterbury Tales*, A 254).

Index 161. St. John's Coll. Cambridge MS. G.28 (195), flyleaf in margin. *Cambridge Middle English Lyrics*, ed. H. A. Person (Seattle, 1953), p. 42, no. 51.

Poem 159. A conventional love poem in rime-royal stanza and the high style (pp. 25, 40, 44). If the rhythm of the repeated last line is uncertain, the other lines are confident and pleasing four-, or five-, stress variations, though of no constant syllabic length. (Note 161.)

S.T.C. 22604. Huntington Lib.: Here folowythe divers Balettys and dyties . . . 4to. n.d. evidently Pynson. *Poetical works of John Skelton*, ed. A. Dyce (London, 1843), vol. i, p. 27.

Poem 160. This poem evinces something of that relish for native words which characterizes Skelton's Scottish contemporary, Dunbar (p. 34), as does its robust low-life comedy (no. 145). Though the lines are shorter than the ten syllables of rime royal, it is interesting that the stanzas have rime-royal rhymes. Skelton: note 161.

S.T.C. 22604. Huntington Lib.: Here folowythe divers Balettys and dyties . . . 4to. n.d. evidently Pynson. *Poetical works of John Skelton*, ed. A. Dyce (London, 1843), vol. i, p. 22.

Poem 161 is from the *Garland of Laurel* (1523) an otherwise poetically dull, allegorical poem in which, after honouring Gower, Chaucer and Lydgate, Skelton calls himself the British Adonis and Homer. Honoured by both Oxford and Cambridge, he was tutor to King Henry VIII before his accession. He died in 1529, aged about sixty-five. This poem has a peculiar delicacy and simplicity. The short lines resemble those of, say, no. 134, but when the rhymes are not interlaced, as here, but follow one upon the other, tumbling out as long as the poet cares, as in his *Philip Sparrow*, they are generally called Skeltonics because they are peculiar to him.

l. 8. Machareus, committed incest with his sister, Canace, in a legend of the Ancient World, while Phedra, l. 15, fell in love with her stepson, Hippolytus, whom she caused her husband, Theseus, to curse when he refused her.

S.T.C. 22610 and 22608. B.M.: A ryght delectable tratise upon a goodly garlande or chapelet of laurell . . . printed R. Faukes (1523); Huntington Lib.: Pithy, pleasaunt and profitable workes of Maister Skelton . . . printed T. Marshe (1568); (etc.) *Poetical works of John Skelton*, ed. A. Dyce (London, 1843), vol. i, pp. 399–400.

Poem 162. This Resurrection hymn succeeds by the natural dignity of its utterance: the images of 'rising', 'driving to a den', 'holding down an enemy's head' and 'sealing a remission' are all from everyday life as well as from religious, and such polysyllabic, Romance words as are used, are used unselfconsciously as part of the normal vocabulary (pp. 25–6). The refrain, slightly varied, closes each well-knit stanza, in which each basically four-stress, octosyllabic line is itself generally self-contained, so that rhyme, sense and rhythm require a pause at the end of each.

Index 3695. B.M. Arundel MS. 285, f.175b; Nat. Lib. of Scotland MS. Advocates 1.1.6, f.34a. C.B. *15c.*, p. 179, no. 113.

Poem 163. The verse form is that of no. 134. The *danger* (p. 44) shown by this mistress is the consequence of that newfangledness which later medieval poets so dreaded.

Index 2518. B.M. MS. Harley 2252, f.84b. R.H.R. *Sec. Lyrs*, p. 138, no. 137; *E.E.L.*, pp. 76–7, no. 37.

Poem 164. Of this, most mysterious and moving of poems, there are three or four other versions recorded by collectors of folk-songs last century and this, but only this version, which is in Richard Hill's commonplace book (p. 29), has this burden. The two-line stanza is rare in a carol but not in a ballad so that it could be that no. 164 is an adaptation of a popular song of a ballad sort by the addition of a burden. It has been argued by Greene that the falcon is Anne Boleyn, whose badge was a falcon, and that this is a reference to her displacement of Catherine of Aragon (l. 2) in the affections of Henry VIII. Greene's interpretation of the details of the stanzas in terms of this situation, as he believes a contemporary would have taken them, is unconvincing: though it is possible to see Catherine in the weeping maiden, why should the falcon bear the husband she has stolen to the place where the deserted wife is abandoned to her grief before the Blessed Sacrament? The poem is rather to be read in terms that, even in Greene's view, it is more likely that it had before its adaptation: they are terms of the Eucharist and the Grail. Thus it has been suggested that in ll. 3–4 it may be Joseph of Arimathea who bears the Grail, the vessel of the Last Supper, to Avalon, Isle of Apples, and that the hall in l. 5 may be the Castle of the Grail Keeper, the Wounded King of l. 9. But ll. 3–4 are the most difficult lines of the poem and the most like those of a ballad, and it may rather be that the orchard is the Church and the hall an aumbry, in which lies Christ, present in every Eucharist, or an Easter Sepulchre where a consecrated Host was laid to rest on Good Friday and 'raised' on Easter Day. From l. 5 onwards the poem makes good sense in these Eucharistic terms, or, more specifically, in these terms of the events of Holy Week, particularly when it is remembered how materialistic was the current, popular conception of the Mass in the late middle ages. The maid of l. 11 will, in this case, be Mary (p. 40). This fine poem has something of the nature of a riddling ballad in which the symbols are suggestive and resonant beyond the sense of any single interpretation, and in which the movement is through layer after layer of mystery to the heart of the matter, satisfyingly disclosed at the end so that it illuminates the whole poem.

Greene discusses the poem in his notes and also in an article in *Medium Aevum*, xxix (1960), pp. 10–21.

Index 1132. Balliol Coll. Oxf. MS. 354, f.165b. Greene, p. 221, no. 322A; *E.E.L.*, p. 148, no. 81.

Poem 165. A ballade of love in the stanza of Chaucer's *Monk's Tale* (pp. 26, 43–5).

Index 2517. Nat. Lib. of Scotland MS. Advocates 1.1.6, f.220a. R.H.R. *Sec. Lyrs*, p. 132, no. 133.

Poem 166. The devotional tradition in which this is written is described pp. 22, 38. This poem attempts dignity in five-stress lines and a complex stanza, that of Chaucer's *Monk's Tale*. ll. 41–8, all end-stopped, have an appropriately slow weightiness.

l. 11, nardus-spikardy; = *nardi spicati* of Vulgate, *Mark* xiv, 3 = 'spikenard'. *l. 24, Locostratus:* = Lithostrotos, of Vulgate, *John* xix, 13 (Hebraice autem Gabbatha). *l. 54, Longus:* Longinus, traditional name of soldier who pierced Christ's side with a spear.

Index 648. B.M. MS. Arundel 285, f.159b; Nat. Lib. of Scotland MS. Advocates 1.1.6, f.33b; Edinburgh Univ. Lib. MS. 205, f.86b. C.B. *15c.*, p. 131, no. 91.

Poem 167. A carol and a drinking song (pp. 35, 42). There is play on the butler's name 'Walter' and 'water' in l. 25.

Index 903. Balliol Coll. Oxf. MS. 354, f.251b. R.H.R. *Sec. Lyrs*, p. 10, no. 14; *E.E.L.*, p. 227, no. 131; Greene, p. 285, no. 421.

Poem 168. A carol of the Christmas Feast (note 78 and p. 35).

Index 1866. Balliol Coll. Oxf. MS. 354, f.223b. Greene, p. 9, no. 11; R.H.R. *Sec. Lyrs*, p. 3, no. 2; *E.E.L.*, p. 234, no. 136.

Poem 169. A variant of this carol is still used in a special ceremony at Queen's College, Oxford, and is sung to a traditional tune.

Index 3313. Balliol Coll. Oxf. MS. 354, f.228a. R.H.R. *Sec. Lyrs*, p. 48, no. 55; Greene, p. 91, no. 132A; *E.E.L.*, p. 235, no. 137.

Poem 170. A carol and a macaronic poem of which the Latin refrain— or one very like it, 'Timor mortis conturbat me', from a service for the dead (no. 146)—and the stanza form are several times found together in poems about death (pp. 35, 41, 44).

Index 1444. Balliol Coll. Oxf. MS. 354, f.229a. Greene, p. 249, no. 372.

Poem 171. More ambitious than no. 84, it develops the subject so that in ll. 25–8 there is an excellent image well opened out, and in ll. 17–20 a picturesque detail added and a comment which points the moral. I have broken the longer lines in which it is written into two.

Index 1226. Balliol Coll. Oxf. MS. 354, f.251a. Greene, p. 94, no. 136B; *E.E.L.*, pp. 239–40, no. 141.

Notes

Poem 172. The paradoxes of the Christian Faith (nos. 28 and 58) are expressed with pleasingly astringent word-play ('What *reason reason* give' and '*Beleeve* and *leave* . . .') and an appropriate air of ratiocination ('this or the other') in the first two stanzas of no. 172, while the rhythm of lines three and four together is peculiarly subtle. The conclusion that, because these paradoxes surpass the power of the human mind, it is to faith that reason must defer, is traditional. There are several earlier instances of a less taut but briefer expression of this idea.

Earlier instances of same idea with verbal echoes (one attributed to Bishop Pecock from whom, therefore, these may derive): C.B. *15c.*, p. 186, no. 119; also Copenhagen: Kongelige Bibliotek Thott 110, f.163a. This poem is scribbled in the records of the abbey of St. Albans (p. 28).

Index 37. Bodl. MS. Rawlinson B. 332 (11670), back of first flyleaf. C.B. *15c.*, p. 187, no. 120.

Poem 173. There is little formally interesting about this poem (p. 27), the impetus of which comes naturally from the course of events. The genuine poignancy of the repeated last lines and its concrete embodiment in the pillow of the last line but one sustains the tone of modest sensuality. (But see pp. 34–5.)

Bodl. MS. Rawlinson C.813 (12653), f.47a. F. M. Padelford, 'The songs of Rawlinson MS. C.813', *Anglia*, xxxi (1908), pp. 360–1, no. 28.

Poem 174. A carol in traditional praise of women (pp. 35, 44).

Index 3782. B.M. MS. Harley 4294, f.81a. Greene, p. 264, no. 396; *E.E.L.*, p. 197, no. 113; R.H.R. *Sec. Lyrs*, p. 31, no. 34.

Poem 175. A perfect poem, superbly confident in all respects, it has many things in common with the ballads, e.g. narrative swiftness, repetition with partial variation and the immediacy of speech. But it makes sophisticated use of them by introducing the ambiguous cuckoo of l. 54 and in the bathetic brevity of the fastidious wanton's 'Alas!'.

Balliol Coll. Oxf. MS. 354, f.251a. *E.E.L.*, p. 251, no. 150.

Poem 176. Though the central idea of this poem was common, I know no earlier instance of its expansion into a full-scale poem. (pp. 34–5.)

Index 1488. B.M. MS. Lansdowne 762, f.3a; C.B. *15c.*, pp. 255–6, no. 162.

Poem 177. A carol of the Christmas Feast (no. 78) of which the stanzas were probably sung by the representative, perhaps the steward, of the host, or *gudman*, of l. 15, and the guests, perhaps, sang the burden.

Index 1873. Balliol Coll. Oxf. MS. 354, f.223b. Greene, p. 77, no. 120.

Poem 178. A carol from Richard Hill's commonplace book (pp. 29, 35) but more widely known since a fragment also occurs elsewhere.

Index 1399. Balliol Coll. Oxf. MS. 354, f.252a; Bodl. MS. Laud Misc. 601 (1491), f.115b (fragment). Greene, p. 277, no. 413.

Poem 179. Such play on the relationship between Mary and the Persons of the Trinity is common (note 28 and p. 40).

Index 1077. B.M. Arundel MS. 285, f.196b. C.B. *15c.*, p. 37, no. 21.

Poem 180. King Henry VIII was a minor composer and, presumably, the poet of this carol which, like several others in the songbook containing it, has music, for three voices, for the burden only. It will not fit the verses which Stevens suggests may have been sung to an already known tune and, moreover, may be a re-working of already current words. The symbolism of holly and ivy, identified with man and woman, is traditional (no. 84). The sexes, however, are not here in conflict but exceptional concord.

B.M. Additional MS. 31922, f.37b. Greene, p. 304, no. 448; Stevens, *Early Tudor Court*, pp. 398–9, no. H33; *Oxford Book of Carols*, music edition, p. 130.

Poem 181. Stevens says that no. 181 was a popular song and suggests that the tenor parts in the collection containing it were later incorporated into settings: for example, masses were written by three composers on this particular tune!

B.M. MS. Royal Appendix 58, f.5a. E.E.L., p. 69, no. 31.

Poem 182. Cornish probably wrote words as well as music and was a professional musician in the court of Henry VIII.

Twenty songs, printed Wynkyn de Worde (1530): B.M. printed book, K.1. e.1. *E.E.L.*, p. 160, no. 89.

Poem 183 follows the Pageant of the Shearmen and Tailors in that version of the religious plays, performed at Coventry, which was corrected by Robert Croo. It was sung, says a rubric (to music in the *Oxford Book of Carols*, no. 22) by women whose children are put to death in the Massacre of the Innocents at the hands of Herod with which the Pageant ends. The date is uncertain.

Date uncertain: Robert Croo's version is dated 1534, but there is in it a reference to a Thomas Mawdycke, which precedes the lyrics, and includes the date 1591.

MS. destroyed in burning of Free Reference Library at Birmingham, 1878. Text from H. Craig, *Two Coventry Corpus Christi Plays*, *E.E.T.S.* E.S. lxxxvii (1957), which is derived from *A dissertation on the pageants or dramatic mysteries anciently performed at Coventry . . .* by Thomas Sharp (Coventry, 1825). Greene, p. 71, no. 112; R.H.R. *Christmas Carols*, pp. 74–6, no. 28.

Poem 184. Wyatt's roundels (pp. 44–6) are not his best poetry but this is probably his best roundel. There is some difficulty, not uncharacteristic of Wyatt's verse, in finding the rhythm of some lines, e.g. l. 6.

B.M. Egerton MS. 2711, f.31b. Wyatt, p. 35, no. 45.

Poem 185. This poem shows Wyatt's place in the English tradition. The form is that of other early Tudor poems (no. 134) and the content and style are scarcely different except for the 'tiger' conceit in ll. 25–8 and the address to his lute. Mention of a lute is no certain evidence that the poem was written to be sung.

Mention of lute: reference may be conventional and the lute, anyway, was an Italian instrument common in England only at a later date. There is known only one early musical setting of any of Wyatt's poems and only some five later ones: no music is known for any of his poems in this anthology (pp. 27, 46). On the other hand, it has been argued by major critics that the music to which it might be presumed such a poem as this was sung would provide the sensuous body of a performance for which the words were made deliberately plain.

B.M. Egerton MS. 2711, f.34a; Additional (Devonshire) MS. 17492, f.12. Wyatt, pp. 37–8, no. 51.

Poem 186. Though it has no burden, this poem has the stanza form of the carol (p. 35), and the lover's symptoms are all those of the 'refined-love' tradition (pp. 44–5). But this poem has imagery that is exceptional in Wyatt, who is more usually 'drab'. It makes the conventional warmly human (e.g. ll. 6–7, 13–15), and what may, perhaps, have been another counter in the love-game of courtly society, for this reason softens into life. Compare the rhythm of ll. 15 and 19 with that of l. 11 in no. 187. Wyatt: p. 46.

B.M. Additional (Devonshire) MS. 17492, f.12b. Wyatt, pp. 99–100, no. 110.

Poem 187. The last stanza makes a perfect end both in its reference to death and in the varied first word of the last line—but it might be asked why, otherwise, as in so many medieval poems, there should be this number and order of stanzas. The plangent, reiterated 'Ons' at the end of each stanza and the beginning of the next is, however, an eloquent bond throughout the poem. It is characteristically colourless; its images, such as they are, are everyday ('Fortune'—pp. 40–1 —'throw me out', 'knit the knot') and, though the poet's mistress speaks intimately in ll. 22 and 27, it is conventionally, and we are given no idea of what she looks like nor more of her character than that she now has a 'newfangled' love. The complaint against the newfangled was a common medieval theme (nos. 19, 96, 134).

l. 11 probably affords an instance of a rhythmical characteristic of Wyatt which has been variously interpreted and valued. In poems of longer lines he often appears to set two stressed syllables together with peculiar effect, sometimes giving to them the weight also of the omitted unstressed syllable. Wyatt: p. 46.

Trinity College, Dublin (Blage) MS. D.2.7, f.138. *Sir Thomas Wyatt and his circle: unpublished poems,* ed. K. Muir, p. 44, no. 33.

Appendix

This is an alphabetical list of types and titles of the Blessed Virgin Mary used in the lyrics of this anthology. Under each entry there is given first, if it is relevant, a reference to where in the Scriptures the pre-figuring symbol is found, and, secondly, one to sample theologians and theological poets who analyse its significance and to services in which it was used (pp. 17–18, 20–2). So this Appendix shall not be too cumbrous full quotations are made only in select cases. Dates are of the time of composition except for Latin hymns in the editions of Dreves and Mone where the date given is that of the earliest MS. they mention. References at the end of each entry are to the relevant poems in this anthology.

BURNING BUSH, OF SINAI
Exodus iii, 2.
12c.: St. Bernard, 'Super "Missus est" homiliae', *P.L.* clxxxiii, col. 63: Quid deinde rubus ille quondam Mosaicus portendebat, flammas quidem emittens, sed non ardens (*Exodus* iii, 2), nisi Miriam parientem et dolorem non sentientem?; Adam, ii, p. 228, ll. 27–32; Hours B.V.M., p. 24: Sext, Antiphon: By the buish that Moises sigh unbrent we knowen that thy preisable maidenhede is kept.
34, l. 19.

CASTLE (but why of Emmaus?)
Luke x, 38–9: (village, Vulgate: castellum).
Pseudo-St. Bernard, 'Sermo in antiphorum "Salve Regina"', *P.L.* clxxxiv, col. 1074; 13c.: Dreves, x, p. 88, no. 108, 7b; *Sarum Missal*, p. 309: the Lucan passage is part of the Gospel for the Mass of the Assumption.
34, ll. 57–8.

CHAMBER
Psalm xix, 5.
12c.: St. Anselm, 'Psalter of Mary', Mone, ii, p. 234, l. 70; Pseudo-Rabanus, *P.L.* cxii, col. 1063.
34, l. 2; 144, l. 30; 1, l. 5.

Appendix

CHASTE VIRGIN, TAMER OF THE UNICORN

12c.: Pseudo-Hugo, 'De bestiis', *P.L.* clxxvii, col. 59: (A unicorn will lay its head in the lap of a virgin and can then be caught.) Sic et Dominus Jesus Christus spiritualis unicornis descendens in uterum Virginis; 14c.: *Meditations*, ll. 26–9; 14c.: Dreves, ix, p. 66, no. 81, 4b.
34, ll. 63–4.

CLOISTER

12c.: Abbot Franco, 'De gratia', *P.L.* clxvi, col. 747: Ne timeas pudori tuo, . . . quia claustra tua sicut in conceptu, ita nec in partu sunt resolvenda; Hours of B.V.M., p. 2: Matins, Hymn.
104, l. 31.

COLUMBA (see DOVE)

DAVID'S KIN (see ROD OF JESSE)

DAWN (see LIGHT, ORIENT (?)) (For *dawn* = Jesus, no. 147)
Song of Songs vi, 10.
Pseudo-St. Bernard, 'Sermo Panegyricus ad B.V.D.' *P.L.* clxxxiv, col. 1012; 11c.: St. Peter Damian, 'Sermones', *P.L.* cxliv, col. 720; *Sarum Missal*, p. 309: Epistle of Mass of Assumption includes *Song of Songs* vi, 10.
12, ll. 9–10.

DEW (see FLEECE OF GIDEON) = Christ
Psalm lxxii (lxxi, Vulgate), 6: (Descendet sicut pluvia in vellus); *Isaiah* xlv, 8: (Rorate, coeli, desuper, et nubes pluant justum); *Psalm* cxxxiii, 3; *Deuteronomy* xxxii, 2.
9c.: Rabanus Maurus, 'De Universo', *P.L.* cxi, col. 328: Ros significat Verbum Domini: ideo quod madida faciat corda hominum terrenorum ad proferendum fructum, ut est illud in Psalmo (cxxxiii, 3). Ros est tenuis ac levis pluvia non per guttas veniens, sed per quasdam minutissimas partes duritiam terrenae ariditatis infundens; *Sarum Missal*, p. 259: Office (Introit) of Mass of Annunciation; *Sarum Breviary*, I, lxxxi: Antiphon in Vespers Second Sunday in Advent; I, clx: Antiphon in Lauds of Vigil of Nativity (preceding *Deuteronomy* xxxii, 2); I, cxviii: Antiphon in Lauds Third Week of Advent.
12, l. 26; 66.

DOOR, GATE, SHUT, OF EZEKIEL
Ezekiel xliv, 2.

12c.: Adam, ii, p. 228, ll. 36–8; a rhymed Office, Mone, ii, p. 11, ll. 151 ff.

34, ll. 49–52.

DOVE

Genesis viii, 11; *Song of Songs* vi, 9.

12c.: Abbot Absalon, 'Sermo in Assumptione B.V.M.' *P.L.* ccxi, col. 246; 14c.: Mone, ii, p. 400, ll. 41–4; *Sarum Missal*, p. 309: Epistle of Mass of Assumption includes *Song of Songs* vi, 9.

34, ll. 13–16; 104, l. 31.

EARTH, UNTILLED

Psalm lxxxv, 11.

12c.: Alanus de Insulis, 'Sermones', *P.L.* ccx, cols. 216–17: (Psalm lxxxv, 11) Terra est Virgo Maria, terra inarabilis; Adam, ii, p. 220, ll. 26–7; 14c.: Mone, ii, p. 414, ll. 49–51.

12, ll. 25–8.

ESTHER

Esther ii, 17.

13c.: St. Bonaventura 'Laus B.V.M.' xiv, p. 186; 14c.: Dreves, ix, p. 58, no. 72, 1b.

34, ll. 43–8.

FLEECE OF GIDEON (see DEW)

Judges vi, 36–40.

12c.: Adam, ii, p. 174, ll. 25–6; p. 168, ll. 49–54: Super vellus ros descendens/Et in rubo flamma splendens,/(Neutrum tamen laeditur,)/Fuit Christus carnem sumens,/In te tamen non consumens/ Pudorem, dum gignitur; Hours B.V.M. p. 21; Tierce, Antiphon; *Sarum Breviary*, I, cvii: Response in Matins of Third Sunday in Advent.

12, l. 26; 34, l. 32.

FOUNTAIN, WELL, SPRING (SEALED, SHUT UP) (see DOOR; GARDEN)

Song of Songs iv, 12; 15.

12c.: Adam, ii, p. 32, ll. 59–60; ll. 63–4; 13c. Dreves, x, p. 104, no. 136, 1b; *Sarum Missal*, p. 308: Epistle of Mass of Assumption includes *Song of Songs* iv, 12 and 15.

179, l. 5; 5, l. 26; 114 (?)

GARDEN ENCLOSED (see DOOR)

Song of Songs iv, 12.

12c.: Adam, ii, p. 228, ll. 33–4; 9c.: St. Paschasius Radbertus, 'Expositio in Matthaeum', *P.L.* cxx, col. 106: (quotes *Song of Songs* iv, 12); *Sarum Missal*, p. 308; Epistle of Mass of Assumption includes *Song of Songs* iv, 12.

107, l. 6.

GATE (see DOOR)

GEM(S)
7c.: Pseudo-Hildefonsus, 'Libellus de corona Virginis', *P.L.* xcvi, cols. 285 ff.; 15c. poem in Mone, ii, pp. 445 f.

144, l. 14; 179, l. 7.

GIDEON (see FLEECE OF GIDEON)

HALL (and LODGING)
8c.: Venantius Fortunatus, *P.L.* lxxxviii, col. 281: 'In laudem S. Mariae Virginis.' . . . Aula Dei . . . Hospitium vitae; 11c.: Dreves, ix, p. 63, no. 78, 4b; *Sarum Missal*, p. 307: Collect of Mass of Vigil of Assumption.

144, l. 27; l. 29.

HILL, MOUNTAIN, OF DANIEL
Daniel ii, 34–5.
12c.: Adam, i, p. 10, ll. 17 ff.: Quid de monte lapis caesus/Sine manu, nisi Jesus/Qui de regum linea/Sine carnis opere/De carne puerperae/Processit virginea?

34, ll. 55–6.

JESSE (see ROD OF JESSE)

JUDITH
Apocryphal *Book of Judith*.
13c.: St. Bonaventura, 'Laus B.V.M.', xiv, p. 186: 'Figurata fuit per Judith'; 14c.: Dreves, ix, p. 58, no. 72, 1b.

34, ll. 37–40.

LAMP
12c.–13c.: Abbot Adam, *P.L.* ccxi, col. 749: Lampas igitur Mariae infrangibilis; 15c.: J. Ryman, Greene, p. 152, no. 207: O lantern of eternall light; 15c.: Mone, ii, p. 284, l. 41.

144, l. 3.

LIGHT, ORIENT (see TWO LIGHTS and DAWN)

13c.: St. Bonaventura, 'Litaniae B.V.M.' xiv, p. 224: Sancta Maria, splendor et lux orientalis.

LILY, AMONG THORNS
Song of Songs ii, 2.
12c.: Mone, ii, p. 297, l. 10: Tu castitatis lilium; Alanus de Insulis, 'Sententiae', *P.L.* ccx, col. 247; Pseudo-St. Bernard, 'Sermo', *P.L.* clxxxiv, col. 1020.
105, l. 8; 144, l. 23(?).

LODGING (see HALL)

MEDICINE
12c.: Mone, ii, p. 260, l. 15; St. Anselm, 'Psalter of Mary', Mone, ii, p. 233, l. 21; Mone, ii, p. 32, l. 53.
104, l. 17; 14, ll. 30–41 (?).

MIRROR, WITHOUT SPOT
Wisdom vii, 26.
15c.: Mone, ii, p. 277, l. 151.
107, l. 5.

MOTHER AND DAUGHTER
Hours of B.V.M., p. 5: first lesson Matins.
5, l. 4.

OLEUM EFFUSUM
Song of Songs i, 3 (Vulgate, 2).
12c.: St. Bernard, 'Sermones in Cantica', *P.L.* clxxxiii, col. 855 (of Jesus not Mary): Sana me, Domine, et sanabor; psallam et confitebor nomini tuo, et dicam: (*Song of Songs* i, 3).
104, l. 17.

PARENS ET PUELLA (see MOTHER AND DAUGHTER)

QUEEN OF HEAVEN(s)
Sarum Missal, p. 390: Gradual of Mass of B.V.M.; Dreves, v, p. 62: Invitation to Matins of a rhymed office.
179, l. 1; 71, l. 12.

RACHEL
Genesis xxix, 16 ff.

13c.: John, p. 104, 'Canticum in laudem virginis gloriose': Uterus Lie faciesque Rachelis; p. 242.

34, l. 53.

ROD OF AARON

Numbers xvii, 8.

12c.: St. Bernard, 'Super "Missus est" homilae', *P.L.* clxxxiii, col. 63: Quid, rogo, virga Aaron florida, nec humectata, nisi ipsam concipientem, quamvis virum non cognoscentem; *Sarum Breviary*, I, cv: Fifth lesson (attributed to St. Augustine) at Matins of Third Sunday in Advent: Virga ergo potuit contra naturam nuces educere; virgo non potuit contra naturae jura Dei Filium generare?

34, ll. 27–8.

ROD, ROOT OF JESSE, KIN OF DAVID

Isaiah xi, 1.

12c.: Adam, i, p. 10, ll. 25 ff.; 13c.: Dreves, x, p. 107, no. 141, 3a; Hours B.V.M., p. 27: None, Antiphon.

34, l. 24; 12, ll. 17 and 41–2; 104, l. 8.

ROSE IN JERICHO, WITHOUT THORNS

Ecclesiasticus xxiv, 14.

12c.: Mone, ii, p. 261, l. 97: Rosa sine spina; Pseudo-St. Bernard, 'Sermo panegyricus ad B.V.D.' *P.L.* clxxxiv, col. 1012: O Maria . . . rosa charitatis; Alanus de Insulis, 'Sententiae', *P.L.* ccx, col. 247; *Sarum Missal*, p. 308: Lesson for Mass of the Assumption includes *Ecclesiasticus* xxiv, 11–13 and 15–20.

5, l. 11; 107, l. 5; 144, l. 8.

SARAH

Genesis xvi.

St. Paul, *Galatians* iv, 22 ff. interprets as an allegory in which Sarah is the New Covenant or Church, and Hagar is the Law or Synagogue (see *Glossa Ordinaria*). What could be said of the Church could be said of B.V.M. 13c.: St. Bonaventura, 'Speculum B.M.V.' xiv, p. 250: O ergo Maria, O Sara nostra; 12c.: Dreves, ix, p. 64, no. 79, 2a.

34, l. 20.

SHIELD

12c.: Richard of St. Victor, 'Sermo in Nativitate, vel Assumptione B.M.V.' *P.L.* clxxvii, col. 980; 15c.: Mone, ii, p. 269, l. 97.

144, l. 17; 8, l. 57; 24, l. 60.

SLING OF DAVID

I Samuel xvii, 40 ff.

13c.: John, p. 104, 'Canticum in laudem virginis gloriose'.
34, ll. 25–6.

STAR, OF THE SEA, OF BLISS, OUT OF JACOB, OF BALAAM (see **TWO LIGHTS**)

Office hymn, 'Ave maris stella', Daniel, i, p. 204; 12c.: St. Anselm, 'Psalter of Mary', Mone, ii, p. 234, ll. 101 ff.: Ave perfusa lumine/ Tuoque digna nomine/Nam quod Maria dicitur/Stella maris exprimitur; Alanus de Insulis, 'Sermones', *P.L.* ccx, col. 201: Ait Balaam: *Orietur stella ex Jacob* (*Numbers* xxiv, 17); Hours B.V.M., p. 27: None, Antiphon; Evensong, Hymn: Hail, sterre of the see.

The star of Balaam was also interpreted as prefiguring Christ (see *Glossa Ordinaria* and *Revelation* xxii, 16: I am the root and the offspring of David, and the bright and morning star.)

5, l. 2; 144, l. 1; 179, l. 1; 107, l. 2.

STONE, PRECIOUS (see **GEM(S)**)

SUN THROUGH GLASS

Sarum Breviary, I, cvi: Matins of Third Sunday in Advent, Lesson Six (attributed to St. Augustine): Specular ergo non rumpit radius solis: integritatem Virginis ingressus aut egressus numquid vitiare poterat deitatis; 15c.: Mone, i, p. 63, ll. 41–4.

34, ll. 73–6.

TABERNACLE

Psalm xix, 4.

12c.: Alanus de Insulis, 'Sermones', *P.L.* ccx, col. 202 (associates B.V.M. with this psalm): St. Anselm, 'Psalter of Mary', Mone, ii, p. 234, l. 71.

104, l. 33.

TEMPLE, OF SOLOMON, OF GOD

Malachi iii, 1; *I Kings* vi.

12c.: Radulphus, 'Homiliae', *P.L.* clv, col. 1340: *Ad templum sanctum suum* (part of the Invitation at Matins of the Purification) id est ad uterum beatae Virginis; St. Anselm, 'Psalter of Mary', Mone, ii, p. 233, l. 17; 13c.: St. Bonaventura, 'Laus B.V.M.' xiv, p. 185; *Sarum Missal*, p. 250: Lesson for Mass of Purification includes

Malachi iii, 1 (the Gospel is *Luke* ii, 22 ff., the account of the Purification).

34, l. 31.

THRONE, OF SOLOMON, OF GOD
I Kings x, 18.

12c.: Abbot Guerricus, 'In Annuntiatione Dominica', *P.L.* clxxxv, col. 117; 13c.: St. Bonaventura, 'Speculum B.M.V.' xiv, pp. 236–7: Thronus vero Salomonis est Maria.

104, l. 52; 144, l. 27.

TOTA PULCHRA
Song of Songs iv, 7.

12c.: Richard of St. Victor, *P.L.* cxcvi, col. 482; St. Anselm, 'Psalter of Mary', Mone, ii, p. 234, l. 97.

104, l. 9.

TWO LIGHTS, STAR AND SUN (see STAR)

13c.: St. Bonaventura, 'Laus B.V.M.' xiv, p. 181: Stella Solem genuisti; *Sarum Breviary*, III, 49: Lesson nine of Matins Conception B.V.M.

124, l. 23; 117, l. 9.

WALL

12c.: Richard of St. Victor, 'Sermo in Nativitate vel Assumptione B.M.V.' *P.L.* clxxvii, col. 980: castrum securitate, murus vel turris fortitudine (etc.).

144, l. 25.

WELL (see FOUNTAIN)

WOMAN CLOTHED WITH THE SUN, OF THE APOCALYPSE
Revelation xii, 1.

12c.: St. Bernard, 'Sermo in Dominica infra octavam Assumptionis B.M.V.' *P.L.* clxxxiii, cols. 429 ff.: text = *Revelation* xii, 1; 15c.: Dreves, x, p. 75, no. 90, 4b.

34, ll. 67–70.

Index of First Lines

(In addition, the first lines of burdens are provided, in italic)

Index of First Lines

Index of First Lines

Index of First Lines

Index of First Lines